To Peter & Areta, two dear, family friends & the wonderful memories of my early years in Chicago

Peter Karavites

PROMISE-GIVING AND TREATY-MAKING

MNEMOSYNE
BIBLIOTHECA CLASSICA BATAVA

COLLEGERUNT

A.D. LEEMAN · H.W. PLEKET · C. J. RUIJGH

BIBLIOTHECAE FASCICULOS EDENDOS CURAVIT

C. J. RUIJGH, KLASSIEK SEMINARIUM, OUDE TURFMARKT 129, AMSTERDAM

SUPPLEMENTUM CENTESIMUM DECIMUM NONUM

PETER (PANAYIOTIS) KARAVITES

PROMISE-GIVING AND TREATY-MAKING

PROMISE-GIVING
AND TREATY-MAKING
HOMER AND THE NEAR EAST

BY

PETER (PANAYIOTIS) KARAVITES

WITH THE COLLABORATION OF

THOMAS WREN

E.J. BRILL
LEIDEN • NEW YORK • KÖLN
1992

The paper in this book meets the guidelines for permanence and durability of the Committee on Production Guidelines for Book Longevity of the Council on Library Resources.

ISSN 0169-8958
ISBN 90 04 09567 5

© *Copyright 1992 by E.J. Brill, Leiden, The Netherlands*

All rights reserved. No part of this book may be reproduced or translated in any form, by print, photoprint, microfilm, ·microfiche or any other means without written permission from the publisher

Authorization to photocopy items for internal or personal use is granted by E.J. Brill provided that the appropriate fees are paid directly to Copyright Clearance Center, 27 Congress Street, SALEM MA 01970, USA. Fees are subject to change.

PRINTED IN THE NETHERLANDS

TO THE MEMORY OF MY PARENTS

THEMISTOCLES AND KALLIOPE

CONTENTS

List of Abbreviations...vii
Preface..ix

Introduction 1
  The Focus..2
    1. The Structural Composition of the Homeric Agreements......3
    2. The Near Eastern Treaties 4
    3. Later Greek Treaty-Making 7
    4. The Mycenaean Gap 8
  The Logic..10
  The Design 13

PART ONE.
THE HOMERIC AGREEMENTS: THEIR CORPUS,
TERMINOLOGY, AND STRUCTURE

I. The Corpus of Homeric Agreements..................................17
  The Homeric Texts..18
    Agreements Nos. 1-23
  The Agreements Compared and Contrasted 41
  The Oral Character of the Homeric Agreements..........................45

II. The Linguistic Evidence...48
  The Significance of *Philotês*..48
  The Interrelation of *Horkia*, *Horkos*, and *Omnyein*..................58
  Conclusion 81

III. The Structure of Homeric Agreements.............................82
  The Preamble 83
  The Recounting of Antecedent History 87
  Stipulations 89
  The Invocation of Gods as Witnesses 98
  Curses and Blessings...104
  Conclusion 107

IV. Other Features of Homeric Agreements...........................108
  Other Maledictions 109
    1. The destruction and transformation of cities...................110
    2. Ravenous wild animals 110
    3. The ravishing of wives...111
    4. The destruction of weapons..111

vi CONTENTS

5. Warriors becoming women 112
6. Refusal of burial 112
7. Devastating flood 113
Ritual 116
Suzerainty Treaties 119

PART TWO.
SOME COMMON CONTENTS AND OTHER FEATURES SHARED
BY NEAR EASTERN AND HOMERIC TREATIES

V. The People 127
The Role of the People 127
Stipulations Concerning the Fate of Fugitives 148

VI. War Conventions 157
The Taking and Sharing of Booty 157
The Use of Surrogates 170
Firing the First Shot 175

VII. Conventions Associated with Treaty-Making 179
Meals 179
Deposition and Recitation 187
The Duration of the Agreement 194

VIII. Conclusion: Continuity or Discontinuity? 201

Bibliography 207
Index of Proper Names and Titles 217
Index of Transliterated Terms 223

LIST OF ABBREVIATIONS

AC	*Antiquité Classique*
AFO	*Archiv für Orientforschung*
ANET	*Ancient Near Eastern Texts Related to the Old Testament,* ed. by J. B. Pritchard et al., 2nd ed., Princeton, 1955
ANNALI	*Annali della Scuola Normale Superiore di Pisa, Classe di Lettere e Filosofia*
AO	*Der Alte Orient*
A.R.M.T	*Archives Royales de Mari*
ATL	*Athenian Tribute Lists,* by B. D. Meritt, H. T. Gery, and M. F. McGregor, Princeton, 1939-53
BASOR	*Bulletin of the American Schools of Oriental Research*
Bengtson	*Die Staatsverträge des Altertums,* by H. Bengtson and H. H. Schmitt, 2 vols., Munich, 1969-75
BoST	*Boghazköi Studien*
BWANT	*Beiträge zur Wissenschaft vom Alten und Neuen Testament*
CAH	*Cambridge Ancient History*
Cauer	F. C. Ameis and C. Hentze, *Homer's Iliad,* ed. by Paul Cauer, 7th ed., Amsterdam, 1965
CBQ	*Catholic Biblical Quarterly*
Erbse	*Scholia Graeca in Homeri Iliadem (scholia vetera),* ed. by H. Erbse, Berlin, 1969
Eust.	*Eustathii Archiepiscopi Thessalonicensis, Commentarii ad Homeri Iliadem Pertinentes,* ed. by Valk van Marchinus, 4 vols., Leiden, 1971-87
	—, *Commentarii ad Homeri Odysseam,* Leipzig, 1825-26
FGrHist	*Fragmente der griechische Historiker,* ed. by F. Jacoby
GdA	*Geschichte des Altertums,* by E. Meyer, 5 vols., Darmstadt, 1965-
HCT	*A Historical Commentary on Thucydides,* by A. Gomme et al., 1945-81
HThR	*Harvard Theological Review*
HUCA	*Hebrew Union College Annual*
HW	*Hethitisches Wörterbuch,* by Johannes Friedrich, Heidelberg, 1952
IG^3	*Inscriptiones Graecae,* vol. 1^3, ed. by D. M. Lewis
JAOS	*Journal of the American Oriental Society*
JEA	*Journal of Egyptian Archaeology*
JNES	*Journal of Near Eastern Studies*
KB	*Keilinschriftliche Bibliothek*
KBo	*Keilschrifttexte aus Boghazköi*
KF(KIF)	*Kleinasiatische Forschungen*

LIST OF ABBREVIATIONS

KIH	*Kleinasien zur Hethiterzeit*
KUB	*Keilschrifturkunden aus Boghazköi*
LCM	*Liverpool Classical Monthly*
MDOG	*Mitteilungen des Deutschen Orient-Gesellschaft*, Berlin
MVAG	*Mitteilungen der Vorderasiatisch-Aegyptischen Gesellschaft*
OCT	*Oxford Classical Texts*
OGI	*Orientis Graeci Inscriptiones Selectae*
OLZ	*Orientalische Literaturzeitung*
PCA	*Proceedings of the Classical Association*
RA	*Revue d'Assyrialogie*
RE	*Real Encyclopädie der classischen Altertumswissenschaft*
RHR	*Revue de l'Histoire des Religions*
RIDA	*Revue Internationale des Droits de l'Antiquité*
SEG	*Supplementum Epigraphicum Graecum*
SF	*Sefire or Sefire Stelae*
Syll.³	*Sylloge Inscriptionum Graecarum*
VAB	*Vorderasiatische Bibliothek*
VT	*Vetus Testamentum*
WO	*Die Welt des Orients, Wissenschaftliche Beiträge zur Kunde des Morgenlandes*
ZA	*Zeitschrift für Assyriologie*
ZAW	*Zeitschrift für die Alttestamentliche Wissenschaft*
ZPE	*Zeitschrift für Papyrologie und Epigraphik*

PREFACE

Scholars of early Greek history customarily work "forward" when evidence exists that promises to elucidate the development of historical events. At other times, constrained by the absence of historical data, they resort to a "backward" analysis, starting from the earliest historical documentation and moving back into the darkness that precedes the earliest documented era. In doing so, they sooner or later come up against the general question of limits concerning what can be said of Archaic civilization: how far, if at all, can scholarly inquiry extend to the time prior to the earliest recorded moment? In particular, can it extend to the Mycenaean era? Many prominent modern historians of Ancient Greece have rejected the latter sort of analysis entirely. However, the present study combines both investigative methods in the belief that they can jointly illuminate the topic under consideration. As a supplement to the "backward" analysis, early material from the history of the Ancient Near East is adduced as collateral evidence to amplify the arguments pertaining to the Mycenaean era.

Several colleagues and friends have helped in the creation of this book. A few of them have already been thanked elsewhere. To them as well as to others who have helped in many ways, grateful acknowledgment is made here. Professors Charles W. Fornara of Brown University, Chester G. Starr of the University of Michigan, Christian Habicht of the Institute for Advanced Study, and Fritz Gschnitzer of the University of Heidelberg, all read earlier drafts of the manuscript and offered suggestions and criticisms. The last-named was also kind enough to send several offprints of his Homeric research, which helped sharpen the focus of some of the arguments in the section on "Popular Participation." Professor Mary Noel, a colleague and friend at Bridgewater State College, went over the manuscript with meticulous care and made many useful corrections and suggestions.

Special gratitude is also due to the staff of the Bridgewater College Interlibrary Loan Service, without whose help this project would have been impossible, as well as to Clement Kuehn of the Classical Studies Department of Loyola University and the staff of the Loyola University Center for Instructional Design, for their advice and other help in the formidable task of preparing the camera-ready copy of the manuscript. A grant from the American Council of Learned Societies and a financial supplement from the Philosophical Society of Philadelphia enabled me to spend the spring semester of 1983 in Munich, doing research at the library of the Seminar für Alte Geschichte, the Kommission für Alte Geschichte und Epigraphik des Deutschen Archäologischen Instituts, and the Staatsbibliothek. The semester in Munich was made especially pleasant as well as useful by the kindness and generous hospitality of Professor Hatto H.

x PREFACE

Schmitt. A fellowship from the Institute for Advanced Study in Princeton, in the spring semester of 1986, enabled me to continue my research.

Finally, special thanks are due to Professor Thomas Wren of the Philosophy Department of Loyola University. His help in the preparation of the manuscript, regarding philosophical issues as well as various technical matters, is acknowledged on the title page of this book.

As is often done in works of this sort, classical Greek has usually been used in citations of more than three words or where emphasis on the original Greek is needed. Otherwise Greek passages are transliterated, even though transliteration raises some awkward problems. For instance, generally the Greek *upsilon* is transliterated as "y." Yet the use of "y" in certain instances would have produced some comical effects, e.g., *toy* for the singular genitive of masculine and neuter article. In these few cases "u" was substituted for "y," thereby avoiding undesirable distractions. Transliteration problems were also presented by the Near Eastern names. The more commonly known names have been spelled in simplified form, as in Gurney's book on the Hittites, with accent marks retained for the others.

Peter Karavites
Bridgewater, Massachusetts

INTRODUCTION

As the sacred ship sailed back from Delos, nearing Athens and bringing with it the time for Socrates' death, his lifelong friend Crito begged him to take the opportunity for an easy and safe escape. To his entreaties Socrates replied with one of history's most famous as well as most moving philosophical arguments. Dismissing all other considerations, he focused on the sheer *rightness* of the act—a category which, in this dialogue at least, is understood solely in terms of what to a Greek was a still more basic category, that of *covenant* or, more generally, *promising*. How, he asked Crito, could he reply if the Laws of Athens were to remind him that he had agreed to be governed by them in deed as well as in word? They would say of his plan to escape:

> You are breaking your covenants and agreements with us, which you made under no compulsion and undeceived. You were not compelled to decide quickly, but you had seventy years in which you could have gone away if you did not like us, or if the agreements did not seem to you just. But you did not prefer Lacedaemon or Crete, which you always declare to be under good laws, nor any other city, Hellenic or barbarian; but you were less out of town than the lame or the blind or others who are maimed: you, so much more remarkably than the other Athenians, like the city and us, the Laws—as is clear, for what city could please without laws? And now, then, will you not abide by your agreements? You will if you obey us, Socrates; do not make yourself ridiculous by leaving the city. (*Crit.* 53A)

This is the voice that Socrates told Crito was humming in his ears, blocking all other voices even as he offered his friend the opportunity for one last word. Significantly, Crito did not take the opportunity. Overcome by not only personal grief but also the moral power of that voice, which spoke to both of them from the most ancient times and was the voice of Greece itself, Crito could only reply: "My dear Socrates, I have nothing to say."

Why he had nothing to say is the topic of this book. Thinkers of later times—moral and political philosophers, theologians, scholars of jurisprudence, and others—would surely not have been reduced to silence as Crito was. To Socrates' argument they would have readily replied that, apart from the dubiousness of any such personification of the laws as parties to a contract, the "rightness" of the proposed escape involved many considerations not addressed, e.g., the fairness and utility of Socrates' death sentence and death sentences in general, and even that of the laws themselves. But for Socrates and Crito, discussion was closed as soon as the issue was cast in the promissory terms quoted above. By trying to escape, Socrates would make himself "ridiculous" in the profoundest possible sense: out of a "miserable desire for a little more life" (53C) he would violate what he considered a sacred agreement.

2 INTRODUCTION

There is an important sense in which all social life presupposes the institution of promising—which is the genus under which fall specific practices and conventions such as treaties, oaths, and less formal agreements. Contrary to what is sometimes suggested in contemporary philosophical literature about "the promising game," there is no place in human life where one can stand on the sidelines, i.e., decide not to play the promising game at all. However, promising assumes a variety of historical and culture-specific forms. These forms vary in the way an agreement is made as well as in the importance attached to keeping them. The ancient Greeks were one of the most promise-conscious of all cultures, as the scene from Socrates' death watch bears out. To be sure, there are important elements in that dialogue that could only have been expressed after the rise of the city state as a political entity and a moral force, which is to say well after the time of Homer and, a fortiori, after the grand pre-Homeric days that are depicted in the *Iliad* and *Odyssey*. But its underlying awareness is that the general practice of stabilizing expectations by means of agreements is indispensable to the social bond, and this awareness goes back to the beginnings of Greek civilization, shaping that civilization over nearly two millennia into the specific normative system and network of social conventions that would eventually produce a Socrates.

THE FOCUS

Of course the Greeks were not the only people to have engaged in this general practice, constitutive as it is of social life per se. Prior to and contemporaneous with the pre-Homeric age of Greece were the promise-making practices of other Mediterranean and Oriental cultures, many of which practices may very well have flowed over into the Greek world. In this as well as other respects the *Iliad* and *Odyssey* are a watershed of cultural streams, including not only those influences which came directly down from Mycenaean times but also those which flowed more remotely and indirectly from Near Eastern sources. Accordingly, this study concentrates on the promise-making practices depicted in the Homeric epics, in the belief that by doing so we can also learn something about times and places adjacent to Homer's. For hundreds of years, scholars have painstakingly explored the contents of these epics, as well as related issues such as their provenance and the identity of their author(s), and they have done so from nearly every conceivable angle. Even so, the present study revisits the Homeric corpus one more time, in hopes that what the poems suggest about the way treaties and agreements were made can help us to understand better not only the internal structure of the poems themselves, but also the social practices of promise-making that existed before, during, and after the Dark Ages when the poems were written.

INTRODUCTION 3

More specifically: The main focus of this book is on three equally prominent themes, outlined below. These are, first, the structural composition of those vows, promises, treaties, and other exchanges described in the *Iliad* and *Odyssey*, here collectively designated as the Homeric agreements; second, their connections with the Near Eastern treaties and covenants; and, third, the impact of the Homeric agreements on the more formal Greek treaties of post-Homeric times. The book also has a secondary focus, which is directed toward a fourth, important but somewhat less prominent theme: the format and structure of the treaties and other promise-making conventions that actually obtained in the Mycenaean world.

1. The Structural Composition of the Homeric Agreements

Except for passing comments, we shall not directly examine the formal structure of Homeric agreements until Chapter 3, which is a sustained review of the different kinds of promise-making that are featured in the *Iliad* and *Odyssey*. However, it is worth pointing out now that neither the third chapter nor the ones preceding it, which concern the corpus of the Homeric agreements (Chapter 1) and their linguistic features (Chapter 2), have any illusions as to the historicity of the epics themselves. They are poems, from the first verse to the last, not chronicles or biographies. Occasionally our analysis may seem to have a biographical ring, especially in speculations about the inner states of the Homeric characters, as expressed in sentences such as "Achilles must have intended to..." or "Agamemnon could not possibly have wished..." But such locutions are merely expository devices for helping us appreciate the poet's intentions, and are not meant directly to assert historical or biographical facts.

On the other hand, this book is squarely based on the background assumption that even poetry can have historical significance. Admittedly, narrative poetry such as Homer's is a form of fiction. Such poems typically do not claim to report historical events, and never claim to be faithful factual records. When poetry, even narrative poetry, is great it is so precisely because it is creative, which means (among many other things) that it has exaggerated, distorted, selected, ignored, and otherwise created a world of its own. Nevertheless, such poetry derives its themes from reality, from which it forms a new synthesis. It is frequently inspired by great events and takes its cue from them. But even when it does not, its settings and characterizations contain hard historical kernels. Thus John Chadwick goes too far when he represents Homeric poetry and history as sealed off from each other, the one concerned only with human values, the other only with facts and events. He is, in short, quite wrong to say that "to look for historical fact in Homer is as vain as to scan the Mycenaean tablets in search of poetry; they belong to

4   INTRODUCTION

different universes."[1] However, he is quite right to refuse to take the narratives literally, although as we shall see in the following chapters historians cannot afford to ignore poetic material altogether, especially when that material is their only source. Whatever might be our views about the genesis, structural composition, and thematic contents of the Homeric poetry qua poetry, there seems no reason to doubt that it contains some references to events of the Mycenaean era, and that it reflects some of the customs, ideas, and practices of that world, in particular those rules that governed pre-Homeric societies at war.[2]

2. The Near Eastern Treaties

The most controversial of our three focal themes is the second, which postulates that there were influences from the Near East on the Mycenaean and later Greek worlds, including the fictional world created by Homer, and—as a corollary to this postulate—that there was considerable continuity between the Mycenaean and Homeric eras. The immediate theme of the *Iliad* unfolds in the Near East, and its non-Greek protagonists are themselves residents of the Near East. In the *Odyssey*, Phoenicians and other Near Easterners frequently appear in the narrative. Moreover, the Homeric worldview shares important general metaphysical or theological features with the oriental worldviews, in that none of them sees any absolute separation between the animate and the inanimate worlds on the one hand, or between the divine and human on the other. For instance, in the Homeric epics the obvious remnants of animism and totemism diminish if not eliminate the distance between man and nature, whereas anthropological gods are organized in societies and lineages resembling human societies and lineages. Furthermore, the biological mixing between gods and men and the emotional ties developed between them seem to be Homeric echoes of the Near Eastern world. Similarly, Homer's divine kingdom is a monarchy, or better, a more or less decentralized empire, which is overseen by a supreme god; so also is the oriental pantheon, where the special competencies are divided among the divine actors and each reigns in his own territory. And so on.[3]

This approach differs markedly from the judgment of such notable scholars as M. I. Finley, who argues that Homer is actually describing his own Dark Age, notwithstanding the reference to an earlier age, as well as W. Leaf and M. P. Nilsson, who have maintained that the *Iliad* shows few or no signs of

---

[1] J. Chadwick, *The Mycenaean World* (Cambridge, 1976) 186.

[2] Fritz Gschnitzer, *Griechische Sozialgeschichte* (Wiesbaden, 1981) 25-26.

[3] Henri Frankfort et al., *Before Philosophy* (Baltimore, 1963) 162; Leon Robin, *La pensée hellenique des origins à Epicure,* 2nd ed. (Paris, 1967) 27.

INTRODUCTION 5

Asiatic (Near East) origins.[4] According to Leaf the scene of the *Iliad* is laid in the Troad, but its point of view is professedly that of the dwellers in Greece proper. In support of this claim, Leaf points out that the poems profess a close acquaintance with the topography of Greece and almost completely ignore that of Asia.[5] In contrast, our study maintains that the Asian influence was real, but leaves it open whether Homer himself was aware of this influence or of specific facts such as the geographical ones cited by Leaf. We have no way of knowing the extent to which Homer was conscious (or oblivious) of the linkage between the Near Eastern peoples and his beloved Achaeans. As noted above, there were surely some contacts between the Mycenaeans and their Near Eastern contemporaries, with veins of influence leading in both directions. But also, before they were noticeable by anyone, small and subtle influences from the East probably quietly oozed and percolated westward in the way a new stream slowly begins to move from its springs through rocks and soil toward a well-defined river bed. Long before the Mycenaeans settled in Greece, the mainland of Greece was inhabited by people of Mediterranean stock, e.g., Pelasgians, Carians, etc., with whose descendants the Mycenaeans lived and interacted with once they arrived. The Pactolus of Homeric poetry has surely been fed by many rivulets whose sources lie deep in history. It is likely that some of these rivulets drew their

---

[4] M. I. Finley, *Early Greece: The Bronze Ages* (London, 1981); W. Leaf, *Homer and History* (London, 1915); and M. P. Nilsson, *Geschichte der Griechischen Religion,* 2nd ed. (Munich, 1955) 1:391. The literature in this area is extensive and varied. For the possible interaction between the Near East and the Mycenaean civilization see also B. C. Dietrich, *Acta Classica* 14 (1965) 11-30; Franz Dirlmeier, RhM 98 (1955) 18-37; C. H. Gordon, AJA 56 (1952) 94; A. Lesky, *Hethitische Texte und griechische Mythos, Anzeiger der Österreiche Akademie der Wissenschaften* (1951) 139-59; A. Lesky, *Eranos* (1954) 8-17. A more recent work, treating the subject of the interrelationship of cultures beyond the Mycenaean times, is W. Burkert, *Die orientalisierende Epoche in der griechischen Religion und Literatur* (SB, Heidelberg, 1984). See also C. H. Gordon, *Hebrew Union College Annual* 26 (1955) 43-108. G. K. Gresseth, CJ 70 (1975) 1-18. H. van Effenteree, *La cité grecque: Des origines à la défaite de Marathon* (Paris, 1985), believes in continuity; see also C. T. Syriopouulos, *Eisagogê eis tên archaian Ellênikên istorian. Oi metabatikoi xronoi apo tên Mykenaikên eis tên archaïkên periodon 1200-700 p. x.* A-B, Bibliotheke tês en Athenais Archaiologikês Etairias, no. 99 (Athens, 1983). For some modern sources in addition to Finley, *loc. cit.,* see also R. A. Crossland, CAH3 vol. 1, pt. 2, chap. 27; R. A. Crossland and A. Birchall (eds.), *Bronze Age Migrations in the Aegean: Archaeological and Linguistic Problems in Greek Prehistory* (London, 1973); J. T. Hooker, *Mycenaean Greece* (London, 1977); G. E. Murray, *Early Greece* (Sussex, 1980); Milman Parry, HSCP 41 (1930) 73-147; Parry HSCP 43 (1932) 1-50; Parry TAPA 64 (1933) 179-99; Pavel Oliva, *The Birth of Greek Civilization* (London, 1981); A. M Snodgrass, *Archaic Greece: The Age of Experiment* (London, 1980); Snodgrass, *The Dark Age of Greece: An Archaeological Survey of the Eleventh to the Eighth Centuries B.C.* (Edinburgh, 1971); C. G. Starr, *The Origins of Greek Civilization 1100-650* (New York, 1961); Lord W. Taylor, *The Mycenaeans* (London, 1983); D. R. Theocharis, *Neolithic Greece* (Athens, 1973); Peter Warren, *The Aegean Civilizations* (Lausanne, 1975).

[5] Leaf, *loc. cit.,* passim.

6INTRODUCTION

waters from the numerous Near Eastern and pre-Mycenaean springs. If so, then Homer's texts are richer than he may have known, since they are sources of insight into other worlds in addition to the Mycenaean one he celebrated.

However, not all the reasons for believing there was a linkage between the Greek and Near Eastern worlds are textual. In their very different ways, common sense and the archaeological spade also demonstrate that there must have been contacts between Mycenae and the Near East. Although it would be farfetched to say that entire institutions, conventions, or practices were the same from one culture to the next, it would be even more farfetched to doubt that they probably shared some common elements. At the very least, it seems plausible to say that—however they may have comported themselves toward each other—the Mycenaeans could not have conducted their international transactions very differently from their contemporaries such as the Hittites and the other kingdoms of the Near East, since these very peoples were the other parties to those transactions.

Archeology provides narrower, though harder, evidence for the same general conclusion, viz., that there were intercultural affinities and that these are best understood as borrowings by the Mycenaeans from Near Eastern cultures. For instance, Persson perceives close Mycenaean parallels in Egyptian rock-cut graves, and attributes the beginnings of the chamber-tomb construction on the mainland Greece to Egyptian influences.[6] There is no doubt that connections between Mycenae and Egypt were very close toward the end of the Middle Helladic period, and that Egyptian practices influenced the burial customs of the Mycenaeans. Similarly, Wace and Blegen have shown that over eight times more Mainland (Helladic) vases than Cretan vases are known to be from Egypt, dating from the Late Bronze I and II periods, i.e., from the sixteenth and fifteenth centuries B.C.[7] The increased number of funeral offerings placed in graves, the example of embalming found in Grave V, the death masks, the ostrich eggs, the box of Egyptian sycamore with the applied figures of dogs in ivory, the Nilotic scene on the Mycenaean inlaid dagger, the sign of Waz on stele from Grave Gamma, perhaps even the idea of sculptured composition on stelae, all indicate a strong Egyptian influence. The suggestion is made, and well supported, that the gold found in the shaft graves of Mycenae was brought from the outside.[8] These borrowings and many others demonstrate the receptivity along with the vitality and dynamism of the Mycenaean culture.

---

[6] A. W. Persson, *Royal Tombs at Dendra Near Midea* (Lund, 1931) 165-75; see also J. L. Myres, *Homer and His Critics* (London, 1958) 157-58.

[7] A. J. B. Wace and C. Blegen, *Klio* 30 (1939) 131-147.

[8] Persson, *Royal Tombs,* 146-95; S. Marinatos and H. Hirmer, *Crete and Mycenae* (London, 1960) 5-6.

INTRODUCTION 7

In view of such considerations, drawn from Homer's text by literary analysis, from the armchair by common sense, and in situ by archeological spadework, our attempt to compare the Homeric agreements with those of the Near East seems in principle to be a fully viable project. Of course it remains to be seen whether its goals will be accomplished, but at least there is no antecedent or methodological reason why they cannot be.

3. Later Greek Treaty-Making

The third theme we shall focus on is that of the impact of the Homeric agreements on post-Homeric Greece, i.e., on the formal interstate treaties that were drawn up from about 700 to 400 B.C. These were years of colonization, commercialization, the development of city-states, and the organization of the hoplite phalanx, all of which demonstrate the dynamism of the Greek world in the centuries after Homer. Nevertheless, we must not exaggerate the contrast between the old and the new: there is no suggestion in what we know of life in post-Homeric Greece and the new Greek colonies that it completely displaced the earlier ways, but only that structures and procedures for the conduct of life which were already in place became more formal and, in many cases, more under the control of the state. One such structure was that of friendship with outsiders, which was an unbounded right for Homeric heroes but in post-Homeric times was subordinated to a citizen's obligations to the *polis*. Another structure or procedure was that of international law, which in earlier times understood the interest of the state or better, national group, to be identified with the individual personalities and attitudes of the ruling class, in contrast to the later view of the *polis* as having interests that transcended those of any individual. Accordingly, seemingly private problems and personal interests such as the abduction of a woman could easily become public matters constituting a legitimate cause for the declaration of war in archaic times, in contrast to the political ethos that marked the rise of the city-states. Even so, there was enough continuity between the Homeric and post-Homeric legal consciousness for the personal interests at stake in romances, kidnappings, and similar events to have been recognized in later times as a sufficient condition for the outbreak of intercommunal hostilities (whatever their real causes might have been). The Greeks of the classical times neither knew nor apparently cared anything more about the origins of those hostilities beyond what was provided in tales such as the abductions of Europe of Tyre, Medea of Phasis, Io of Argos, and Helen of Troy (Hdt. 1.1 ff.).

But the change that most concerns us is, of course, that which institutionalized the structures and procedures of promise-making, specifically, the development of those interstate promises which go under the title "treaties." (Terminology is somewhat loose both in Homer and in the present study, in that although treaties are usually formal arrangements,

8 INTRODUCTION

terms such as "treaty," "agreement," "promise," and "pact" are often used interchangeably: there seems no need to create a special technical terminology for our study. A similar elasticity is found in the term "covenant," which is sometimes used to advert to formal treaties, and sometimes to one-sided promises, as in God's covenant with Abraham in Gen. 15.)

As G. Ténékidès has pointed out, treaty-making falls under the general rubric of international law, and for the existence of international law two conditions are generally required: the existence of sovereign states, and a condition of war or peace obtaining among them that is based on some common principles.[9] To some extent these two conditions existed in the Homeric era, but the notion of the state was still quite vague, such that the Homeric states constituted a loose association under a minimum of common rules.[10] Furthermore, those common rules were not codified, but rather were the products of custom, which was the only law prevalent at the time. However, in spite of the relatively informal nature of international law and interstate treaties in Homeric times, they were considered no less binding upon the parties than were the more carefully wrought laws and treaties of classical Greece.

As we shall see in Part Two (as well as in Chapter 4), what accounted for this continuity was a common factor that was shared, synchronically, by the formal and informal agreements of each period and, diachronically, by the interstate treaties that were drawn up between Homeric groups (including not only the several Greek nations but also the Trojans and, as we shall see, their Near Eastern contemporaries) and those more legalistic treaties drawn up in later centuries by Athens, Sparta, and other politically articulated city-states. This shared factor was what, for lack of a better term, we shall consider under the sobriquet, "the aristocratic spirit," and which we shall find to be a powerful interpretative concept, capable of unifying the otherwise disparate Homeric agreements with each other, with the post-Homeric treaties, and even with the Near Eastern treaties, all of which seem to have been pervaded by a similar spirit.

4. The Mycenaean Gap

As noted above, besides the three themes that are the joint object of the primary focus of this study, a fourth (and again controversial) theme is considered, albeit without the same sharpness of detail as the first three. This

---

[9] G. Ténékidès, *Droit international et communautées fédérales dans la Grèce des cités (Ve-IIIe avant J.C.)* (Leyden, 1957).

[10] T. Sorgen-Grey, *De vestigiis iuris gentium homerici* (Leipzig, 1871) passim; M. I. Finley speaks of a break between Mycenae and the Homeric world, *Early Greece, The Bronze and Archaic Age* (London, 1970) passim; M. M. Austin and P. Vidal-Naquet, *Economic and Social History of Greece* (Berkeley and Los Angeles, 1977), especially the first three chapters.

INTRODUCTION 9

is the "protohistorical" theme of promise-making in Mycenaean times.[11] Given the dearth of written information about the Mycenaean era, any attempt to understand its social conventions may seem brash, to say the least. Of course there must have been *some* agreements struck in the course of the wars, raids, disputes, and other common enterprises that obviously took place, but this would be true of any civilization, and tells us nothing about the Mycenaeans per se. Similarly, archaeologists have unearthed pre-Homeric tombs, artifacts, and even documents (i.e., tablets with writing), but nothing that tells us about Mycenaean treaties or related social conventions. Whether or not it is true that writing itself was a lost art during most of the Dark Ages, there certainly are no chroniclers like the Venerable Bede to whom we may turn. But just as the astronomer can triangulate from other sightings to the existence and locations of dead stars and even conjecture as to their constituent features, we can triangulate to the Mycenaean treaty conventions by using, on the one hand, the relatively informative written records of contemporary (and earlier) Near Eastern cultures and, on the other hand, certain hints gleaned from Homer.

True, Homer was not a chronicler. Equally true, the Hittites and other Near Eastern peoples were not Greeks, nor much interested in writing about the Greeks even though they arranged treaties with them (assuming it is indeed the Mycenaean Greeks who are named by such terms as the Hittite's "Ahhiyawa"). But the linkages are there, to be seen if one only looks for them. We know that there were (A) Near Eastern cultures, some of whose legal systems reach back into the third millennium B.C. or beyond. During the second millennium some of these peoples lived alongside and must have interacted with (B) the sophisticated and aggressive Mycenaean civilization that lasted almost a thousand years, counting from the time the first rough tribes migrated southward until its collapse at the end of the twelfth century,[12] with its zenith apparently being sometime in the thirteenth century. Highlights of the latter period were reflected in (C) the poetic retrieval in the *Iliad* and *Odyssey*, around 800 B.C., of those great earlier times. Of course it would be fallacious to infer anything about the nature of B solely from what we know of A, since temporal and geographical proximity do not of themselves imply similarity. It would be likewise fallacious to read straight

---

[11] The archaeologist J. N. Coldstream argues that the term "protohistory" is a "useful word, already accepted in several European languages, though hardly at all in English." It is defined by him as a form of historiography, i.e., as "an attempt to gain an historical insight into a period without contemporary written records by confronting its archeological evidence with the memories preserved in later literary sources." *The Formation of the Greek Polis: Aristotle and Archeology* (Opladen, 1984) 7.

[12] We do know that the Mycenaeans had extensive commercial relations, especially with the East, and that gold found in Mycenaean graves reflects Mycenaean wealth procured from such trading contacts.

10   INTRODUCTION

back to B from C, since the Homeric epics were neither meant to be taken as history nor produced in a time or social milieu already known on independent grounds as being close to the Mycenaean age. However, we *can* infer, tentatively but not at all fallaciously, to the nature of B if we move to it from A and C simultaneously.

This is really a very conservative claim, which can be stated more carefully, if somewhat ponderously, as follows. If (1) when the A-B relationship is reconstructed by the usual tools of historical scholarship (one of which tools is that of common sense), certain patterns emerge giving rise to hypotheses about Mycenaean conventions and, if (2) these hypotheses agree with those formed from patterns emerging when the C-B relationship is reconstructed by literary analysis supplemented by historical scholarship (again, using common sense as one of the literary and historical tools), then (3) we have a relatively strong albeit non-definitive reason for accepting these hypotheses. This last point is all the more compelling once we recognize that, in the present disposition of historical knowledge, to "accept" these hypotheses is the equivalent of preferring them to the alternative of no hypotheses at all. Concerning such an alternative, we may say what Chadwick said about the problem he faced in trying to interpret certain documents that somehow survived the Mycenaean collapse:

> Some of my colleagues will doubtless think I have in places gone too far in reconstructing a pattern which will explain the documents. Here I can only say that some pattern must exist, for these are authentic, contemporary sources; and if the pattern I have proposed is the wrong one, I will cheerfully adopt a better one when it is offered. But what I do reject is the defeatist attitude which refuses even to devise a pattern, because all its details cannot be proved. The documents exist; therefore the circumstances existed which caused them to be written, and my experience has shown me that these are not altogether impossible to conjecture.[13]

THE LOGIC

In other words, there is no gainsaying the fact that this study necessarily involves some conjecture, owing to the paucity of hard evidence available concerning the Mycenaean era. However, it does not follow from this rather inconvenient fact that whatever conjectures are made will be logically circular, although that sort of objection is sometimes lodged against studies of this sort. Whereas the paucity of data is a genuine and discomfiting problem about which one can only say, with Chadwick, that it would be "defeatist" to refuse to speculate at all, no such modesty or feelings of discomfiture are called for in the second case. More specifically: studies that

---

[13] Chadwick, *loc. cit.*, x.

INTRODUCTION
11

are long on speculation and short on so-called hard evidence are sometimes quite unfairly dismissed on the grounds that they can only be circular, that their meager data are gathered and arranged as evidence using certain criteria that are then "proven" to be common features of the instances selected. In the present case, the circularity objection would go something like this: certain relatively formal agreements of the Ancient Near East, especially Hittite treaties, have been taken as a model of promising or treaty-making, according to which certain relatively informal agreements in the Homeric epics have been (1) selected and then (2) reconstructed. Then (so the objection goes) the "hypothesis" is made that because the reconstructed Homeric agreements are significantly similar to the earlier Near Eastern treaties, they are probably derived from those treaties, either directly or via the interaction between pre-Homeric Greeks and their Near Eastern contemporaries. But then, supposedly, this hypothesis is really a pseudo-hypothesis. Nor is there any question of "probability," an empirical concept, since the point of the circularity objection is that it is not probable but instead only vacuously true that Homeric agreements selected and reconstructed in terms of some other culture's treaty-making conventions will resemble the treaties of that culture. Furthermore, since this "resemblance" would obtain regardless of the century to which the original model belonged—the model could, so to speak, just as well be Benthamite as Hittite—one could hardly go on to assert a causal relationship, for even the most indirect sort of influencing necessarily takes place along a temporal line.

There are at least two excellent reasons for utterly rejecting this circularity objection, one specific to this study and directed to the charge of biased selection, and the other involving the very notion of what it means to write history and directed to the charge of biased reconstruction. (Only because each of these two reasons constitutes an important insight is it worthwhile here to consider either aspect of the general objection.) The first reason is that in the present study, the Homeric agreements comprised by the corpus presented in Chapter 1 have not been "selected" at all, in the sense that only those agreements that fit Near Eastern (or any other) criteria were included. Consequently, the objection is a non-starter insofar as it alleges a biased or question-begging selection procedure. As we shall see, there seem to be over twenty episodes in the *Iliad* and *Odyssey* that are or involve promises, some of which are interstate or at least intergroup agreements and some of which are personal, even trivial arrangements. However, although the corpus seems complete as it stands, it may well happen that subsequent scholarly inspection of the epics will reveal other promises that have not been taken into account here, in which case they would be added to the corpus of this study without further question. That is, they would not first be tested for "fit" with the Near Eastern model, though they certainly would need to be carefully examined in order to determine whether the speech acts in question

12 INTRODUCTION

were indeed promises rather than predictions, velleities, words of encouragement, or other sorts of performatives. (Of course utterances are often combinations of several simultaneous speech acts, e.g., promising, predicting, encouraging, or flattering, in which case the relevant question would only be: Of the several things being done by the speaker, is any one of them tantamount to a promise?)

As scholars of linguistic pragmatics know only too well, what counts as a certain kind of performance in one speech community need not have that significance in another community. And so there may be no completely culture-transcending criteria for establishing whether a certain set of words is "really and truly" a promise (or any other sort of speech act), just as there may be no transcendent criteria for establishing the "true nature" of any other social or natural phenomena, Plato notwithstanding. But that is not our concern here, nor is it the force of the objection cited above. The present study assumes a tacit sense on the part of the reader concerning what it means to make a promise, which is why the family of promise-making acts discussed in these pages (treaties, oaths, compacts, and other sorts of agreements) are for the most part left undefined. If this sort of assumption be disallowed, then there is indeed no point in reading further—not because the circularity objection has been upheld, but because this or some very similar assumption of shared meanings is a necessary condition for the possibility of any discourse whatsoever.

The second reason for rejecting the circularity objection is more fundamental. It concerns the (often poorly understood) general question of what constitutes historical knowledge, and in the present context takes up the allegation that, because Homeric agreements are here interpreted and "reconstructed" in terms of another culture, it therefore would be viciously circular to go on and make even the most tentative inferences about their historical or causal links with that other culture. Although it presents itself as a general principle of historical inference, this aspect of the circularity objection also fails, for the very basic reason that, in a certain very important sense, *all* historiography is circular, though not viciously so—at least not usually. This last point is not so obvious when the historical issues are narrow and the historian's questions employ categories that are very familiar, either because our physical situation makes radically alternative categories virtually unthinkable (everyone "just knows" what a parent is), because our social situation is itself defined by certain agreed-upon parsings of history ("The Renaissance," "The Depression," "World War II"), or just because we lack imagination (national, sexual, and other forms of chauvinism). But the point is easy to appreciate when the issues are broad and the questions slightly off-key. For instance, the question "How many favorites did Louis XIV have, and who were they?" is a question of the first sort, which a historian can address without much fear of being accused of elemental

INTRODUCTION   13

circularity. But "What is a favorite?" is a question of the second sort. Even to ask it, much less to attempt an answer, is to structure one's initial thought in terms of the anticipated conclusions. Paul Veyne has distinguished these two questions as belonging, respectively, to a history of events and structural history, with the further suggestion that the simple term "history" is more aptly used for the latter.[14] But neither sort of historical narrative directly corresponds to what P. Munz calls the *res gestae*, i.e., (the totality of) what actually happened, since historians have no way of looking at *res gestae* and, by looking, deciding whether any particular historical narrative is true.[15]

Instead, what they must do—as the present study illustrates—is look for correspondences between narrative and narrative. Some of these narratives are small stories and some large, but all are created and subsequently understood by means of selection criteria and other principles of intelligibility that any historical account (be it a diary, a public decree, an inscription, or a historical treatise) assimilates in basically the same way that an individual person assimilates his or her native language.

THE DESIGN

The book itself is separated into two main parts, concerned in turn with the structure and the contents of the ancient promise-making conventions. The first part begins with the identification of the Homeric agreements, establishing their corpus and providing a brief commentary on each agreement (Chapter 1). It then analyzes the significance of a few of the terms employed by the treaties and their relationship to the Near East (Chapter 2), and goes on to explain some of the structural aspects common to the Homeric agreements and their Near Eastern counterparts (Chapter 3). Part One finishes with a structural comparison of the Homeric agreements with such Near Eastern agreements as the Hittite, Sfire, Esarhaddon, and so on, on the one hand, and with some of the Greek post-Homeric treaties, on the other (Chapter 4). The second main part of the book consists in a serial analysis of some of the non-structural features or contents, i.e., stipulations and procedures, common to Homeric agreements and their Near Eastern and post-Homeric counterparts. The first content domain to be considered is that of stipulations concerning the people, including fugitives (Chapters 5), and the second domain is that of what for lack of a better term may be called war

---

[14] "For history the role of favorite is not the explanation of the story of Villeroi but, on the contrary, the fact to be explained.... History of events is political actuality gone cold." P. Veyne, *Writing History: Essay on Epistemology*, trans. by M. Moore-Rinvolucri (Middletown, 1984) 221-22.

[15] P. Munz, *The Shapes of Time: A New Look at the Philosophy of History* (Middletown, 1977) 209 ff.

14 INTRODUCTION

conventions (Chapter 6). Another set of conventions, which are not specific contents but rather general procedures for making and guaranteeing treaties in the Near East and Greece, is then discussed (Chapter 7), followed by some concluding remarks (Chapter 8).

Scholars will understandably differ with many points expounded in this work, as well as with the decision not to deal with certain topics that have clear importance in their own right, especially several legal questions associated with treaty-making in the ancient world. Some will regret the lack of any close discussion of the authorship, composition, and dates of the Homeric epics. But this book is not much concerned with such problems, which have already been exhaustively treated by classicists. In spite of its debt to philological scholarship, its questions are fundamentally historical ones, concerned with the early common origins of certain practices associated with promising and treaty-making and the viability of these practices. It assumes without demurral the prevailing scholarly view that the Homeric epics were composed sometime in the latter part of the Dark Ages (1150-750 B.C.) and that the *Odyssey* is the younger of the two compositions. Occasional references to the name of Homer constitute a topos more than an acknowledgment of any so-called "unitarian" theory: authorship of the epics is a subject that is not addressed here. The question of "younger" or "older" passages in the Homeric corpus is of somewhat greater relevance to this study, but even this question is suspended, since its answer would not much affect the general arguments here advanced. Indeed, if it should turn out that some of the passages included in our corpus of Homeric agreements are much younger than the others, that fact would itself illustrate one of the principal themes of this study, viz., that the structures and practices under discussion here were enduring features of Greek and Near Eastern civilizations, rather than merely the poetic fancies or short-term social arrangements of Homer's own time.

PART ONE

THE HOMERIC AGREEMENTS

Their Corpus, Terminology, and Structure

CHAPTER ONE

THE CORPUS OF HOMERIC AGREEMENTS

In the discussion that follows we shall try to isolate the corpus of those vows, promises, treaties, and other exchanges between Homer's dramatis personae that are here collectively referred to as the *Homeric agreements.* Each agreement is accompanied by a brief commentary, which not only fills out the narrative but also discusses whether the agreement involves equal parties (parity) or unequals (suzerainty).

Whereas in the Near Eastern treaties the lines drawn between these two types of covenants may be easy to detect, the same is not true of the Homeric agreements. The reader should bear in mind that although most of the Near Eastern treaties would easily fall under the formal category of what are in modern times internationally recognized as treaties, the same is not necessarily so with the Homeric agreements.[1] If nothing else, we may be sure that the Homeric literature was not intended to reproduce legal documents, although it certainly reflects many of the customs of the age and preceding times, including the way Greek people made agreements. Thus, whatever position Agamemnon might actually have held during the Trojan campaign, in the Homeric epics he is represented as the *primus inter pares,* who leads with the consent and approval of the other Homeric kings. Consequently, the original agreement of the Greeks by which Agamemnon was designated the supreme commander of the Greek troops (regardless of whether his position as the king of Mycenae made him the paramount figure in the Mycenaean world or not) was voluntary.

In the Homeric context, therefore, any agreement made between him and any of the other Greek kings in Troy must be considered a parity arrangement, despite the obviously superior position of Agamemnon. In other instances, such as agreements between gods and human beings or between superior and inferior gods, it is easier to decide the type of the agreement, although not all such cases, for instance that of Hera and Sleep, are as clear as they first seem. In more complicated instances, the question of what type of agreement is involved has to be resolved case by case, with close scrutiny of the circumstances of the particular occasion.

It goes without saying that the agreements between gods or gods and human beings are fictional and in that sense cannot be taken literally; but

---

[1] There is no unanimity about the division of the Near Eastern treaties. In his *Zur staatsrechtlichen Wertung der hethitischen Verträge* in *Meisner's Festschrift* (Leipzig, 1929) 2:180-86, Schachermeyr provides six categories for the Hittite treaties. Korosec, *Hethitische Staatsverträge* (Leipzig, 1931) 4-11, makes what seems a more plausible classification of the Hittite treaties.

although events and persons may be fictional, there is little doubt that the type of agreement concluded reflected the profound convictions and real practices of the background culture which gave rise to such agreements. For instance, it matters little whether Agamemnon's failure to agree to Chryses' demands produced the plague sent by Apollo or whether the plague actually resulted from some sort of virus that happened to strike the Achaean camp sometime after the encounter between Agamemnon and Chryses, or even whether the episode is a fictional recourse, given the fact that the Greeks and other people of the Near East believed that plagues and other sorts of misfortune could be visited upon them as divine punishment for some moral infraction. Similarly, it matters little that the pacts between Circe and Odysseus and Hera and the river Xanthus were fictional. What is important is that they probably reflected real circumstances among human beings, from which the ancients, like us, extrapolated in order to describe the economy of the gods.

A. THE HOMERIC TEXTS

Agreement No. 1: Achilles' oath

> "ὦ 'Αχιλεῦ, κέλεαί με, Διίφιλε, μυθήσασθαι
> μῆνιν 'Απόλλωνος ἑκατηβελέταο ἄνακτος·
> τοιγὰρ ἐγὼν ἐρέω· σὺ δὲ σύνθεο καί μοι ὄμοσσον
> ἦ μέν μοι πρόφρων ἔπεσιν καὶ χερσὶν ἀρήξειν·
> ἦ γὰρ ὀΐομαι ἄνδρα χολωσέμεν, ὅς μέγα πάντων
> 'Αργείων κρατέει καί οἱ πείθονται 'Αχαιοί."
> ...
>
> "οὔ τις ἐμεῦ ζῶντος καὶ ἐπὶ χθονὶ δερκομένοιο
> σοὶ κοίλης παρὰ νηυσὶ βαρείας χεῖρας ἐποίσει
> συμπάντων Δαναῶν, οὐδ' ἤν 'Αγαμέμνονα εἴπῃς,
> ὃς νῦν πολλὸν ἄριστος 'Αχαιῶν εὔχεται εἶναι."
> *Il.* 1.74-79, 88-91

The first of the Homeric agreements that we shall consider is found at the beginning of the *Iliad*, with the Achaean assembly convened to discuss the means whereby the Achaean troops could escape the decimating plague that had befallen them. As frequently happened in times of crisis, the Greeks decided to consult the gods. Calchas, the seer, was asked to prophesy, but since he supposedly knew that his predictions would anger Agamemnon, he refused to do so at first, but then, pressured by Achilles, decided to speak out.[2] However, even after the command of Achilles he would not engage in prophecy before he had received certain guarantees of protection, irrespective of who might be vexed by his predictions. He thus asked for an agreement (*synthêkên epi boêtheiai*), for this is the meaning of the verbal form *syntheo*. And not only did he ask for an agreement in front of all the Achaeans, but that it be a *sworn* agreement (*kai moi omosson*). Its terms required that Achilles would protect Calchas wholeheartedly (*prophrôn ... arêxein*) from physical as well as verbal attacks, regardless of the social or political station of the attacker. Furthermore, he demanded that the agreement be of long duration (*metopisthen echei koton*) for one never knew how long the grudge of his enemies might last. The terms set by Calchas before he prophesied can then be summarized as follows: he required (1) an agreement, (2) a sworn agreement, (3) wholehearted support, (4) support of long duration, (5) protection against physical and verbal abuse, and (6) total protection.

Achilles quickly agreed to all the demands set by Calchas. However, a somewhat surprising qualification was attached to these assurances. Although the use of the locution οὔ τις ἐμεῦ ζῶντος καὶ ἐπὶ χθονὶ δερκομένοιο makes Achilles' promise appear to be a life-time commitment, the *koilêis para nêusi* limits its coverage to the Greeks' stay in Troy. Was Achilles being cautious, hedging his bets as it were? Not necessarily. This limitation, seemingly so out of character for Achilles, may have been meant to remind everyone that Calchas had little to fear after the departure of the Greeks from Troy, for Agamemnon might have been *aristos en stratôi* but after the termination of the campaign his power would be once again limited to Mycenae.[3] Eventually, the prediction of Calchas led to a dissension which on the surface appeared to be personal and psychological, although in fact it essentially involved legal and political matters between two independent kings who found themselves antagonistically posed. As Erbse has pointed out, even if the comment by Achilles was not arrogantly meant but only intended to mean something like "If I may say so I would protect you against all, including Agamemnon," it placed Achilles in a difficult position from which he could not retreat without loss of face in front of the whole army, when it turned out that the real culprit was none other but Agamemnon himself.[4] In the course of the dispute Achilles took an oath that would end

---

[2] The Romans, like Achilles, frequently swore on the scepter of Jupiter that they would fulfill the conditions agreed to; Cic. *Fam.* 7.2. The wrath of Achilles sets the stage for later instances where the dangerous wrath of kings against carriers of undesirable news became commonplace; see Sophocles' *Oedipus King* and Euripedes' *Bacchae*; G. S. Kirk, *The Iliad: A Commentary*, vol. 1 (Cambridge, 1985) ad *Il.* 1.74-83, believes that the theme existed in epic tradition before Homer's time and that kings were prone to be angry at mere disagreement; *Il.* 2.195-97; 9.32.

[3] Eust. ad *Il.* 1.77-83.

[4] Erbse ad *Il.* 1.90.

20 THE CORPUS OF HOMERIC AGREEMENTS

his cooperation with the other Achaeans. This action disrupted the unity of the Achaean camp, and made what was originally a personal quarrel a grievous dispute of interest to all.

Agreement No. 2: Nestôr's speech

"οὐδέ τοι ἐκτελέουσιν ὑπόσχεσιν ἥν περ ὑπέσταν
ἐνθάδ' ἔτι στείχοντες ἀπ' Ἄργεος ἱπποβότοιο,
Ἴλιον ἐκπέρσαντ' εὐτείχεον ἀπονέεσθαι."
                                                Il. 2.286-88

"πῇ δὴ συνθεσίαι τε καὶ ὅρκια βήσεται ἥμιν;
ἐν πυρὶ δὴ βουλαί τε γενοίατο μήδεά τ' ἀνδρῶν,
σπονδαί τ' ἄκρητοι καὶ δεξιαί, ἧς ἐπέπιθμεν·"
                                                Il. 2.339-41

Odysseus and Nestor advised the Achaeans to put aside any thought of returning home, urging them to go on with their campaign against Troy. Any thought of departure would be premature, for departure would convert their earlier compacts and oaths to empty words.[5] The terms of the agreement adverted to by Nestor are not spelled out here but they apparently contained the stipulation that the supreme command would be entrusted to Agamemnon (*Il.* 2.344); it also included Agamemnon's obligation to consult the other Greek leaders about common problems, and the promise of all parties to remain in Ilium until the capture of Troy.[6] Presumably the compact was solemnized in the usual manner, by the sacrifice of animals and the pouring of unmixed wine.[7]

The use of *synthesie* is similar to *syntheo kai moi omosson* in *Il.* 1.76, while the *mêdea andrôn* is here employed euphemistically as a way of saying either "our" or "your" decisions. Nestor preferred to express himself this way to make his statement more palatable. The reference to unmixed wine used in the libations in connection with agreements was meant to symbolize the straightforward character of the exchanged promises. The practice of clasping the right arm was a gesture complementary to the oaths just taken, a token of

---

[5] For the use of *pyri* and allusions to the above treaty see *Il.* 5.215; 8.229; 13.219 ff. The "promise" referred to in line 286 was the general commitment by the army to see the expedition to a successful end. This pledge was given prior to the Achaean departure from Argos or Aulis, and is not identical with the earlier famous vow of Helen's suitors; Kirk, *The Iliad,* ad *Il.* 2.286-88.

[6] Leaf *ad loc*; for the promise to Agamemnon see *Il.* 2.284 ff.; see also Vergil's *Aen.* 4.426; Ameis and Hentze, note on *Il.* 2.339.

[7] For *akrêtoi* see *Il.* 4. 159. Odysseus pretentiously criticized Agamemnon on the grounds that the latter's decision to return home ostensibly constituted a violation of the Achaean oath which specified that there would be no return until Troy had been captured, *Il.* 2.286-88.

THE CORPUS OF HOMERIC AGREEMENTS 21

friendship and unity of spirit. Here *hypestan* stands for *hypestêsan*, which is equivalent to *hypeschonto* and *hypemeinan*. Odysseus was here accusing the Greeks of breaking their earlier promise to Agamemnon not to return home before they had destroyed Ilium. Nestor, on the other hand, was charging them outright with a flagrant violation of their oaths (*epiorkia*), since they had not only promised but also sworn to capture Troy before they returned home. Furthermore, they had poured forth libations and had given their right hands in confirmation of their oaths. He is thus implying that, had they not gone through these procedures, Agamemnon might not have undertaken the campaign.[8]

The aforementioned agreement seems to have been predicated upon an earlier one following the competition for the hand of Helen. According to Stesichorus, before Helen's father gave his daughter away to one of the suitors, he had them all bound to an oath that they would come to Helen's assistance if any adversity befell her.[9] The story sounds like one of several apocryphal tales invented ex post facto to explain the Trojan expedition. However, it may contain some kernel of truth, since Stesichorus's story

---

[8] Bekker ad *Il.* 2.340.

[9] The agreement is mentioned in Stesichorus, D. L. Page, *Lyrica Graeca,* OCT, No. 60. For a similar event see also Hdt. 6.126 ff. For the dates of Stesichorus see Plat. *Phaedr.* 243A ff.; *Rep.* 9.586C; *Epistl.* 3.319E; Suidas s.v. Stesichorus; *Marm. Par.* 50; Quint. *Instit.* 10.1.62; Dion. Hal. *Vett. Gens.* 2.27; Thuc. 1.91.1; Isocr. 10.40; Paus. 3.20.9; Apollod. 3.10.9. Thucydides' view is that the various Achaean leaders followed Agamemnon because of his military and economic superiority, which inspired them with awe. This is not the picture one gets from Homer. Achilles is definitely not afraid of Agamemnon, nor are the other leaders. Acceptance of Thucydides' view should not be interpreted (*ou tosouton*, Thuc. 1.9.1) in such manner as to make Peleus a subject of Agamemnon and Achilles Agamemnon's subordinate. As the son of Peleus, Achilles possessed a prominent place in the council of elders, οὕνεκα βουλῇ ἀριστεύειν ἁπάντων; *Il.* 11.627. Since Peleus was still ostensibly alive and reigning over the Myrmidons, Achilles could not be considered as yet as *anax*, except in an indirect manner, i.e., as plenipotentiary of his father in Troy. Achilles' position is somewhat akin to that of Hector whose father is also unable to lead the troops because of old age but still remains the active ruler of Troy. Otherwise, the state of the Myrmidons is similar to that of Agamemnon's in that it enjoys the two main characteristics of a Homeric state: territorial independence and an active dynastic legitimacy. Pylos, the land of Nestor, Crete, the kingdom of Idomeneus, and Ithaca, the country of Odysseus are other examples of this independent status, L. Palmer, *Mycenaeans and Minoanss,* 2nd ed. London, 1965) 36; Mabel Lang, *The Palace of Nestor at Pylos in Western Messenia* (Princeton, 1966) 23. Perhaps the recommendation of Odysseus provides a better answer to the problem of unity vs. pluralism in the Achaean community. When Odysseus utters the apophthegmatic suggestion εἷς κοίρανος ἔστω εἷς βασιλεὺς, *Il.* 2.204-205, he does not advert to the internal authority of a state, for this is not essentially in doubt, but to the situation in Troy. Accordingly Odysseus struck down Thersites when he raised doubts about the right of Agamemnon to rule. What Odysseus wanted to make clear and to impress upon all the leaders is the idea of a unified military command in the context of a wider hegemonic policy, on which the success of the common enterprise depended. Because the army is not completely integrated but retains its individual ethnic physiognomy, it required a unity of command if it were to act effectively.

22 THE CORPUS OF HOMERIC AGREEMENTS

bears comparison with a similar contest organized by the Sicyonian Cleisthenes in the sixth century B.C., the historicity of which is in little doubt.

The agreement referred to by Nestor implied a mutuality of obligations between leader and followers, in that failure to abide by these obligations could eventually lead to a fissure in the Greek ranks similar to the break between Achilles and Agamemnon. Although Agamemnon told Achilles to leave if he wished, any notion of using force to keep Achilles in the alliance would have been out of question, for the use of force would have been contrary to the spirit of independence prevailing among the participating kings in the expedition. There is little doubt that the pledge to Helen's father overshadowed the spirit of voluntarism, but, as will be shown later, Achilles had not taken the oath to Helen's father, and the customary law (*themistes*) imposed a set of mutual obligations, whose violation freed the injured party from his obligation to the alliance.

Agreement No. 3: Alexander's proposal

"κέκλυτέ μευ, Τρῶες καὶ ἐϋκνήμιδες Ἀχαιοί,
μῦθον Ἀλεξάνδροιο, τοῦ εἵνεκα νεῖκος ὄρωρεν.
ἄλλους μὲν κέλεται Τρῶας καὶ πάντας Ἀχαιοὺς
τεύχεα κάλ' ἀποθέσθαι ἐπὶ χθονὶ πουλυβοτείρῃ,
αὐτὸν δ' ἐν μέσσῳ καὶ ἀρηΐφιλον Μενέλαον
οἴους ἀμφ' Ἑλένῃ καὶ κτήμασι πᾶσι μάχεσθαι.
ὁππότερος δέ κε νικήσῃ κρείσσων τε γένηται,
κτήμαθ' ἑλὼν ἐῦ πάντα γυναῖκά τε οἴκαδ' ἀγέσθω·
οἱ δ' ἄλλοι φιλότητα καὶ ὅρκια πιστὰ τάμωμεν."
Il. 3.86-94

On behalf of his brother Alexander, Hector proposed a duel to the Greeks. It is noteworthy that, in transmitting his brother's message, Hector did not simply say κέκλυτέ μευ μῦθον but rather μῦθον Ἀλεξάνδροιο. His reason for underscoring the provenance of the proposal may well have been his awareness of its unjust nature, since what Alexander was proposing involved fighting for what he had unjustly taken away, in contrast to Menelaus, whose battle would be to get back what he originally and quite justly possessed. In this context, Homer shows that Hector was not simply glad about the impending *monomachia* but overwhelmed with joy. Presumably, Hector's hope was that one of two results would follow: Paris would either kill Menelaus or be killed by him. In either case, both Trojans and Achaeans

THE CORPUS OF HOMERIC AGREEMENTS 23

hoped to see the end of the war, for according to Eustathius's reference ὀλίγῳ κακῷ ἔοικε νεῖκος ἀναιρεῖν.[10]

The stipulations of the agreement were as follows: (1) Helen and her possessions would go to the winner; (2) if Menelaus won, the Greeks would take Helen and return to their land; (3) the Trojans would remain thereafter unmolested in their land; (4) friendship and peace would reign between the two peoples. To solemnize the agreement both sides agreed to a sacrifice. The Greeks accepted the proposals on the condition that Priam himself would be present at the ceremony, inasmuch as the Greeks had no faith in Priam's sons whom they considered overweening and unreliable.[11] In fact, not all of Priam's sons were such, as the example of Hector demonstrates. Priam had ostensibly fifty sons and, as happens in most families, some were more admirable than others. Those who exhibited the nobility of their class and ancestry were held in high esteem among the Trojans. The virtues of these able princes best represented the ideals of their age and society. Others, however, were less admirable, as Priam himself was the first to admit. Priam's negative comments regarding several of his surviving sons were remarkably harsh: he described them as liars, dancers, nimble of foot (most probably denoting an effeminate quality somewhat alien to the requirements of the age and culture), robbers of lambs and kids even from their own folk (*Il.* 24.259 ff.) Among those harangued by Priam for disgracing the family's name was Paris, whom Menelaus must have had in mind when he remarked that Priam's sons were unreliable. In view of Paris's reputation, then, it is little wonder that the Greeks asked for Priam's presence at the solemnizing ceremony.

The agreement further specified the type of animals to be sacrificed, namely two lambs, one a white ram and the other a black ewe, to be sacrificed to the Sun and Earth respectively, with a third lamb to be sacrificed to Zeus. Significantly, the duel agreement did not merely comprise terms for the settlement of the quarrel itself; it also entailed *philotêta* (*hospitium*), i.e.,

---

[10] Eust. ad *Il.* 3.76. Obviously the quotation belongs to some other ancient source which is not extant.

[11] Duels as a means of solving personal, social, political, and other types of disputes were frequent occurrences in the Ancient Near East; G. R. Driver, *Canaanite Myths and Legends in Old Testament Studies* (Edinburgh, 1956) 3:12 f., 20 ff.; CAH³ 2:156. As C. Phillipson has said, a certain artistic ideal was realized in the single combat between leading protagonists or distinguished warriors who played the fitting part of the protagonists of a tragedy, while their respective armies took the role of the spectators and judges of fair play; Phillipson, *The International Law and Custom of Ancient Greece and Rome* (London, 1911) 2:209. See also M. R. Davie, *The Evolution of War, A Study of Its Role in Early Societies* (New York, 1968) 177-78; T. D. Seymour, *Life in the Homeric Age* (New York, 1907) 581-82; Strabo 13.1.38, 8.3.33; Plut. *Moral.* 855B; Aristl. *Rhet.* 1.15; Diog. Laert. 1.74. For single battles see also Eur. *Phoen. Women* 1225-40; *Heracleides* 802 ff.; FGrHist. 70 F 116; Hdt.7.104.3, 9.26.3-5.

24   THE CORPUS OF HOMERIC AGREEMENTS

friendship and alliance to prevail thereafter between the two enemies.[12]
Menelaus seemed to doubt that the Trojans would honor the agreement were
he the victor; but he could not turn down the proposal, since he realized that
the Achaeans had already suffered much on account of his personal
vicissitudes and that they were eager to return to their homes. Faced with this
dilemma, Menelaus decided to risk his life, trusting in the aid of the gods
because he believed that right was on his side.[13] His request that Priam
should take the oath instead of Paris was intended to strengthen his position
in the eyes of the gods and of the combatants on both sides, in case Paris
violated the agreement. If that happened, Menelaus and the Achaeans would
be further convinced of the justice of their cause, while conversely the
Trojans would be exposed for their faithlessness and deceit. With the justice
of Menelaus's case newly strengthened, the Achaeans would be readier than
before to fight for the violated oaths, whereas the Trojans would subsequently
labor under the fear of divine punishment.

Notified by the herald Idaeus, Priam went to the plain where Agamemnon
and the Greeks were waiting to take the oaths. In the invocation of the gods
as witnesses, Agamemnon once more repeated the stipulations for all to hear
adding a new condition not mentioned in the original proposal: the payment
of compensation to the Greeks without which, even if Menelaus won,
Agamemnon vowed to stay in Troy until a successful outcome of the war had
been reached.[14]

In *Il.* 3.245 and 3.269 the oath offerings included wine as well as the
sacrificial victims; *pista* stressed the obligation to abide by the promises
given, while *horkia temnein*, properly speaking, signified the victims for the
sacrifice. However, the original signification of the phrase *horkia temnein*
ultimately became so conventional that it was identified with the treaty
itself.[15] Finally, Agamemnon slew the sacrificial sheep, poured wine from
the cups and, raising his hands, prayed that the violator's brains be poured
forth like the wine. According to Homer a just curse never failed to
materialize sooner or later. This stress on the concept of the eventual meting
out of justice contributed in no small part to Homer's reputation as the
educator of Greece, since he praised certain divine forces as witnesses of the
oaths and as punishers of the oath-breakers. Here he has Helios witness the
oaths because of the prevalent belief that Helios could see everything.[16] The

---

[12] Erbse ad *Il.* 3.97; Cauer ad *Il.* 3.10; Bekker ad *Il.* 3.98; Leaf and Bayfield ad *Il.* 3.19-98.

[13] Bekker ad *Il.* 3.97-99.

[14] *Il.* 3.286; Eust. ad *Il.* 3.273.

[15] *Il.* 3.94, 256, 4.269; Erbse ad *Il.* 3.269; Leaf ad *Il.* 3.246.

[16] For the same reason it is said that the Bithynians held court seated facing the Sun; Eust.
ad *Il.* 3.276-77. By inference, devious business was transacted in the dark not to be seen by
the Sun. Similarly, Agamemnon invoked Zeus of Ida as witness, for Zeus of Ida was

THE CORPUS OF HOMERIC AGREEMENTS 25

curse included the children and wives of the guilty, although a different punishment was invoked for them.[17] The cutting of the hair from the sacrificial animals (*Il.* 3.271-74) and its distribution to the participants in the oath symbolized the death of the participants should they breach the agreement.[18]

Unaware that the eventual withdrawal of Alexander from the duel was the result of Aphrodite's intervention, the Achaeans appealed to the Trojans and their allies for the fulfillment of the agreement under discussion here (*Il.* 3.56-60). But the Trojans refused to comply with the Achaean request, instead proposing what seemed to the Achaeans a rather obvious subterfuge, namely, the stipulation specifying death (*sphagê*) as the criterion of victory.[19] Even Hector, the bravest and most fair-minded of the Trojans, accepted this technicality in the treaty's language in order to ignore Agamemnon's request for the return of Helen, suggesting instead another duel. To complicate matters further, Pandarus hurled an arrow with the purpose of killing Menelaus, an act perceived by the Greeks as an additional treachery on the part of the Trojans.[20]

Agreement No. 4: Idomeneus's promise

"'Ατρείδη, μάλα μέν τοι ἐγὼν ἐρίηρος ἑταῖρος
ἔσσομαι, ὡς τὸ πρῶτον ὑπέστην καὶ κατένευσα·
ἀλλ' ἄλλους ὄτρυνε κάρη κομόωντας 'Αχαιούς,

---

considered the giver of life. Agamemnon also called upon the rivers and the Earth, the first as the provider of liquids, the second as the giver of food. In short, Agamemnon called upon all the gods, the Sky, Earth and subterranean deities to witness the transaction; Eust. ad *Il.* 3.273 ff.

[17] In the Homeric times for someone's wife to become another's slave was considered a fate worse than death. For the symbolism of the curses and the swearing see Soph. *Aias* 1179; Theocr. 2.21-23; Livy 1.24; 21-45; Gen. 15.9 ff.; Cauer ad *Il.* 3.273; Leaf ad *Il.* 3.269; Eust. ad *Il.* 3.273. The invocation of all the gods recalls the extensive list of gods in the Hittite and other Near Eastern treaties. Similarly the use of *pantôn* in the treaty between Hannibal and Philip V of Macedon points to the persistence of formulas employed in the making of treaties, M. L. Barré, *The God-list in the Treaty between Hannibal and Philip of Macedonia. A Study in Light of the Ancient Near Eastern Treaty Tradition* (Baltimore, 1983) 93, 100-101. Some of the remarks by A. H. Chroust, *Classical et Mediaevalia* 15 (1954) 75 may also be appropriate here. On the other hand, Chroust considers the reference to and invocation of rivers, harbors and waters rather unusual among the Greeks, thus ignoring Homer. He also seems to err when he views Hannibal's invocation of the gods (Polyb. 7.9.3) as traditional for the "oriental Carthaginians" but totally alien to the diplomatic or legalistic language of the Greeks. He cites as evidence W. R. Smith, *Lectures on the Religion of the Semites* (New York, 1957) 169 and R. Laqueur, *Hermes* 71 (1934) 467 ff.

[18] Eust. ad *Il.* 3.271-74. For self-cursing see Arist. *Ach.* 833; *Clouds* 40; *Peace* 1063; *Plutos* 526; Soph. *Aias* 1177-79.

[19] *Il.* 3.281-84; Erbse *ad. loc.* The verb *katapephnê* denotes *sphagê*.

[20] *Il.* 4.157; Bekker *ad loc.*; P. Wolf, *Mus. Helv.* 11 (1954) 231-42.

26   THE CORPUS OF HOMERIC AGREEMENTS

ὄφρα τάχιστα μαχώμεθ', ἐπεὶ σύν γ' ὅρκι' ἔχευαν
Τρῶες·"

Il. 4.266-70

After the refusal of the Trojans and their allies to honor the duel agreement, Agamemnon urged the Achaeans to resume the fighting. Thereupon, Idomeneus promised to stand by Agamemnon and to honor the pledges he had given, most probably prior to the Achaean departure for Troy when Agamemnon solicited Achaean aid against the Trojans.[21] Idomeneus's pledge is clearly intimated by the *hypestên kai kateneusa* while the recent agreement between the Achaeans and Trojans is hinted by the *horkia echeuan*.

It should also be noted that the Trojans were not consistent in their attitudes toward oath-breaking, as is clear from an incident following the Hector-Aias duel (*Il.* 7.348-53). When the Trojans assembled in order to give thanks to their gods for returning Hector safely to them, Antenor grasped the opportunity to urge his compatriots to return Helen and her possessions to their rightful owners, inasmuch as the continuation of fighting would constitute an *epiorkia* in view of what had already transpired in the Menelaus-Alexander duel. However, the incident also reveals hardheartedness on the Trojans' part, since Antenor's suggestion fell on deaf ears.

Agreement No. 5: Apollo and Athena's agreement

"νῦν μὲν παύσωμεν πόλεμον καὶ δηϊοτῆτα
σήμερον· ὕστερον αὖτε μαχήσοντ', εἰς ὅ κε τέκμωρ
'Ιλίου εὕρωσιν."

...

"'Έκτορος ὄρσωμεν κρατερὸν μένος ἱπποδάμοιο,
ἤν τινά που Δαναῶν προκαλέσσεται οἰόθεν οἶος
ἀντίβιον μαχέσασθαι ἐν αἰνῇ δηϊοτῆτι,
οἱ δέ κ' ἀγασσάμενοι χαλκοκνήμιδες 'Αχαιοὶ
οἶον ἐπόρσειαν πολεμίζειν 'Έκτορι δίῳ."
"Ὡς ἔφατ', οὐδ' ἀπίθησε θεὰ γλαυκῶπις 'Αθήνη·
τῶν δ' 'Ελενος, Πριάμοιο φίλος παῖς, σύνθετο θυμῷ
βουλήν, ἥ ῥα θεοῖσιν ἐφήνδανε μητιόωσι·

Il. 7.29-31, 38-45

Apollo and Athena agreed to provoke Hector into a duel against any one of the Achaeans. The Achaean who was eventually selected to fight Hector was Aias. Once their agreement about the duel was made, the two gods, in the

---

[21] Kirk, in *The Iliad*, thinks that *kateneusa* in 1.267 adverts to the general oath taken by Helen's suitors of whom Idomeneus was one; Hesiod, *Echoiae*, frg. 204, 1.56. Kirk's view is debatable.

THE CORPUS OF HOMERIC AGREEMENTS 27

guise of vultures, perched themselves on the oak tree by the Scaean gate to watch the course of the duel.[22]

While *tekmôr* means, in general, that which has been established, or whatever has been set as the assigned goal, here it seems to have the more specific meaning of "the limit set by fate for Ilios," or even "the goal set for themselves by the Greeks with regard to Ilios." Ameis accepts the latter on the analogy of *Il.* 2.472. Leaf (*ad loc.*) feels that the voice of the verb accompanying *tekmôr* may make the difference. In *Il.* 2.472 the verb *heureto* is in the middle voice while here it is in the active (also in *Il.* 1.48, 418). The absence of constraint in the formulation of the agreement as well as its immediate enforcement did not require an oath on the part of the gods, nor was one taken. In other times, when one of the parties was asked to grant a favor to another in return for a compensation, the asking party was expected to swear an oath that it would reciprocate and that it would not break its promise.

Agreement No. 6: Hector's challenge

"ὧδε δὲ μυθέομαι, Ζεὺς δ' ἄμμ' ἐπὶ μάρτυρος ἔστω·
εἰ μέν κεν ἐμὲ κεῖνος ἕλῃ ταναήκεϊ χαλκῷ,
τεύχεα συλήσας φερέτω κοίλας ἐπὶ νῆας,
σῶμα δὲ οἴκαδ' ἐμὸν δόμεναι πάλιν, ὄφρα πυρός με
Τρῶες καὶ Τρώων ἄλοχοι λελάχωσι θανόντα.
εἰ δέ κ' ἐγὼ τὸν ἕλω, δώῃ δέ μοι εὖχος Ἀπόλλων,
τεύχεα σύλησας οἴσω προτὶ Ἴλιον ἰρήν,
καὶ κρεμόω προτὶ νηὸν Ἀπόλλωνος ἑκάτοιο,
τὸν δὲ νέκυν ἐπὶ νῆας ἐϋσσέλμους ἀποδώσω,
ὄφρα ἑ ταρχύσωσι κάρη κομόωντες Ἀχαιοί,
σῆμά τε οἱ χεύωσιν ἐπὶ πλατεῖ Ἑλλησπόντῳ."
Il. 7.76-86

Hector proposed a duel between himself and one of the Achaeans on the condition that the victor, after stripping the victim's armor, would return the body for burial. The Greeks accepted Hector's challenge and proceeded to cast lots among themselves to determine Hector's opponent. The lot fell on Aias the Telamonian, who was assured by Hector of a fair and open fight according to the rules of the agonistic age appropriate to gentlemen.[23] Although, this was a duel to the death, neither of the opponents turned out to be capable of inflicting death on his opponent.

---

[22] This oak tree was an important landmark featured several times in the *Iliad* (5.237, 693; 7.22, 60). This is strictly an interpersonal agreement (a matter of consensus?) without any mutual obligations. See also Kirk, *The Iliad: A Commentary* 2, *ad loc.*

[23] *Il.* 7.243-44; Erbse *ad loc.*; Eust. *ad. loc.*

28 THE CORPUS OF HOMERIC AGREEMENTS

The single battle lasted until darkness fell, at which point the combatants agreed to separate amicably. The suggestion for the termination of the duel had to have the prior approval of Hector, who was the challenger (*Il.* 7.284-85; Bekker, ad *Il.* 7.86). Hector not only embraced the suggestion but even recommended that the duelists exchange gifts as tokens of their friendly parting. Although neither of the combatants suffered injury or death, the duel was considered as having reached a legitimate resolution. However, both parties parted with the undefined hope that someday they might meet again to finish what they were unable to finish this time. Unlike the Menelaus-Alexander agreement, which involved deeper moral and social issues, this later duel seems to have been nothing more than a trial of skills. Once both parties were satisfied that one opponent proved a match for the other, they needed to go no further.[24]

Although this duel had no great relevance to the issues and no significance for the outcome of the war, the rules of agonistic etiquette seemed to have required the challenger's consent to terminate the fight. Hector, with his reputation at stake (*synetou ontos Hectoros*), did not wish to comply too eagerly with the herald's suggestion lest he give the impression that he had been eager to quit the battle. He tactfully asked for the approval of Aias before he agreed to have the duel ended. Aias, somewhat ahead in the fight at that point and afraid that his reputation might be tarnished by his quick acceptance of the herald's proposal, gave his conditional endorsement upon Hector's open admission that he would consent to putting an end to the battle (Eust. ad 7.274). The Greek herald Talthybius seems to have been ambivalent about terminating the fight because Aias had the advantage at that point. However, at the end Talthybius reluctantly agreed to have the duel stopped (Eust. ad. *Il.* 7.274).

Agreement No. 7: Idaeus's proposal

"Ἰδαῖ', ἦ τοι μῦθον Ἀχαιῶν αὐτὸς ἀκούεις,
ὥς τοι ὑποκρίνονται· ἐμοὶ δ' ἐπιανδάνει οὕτως.
ἀμφὶ δὲ νεκροῖσιν κατακαιέμεν οὔ τι μεγαίρω·
οὐ γάρ τις φειδὼ νεκύων κατατεθνηώτων
γίγνετ', ἐπεί κε θάνωσι, πυρὸς μειλισσέμεν ὦκα.
ὅρκια δὲ Ζεὺς ἴστω, ἐρίγδουπος πόσις Ἥρης."
                                                    Il. 7.406-11

Following Antenor's recommendation for the return of Helen, a new effort was made at a negotiated peace. The negotiations aimed at a double understanding. The first part contained Alexander's proposal for the return of Helen's possessions but not Helen herself, and included a rider for a truce to

---

[24] Leaf and Bayfield, 288; Bekker ad *Il.* 7.242.

THE CORPUS OF HOMERIC AGREEMENTS   29

permit the burial of the dead. The Trojans were ready to return Helen's property and offer compensation as the Greeks had earlier demanded (*Il.* 3.286). Idaeus was thus dispatched to the Greek camp to announce the proposals and to receive the response of the Greeks (*Il.* 7.385-97). (It is for this reason that the agreement is here referred to as "Idaeus's Proposal," even though it originated with Priam and other Trojans.) Interestingly, Idaeus did not limit himself strictly to the instructions he had received but proceeded to express his sentiments—which, no doubt, reflected the sentiments of many other Trojans—by damning Alexander in front of the Greeks and thereby inappropriately informing the Achaeans that most of the Trojans were in favor of Helen's return.[25]

The Greeks rejected the idea of compensation while they agreed to a truce for the burial of the dead. This truce was sealed by *horkia*, in which Zeus was invoked as witness. The absence of the formula *horkia pista temnein*, customary in the sacrificial ceremonies, signifies the conclusion of an informal agreement without the solemnization by sacrificial animals. Agamemnon simply raised his staff to all the gods as he invoked Zeus to be the witness. The Trojans did not swear to the agreement; they did not have to do so. It is not, clear, however, why Agamemnon raised his staff to all the gods when only Zeus, the presiding deity, is named.[26]

Agreement No. 8: Hector's pledge to Dolon

"ἀλλ' ἄγε μοι τὸ σκῆπτρον ἀνάσχεο, καί μοι ὄμοσσον
ἦ μὲν τοὺς ἵππους τε καὶ ἅρματα ποικίλα χαλκῷ
δωσέμεν, οἵ φορέουσιν ἀμύμονα Πηλεΐωνα,
σοὶ δ' ἐγὼ οὐχ ἅλιος σκοπὸς ἔσσομαι οὐδ' ἀπὸ δόξης.
τόφρα γὰρ ἐς στρατὸν εἶμι διαμπερές, ὄφρ' ἂν ἵκωμαι
νῆ' Ἀγαμεμνονέην, ὅθι που μέλλουσιν ἄριστοι
βουλὰς βουλεύειν, ἤ φευγέμεν ἠὲ μάχεσθαι."
"Ὣς φάθ', ὁ δ' ἐν χερσὶ σκῆπτρον λάβε καί οἱ ὄμοσσεν·
"ἴστω νῦν Ζεὺς αὐτός, ἐρίγδουπος πόσις Ἥρης,
μὴ μὲν τοῖς ἵπποισιν ἀνὴρ ἐποχήσεται ἄλλος
Τρώων, ἀλλά σέ φημι διαμπερὲς ἀγλαϊεῖσθαι."
                    Il. 10.321-331

Hector needed somebody to undertake a spying mission in the Achaean camp, for which Dolon volunteered, enticed by the promise of the best horses around, not excluding those of Achilles. Homer underscored Dolon's avarice by the use of the adjective *polychrysos, polychalcos* (*Il.* 19.315). Dolon offered Hector the staff he was holding at the moment as the speaker. The

---

[25] *Il.* 7.390; Bekker ad 7.390.
[26] For the raising of the scepter in oath-taking see also *Il.* 1.234; 10.328.

30 THE CORPUS OF HOMERIC AGREEMENTS

staff was customarily passed on to the would-be speaker by a herald as a sign of the recognition of his right to address the assembly (*Il.* 10.328, 1.234, 18.505). Kings of the heroic era swore by their scepter, their ensign of office, which they raised to the gods invoking their punishment if they violated their oaths (Ameis and Hentze *ad loc.*). Hector therefore raised the staff given to him by Dolon and took an oath in the name of Zeus to fulfill his pledge to Dolon. Dolon did not have to take an oath, for the simple reason that the agreement was made to assure him that Hector would fulfill his end of the bargain once Dolon accomplished what Hector had asked him to do. The same is true of agreement No. 10, where the one doing the asking is Hera, who also makes certain promises in exchange for the favor she asked. Hypnos has to be reassured that Hera would deliver her promises once she received what she wanted. In both cases, the asker of the favor has to swear as a safeguard that the promise made will be carried out.

Agreement No. 9: The alliance between Orthryoneus and Priam

πέφνε γὰρ 'Οθρυονῆα Καβησόθεν ἔνδον ἐόντα,
ὅς ῥα νέον πολέμοιο μετὰ κλέος εἰληλούθει,
ᾔτεε δὲ Πριάμοιο θυγατρῶν εἶδος ἀρίστην,
Κασσάνδρην, ἀνάεδνον, ὑπέσχετο δὲ μέγα ἔργον,
ἐκ Τροίης ἀέκοντας ἀπωσέμεν υἷας 'Αχαιῶν.
τῷ δ' ὁ γέρων Πρίαμος ὑπό τ' ἔσχετο καὶ κατένευσε
δωσέμεναι· ὁ δὲ μάρναθ' ὑποσχεσίῃσι πιθήσας.
Il. 13.363-69

Othryoneus asked for and was promised the hand of Cassandra. In return, he pledged to help drive the Achaeans out of Troy. This marriage implied a politico-military alliance between the two families. Unfortunately, Idomeneus killed Othryoneus before the latter could effect any change in the military equilibrium, and so Idomeneus deprived the Trojans of their most recent ally.[27] The alliance seems to have been a simple gentlemen's agreement in which no *horkoi* or *horkia pista* were deemed necessary beyond the promises given by both parties. However, this is an unusually difficult text. The term *endon* seems to distinguish Othryoneus from other allies, but most of the explanations offered of this passage seem unsatisfactory.[28] The true location of Kabesos is equally problematic. The term *eidos aristên* is taken by many to refer to Cassandra's ability to predict (*mantikês eidêsin*), not to her beauty. The *anaendon* admits a double interpretation: the phrase can refer

---

[27] Bekker ad *Il.* 13.364; Erbse ad *Il.* 13.364; FGrHist. 1.169; Eust. ad *Il.* 13.363-69. For sarcastic gloating over one's victim, compare Idomeneus's comments to Judges 5.28-31; C. H. Gordon, *Homer and the Bible*, 89.

[28] Eust. ad *Il.* 13.363; Leaf ad *Il.* 13.363.

THE CORPUS OF HOMERIC AGREEMENTS 31

to gifts given by a groom or to the usual dowry of a bride. Since the latter seems to be more appropriate here, the passage indicates Othryoneus was willing to accept Cassandra without the usual dowry (Eust. *ad loc.*).

Agreement No. 10: Hera's oath

"ἐγὼ δέ κέ τοι ἰδέω χάριν ἤματα πάντα.
κοίμησόν μοι Ζηνὸς ὑπ' ὀφρύσιν ὄσσε φαεινώ,
αὐτίκ' ἐπεί κεν ἐγὼ παραλέξομαι ἐν φιλότητι.
δῶρα δέ τοι δώσω καλὸν θρόνον, ἄφθιτον αἰεί,
χρύσεον· Ἥφαιστος δέ κ' ἐμὸς πάϊς ἀμφιγυήεις
τεύξει' ἀσκήσας, ὑπὸ δὲ θρῆνυν ποσὶν ἥσει,
τῷ κεν ἐπισχοίης λιπαροὺς πόδας εἰλαπινάζων."
                                                      Il. 14.235-41

"ἀλλ' ἴθ', ἐγὼ δέ κέ τοι Χαρίτων μίαν ὁπλοτεράων
δώσω ὀπυιέμεναι καὶ σὴν κεκλῆσθαι ἄκοιτιν."
Πασιθέην, ἧς αἰὲν ἱμείρεαι ἤματα πάντα.
Ὣς φάτο, χήρατο δ' Ὕπνος, ἀμειβόμενος δὲ προσηύδα·
"ἄγρει νῦν μοι ὄμοσσον ἀάατον Στυγὸς ὕδωρ,
χειρὶ δὲ τῇ ἑτέρῃ μὲν ἔλε χθόνα πουλυβότειραν,
τῇ δ' ἑτέρῃ ἅλα μαρμαρέην, ἵνα νῶϊν ἅπαντες
μάρτυροι ὧσ' οἱ ἔνερθε θεοὶ Κρόνον ἀμφὶς ἐόντες,
ἦ μὲν ἐμοὶ δώσειν Χαρίτων μίαν ὁπλοτεράων,
Πασιθέην, ἧς τ' αὐτὸς ἐέλδομαι ἤματα πάντα."
                                                      Il. 14.267-76

Cajolery and deviousness were practiced not only by men but by the Homeric gods as well. In the above compact between Hera and Sleep, Hera used her persuasive power and some underhanded diplomacy to extract a favor from Sleep. If Sleep consented to grant her the favor, Hera promised him an imperishable throne of gold made by Hephaestus, along with a footstool on which Sleep would rest his feet during his wine-drinking sessions. Sleep balked, however, because what Hera wanted involved putting Zeus to sleep, a very risky proposition. Sleep had all too bitter memories of similar experiences in the past. But Hera was not to be put off so easily. She reacted to his refusal by improving her bait, promising him the charms of Pasithea, one of the Graces. This turned out to be too great a temptation for even lethargic Sleep to resist and so, succumbing to Hera's blandishments, he gave in to her mischievous demand. However, the deal was not concluded until Hera took the oath Sleep had demanded as security for the fulfillment of her part of the bargain. Hera had to swear by the inviolable waters of the Styx as she laid one of her hands on the Earth and the other on the simmering Sea. The touching of the waters of the Styx and the Sea signified that all the gods below would serve as witnesses to their pact. It is clear that

32 THE CORPUS OF HOMERIC AGREEMENTS

neither could swear by the name of Zeus as was customary with men, especially since both were bent upon duping him.[29]

Agreement No. 11: Achilles' conditions

"ἀλλὰ καὶ ὥς, Πάτροκλε, νεῶν ἀπὸ λοιγὸν ἀμύνων
ἔμπεσ' ἐπικρατέως, μὴ δὴ πυρὸς αἰθομένοιο
νῆας ἐνιπρήσωσι, φίλον δ' ἀπὸ νόστον ἕλωνται.
πείθεο δ' ὥς τοι ἐγὼ μύθου τέλος ἐν φρεσὶ θείω,
ὡς ἄν μοι τιμὴν μεγάλην καὶ κῦδος ἄρηαι
πρὸς πάντων Δαναῶν, ἀτὰρ οἱ περικαλλέα κούρην
ἄψ ἀπονάσσωσιν, ποτὶ δ' ἀγλαὰ δῶρα πόρωσιν.
ἐκ νηῶν ἐλάσας ἰέναι πάλιν· εἰ δέ κεν αὖ τοι
δώῃ κῦδος ἀρέσθαι ἐρίγδουπος πόσις Ἥρης,
μὴ σύ γ' ἄνευθεν ἐμεῖο λιλαίεσθαι πολεμίζειν
Τρωσὶ φιλοπτολέμοισιν· ἀτιμότερον δέ με θήσεις·
μηδ' ἐπαγαλλόμενος πολέμῳ καὶ δηϊοτῆτι,
Τρῶας ἐναιρόμενος, προτὶ Ἴλιον ἡγεμονεύειν,
μή τις ἀπ' Οὐλύμποιο θεῶν αἰειγενετάων
ἐμβήῃ· μάλα τούς γε φιλεῖ ἑκάεργος Ἀπόλλων·
ἀλλὰ πάλιν τρωπᾶσθαι, ἐπὴν φάος ἐν νήεσσι
θήῃς, τοὺς δ' ἔτ' ἐᾶν πεδίον κάτα δηριάασθαι."

Il. 16.80-96

Yielding to Patroclus's solicitations, Achilles agreed to allow his fellow warrior to defend the Achaeans, even giving him his armor. Nonetheless, Achilles set certain conditions, one of which was that Patroclus would ward off the Trojans but not chase them back to Troy. To do so would have automatically deprived Achilles of the honor he had reserved for himself. Thus Patroclus's glory was to be subordinated to Achilles' ambition. Patroclus was to save the ships but not to relieve the Greeks from the stress of battle. This limited mandate reflected the typical Greek stubbornness and

---

[29] See *Il.* 13.755 where Styx is the dread river of oath; Paus. 1.1.18. For the binding force of oath see Hesiod's *Theog.* 793-803; 785. Also cf. Serv. *Aen.* 6.565: *Fertur namque ab orpheo quod dii peierantes per stygam Paludem nouem annorum spatio puniuntum in Tartaro. Unde ait Statius et styx peniuria diuum arguit.* This testimonium is supported by Pseudo-Galen (Porphyry) *ad Caurum* 35.2; *Orhp.* frg. 115 without the mention of Styx. Whenever a god perjured himself, he was allegedly banished from the company of the immortals for 30,000 seasons and underwent a cycle of mortal lives as an animal, human, plant, fish, etc. Also Erbse ad *Il.* 14.235 and Bekker ad *Il.* 14.234 and 271; Leaf ad *Il.* 14.271; J. G. Frazer, *Pausanias's Description of Greece* (New York, 1896) 4:253. Water was supposed to be fatal to life, and hence an oath in the name of the waters of the Styx was a "sort of poison-ordeal" since the water would kill the person who foreswore himself, but spare him who swore truly. In Hdt. 6.74 there is a case, the only one recorded in history, where the Arcadians were asked to swear by the Styx. There is thus the possibility that when the poets made the gods swear by the Styx, they were only transferring to heaven a practice which had long been customary on earth.

THE CORPUS OF HOMERIC AGREEMENTS   33

petty personal spite for which eventually Achilles would pay with the loss of his friend.

The reader will recall that Achilles had already (in Book 9) rejected the very thing which he is now anxious to secure. Now the danger was (as Phoenix warned him, *Il.* 9.601-605) that the Greeks might be victorious without him, in which case Achilles would forfeit his revenge and the gifts of Agamemnon as well. Patroclus therefore was only to relieve the immediate danger and to leave him to do the rest on his own terms (*epi dôrois*, *Il.* 9.602). Afterwards (*Il.* 19.147 ff.) Achilles treated the gifts with as much disdain as ever; the change was consistent with his nature, because Achilles' grief for Patroclus filled his mind with the same absorbing force as his wrath against Agamemnon had created. The present passage may be understood as showing him in a calmer mood, when the glory and rewards of victory have their natural place in his thought. This agreement is somewhat different than others since the contractants are not only close personal friends, but one is also subordinate to the other. However, to the extent that Patroclus enters into this agreement of his own freewill and accepts freely the terms entailed in the agreement, the agreement fits under the general rubric of the chapter.

Agreement No. 12: Hera and Athena's agreement

"ἦ τοι μὲν γὰρ νῶϊ πολέας ὠμόσσαμεν ὅρκους
πᾶσι μετ' ἀθανάτοισιν, ἐγὼ καὶ Παλλὰς 'Αθήνη,
μή ποτ' ἐπὶ Τρώεσσιν ἀλεξήσειν κακὸν ἦμαρ,
μηδ' ὁπότ' ἄν Τροίη μαλερῷ πυρὶ πᾶσα δάηται
καιομένη, καίωσι δ' ἀρήϊοι υἷες 'Αχαιῶν."
Il. 20.313-17

In this relatively straightforward passage, Hera refers to an agreement between Athena and herself. Made in the presence of the other gods, it was not to ward off destruction from Troy even though the city was consumed by fire set by the Achaeans.

Agreement No. 13: Xanthus's pledge

"'Ήρη, τίπτε σὸς υἱὸς ἐμὸν ῥόον ἔχραε κήδειν
ἐξ ἄλλων; οὐ μέν τοι ἐγὼ τόσον αἴτιός εἰμι,
ὅσσον οἱ ἄλλοι πάντες, ὅσοι Τρώεσσιν ἀρωγοί.
ἀλλ' ἦ τοι μὲν ἐγὼν ἀποπαύσομαι, εἰ σὺ κελεύεις,
παυέσθω δὲ καὶ οὗτος· ἐγὼ δ' ἐπὶ καὶ τόδ' ὀμοῦμαι,
μή ποτ' ἐπὶ Τρώεσσιν ἀλεξήσειν κακὸν ἦμαρ,
μηδ' ὁπότ' ἄν Τροίη μαλερῷ πυρὶ πᾶσα δάηται
καιομένη, καίωσι δ' ἀρήϊοι υἷες 'Αχαιῶν."
Il. 21.369-76

34 THE CORPUS OF HOMERIC AGREEMENTS

Angered by Achilles' conduct, the river Xanthus rushed after him and brought him to a point of desperation. As Achilles seemed about to succumb to the superior might of the river, Hera saved him by sending Hephaestus's fire to consume the waters of the river. The intensity of the heat proved so overwhelming that the river-god pleaded with Hera to spare him this conflagration. He apologized for having helped the Trojans and excused himself by asserting that he was not as great a culprit as some others had been in respect to helping the Trojans. Xanthus further pledged to refrain from his pursuit of Achilles if only Hephaestus quenched his fire. He was also ready to take an oath not to ward off the day of doom from the Trojans, even if all of Troy burned to the ground. Hera accepted Xanthus's promises and the agreement implied in the oath (ὀμοῦμαι) was consummated.

Agreement No. 14: Hector's proposal

"ἀλλ' ἄγε δεῦρο θεοὺς ἐπιδώμεθα· τοὶ γὰρ ἄριστοι
μάρτυροι ἔσσονται καὶ ἐπίσκοποι ἁρμονιάων·
οὐ γὰρ ἐγώ σ' ἔκπαγλον ἀεικιῶ, αἴ κεν ἐμοὶ Ζεὺς
δώῃ καμμονίην, σὴν δὲ ψυχὴν ἀφέλωμαι·
ἀλλ' ἐπεὶ ἄρ κέ σε συλήσω κλυτὰ τεύχε', 'Αχιλλεῦ,
νεκρὸν 'Αχαιοῖσιν δώσω πάλιν· ὣς δὲ σὺ ῥέζειν."
                                                Il. 22.254-59

Before their final battle, Hector proposed an agreement to Achilles whereby both would invoke the gods as the best witnesses and guardians of covenants (literally to give one another to their respective gods). Hector was ready to promise that in case of victory he would do no harm to his opponent's body beyond the traditional stripping of its armor and that he would deliver it for burial. Achilles, on the other hand, was to show the same respect for Hector's body if the gods gave Achilles the victory. The proposal fell on deaf ears, since Achilles, enraged over the death of his friend Patroclus, was in no mood to listen to the customary suggestions. Similar terms had been proposed by Hector when in *Il.* 7.76 ff. he had challenged the best of the Achaeans to fight a duel with him. The use of *epidometha* served to invoke one another's gods as witnesses, denoting the offer of a guarantee to the other side exactly as in *Il.* 3.276, where Zeus, the god of Ida, was named as witness and the local rivers as divinities invoked to represent the Trojan side. The use of *harmonia* here is remarkable, since the word denotes the act of collecting and fitting disparate parties together in a harmonious whole (Eust. ad *Il.* 22.255; Bekker *ad loc.*). That *harmonia* was a sworn treaty becomes obvious from Achilles' answer to Hector, οὐδέ τι νῶϊν ὅρκια ἔσσονται (*Il.* 22.265-66).

THE CORPUS OF HOMERIC AGREEMENTS

Agreement No. 15: Achilles and Priam's arrangement

"ἀλλ' ἄγε μοι τόδε εἰπὲ καὶ ἀτρεκέως κατάλεξον,
ποσσῆμαρ μέμονας κτερεϊζέμεν Ἕκτορα δῖον,
ὄφρα τέως αὐτός τε μένω καὶ λαὸν ἐρύκω."
Τὸν δ' ἠμείβετ' ἔπειτα γέρων Πρίαμος θεοειδής·
"εἰ μὲν δή μ' ἐθέλεις τελέσαι τάφον Ἕκτορι δίῳ,
ὧδέ κέ μοι ῥέζων, Ἀχιλεῦ, κεχαρισμένα θείης.
οἶσθα γὰρ ὡς κατὰ ἄστυ ἐέλμεθα, τηλόθι δ' ὕλη
ἀξέμεν ἐξ ὄρεος, μάλα δὲ Τρῶες δεδίασιν.
ἐννῆμαρ μέν κ' αὐτὸν ἐνὶ μεγάροις γοάοιμεν,
τῇ δεκάτῃ δέ κε θάπτοιμεν δαινῦτό τε λαός,
ἐνδεκάτῃ δέ κε τύμβον ἐπ' αὐτῷ ποιήσαιμεν,
τῇ δὲ δυωδεκάτῃ πολεμίξομεν, εἴ περ ἀνάγκη."
Τὸν δ' αὖτε προσέειπε ποδάρκης δῖος Ἀχιλλεύς·
"ἔσται τοι καὶ ταῦτα, γέρον Πρίαμ', ὡς σὺ κελεύεις·
σχήσω γὰρ πόλεμον τόσσον χρόνον ὅσσον ἄνωγας."
Ὥς ἄρα φωνήσας ἐπὶ καρπῷ χεῖρα γέροντος
ἔλλαβε δεξιτερήν, μή πως δείσει' ἐνὶ θυμῷ."

Il. 24.656-72

In a noble gesture, characteristic of the best practices of the age of aristocratic Greek warriors, Achilles offered the aged Priam a truce for the duration of Hector's funeral ceremonies. Priam had only to name the number of days he needed for the funeral of his son. The arrangement somewhat resembles a suzerainty treaty, for although Priam was an independent king, he was completely at the mercy of his opponent in this instance. No oath is given here because no oath is necessary. The stronger of the parties initiated the offer, and Priam had not the slightest doubt of Achilles' intention to fulfill his promise. The sad funerary occasion further helps to make the taking of oaths unnecessary. A gentleman's word was a contract and this contract was sealed merely by the clasping of hands, a gesture expressive of kindliness as well.[30]

This scene is reminiscent of a similar scene in Sophocles' *Philoctetes*, where Neoptolemus promised to take Philoctetes along on his ship. Philoctetes then asked Neoptolemus for a clasping of hands in confirmation of the promise. To have put Neoptolemus through the test of an oath would have been ungentlemanly, particularly since it was Neoptolemus who had made the promise.

---

[30] *Il.* 24.671-72, 778-81; 7.108; *Od.* 18.258. Modern Greeks clasp hands as token of confirmation of oral agreements, accompanying the gesture with the expression *kolla to!* meaning "Give me your hand." The practice of giving one's hand in confirmation of his word was not exclusive to the Near East. It is found among the Romans (*dexteratum iunctio*) as a symbol of faith, Tac. *Annales* 2.58, 71, and also among the ancient Celts, A. Momigliano *Annali* 14 (1984) 875-86. Also Gregory Nazianzus, *De Pace*, Discourse XII (30), p. 35, col. 1165, (ἰδού δεξιὰς δίδομεν ἀ λλήλοις), and the Scholion, *En mutues dextras, inspectantibus vobis.*

36   THE CORPUS OF HOMERIC AGREEMENTS

The agreement between Achilles and Priam consisted chiefly of the stipulations cited in the text of No. 15, which Achilles worked out with Priam. However, accompanying these stipulations and intimately connected with them is another declamation, recounting the antecedent history underlying the stipulations of the compact. Also accompanying the stipulations was an important clause requiring the cessation of hostilities until the end of the funeral ceremonies. Since there was no oath, there was no need for any curses or blessings, nor for any invocation of the gods as witnesses, as was otherwise customary with reciprocal agreements where both parties, regardless of their status, assumed certain responsibilities.

Achilles offered the truce even though he suspected that his commander would not like it. Moreover, he acceded to a magnificent burial by giving Priam an unprecedented eleven-day truce. Some scholars have noted a mocking tone in Achilles' speech (*epikertomeôn*) owing to what they consider its obscure wording, presumably used by Achilles because he suspected that Agamemnon would try his best to thwart him at every opportunity when he finally heard of the agreement with Priam.[31] This hypothesis is further strengthened by the vision of Hermes, who urged Priam not to sleep in Achilles' hut but to depart immediately lest Agamemnon find out about his presence and thwart his departure until he paid thrice the ransom given to Achilles (*Il.* 24.683 ff.).

Agreement No. 16: Menelaus's promise

ἐν Τροίῃ γὰρ πρῶτον ὑπέσχετο καὶ κατένευσε
δωσέμεναι, τοῖσιν δὲ θεοὶ γάμον ἐξετέλειον.
Od. 4.6-7

Telemachus's arrival in Sparta on a fact-finding mission about his estranged father coincided with the nuptials of Menelaus's daughter to Achilles' son. The marriage was the fulfillment of a promise made to Achilles by Menelaus in Troy. Clearly, here as in other cases a gentleman was bound by his word and no solemnization of the agreement was needed to guarantee its execution. Any further formalities attendant upon a gentleman's pledge might even have been considered offensive, giving the impression that his word could not be

---

[31] Leaf ad *Il.* 24.649, 662-63. Lines 662-63 are rejected by some scholars as giving a wrong reason for the length of time needed, viz., that it would take them so long to collect the wood, whereas really nine days of mourning were demanded by ancient customs. See Plut. *Lyc.* 27.2, where Lycourgos limited the days of mourning and the funeral arrangements to eleven days. Allegedly the Homeric interpolator being ignorant of this held it necessary to supply an explanation of the length of time required. Others reject this skepticism because they do not find the length of time for the collection of wood unreasonable.

THE CORPUS OF HOMERIC AGREEMENTS 37

trusted. A simple nodding of the grantor's head sufficed to get the oral contract sealed.

Agreement No. 17: Calypso's promise

"οὐδ' ἂν ἐγὼν ἀέκητι σέθεν σχεδίης ἐπιβαίην,
εἰ μή μοι τλαίης γε, θεά, μέγαν ὅρκον ὀμόσσαι
μή τί μοι αὐτῷ πῆμα κακὸν βουλευσέμεν ἄλλο."
Od. 5.177-79

Calypso announced to her prisoner-guest her decision to let him return home. In the light of his earlier experiences, Odysseus did not believe her until she swore a mighty oath not to plot further mischiefs against him. Calypso was amused by Odysseus's suspicions, because this time she meant to fulfill her promise, even though she did not divulge to him that she had no alternative since the gods ordered her to release him. She skillfully let Odysseus believe that she was acting on her own. She smiled at Odysseus's incredulity because she knew that there is no one like a trickster for suspecting trickery. Calypso swore the oath in the name of the Earth and Heaven and the Styx, the greatest and deadliest of oaths. The powers invoked represented all that existed in Heaven and Earth and below the Earth. The inclusion of the Styx contributed to the dreadfulness of the oath because the Styx reminded one of death and implied the loss of immortality even for the gods.

The forces invoked here bring to mind the second commandment of the Mosaic Law, where the heaven above, the earth beneath, and the water under the earth are cited (Exod. 20.4; Deut. 4.10-18). The seriousness of this type of oath was underscored by Hesiod (*Theog.* 793 ff.), who wrote that any god who violated an oath such as that taken by Calypso was condemned to a year's unconsciousness and nine years of banishment from the Olympian council. For human beings the penalty for perjury was punishment and torment on this earth and in the hereafter.[32]

Agreement No. 18: Circe's oath

"'οὐδ' ἂν ἐγώ γ' ἐθέλοιμι τεῆς ἐπιβήμεναι εὐνῆς,
εἰ μή μοι τλαίης γε, θεά, μέγαν ὅρκον ὀμόσσαι
μή τί μοι αὐτῷ πῆμα κακὸν βουλευσέμεν ἄλλο.'"
Od. 10.342-44

Astonished because her charms failed to bewitch Odysseus, Circe panicked at his onslaught and proposed that he should put his sword away so that the two

---

[32] E. Rohde, *Psyche*, trans. by W. C. K. Guthrie (New York, 1966) 41; Eust. ad *Od.* 5.184; Standford *ad loc.*

38 THE CORPUS OF HOMERIC AGREEMENTS

could make love. Forewarned by the gods that such a suggestion might constitute another trap on Circe's part, Odysseus makes her swear that she would not plot any mischief against him. Only when she finished swearing the oath did Odysseus accommodate her desire.

Agreement No. 19: Odysseus's oath

> "'ἀλλ' ἄγε νῦν μοι πάντες ὀμόσσατε καρτερὸν ὅρκον·
> εἴ κέ τιν' ἠὲ βοῶν ἀγέλην ἢ πῶυ μέγ' οἰῶν
> εὕρωμεν, μή πού τις ἀτασθαλίῃσι κακῇσιν
> ἢ βοῦν ἠέ τι μῆλον ἀποκτάνῃ· ἀλλὰ ἕκηλοι
> ἐσθίετε βρώμην, τὴν ἀθανάτη πόρε Κίρκη.'
> Ὣς ἐφάμην, οἱ δ' αὐτίκ' ἀπώμνυον, ὡς ἐκέλευον.
> αὐτὰρ ἐπεί ῥ' ὄμοσάν τε τελεύτησάν τε τὸν ὅρκον."
> *Od.* 12.298-304

On the surface, the meeting of minds cited in this passage seems to be a suzerainty agreement since Odysseus was a king and those of the other party were his subjects. But in this instance Odysseus dealt with his subjects as if they were his equals. Actually, Odysseus found himself in a very delicate position where he had to use persuasion rather than fiat, particularly since the ex post facto punishment would have been useless to his cause. Consequently, he employed his only resort, an oath in the name of the gods. The term *apômnyon* points to a negative oath, their swearing that they would not do what Odysseus had asked them not to do (*Od.* 10.45; 2.377-78). In the final line, *omosan* refers to the taking of the oath demanded of them by Odysseus. The text initially conveys the impression that the stipulation was tautological with the oath itself, but the use of *omosan* in the last line hints at the use of some traditional formula whereby Zeus and perhaps other gods and most probably Helios had been invoked as witnesses to the agreement.

The language is somewhat complicated here. Elsewhere in Greek the μὴ of the oath goes with the indicative, e.g., in *Il.* 15.4, μὴ δι' ἐμὴν ἰότητα Ποσιδάων ἐνοσίχθων πημαίνει Τρῶάς τε καὶ Ἕκτορα, and in Hymn. *Merc.* 275-76, ὀμοῦμαι, μὴ μὲν ἐγὼ ... ὑπόσχομαι, μή τε τιν' ἄλλον ὄπωπα. The same is true in *Theog.* 659, ὀμόσαι ὅτι μήποτε πρᾶγμα τόδ' ἔσται, Arist. *Birds 195*, μά γῆν ... μὴ 'γώ νόημα κομψότερον ἤκουσα πω; Lys. 917, μὴ σ' ἐγὼ ... κατακλινῶ χαμαί; Eccles. 1000, μὴ 'γώ σ' ἀφήσω. Also, μὴ is used with ὄμνυμι and the future infinitive in *Od.* 5.178-79 and with the subjunctive here (*Od.* 1.310) though one would expect an infinitive.

Agreement No. 20: Odysseus's rhêtrê

> "ἀλλ' ἄγε νῦν ῥήτρην ποιησόμεθ'· αὐτὰρ ὄπισθε
> μάρτυροι ἀμφοτέροισι θεοί, τοὶ Ὄλυμπον ἔχουσιν.

THE CORPUS OF HOMERIC AGREEMENTS   39

εἰ μέν κεν νοστήσῃ ἄναξ τεὸς ἐς τόδε δῶμα,
ἕσσας με χλαῖνάν τε χιτῶνά τε εἵματα πέμψαι
Δουλίχιόν δ' ἰέναι, ὅθι μοι φίλον ἔπλετο θυμῷ·
εἰ δέ κε μὴ ἔλθῃσιν ἄναξ τεὸς ὡς ἀγορεύω,
δμῶας ἐπισσεύας βαλέειν μεγάλης κατὰ πέτρης,
ὄφρα καὶ ἄλλος πτωχὸς ἀλεύεται ἠπεροπεύειν."
Od. 14.393-400

The *rhêtrê* proposed by Odysseus contained two conditions. First, if Odysseus's information proved correct, Eumaeus would have to clothe him in cloak and tunic and send him off to Dolichium, Odysseus's alleged destination. Secondly, if Odysseus lied, Eumaeus would be free to have him killed. Eumaeus rejected the proposed agreement because he considered the second stipulation unpalatable, particularly for a host. The striking use of the *rhêtrê* for agreement denotes an accord on specific and mutually agreed upon terms.[33]

Agreement No. 21: The Phoenicians' pledge

"'Ἦ ῥά κε νῦν πάλιν αὖτις ἅμ' ἡμῖν οἴκαδ' ἕποιο,
ὄφρα ἴδῃ πατρὸς καὶ μητέρος ὑψερεφὲς δῶ
αὐτούς τ'; ἦ γὰρ ἔτ' εἰσὶ καὶ ἀφνειοὶ καλέονται.'
Τὸν δ' αὖτε προσέειπε γυνὴ καὶ ἀμείβετο μύθῳ·
"Εἴη κεν καὶ τοῦτ', εἴ μοι ἐθέλοιτέ γε, ναῦται,
ὅρκῳ πιστωθῆναι ἀπήμονά μ' οἴκαδ' ἀπάξειν.'
"Ὣς ἔφαθ', οἱ δ' ἄρα πάντες ἐπώμνυον ὡς ἐκέλευεν.
αὐτὰρ ἐπεί ῥ' ὄμοσάν τε τελεύτησάν τε τὸν ὅρκον,
τοῖς δ' αὖτις μετέειπε γυνὴ καὶ ἀμείβετο μύθῳ·
'Σιγῇ νῦν, μή τίς με προσαυδάτω ἐπέεσσιν
ὑμετέρων ἑτάρων, ξυμβλήμενος ἤ ἐν ἀγυιῇ,
ἤ που ἐπὶ κρήνῃ· μή τις ποτὶ δῶμα γέροντι
ἐλθὼν ἐξείπῃ, ὁ δ' ὀϊσάμενος καταδήσῃ
δεσμῷ ἐν ἀργαλέῳ, ὑμῖν δ' ἐπιφράσσετ' ὄλεθρον.
ἀλλ' ἔχετ' ἐν φρεσὶ μῦθον, ἐπείγετε δ' ὦνον ὀδαίων.
ἀλλ' ὅτε κεν δὴ νηῦς πλείη βιότοιο γένηται,
ἀγγελίη μοι ἔπειτα θοῶς ἐς δώμαθ' ἱκέσθω·
οἴσω γὰρ καὶ χρυσόν, ὅτις χ' ὑποχείριος ἔλθῃ·
καὶ δέ κεν ἄλλ' ἐπίβαθρον ἐγὼν ἐθέλουσά γε δοίην.
παῖδα γὰρ ἀνδρὸς ἑῆος ἐνὶ μεγάροις ἀτιτάλλω,
κερδαλέον δὴ τοῖον, ἅμα τροχόωντα θύραζε·
τόν κεν ἄγοιμ' ἐπὶ νηός, ὁ δ' ὑμῖν μυρίον ὦνον
ἄλφοι, ὅπῃ περάσητε κατ' ἀλλοθρόους ἀνθρώπους.'"
Od. 15.431-53

Phoenician pirates arrived at the island of Syria where they met the local king's maid, herself from the Phoenician city of Sidon, and promised her that

---

[33] Dindorf ad *Od.* 14.394-400; Eust. ad *Od.* 14.393.

40 THE CORPUS OF HOMERIC AGREEMENTS

they would take her back to her parents in Sidon, if that was her desire. The maid was pleased, but before she agreed to their suggestion she had them pledge that they would bring her safely home instead of selling her to somebody else. After the pirates took the oath, she advised them to keep out of her sight until the day they were ready to depart, lest they arouse suspicion. However, once their departure became imminent, they were told to notify her so that she would come along with as much gold as she could get, together with the royal child, to be sold as part of their reward for their benefaction. In the agreement the oath preceded the promises for the gold and the child because these rewards were subsequent to the offer of the pirates and not stipulations of the original agreement.[34]

Agreement No. 22: Odysseus's covenant

> ὅρκια δ' αὖ κατόπισθε μετ' ἀμφοτέροισιν ἔθηκεν
> Παλλὰς 'Αθηναίη, κούρη Διὸς αἰγιόχοιο,
> Μέντορι εἰδομένη ἠμὲν δέμας ἠδὲ καὶ αὐδήν.
>
> *Od.* 24.546-48

The *Odyssey* concludes with another of the many theophanies. After the murder of the pretenders, Pallas Athena appeared and advised Odysseus to reconcile himself to the people of Ithaca, thereby putting an end to the internecine war raging on the island. The solemn covenant between the two parties which followed Athena's advice was consecrated by the goddess herself. The phrase *horkia ethêken* instead of the more customary *horkia etamen* is appropriate here, since one would not expect a goddess to cut an animal in sacrifice and to pronounce the oaths in association with the cutting process practiced by men. The oaths administered by Athena are to be inviolable, thereby opening the way to *ploutos* and *eirênê* prescribed by Zeus in *Od.* 24.485-86. Odysseus was delighted by the advice of Athena and conformed to it because as the victor he would be seen to extend a conciliatory hand to the vanquished. The peace proposed had much better prospects of success if the victor appeared to be concerned with the welfare of his subjects and wanted to spare them from further bloodshed.

Agreement No. 23: Zeus's promise

> "ὅς πρὶν μέν μοι ὑπέσχετο καὶ κατένευσεν
> Ἴλιον ἐκπέρσαντ' ἐϋτείχεον ἀπονέεσθαι."
>
> *Il.* 2.112-13

---

[34] For the island of Syria(e), see J. D. Muhly, *Berythus* 19 (1970) 41; W. B. Standford, 2:256 ff.; Strabo 10.5.8; L. A. Stella, *Archaeologia Classica* 4 (1952) 72-76; H. L. Lorimer, *Homer and the Monuments* (Oxford, 1950) 80 ff.

THE CORPUS OF HOMERIC AGREEMENTS   41

Our final case of promising is that reported by Agamenon, who speaking to the assembly of the Achaeans, informed them that Zeus had earlier promised him the conquest of Troy. Zeus sealed his promise with a nod of his head and lightning on the Achaeans' right side. This promise can be regarded as an agreement between two unequal parties, the senior party giving the promise and the junior accepting and agreeing with it.

B. THE AGREEMENTS COMPARED AND CONTRASTED

Of the above agreements, at least two of those from the *Iliad*, Nestor's speech and Alexander's proposal (Nos. 2 and 3), seem to have been contracted for the purpose of making war. The same is true of Idomeneus's promise (No. 4), cited by Stesichorus, which was contingent upon Helen's betrothal. Not only were the suitors obligated to defend (*epamynein*) Helen but they were also obligated to go to the extreme of an overseas campaign. Nestor's speech (No. 2) explicitly mentions *synthesiai, horkia,* and *spondai,* signifying a formal agreement made by the Greeks prior to their departure for Troy. This agreement spelled out the objectives of their enterprise. Similarly, the compact between Agamemnon and Idomeneus (No. 4) alluded to another type of agreement, most probably a personal agreement between Agamemnon and each of the Achaean leaders. It is very possible that these seemingly separate personal agreements were envisioned as one general agreement made by the assembled Achaean kings prior to their departure for Troy, most probably at Aulis. The use of the verb *machêsometha* in Idomeneus's promise denotes the aggressive character of the personal treaties, although in the eyes of the Greeks their undertaking was just, considering the moral transgression committed by Paris. By going to war against the Trojans the Greeks would be defending the violated honor of a colleague, as well as upholding their own aristocratic traditions. Though apparently an offensive action, their war was fundamentally a defense of themselves, their families, and their institutions. In both instances, the treaties do not seem to illustrate disparity in rank, despite the preeminent position of Agamemnon: they appear to be parity treaties. If Agamemnon had the overall command of the Achaean troops, he enjoyed that position as a result of reciprocal understanding by all those who consented to campaign with him.

Alexander's proposal, Hector's challenge, and his later proposal (Nos. 3, 6, and 14) are duel agreements between Achaeans and Trojan leaders, containing binding stipulations for the resolution of the war as well as provisions for future alliance and friendship between the erstwhile enemies (*philotêta*). Hector's challenge differs from Nestor's speech (No. 2) in that it contains no express stipulation for the resolution of the conflict between Achaeans and Trojans, although the death of Hector would have certainly deprived the Trojans of their major champion and would have probably changed the sequel of the war. Since, without Hector's bravery and leadership, the Trojans probably would not have been able to rival the aggressiveness of the Greeks on the battlefield, to continue the war would require switching to a defensive strategy behind their own walls.

The Homeric duel epitomizes the agonistic spirit prevalent in the aristocratic era, during which men fought for the sake of competitive purposes and the honor of victory. In the agreement are provisions for respecting certain rules of the game, rules which had been part and parcel of the men's personal lives and their public times. Among the rights of the victor was the privilege to strip the defeated warrior of his armor as a trophy of victory, just as today the heads or skulls of wild animals are preserved as trophies. The body of the defeated was to be returned to his people for proper burial. The right to burial could not be denied to the dead, even one's enemies, a theme dramatized much later in Sophocles' *Antigone*. In this respect, Achilles' initial refusal to allow Hector the proper burial rites ran counter to the ethos of his age, his exalted lineage, and the rules regulating the relations of the aristocratic age. In no small way, Achilles acted in flagrant disregard of the spirit of the times, and his actions were not to be tolerated by the gods.

Idaeus's proposal (No. 7) was the product of a compromise between Antenor's recommendation that Helen and her treasures be returned to the Greeks and Alexander's categorical refusal to consider any suggestion dealing with the return of Helen. On the heels of this altercation in the Trojan assembly, Priam suggested a compromise proposal: the return of Helen's property plus adequate compensation for the injustice committed by Paris. In addition, Priam moved for a truce to permit the burial of the dead of both sides. Priam's motion was accepted by the assembly, and Idaeus was subsequently dispatched to the Greeks to transmit the decision. Oddly, Idaeus did not simply impart the Trojan decision but editorialized on it by confiding to the Greeks the feeling of the Trojans concerning Paris.

Idaeus's comment suggests the openness of the Homeric societies, although the wisdom of such a comment by an ambassador is questionable. Such a piece of news imparted to enemies could only encourage them to persevere in their cause. Indeed, Homer has the Greeks reject the idea of compensation alone, although they granted the Trojan request for a truce in order to bury the dead.

The common element of the agreements discussed thus far is equality. This is especially evident in the last three compacts discussed, which were voluntarily entered into precisely because of the equality assumed to exist between the duelists. In all three instances the opponents were fairly well matched in strength (with perhaps a slight imbalance in the third case), as the agonistic rules demanded. This element of equality or the appearance of it

THE CORPUS OF HOMERIC AGREEMENTS 43

also served to bring about a reconciliation between the two antagonistic sides at the end of the *Odyssey,* agreement No. 22. For though Odysseus and his friends seemed to enjoy the upper hand at the moment of the reconciliation agreement, they yielded to the goddess's advice and were ready to treat their opponents as equals because a treaty which did not completely humiliate the opponent had the best chance of providing a permanent peace. The factor of parity (*homoiiou polemoio, Od.* 24.543) was the more essential at that juncture since it concerned an internecine strife and anything but equal treatment of the opposite side might have had disastrous consequences for the future of Ithaca. For this purpose, Homer has Zeus intervene just in time to save the situation, and has Athena speak of *neikos homoiiou polemou.* The oaths administered by the goddess guaranteed the inviolable character of the agreement and the way was thus opened for the customary friendship (*philotês*) attendant upon reconciliation of enemies in other circumstances as well, and for the *ploutos* and *eirênê* prescribed by Zeus (*Od.* 24.485-86).

The parties involved in the arrangement described in Hera and Athena's agreement and Xanthus's pledge (Nos. 12 and 13) possessed disparate physical strength and social positions; consequently, these two compacts are between unequals. Patroclus was definitely inferior to Achilles in martial qualifications and political standing. He acted at the consent of his friend and received definite instructions from him with which he promised to comply in order to avoid any damage to his friend's reputation. In Xanthus's pledge the river acknowledged the superiority of fire and sued for peace, promising in return to refrain from further pursuit of Achilles. In effect, this agreement is a form of capitulation by which the capitulating party surrenders to the mercy of the opponent in an effort to save himself. However, it was not an unconditional surrender, for Xanthus managed to negotiate an agreement before his surrender despite the obvious superiority of his opponent.

On the three other occasions (respectively, Nos. 9, 16, and 15), we also find an inequality relationship, although the parties involved were independent of each other and to that extent equal. Two of these cases involved marriage arrangements which, at least in one instance, led to a military alliance. In the first case, the alliance between Othryoneus and Priam (No. 9), Othryoneus asked Priam for Cassandra's hand, whereupon Priam, with an Olympian move of his head, consented. How weighty this military alliance proposed by Othryoneus would have been for the future of the war is not clear, but what is clear is the implication that alliances of this sort were not rare in the Greek or Near Eastern world. In the second case (No. 16), Menelaus promised his only daughter to the son of Achilles in gratitude for the father's role in the Trojan campaign. Here the military cooperation pre-existed the marriage agreement, but there is no doubt that with the bond between the two parties thus strengthened, military cooperation and the alliance would continue to grow to the benefit of both parties. It is significant that the same sign was used in both cases to indicate consent to the future nuptials, i.e., the nodding of the head.

The third of these agreements, that between Achilles and Priam (No. 15), was a noble gesture by one party to the other. In this agreement the freedom of the recipient is limited by the particular circumstances in which the gesture was made and the customs of the age. Priam was Achilles' guest, and it would have seemed inappropriate for him to turn down a kindness of his host, which, after all, coincided with his own desire.

To another category altogether belong the purported deals between the gods, or those between demonic beings and men, wherein men, with the advice and support of the gods, were enabled to stand on an equal footing with the divinities. The arrangements described in agreements Nos. 10, 12, 16, and 19 are of such form. For instance, the parties involved in Hera's oath (No. 10) were the Olympian Hera and the non-Olympian Sleep. Though obviously a lesser god than Hera, Sleep could act here as her equal for the double reason that (1) Hera had asked for a favor which fell within Sleep's purview, and (2) the latter feared that Hera's request would put him into trouble with Zeus. Sleep's fear of Zeus initially prompted him to reject Hera's request, which in turn forced Hera to resort to cajolery and bribery in order to extract the favor she sought.

Similarly, Hera and Athena's agreement (No. 12) describes a compact made sometime earlier by Hera and Athena. There was no mention of an oath, but only the comment that both had made the compact in the presence of all the gods, a factor that made the taking of an oath superfluous since the presence of the gods served as sufficient guarantee of the agreement.

The next two agreements, Calypso's promise and Odysseus's oath (Nos. 17 and 19), were the result of tensions and mutual suspicion between Odysseus and two minor divinities who sought to block his return home. To allay Odysseus's suspicions Calypso had to swear a dreadful oath in the name of the Styx. Circe's oath-content was not given; we are only told that Odysseus asked Circe to swear a mighty (*megas*) oath. Since this use of the term *megas* is another way of saying *deinotatos*, it seems that the name of the Styx must have been invoked. Significantly, in both cases only one of the parties was required to take the oath, as was also the case in Achilles' agreement (No. 11). Furthermore, we may note that in all three instances the party taking the oath had the power to grant the favor asked.

Finally, Odysseus's *rhêtrê* (No. 20) was an agreement proposed between persons of supposedly lower class and origin. That the proposal failed to materialize was owing to the moral scruples preventing one of the two parties from putting the other to the test. Nevertheless, the proposed compact followed the customary format of personal agreements; the Olympian gods were to be invoked as witnesses to the veracity of the terms and as avengers in the event of chicanery.

THE CORPUS OF HOMERIC AGREEMENTS 45

C. THE ORAL CHARACTER OF THE HOMERIC AGREEMENTS

At this point in the discussion it is probably worth taking the risk of elaborating the obvious, in order to show the importance of attending to the textual evidence. Despite the well-attested and universally accepted fact that some of the material of the Homeric poetry had been orally transmitted down to around 800 B.C., one should not take it for granted that any individual Homeric agreement was an oral compact. Instead, one should examine the language of the Homeric agreements on a case-by-case basis in order to ascertain whether they are indeed presented as oral arrangements rather than written pacts.

For instance, we see in Alexander's proposal (No. 3) Hector asking the Greeks to hear (*keklyte*) from him the words of Alexander.[35] Clearly this was an oral transaction. Similarly, in Nestor's speech (No. 2) the references to *horkia*, *mêdea*, and *boulae* imply oral exchanges, and this view is further supported by the *akrêtoi spondai* and the giving of the right hand as ratification of the arrangements. Reliance on the giving of the right hand usually accompanies an oral agreement. The only question about the oral nature of the transaction is one that arises from the use of the term *synthesiê*, about which more will be said a bit later. The formulaic phrase *hypestên kai kateneusa* in Idomeneus's promise (No. 4) implies assent to something by the nodding of one's head supposedly in imitation of the Olympian gesture in which Zeus's silent nodding of the head enhances his magnificence as the Father of gods and men. The lines in *Il.* 7.67-75 (No. 6) are free of any suggestions or connotations of a written pact, and the same is true about the text (*Il.* 7.368-89) preceding No. 7, the proposal carried by Idaeus to the Greek camp and announced in the assembly by the Trojan herald (*meteeipen*).[36] The envoy also stated that Priam had ordered him to inquire (*eipein*) whether the Achaeans would agree with Paris's latest proposal and Priam's addendum regarding the burial of the dead.[37] The Achaean answer to the herald is also understood to be given orally.[38] Regarding the suggestion about the truce for the burial of the dead, Agamemnon agreed with it by raising his staff toward the gods as a sign of ratification. Significantly, Agamemnon did not need the approval of the assembly for this truce. *Mytheomai* is the verb used by Hector in his suggestion for a duel with one of the Achaeans, while Othryoneus's promise to perform important work (*hypescheto mega ergon*) for the hand of Cassandra likewise denotes an oral bargain. By the same token, Priam merely promised and nodded agreement

---

[35] *Il.* 3.86: κέκλυτέ μευ ... μῦθον Ἀλεξάνδροιο. Ἄλλους μὲν κέλεται...
[36] *Il.* 7. 367-69: μετέειπε · ... κέκλυτέ μευ ... ὄφρα εἴπω.
[37] *Il.* 7.374: μῦθον Ἀλεξάνδροιο.
[38] *Il.* 7.406-97: ἦ τοι μῦθον Ἀχαιῶν αὐτὸς ἀκούεις ὡς τοι ὑποκρίνονται.

46 THE CORPUS OF HOMERIC AGREEMENTS

(*hyspescheto kai kateneuse, Il.* 13.366, 368-69). In both instances the verb *hypescheto* alludes to the oral character of the agreement and so does *kateneuse*. The same is true of agreements Nos. 16 and 21, Menelaus's promise and the Phoenicians' pledge, which are self-evidently oral. Nor is there any doubt of the oral character of the conditions set by Achilles in agreement No. 11, although it was an agreement made not between gods but humans, friends at that, who had different degrees of political influence and military might. Whether or not one interprets this particular agreement as a *diktat*, there cannot be any doubt that the absence in it of those formalities essential to written settlements, namely oaths, confirms its oral character. Finally, the circumstances in Odysseus's *rhêtrê* (No. 20) point only to an oral exchange between the two parties. The conclusion is then obvious. Inspection of the textual evidence shows no reference in any of the Homeric agreements discussed so far in this section that would lead us to think of any of them as written documents. Furthermore, the textual evidence points in the same direction in the cases of the three agreements not yet discussed (Nos. 2, 14, and 20), where a few terms occur that could, in different contexts, be thought to refer to a written pact. For the sake of thoroughness, we shall now turn to these terms, *synthesiê, harmoniê, rhêtrê*, and *synêmosynê,* in order to evaluate the possibility that in the three agreements just mentioned there is any reference to a written pact.

Fortunately, our task is made easier by the fact that these terms are rather rare in Homer. Outside of Nestor's speech (No. 2), the word *synthesiê* appears only once in Homer, where it clearly denotes an oral command by Diomedes to his chariot-driver (*Il.* 6.319). *Harmoniê* is equally rare in Homer, appearing twice in the *Odyssey* with the meaning "fitting together."[39] In the *Iliad*, the only other instance of this term is in Hector's proposal (No. 14), where obviously nothing more than a verbal gentlemen's agreement is implied. As for the term *rhêtrê*, it only occurs in connection with one of Odysseus's agreements, No. 20 (*Od.* 14.393), where it denotes "speech," "word," or an "oral agreement" and nothing else beyond the fundamental notion of mutuality.[40] The same is true of *synêmosynê* ("swearing together"), which appears only once in Homer (*Il.* 22.261) and there with the meaning of "agreement," in a context which makes it evident that an oral agreement is meant.

These brief comments reinforce what was said above about the other Homeric agreements, namely, that when one looks at the texts one sees for oneself that they are oral rather than written compacts. But as we shall see in

---

[39] *Od.* 5.248; 5.361.

[40] Eust. ad *Od.* 14.393: ἐπὶ ῥητοῖς καὶ ὁμολογουμένοις πράγμασι συνθήκη καὶ ὁμολογία.

the following chapter, this is only one of several conclusions to be drawn from the linguistic evidence. Specifically, a closer textual analysis of certain key terms associated with the Homeric agreements will enable us to understand better the political, social, and moral motives behind them.

CHAPTER TWO

THE LINGUISTIC EVIDENCE

Although we have no specimens of formal treaties made during the Dark Ages or preceding Greek times, the less formal agreements contained in the Homeric epics provide us with useful examples of the typology of agreements prevalent during these earlier periods. The inter-ethnic agreements described by Homer reflect the earlier international treaties, while the more personal agreements made in the epics reflect the interpersonal relationships of the pre-Homeric aristocratic times. Both groups of agreements afford us a glimpse into the promise-giving practices of that earlier world, and suggest some of its social, political, economic, and military relationships. The oral nature of these agreements, remarked on at the end of the last chapter, indicates the very great importance of the spoken word in personal relations in the Heroic age. In the present chapter we shall analyze more closely some of the terms employed in these agreements, which will help us understand more fully the implications of their terminology as well as the culture which produced that terminology. The first term we shall consider is *philotês*, which has a wide gamut of nuances in the field of human relationships and which of all terms is probably the one most central to our subject. We shall then consider three other important terms and their interrelations with each other, viz., *horkia*, *horkos*, and *omnyein*.

A. THE SIGNIFICANCE OF *PHILOTÊS*

Upbraided by his brother Hector for his cowardly behavior in the Trojan War, Paris decided to engage the formidable Menelaus in a single battle in the presence of the two rival armies. The major stipulations of this agreement were that the victor would carry Helen off to his own house along with her possessions, while the two armies would make a treaty of peace and friendship and would withdraw to their respective lands (*Il.* 3.67-73). Unfortunately, the duel turned out differently than expected, because the goddess Aphrodite intervened on Paris's behalf just as Menelaus was about to dispatch him. Thus Paris miraculously escaped death, while the friendship and peace originally anticipated in consequence of the duel failed to come about.

The use of the term *philotês* in the negotiations between Achaeans and Trojans is remarkable, as *philotês* was meant to convey the state of good will that ought to characterize the making of the agreement itself as well as the type of relations that were supposed to ensue the making of the agreement. In fact, as we shall see, *philotês* is a many-sided term used by Homer and others after him, in a variety of circumstances, almost all of which express a

THE LINGUISTIC EVIDENCE

49

positive and friendly feeling. An analogous state of friendliness is conveyed in the near Eastern treaties by the term for "brotherhood" or "fraternity," a term which appears to have been technical but sufficiently flexible to accommodate many nuances of meanings and a variety of relationships in the diplomatic language of the Near Eastern potentates. Because of the manifest importance of the term *philotês* in the Homeric texts, an effort will be made here to explicate some of its nuances and to compare it with the concepts of "brotherhood" or "fraternity" found in the Near Eastern treaties. This brief analysis of *philotês* will primarily focus on the moral and legal implications, especially the implications which carried over to the international relations of the times. Let us then begin with a rapid review of the Near Eastern terms for "brotherhood."

One of the most striking instances relating to brotherhood is the treaty between Ramses II and Hattusilis III (ca. 1280 B.C.), which declared at the outset that its purpose was to secure good peace and brotherly relations between the two kings and their respective peoples.[1] The good relations were intended to endure beyond the life-span of the two kings, as their successors were to continue the brotherhood initiated by the signatories.[2] The treaty and its resultant brotherhood were expected to prevail for all time to come. Again, in the famous Tawagalawas Letter, the king of Ahhiyawa, whoever he may have been, is addressed as "my brother," which seems to have been the standard address among sovereigns of the time, e.g., the kings of Egypt, Babylonia, Assyria, Mitanni, and Hatti. Likewise, this is so in their letters found at Amarna and Bogazköy, since the political relationship between allied rulers was conceived of as one of kinship, either of "fraternity" (*ahûtum*) or "sonship." It has been suggested that brotherhood was invoked between rulers of equal status, whereas "paternity" (*abûtum*) and "sonship" (*marûtum*) expressed subordination, in particular that of a vassal to his overlord or "father," a relationship which might alternatively be interpreted as a relationship of service. In this context, the title of "brother" given by the Hittite king to the Ahhiyawan king acknowledges equality of rank and the greatness of the Ahhiyawan king. But as the correspondence between the Pharaoh and the king of Cyprus shows, that form of address could also be used between rulers of unequal rank. Munn-Rankin, who has examined the Mesopotamian evidence in detail about this problem, has come to the conclusion that although dependence of a vassal on his overlord was expressed in terms of sonship, "fraternity" and "sonship" were not strictly technical terms and therefore are not reliable guides to political status, so that

---

[1] Weidner, *Polit. Dok.*, 27; Korosec, RIDA 22 (1975) 55-56; E. Bickerman, AJPh 73 (1952) 8-9.

[2] Weidner, *Polit. Dok.*, 27; S. Langdon and A. H. Gardiner, JEA 6 (1920) 186-87, 188-89.

50 THE LINGUISTIC EVIDENCE

overlords would often address vassals as brothers and vice versa.[3] In one sense, the term connotes a technicality, that is, the establishment of friendly relations (brotherhood) as a result of some cooperation or by the successful conclusion of a treaty. In every case in which the term is used by one ruler for another there is evidence that the two were already in treaty relations, or else that they had been or were currently engaged in joint military operations, an activity that presupposed the existence of some agreement.[4] Moreover, the concept of brotherhood was not confined to rulers, but rather was also applicable to their people.[5]

In the Amarna Letters (ca. 1500 B.C.), one encounters the same desire for brotherly relations.[6] The ruler Kadašman-Harbe and Amenophis III exchanged gifts as tokens to remind each other of their brotherhood and to show that brotherhood and peace were not simply words but a binding relationship. Especially informative in this respect is the remark of the Babylonian king Burnaburias II, who wrote to Amenophis IV: "Between kings, brotherhood, good friendship, peace and good relationships are established when the precious stones are heavy, the silver is heavy, and the gold is heavy."[7] It is evident from a letter in the archives of Mari that the concept of brotherhood and friendship entailed a very close relationship which ought to have prevailed between physical brothers, but in actual fact this was not always the case. In this letter Išme-Dagan, son and successor of the Assyrian king Samši-Adad I (ca. 1800 B.C.) suggested to his blood-brother and ruler of Mari, Yašmah-Adad, that they swear an oath of brotherhood between themselves.[8] In this respect, the relationship that flowed from this form of brotherhood was seen as deeper than the physical relationship itself. A by-product of this brotherly relationship in the Ancient Near East was the use of a form of address in the diplomatic correspondence of the parties involved. The sender of the letter described himself as the brother of the addressee (ahûka: your brother).[9] Refusal to employ the form of address could be

---

[3] H. G. Güterbock, AJA 87 (1983) 135; KUB 14.3; AU 2-19.

[4] Munn-Rankin, *Diplomacy,* 76, 83-84.

[5] Weidner, *Polit. Dok.,* 129.

[6] Knudtzon, *Die El-Amarna Tafeln,* 81; Korosec, RIDA 22; Langdon and Gardiner, JEA 6 (1920) 186-89.

[7] Knudtzon, *Die El-Amarna Tafeln,* 89.

[8] G. Dossin, ARMT 4 (Paris, 1954), 21-26. For the persistence of the idea of Near Eastern brotherhood see also H. C. Trumbull, *The Blood Covenant* (New York, 1885) 5, as well as N. Kazantzakis's first chapter of *Captain Michael,* concerning the brotherhood between Michael and Nouri.

[9] Korosec, RIDA 22, 57; Weidner, *Polit. Dok.,* 26 where the term used is *Ahu-ut(ti).* See also W. L. Moran, JNES 22 (1963) 13-17; D. R. Hillers, BASOR, 176 (1964) 46, where *Tabuta epesu* is a phrase commonly meaning "to make a treaty." Also Klaus Baltzer, *The Covenant Formulary,* trans. by D. E. Green (Philadelphia, 1971) 1-8; J. Gelb, B.

THE LINGUISTIC EVIDENCE 51

interpreted as an offense by the addressee. Similarly, as the Hittites discovered to their chagrin, refusal to accept this form could lead to undesirable consequences for the addressee. When the Assyrian King Adad-nirari I (ca. 1305-1274 B.C.) expressed the wish to establish friendly relations with the king of the Hittites, he dispatched a letter to the Hittite king inviting him to a meeting and containing a proposal of mutual friendship, following which brotherhood would have been unquestionably inaugurated between the two kings.[10] Unfortunately, for reasons that are not entirely clear, this friendly gesture was briskly rejected by the Hittite king with the result that a hostile climate between the two countries was created, extending into the reign of the next Hittite king whose name was Tudhaliyas IV (ca. 1250-20 B.C.). Tudhaliyas did not hesitate to send a missive to his young Assyrian counterpart Shalmanezer I (ca. 1273-44 B.C.), in which he addressed Salmanezer as brother, in hopes of repairing the damage done by his predecessor and thereby averting war between the two countries.[11] The effort failed: Assyria remained the enemy of the Hittites.

Unlike the concepts of modern diplomacy which frequently aim at establishing channels of communication and building bridges over enormous ideological gaps and historical enmities, by their very nature the concepts of *philotês* and brotherhood precluded the possibility of friendly relations with a friend's enemy and often even the appearance of such contacts. Positive intervention on behalf of a friend was the natural expectation of the state of *philotês*. Thus early in his reign, the Babylonian king Kurigalzu, an ally and "brother" of the Egyptian king Amenophis III (first half of the fourteenth century B.C.), refused to entertain a proposal by would-be Canaanite rebels who had sent an embassy to Babylonia with instructions to sound out the Babylonian king about an insurrection against their Egyptian overlord. The reply of Kurigalzu demonstrated in no uncertain terms his faithful adherence to his promise of brotherly devotion to his Egyptian counterpart and his loyalty to their treaty: "If you cherish hostility to the king of Egypt, my brother, and wish to ally yourself with another, shall I not come and shall I

Landsberger, A. Leo Oppenheim, and E. Reiner (eds.), *The Assyrian Dictionary* (Chicago, 1964); s.v. *Ahu*; Chroust, *Class. et Med.* 15 (1954) 87; E. Bickerman, AJPh 73 (1952) 96; Bickerman, TAPA 75 (1944) 96.

[10] KUB 13, 102; E. Laroche, *Catalogue des textes hittites. Textes et commentaires* (Paris, 1971) 24. Among the possibilities are Muwatallis and Hattusilis III, Korosec, RIDA 22, 57.

[11] KUB 23, 99; 103; H. Otten, *Ein Brief aus Hattusa an Babu-ahu-iddina*, ATO (Graz, 1959-60) 39-46; Korosec, RIDA 22, 58. Refusal to receive ambassadors meant that any treaties subsisting between the states concerned were immediately broken off. Frequently, this rupture signified steps preliminary to war. Where there was no existing treaty refusal to receive ambassadors implied the determination to remain without any regular relations with the other party. Something similar occurred in later times. Thus in 168 B.C. the Romans indicated their intention to discontinue their relationship with the Rhodians by refusing to receive the Rhodian ambassadors; Liv. 45.20.4-10. Also cf. Polyb. 33.11.1-7; Diod. 31.23.

52   THE LINGUISTIC EVIDENCE

not plunder you? For he is in alliance and brotherhood with me."[12] Such
loyalty was not supposed to be broken even by death. A deceased king was to
be mourned by all his "brothers" and allies. Messages of condolences were
expressed to the widow and the king's son and successor, together with
messages of congratulation to the new king on his accession. At the same
time, it was firmly understood that the brotherhood and alliance that existed
among them and the new king's predecessor would continue and would be
renewed tenfold.[13]

When one turns to the Homeric epics, one finds that the concept of
philotês exhibits an even greater range of vitality. While the concept did
reflect a special bond of friendship among the Homeric heroes, it was not
limited to that meaning as the Near Eastern meaning of brotherhood seems to
have been. *Philotês* appears as a broad concept with a great variety of
possible nuances. As is clear from the *Iliad*, it could refer to the act of
courting, which naturally presupposed amiability between the two individuals
involved, and it could likewise refer to a newly contracted friendship between
two persons.[14] This type of friendship could be the offshoot of diverse
circumstances, e.g., hospitality extended to one of the parties by the other (*Il.*
3.345). The relationship which was the normal consequence of acts such as
hospitality, was tantamount to *philotês* even when the term itself was not
used to describe the ensuing friendship. Thus when Diomedes noticed
Glaucus for the first time on the battlefield, his intuitive sense led him to
inquire about the identity of his opponent, eventually discovering that his
own father Tydeus had once entertained Glaucus's grandfather Bellerophon in
his home for twenty days.[15] According to the story, upon Bellerophon's
departure Tydeus and Bellerophon exchanged gifts of friendship, a friendship
that was conceived as binding the two families forever.[16] Consequently,

---

[12] CAH3 2.1.467; 482; A. Ungnad, *Archiv für Keilschriftforschung* 1 (1923) 202-203.

[13] Knudtzon, *Die El-Amarna Tafeln* 245; E. F. Campbell, *The Chronology of the Amarna
Letters* (Baltimore, 1964) 46, n. 44; C. Virolleand, *Revue d'Assyriologie et Archeologie
orientale* 38 (1941) 1-3. For some exaggerated as well as bizarre expectations of friendship
see Knudtzon, *Die El-Amarna Tafeln,* 149-73.

[14] *Il.* 2.232; 3.441; 6.161, 165.

[15] *Il.* 6.215; Boisacq, *Dictionnaire étymologique,* s.v. *xeinos*; Nilsson, *Geschichte der
Griechischen Religion* 1:391; F. Robert, *Homère* (Paris, 1950) 215-19. It is interesting that
the term *xenia* was similarly employed in the fifth century in association with the making of
alliances. Like the Homeric *philotês, xenia* was a state preceding the contracting of
alliance, Hdt. 1.69.2-3. In both cases friendship and hospitality are mentioned first. They
seem to be the preconditions without which the making of an alliance could not be really
understood.

[16] The tie of hospitality contracted between host and guest was a sacred one and
transmitted from father to son (*Od.* 1.181, 15.197). For hereditary ties of friendship and
hospitality see also Thuc. 8.6.4, 2.13.1. According to the Greek Law of Nations, however,
it was permissible for an ally to give military assistance to an enemy as long as the territory

THE LINGUISTIC EVIDENCE 53

although their own meeting took place on the Trojan battlefield, Diomedes and Glaucus refused to fight against one another and once more exchanged gifts in commemoration of their ancestral friendship, promising to avoid each other's spear in the future. Their clasping of hands and renewed pledges of faith served to demonstrate to all present that despite their being on opposite sides, they would continue to cultivate the old relationship.

Objections may be in order at this point, and, on the surface, they may seem justified. The terminus technicus used by Homer in the Diomedes-Glaucus episode (if it is permissible to speak of termini technici in poetry) is *xeniê* (guest-friendship), not *philotês*. But the use of *xeniê* here does not rule out the relationship implied by *philotês* in the aristocratic world. *Xeniê* and *philotês* are not mutually exclusive or radically different relationships; on the contrary, in the world described by the *Iliad* the two relationships seem very similar to each other. In fact, guest-friendship and marriage were the two fundamental devices for the establishment of alliances among nobles and chieftains.[17] Both institutions were always sealed by the partaking of the same nourishment, and people in Ancient Greece and the Near East believed that a bond of alliance and friendship was formed between those who partook of the same table (but more about this subject later). In the making of an alliance, the parties involved sat down to a common meal or, if this was not possible for both parties, the official envoy(s) responsible for the conclusion of the treaty represented the king at the ceremonial dinner.

In such instances, the term *philotês* was used to underscore the friendly feelings and reciprocal relationships. It was also used in other contexts, e.g., to indicate a liking toward somebody irrespective of reciprocal feelings. In the *Iliad* (3.453) it is stated that the Trojans considered Paris the architect of their troubles, and that for this reason Troy had no liking or *philotês* for him (οὐ μὲν γὰρ φιλότητί γ' ἐκεύθανον). Conversely, when the other Greeks were pressed by the Trojans (*Il.* 9.630; 13.636), Achilles was expected to put aside his anger and go to their aid because of the *philotês* nurtured by the Greeks for Achilles. When he refused, preferring rather to spite Agamemnon, the representatives of the Greeks complained that Achilles placed his personal feelings over the obligations of *philotês*.[18] Similarly, when Phoenix exhorted Achilles to cease his wrath and help the Greeks, Achilles, still greatly agitated, advised Phoenix to be careful how he spoke lest he change Achilles'

---

of the latter remained inviolate, Bickerman, AJPh 73 (1952) 13; 1 Sam. 18.4; C. H. Gordon, *Homer and the Bible*, 88-89.

[17] Eust. ad *Il.* 9.630. G. Herman, *Ritualized Friendship and the Greek City* (Cambridge, 1987) in his sections on *Xeniê* and *Philotês*.

[18] *Il.* 9.612-15; also J. Fitzmyer, S.J., CBQ 20(1959) 444; Fitzmyer, JAOS 81 (1961) 181; Friedrich, *Die Staatsverträge* 1:55; 2:13, 117, 119.

54 THE LINGUISTIC EVIDENCE

love for him to hate. The best thing for Phoenix to do, he declared, would be to cross the man who had crossed Achilles.[19]

The most striking use of *philotês*, however, is that of designating an extremely close bond forged in the course of resolving political or military hostilities. Thus, when Alexander proposed the duel between himself and Menelaus in order to resolve the feud between the Greeks and the Trojans, he attached to his proposal a condition aimed at establishing *philotês* between the two rival camps (*Il.* 3.73, 94). Like the *philotês* contracted as a result of hospitality between the families of Tydeus and Bellerophon, the *philotês* envisioned here was expected to be eternal. The arrangement did not rest on a juridical basis but was universally recognized to be under the protection of the gods (especially Zeus *xenios*) and received the sanction of religion in general, both of these supporting factors being considered no less effective than the sanction of law. A deliberate violation of *philotês* by a gentleman was a contradiction in terms, one that would subject the offender to public infamy and divine retribution whereby the entire family's name was besmirched for all times.

As the Diomedes-Glaucus incident signifies, the ties of *philotês* were not strained even when relations between nations were hostile. In Book 7 of the *Iliad*, Hector proposed still another duel as a relief from the drabness of the fighting. Darkness fell, however, before the duel reached a resolution. In view of these circumstances, Hector proposed that the duelists part in *philotêti*.[20] Similarly, following the slaughter of the suitors by Odysseus, a reconciliation in *philotêti* was effected between Odysseus and the people of Ithaca through the intervention of the gods.[21] In the above two cases the term *philotês* implies a transition from an earlier negative state to something positive. Whether the situation concerned a social or political association between two persons, families or groups, a positive bond between the two parties was forged. *Philotês* changed the position of the parties from a state of enmity to one of explicit and steadfast friendship. The newly established state restrained the parties from injurious action against each other, since to perpetrate injury would run contrary to the very idea of friendship and brotherhood. Consequently, *philotês* went beyond the formal compliance with specific obligations. It was more than merely abiding by the minimum rules—usually negative—of moral obligations. It provided a positive and robust standard of how one should think and feel when one helped a partner in need: hence *philotês* carried the auxiliary connotations of kindness, mercy, promptness, and selflessness in the discharge of one's obligations. It called

---

[19] *Il.* 7.303: ἐν φιλότητι διέτμαγεν ἀρθμήσαντε.

[20] *Od.* 24.474: φιλότητα μετ' ἀμφοτέροισι τίθησθα.

[21] Weidner, *Polit. Dok.*, 71-73.

THE LINGUISTIC EVIDENCE 55

upon the partners to go to the extreme of risking personal danger for the sake of each other. Although the case of Phoenix and Achilles points to a somewhat rigid interpretation of *philotês* in Homeric times, the example of Diomedes and Glaucus demonstrates that the interpretation of the concept was wide and flexible enough to allow sufficient ground for accommodation. In the instance of a political-military relationship between a lord and his vassal, it would be logical to surmise that the vassal carried the obligation to follow his lord and to fight his lord's enemy. Furthermore, the vassal was expected to have the same friends and enemies as the lord. In practice, whereas care was taken to spell out in detail the obligations of the vassal to his lord, a much briefer omnibus clause enjoined the vassal to be genuinely friendly in spirit as well as in action: in short, failure to be friendly in spirit was regarded as contrary to the agreement itself.[22]

That the personal ties stemming from *philotês* overarched the mere formality of obligations is manifest in the sentiments of Menelaus for Odysseus. To express his overwhelming feelings of indebtedness, Menelaus offered Odysseus an entire district within his kingdom to which Odysseus and his people could migrate and where they could live in freedom. By this act Menelaus intended to express his gratitude for Odysseus's role in the Trojan campaign and to achieve for himself the pleasure of permanent association with Odysseus.[23] A similar display of friendship for Odysseus was shown by the Phaeacian Alcinous, who entertained Odysseus in his palace, showering him with gifts given with a loving heart. Alcinous considered Odysseus very dear, and regarded their newly contracted friendship and the pleasure thereof as better than any relation between brothers (ἀντὶ κασιγνήτου).[24] This "more than brother" relationship is reflected in the meaning of *philotes*. Since the noun *philia* does not appear in Homer (or Hesiod) there is no other term that better exemplifies the new bond between two persons and the personal or political relationship emerging therefrom. In Od. 8.545, Alcinous admits that for the sake of Odysseus, his dear friend and honor guest, everything has been readied, his departure, and the gifts of friendship, which Alcinous and his noblemen friends gave Odysseus out of the pleroma of their hearts (φίλα δῶρα, τὰ οἱ δίδομεν φιλέοντες). Only shortly before, Odysseus had arrived

---

[22] Menelaus's objective was to substitute for the arid land of Odysseus in Ithaca a more fruitful one. All of Odysseus's people were to be moved because to move Odysseus only would constitute exile for him, Dindorf ad *Od.* 4.175.

[23] *Od.* 8.546, 585-86; Dindorf *ad loc.*

[24] The classical formula τοὺς αὐτοὺς ἐχθροὺς καὶ φίλους ἔχειν (in Latin *ut eosdem amicos et hostes haberent*), used in connection with interstate relations, does not carry the parity implication present in the Homeric world. While internally the allied cities preserved their autonomy (at least some of them) externally they were deprived of their right to act as sovereign states and had to follow the leadership of the dominant city; Phillipson, *The International Law and Custom,* 1:104.

56 THE LINGUISTIC EVIDENCE

as a stranger and was perceived with an enemy-like hostility. Now, he departs as a "bosom" friend.

Reconciliation and Moderation

The assumption on the part of the Greeks that friendship would follow the resolution of a conflict between two erstwhile rivals may partially account for the beginnings of that important tradition that dictated moderation on the part of the victor toward the vanquished. Even among enemies, opposition should not be considered irreconcilable and room should always be left for future reconciliation.

Naturally the Greeks were not always as magnanimous in victory as their tradition of moderation required, nor did they always leave open the possibility of reconciliation and friendship with the enemy. This was especially the case where preconditions for *philotês* did not exist. The conduct of Achilles is illustrative enough. Rabid with anger over Patroclus's death, Achilles was unyieldingly bent upon revenge. Nothing less than the death of Hector would satisfy him. In his enraged state there was no room for any of those qualities that elevated Man above beast. Hector's civil proposal to respect long-established human conventions was peremptorily denied by Achilles, a denial accompanied by the remarkable comment that it is unnatural for lions and men to make agreements of faith or wolves and lambs to establish concords. Rather, their natural condition is that of a state of perpetual enmity. The important structural pre-conditions of reasonableness and moderation, those generally common denominators that lead to the state of *philotês* and make agreements possible, had ceased to be operative in the state of agitation to which Achilles had fallen (*Il.* 22.261-62).

Failure, however, to abide by certain conditions does not necessarily negate the value of the principle, and in this case the principle of *philotês*, which had become a strong tradition by Homeric times, is to remain such throughout Greek history. Thus Plato's suggestion (*Rep.* 471A) that the Greeks should conduct their quarrels always with an eye toward reconciliation (ὡς διαλλαγησόμενοι) only continues a Greek practice which clearly goes back to the Homeric era, if not earlier. As a matter of fact, Plato's admonition regarding reconciliation addressed as it was predominantly to the Greeks seems narrow-minded when contrasted with the Homeric *philotês* which knew no ethnic bounds. The term itself in connection with interstate agreements prevailed down to the beginnings of the fifth century, when it began to be slowly displaced by the more frequent use of *philia*.[25] This latter word, combined with συμμαχία (φιλία καὶ συμμαχία) or σπονδὴ

---

[25] In spite of the alterations in the concept of *philotês* wrought by the passage of time and the emergence of the city-states in Greece, the aristocratic ideal and its obligations are not completely extinct in the fifth century B.C.

THE LINGUISTIC EVIDENCE 57

(σπονδὰς καὶ φιλία) seems best exemplified in the texts containing the treaty relations of the city-states in classical times.[26] Consequently, the traditional aristocratic principle of *philotês* which had so strongly influenced the personal and interstate relations of the Homeric world found an express formulation in the written treaties of later centuries, when personal relations had been largely replaced by the interstate treaties. Once this change took place the obligations of *philotês* became important as accoutrement of the contractual stipulations of impersonal nature.

In sum, like brotherhood, *philotês* was an extremely complex and always positive concept. Both expressed the declaration of peaceful and friendly intentions of the parties bound by this state of affairs. Brotherhood had a variety of meanings chiefly within the social and political sphere, but it seems to have obtained exclusively between men (no brotherhood between women is mentioned) in the social field and between rulers politically; in contrast, *philotês* could obtain between men and women, at least socially. Within the political sphere brotherhood seems to have denoted a variety of relationships and therefore seems to have been a technical term with a specified number of uses, not all of which implied political or military parity. *Philotês*, on the other hand, remained a less technical term, and owing to its lack of formality was capable of expressing a wide variety of relationships in the political, social, and sexual area. Like brotherhood, *philotês* denoted politically a positive condition that determined the character of the activities that followed and nullified all potential aggression. The expansive state of the soul flowing from the state of *philotês* could lead to enduring relationships that took the place of legal arrangements and superseded the mere formality of legality. Whereas in classical times agreements were formally spelled out, such that the signatories to written treaties were expected to adhere to explicit stipulatory agreements, in the time of the epics and probably before that time as well the meaning of *philotês* went beyond the formal agreement. It required that the contractant should render to the other party whatever he would have liked the other to do to him. In the same manner, *philotês* denoted a positive attitude in the area of sexual relationships, a phenomenon with which we are not much concerned here. What is of interest, however, in this area is that *philotês* was also a positive condition that determined the character of the activity that followed, namely, its pleasurable and voluntary character.[27] Indeed, *philotês* itself was originally personified as the offspring of such a sexual union (*Theog.* 224). By the time

---

[26] Hesiod *Theog.* 224.

[27] References in Homer and Hesiod to sexual *philotês: Il.* 2.232; 3.441; 6.25, 161, 165, 209, 216, 314, 331, 353, 360; 15.32; 24.130; *Od.* 2.271; 5.126, 227; 8.313; 10.335; 11.284; 15.421; 19.226; 23.330; Hesiod *Theog.* 125, 306, 336, 375, 380, 405, 625, 920, 927, 941, 1009, 1018; Sc. 36.

58 THE LINGUISTIC EVIDENCE

of the heroic era *philotês* became a state of mind that transcended the sexual passion. For this reason *philotês* was not considered equivalent to *eros*, and Hesiod did not use the term *eros*, except for one questionable instance in Hesiod.[28] It goes without saying that sexual acts took place when the preconditions of *philotês* did not obtain, but in those instances the acts performed were characterized as *ater philotêtos ephimerou* (*Theog.* 132; Sc. 15), the results of sheer animal drive or of basic necessity.

To return to our main interest in *philotês* and the incident with which the discussion of *philotês* began, we may recall that the expectations stemming from *philotês* explain the special twist taken in the story of the duel between Menelaus and Alexander. If the duel had been fought to its natural conclusion, that is, to the death of one of the duelists, the stipulated *philotês* which served as a pre-condition for the duel would have ipso facto terminated the hostilities which were destined to end only with the destruction of Troy. Thus the fighting of the duel to its conclusion would have resulted in that very *philotêta* which could only have defeated destiny itself. Such was the use of *philotês* in the making of the Homeric agreements. *Philotês* was a central term in the making of agreements in the ancient world, but other terms were also very important. Three such terms were *horkia*, *horkos*, and the verb *omnyein*. Let us therefore quickly survey the ways these terms were used in the Homeric contractual relations.

B. THE INTERRELATION OF *HORKIA*, *HORKOS*, AND *OMNYEIN*

As we have seen, in the Homeric world agreements were oral, sanctioned as a rule by religious ritual. The good of society itself demanded that promises be adhered to, and to that effect forms and procedures were devised by which parties to a promise or agreement sought to guarantee those promises. These procedures were most closely associated with religion and understood as oaths. An oath was a conditional self-cursing or self-blessing, that is, an appeal to the gods to reward the oath-taker if he kept his pledge or punish him if he defaulted, and it became the legal formula which made the promise binding. Since the punishment by the guarantor was usually believed to take the form of natural calamities such as plague, drought, and famine that struck the entire tribe or community, the concept of tribal or corporate responsibility was a strong feature of the early stages of legal thought in the ancient world. Thus, the religious obligations tended to become legal obligations, and the practice of taking oaths acquired an extraordinary vitality

---

[28] Hesiod frg. 298 in OCT (if indeed this fragment is part of Hesiod's poetry). In *Il.* 3.441-2 both terms are used in an interesting combination where *Philotês* signified the end of bickering and a change from a negative mood to a positive one where *eros* adverts to sexual love or desire. See also Il. 14.294; 315; 13.638; 24.227; Od. 18.212.

THE LINGUISTIC EVIDENCE   59

and influence. This was particularly so in the international realm, where a treaty upheld by an oath continued to be binding, since it was in this realm of human affairs that adequate legal procedures were most scarce. References to international treaties (including those between city-states) are found as early as the Old Sumerian Texts of the third millennium B.C. Owing to the contingencies of transmission or excavation adequate source material for the study of international agreements probably exists only from the Hittite Empire, more specifically from ca. 1450-1200 B.C. Obviously, the Hittites themselves did not originate the treaty-making format. On the contrary, there is abundant evidence that they themselves borrowed many features of this format from other Near-Eastern civilizations. Some of these features will be pointed out in the following discussion, which takes up in turn the nouns *horkia* and *horkos*, and then the verb *omnyein*.

1. Horkia

Scholars have long argued about whether the two terms *horkia* and *horkos* define different legal or political phenomena, and if so, about the nature of the phenomena they define.[29] Some scholars have maintained that *horkos* referred primarily to oaths, a view which seems to be supported by the use of the term in Homer, while *horkia* referred to the treaties and the sacrificial animals employed in making them official. Modern scholars have not always followed this apparent distinction in the meanings of *horkos* and *horkia* in their analysis of the various passages containing these terms. Frequently *horkia* has been interpreted simply as "oath," an interpretation which fails to distinguish it from *horkos*. Are these terms then interchangeable? Is *horkos*

---

[29] J. Plescia, *The Oath and Perjury in Ancient Greece* (Tallahassee, 1970) 58; M. Leumann, *Homerische Wörter* (Basel, 1950) 263, defines *horkia temnein* as as "'beschworen' eigentlich, 'das Eidopfertier schlachten.'" Leumann (pp. 79-84) discusses *epiorkos* and analyzes briefly the term *horkia* which he nearly identifies as *horkos*. In *The International Law* Phillipson distinguishes at times between *horkos* and *horkia* as belonging to oaths and treaties respectively; he nonetheless translates *horkia etamon* as "pledges these oaths," and κατὰ δ' ὅρκια πιστὰ πάτησαν (*Il.* 4.157) as "trampled upon the trusty *horkia*" as either treaty or oath. Mulder, RhM 79 (1930) 15 takes a similar view, as does W. Arend, *Die typischen Szenen bei Homer* (Berlin, 1933) 122-23; similarly R. Hirzel, *Der Eid* (Leipzig, 1902), considers *horkia* briefly and inclines toward the view that *horkia* fall within the category of words associated with oaths. More recently D. Cohen, RIDA (1980) 49-68 made an excellent attempt to distinguish between *horkos* and *horkia*. According to him *horkia* denotes the treaties and the sacrificial animals employed in the contracting of treaties but almost never oaths, with perhaps a single exception. *Horkos* and *horkia* "are never interchangeable (in the *Iliad*) and although perhaps perceived as related in some general sense, describe two fundamentally different legal phenomena which must be scrupulously distinguished in order to appreciate the range of meaning which each word may convey in the legal and non-legal context in which it typically occurs." Cohen further makes the interesting assertion that the word *horkia* implied the existence or creation of relationship between two or more autonomous parties. The use of *horkia* therefore is not appropriate in cases involving subordination or equality between friends (p. 51, n. 5). Consequently, *horkia* is employed when the emphasis is generally upon relationships.

60 THE LINGUISTIC EVIDENCE

tantamount to *horkia* and vice versa, or is one of these merely a subcategory of the other? The answer lies in the Homeric context, but a few preliminary remarks are in order. First of all, irrespective of their identity or disparity, *horkos* and *horkia* normally occur in different contexts, only once appearing together.[30] Secondly, *horkia* is to be found much more frequently in the *Iliad* than in the *Odyssey*, occurring predominantly in the first half of the *Iliad* (Books 1-12), where the type of agreements requiring the use of *horkia* are made. Conversely, references to *horkos* are more frequent in the second half of the *Iliad*. In contrast, the presence of *horkos* in the *Odyssey* is more evident than *horkia* and its spread is more even in the *Odyssey* than *horkia* in the *Iliad*. Finally, let it be noted here that the singular of *horkia* (*horkion*) appears only once in Homer.[31] It stands juxtaposed to other terms associated with oaths and the making of agreements in the Near East and in the Greek world. The slaughter of lambs, the pouring of unmixed wine, the clasping of the right hand were all components of the treaty-making process, although they did not all appear together in most cases. *Horkion* is a term denoting a part (the blood of the sacrificial victims) rather than the whole animal. Thus the singular form *horkion* is not interchangeable with either *horkos* or *horkia*. Consequently, it does not describe the same fundamental religious and legal phenomena and does not serve the same purpose.

The next question pertains to the plural *horkia*. The discussion of *horkia*, however, is intended to be selective rather than all-inclusive.[32] The meaning of the term is fairly evident when *horkia* occurs in *Od.* 19.302 where Odysseus, disguised as a beggar, tells Penelope that her husband is safe and will presently return to his friends and native land. Penelope was understandably doubtful about the news since she had definitely heard these optimistic predictions many times before. Accordingly, Odysseus needed to back his assurances by the typical oath in the name of Zeus, the highest and mightiest of the gods. The phrase used by Odysseus is *horkia dôsô*, and it is the only time it appears in the *Odyssey*. Since it was unthinkable for a guest of purportedly much lower status to presume to offer his hostess a treaty or to make a bargain with her, the most reasonable translation of *horkia* in this context is that of "to give a promise," or perhaps even better "to give you an oath" in confirmation of his statement.[33] In this instance, therefore, *horkia* is tantamount to *horkos*.

---

[30] Cohen, RIDA, 50.

[31] ὄρκιον αἷμά τε ἀρνῶν, *Il.* 4.158. It refers to the blood of the victims, and for this reason the singular form is used.

[32] *Il.* 2.124, 339; 3.73, 94, 105, 245, 252, 256, 280, 299; 4.72, 155, 158, 269, 271; 7.69, 351, 411; 22.262, 266; *Od.* 19.302; 24.483, 546.

[33] E. Bickerman, *Archive d'histoire du droit oriental* (1950) 133-56.

THE LINGUISTIC EVIDENCE 61

Another atypical phrase in the last book of the *Odyssey, horkia ...
ethêken*, is of interest (546). The subject of the verb is goddess Athena, who
placed (*ethêken*) the *horkia* on both sides into which the people of Ithaca had
been divided after the macabre slaughter of the suitors. Although not
impossible, it would have been rather awkward for Athena to compel both
sides to swear, unless for the purpose of agreeing to a peace. The expression
horkia ethêken would then logically translate as "imposed peace" between the
two enemy camps. We know indeed from an earlier passage that this peace
contained a compromise formula worked out by the gods, in accordance with
which the Ithacans would recognize Odysseus as their legitimate king once
again 'and would live in peace and friendship thereafter (*Od.* 24.483-86). This
is the compromise imposed here by Athena. Clearly, what we have at this
point is a reconciliatory agreement with a sacrifice.

In two other instances the meaning of *horkia* admits of no doubt. In the
first instance *Il.* 3.245 the Trojan herald carried through the city of Troy the
horkia pista of the gods. The poet proceeded to explain what these were,
namely, two lambs for the sacrifice and the wine. The use of the verb *pherô*
and the enumeration of the holy items transported by the heralds illustrate
that *horkia* refers to the sacrificial animals and the wine. The same is true of
Il. 3.269 where the reference of *horkia* is clearly to the sacrificial animals
indicated in *Il.* 3.245.

However, the most frequent use of *horkia* in Homer is in combination
with the adjective *pista* and the verb *temnein*.[34] In Book 2 of the *Iliad*,
Agamemnon, testing the martial stamina of the Achaeans, discussed a
hypothetical situation during which a truce with the Trojans might be held
(*horkia pista temnein*) for the purpose of counting the troops. *Horkia pista
tamontes* (*Il.* 3.256) is a traditional phrase for oath-taking, used in the most
solemn form in which a sacrificial victim or victims were slaughtered. The
victims embody the oaths and can be called *horkia pista* (*Il.* 2.69; 3.245).
That *horkia* could point to a treaty or reconciliation agreement is obvious
from the formerly discussed combination *horkia ethêken*. Moreover, the use
of *horkia* in this instance resembles the situation in Book 7 in which
Agamemnon agreed to a temporary truce for the purpose of burying the dead
(411).[35] In both cases the nature of the transaction was of a short duration and
for a determinate objective.

In Book 3 Hector became the emissary of a duel proposal which was
suggested by Paris and seems to have enjoyed the universal support of the

---

[34] *Il.* 2.124; 3.73, 94, 105, 252, 356; 4.155; 19.191; 24.483. See also G. S. Kirk, *The
Iliad* ad *Il.* 3.73-75.

[35] *Il.* 7.411; the term *horkia* is not accompanied by the verb *temnein*.

62   THE LINGUISTIC EVIDENCE

Trojans (*Il.* 3.59 ff.).[36] Paris and Menelaus would fight a single duel, and the apple of discord would belong to the victor. The others, Achaeans and Trojans, would become reconciled and "cut the *horkia*," following which the Achaeans would return to their homes. Since Priam's unruly sons, especially Paris, did not inspire confidence, the Achaeans demanded that Priam himself should "cut" the *horkia*. There was of course a still more weighty reason that the presence of Priam was required. If Agamemnon was to represent the Greeks in the taking of oaths, protocol dictated that his Trojan counterpart be present. In fact, because of Priam's advanced age, on the battlefield supreme military command was exercised by his son Hector, but Priam still was the ultimate authority of Troy. Thus a herald was dispatched to ask Priam to come *ophr' horkia temnêi*. The term *horkia* here plainly denotes the sacrificial victims to be used in the oath-taking ceremony and, by extension, the treaty.

Hence we see that the term *horkia* admits of a multiple translation: (1) a pledge accompanied by an oath, (2) sacrificial victims and objects used during the oath-taking ceremony, and, by extension, (3) the treaty itself. But what about the locution *horkia temnein*? Just what does it refer to, and how did it emerge? Does the verb *temnein* designate the cutting of the victim's throat? These are pertinent but difficult questions since Homer uses the formulas *horkia temnein* or *horkia pista temnein* but does not give any clues as to their provenance. From other evidence that we have, however, it appears that the formulas are older than the Homeric writings, and that these formulas may be associated with similar formulas used in the Ancient Near East prior to Homer. Greek evidence is found in sources later than Homer but it alludes to times earlier than the Homeric war. The investigation of this evidence may turn out to be significant in the elucidation of the dilemma regarding *horkia temnein*.

According to a story in Stesichorus, Tyndareos, Helen's father, had asked all those who sued for his daughter's hand to stand on the *tomia* of a horse he had sacrificed and to swear that they would go to the aid of his daughter and her future husband—whoever he might be—if any injustice befell them.[37] Pausanias also mentioned the Boar's Tomb, which he located in the area of

---

[36] Also *Il.* 3.73, 94, 105, 107, and so on. For *horkia* see Nilsson, *Geschichte der Griechischen Religion* 1:139; P. Stengel, *Opferbraüche der Griechen* (Leipzig, 1919) 19, 78; his *Die Griechischen Kultusaltertümer* 2nd ed. (Munich, 1920); and also his article in *Hermes* 49 (1914) 90-92; Kurt Latte, *Heiliges Recht* (Tübingen, 1920) 35; Arist. *Lys.* 185; Aischin. 2.87 (p. 264); Dem. 23.68 (p. 642); Dion. Hal. 5.1; Hesychius, s.v. *tomia*; Plescia, *The Oath of Perjury*, 2.

[37] Paus. 3. 20.9 claims to have seen the tomb of the horse; Stesichorus, frg. 14. About horse sacrifices to Helios, Stengel, *Die Griechischen Kultusaltertümer*, 136, says that they were not Greek in origin and that wherever they were made, they imitated Persian custom. Also see Paus. 3.20.5 and Aesch. *Scholia in Eum.* 450, which is not very reliable.

THE LINGUISTIC EVIDENCE   63

the Messenian Stenyclerus, where, according to the story, Heracles took and gave oaths to the sons of Neleus, standing on the pieces of a boar (*tomiôn kaprou*).[38] Pausanias further described how athletes along with their fathers, brothers, and trainers took an oath in Olympia while standing on the pieces of a boar beside the image of Zeus, surnamed the oath-god, swearing that they had followed the training regulations for the last ten successive months. A similar story is related in connection with the campaign of the Greeks against Troy. Before the Greeks departed for Troy, Calchas cut a boar into two parts at the market place and had each man pass with drawn sword between the two pieces in such a manner as to have his sword smeared with the victim's blood. The ritual is supposed to have symbolized sworn enmity towards Priam's people.[39] As we shall see, this story related to later Greek stories as well as stories of Near-Eastern provenance. Among the Israelites, for example, a common way of establishing a covenant was to cut up the animal and pass between the parts. Jeremiah tells us that this is how king Zedekiah of Judah, his princes, his priests, his eunuchs, and all the people of the land made an agreement between them to free their Hebrew slaves. In the participants' minds, this cutting of a calf had the effect of subjecting them to a possible curse. When, shortly afterwards, they violated the agreement, Jeremiah announced to them God's judgment: "I will make you an object of horror to all the kingdoms of the earth. And these men who have infringed my covenant, who have not observed the terms of the covenant made in my presence, I will treat these men like the calf they cut in two to pass between the parts of it" (Jer. 34.18). Here as in the case of Greeks, oaths and agreements are solemnized by the ritual slaughter of animals, the severed parts of which served to underscore the awesomeness of the oath taken. In both instances of *tomia* or the cutting of the animal in half, a severance is involved, and this severance may be responsible for the use of the verb *temnein*. Of course the slitting of an animal's throat is not, strictly speaking, a "severance," but it is so in an extended sense, in that it cut off the life of the animal notwithstanding the fact that no part of the animal was separated from the rest, as when the animal is divided into parts.

The stories of Calchas and Jeremiah are not unique. A similar story in the Old Testament appears in Gen. 15.10, while Herodotus describes the cutting up of one of the sons of Pythius for a different reason. Herodotus's story has

---

[38] Pausanias is in a way apologetic because he forgot to ask how the remains of the boar were disposed of after the oath. The custom forbade the eating of an accursed animal. In support of this he mentions the boar on which Agamemnon took an oath that he had not touched Briseis. The boar was thrown into the sea by the herald; Paus. 5.24.11. Also cf. Dem. 49.10.

[39] See J. G. Frazer, *Pausanias' Description of Greece*, 4:367-68. For something similar see Dem. 23.28; Arist. *Lys.* 86 ff.; Aesch. *Seven against Thebes* 43 ff.; Xen. *Anab.* 2.2.9.

64 THE LINGUISTIC EVIDENCE

the appearance of a legend, but Herodotus would not have mentioned such an absurd story without an explanation unless stories of this type were familiar to the Greeks and Persians. Since the story is considered legendary, the origins of the practice in the story must go far back in history.[40] Plato employs a parallel expression, not in association with a treaty but in connection with serious constitutional matters among the citizens of his purported state (*Laws* 753 D, διὰ τομίων πορευόμενος). His phrase is similar to the Hebrew, and unless the history of the locution was very familiar to the Greeks, Plato would not have used it. Similarly, the Latin *foedus ferire* stands substantially close to the Hebrew, and some scholars think that it travelled directly from the Near East to the Romans through the Carthaginians. For these scholars the Greek σπονδὰς τέμνειν appearing in Euripides' *Helen* (1235) is unique, but this writer does not share this view.[41]

Horkia temnein, then, stood not for just any oaths or agreements, but for those solemnized by the ritual slaughter of animals, though not always horses and boars, and reflected the ancient practice of standing upon the animal's genitals (*tomia*) or passing through the severed parts.[42] The expression continued even when the practice of standing on *tomia* had fallen into disuse, since in Homer it is not certain that the participants in a sacrifice connected with an agreement stood on the *tomia* of the sacrificial animal.

---

[40] See Hdt. 7.39.3; 4.84 for a more gruesome story. How and Wells, *A Commentary on Herodotus* (Oxford, 1912) *ad loc.*, are skeptical of the story and so is R. W. Macan, *Herodotus* (London, 1895-1908) *ad loc.* and lxiv ff. How and Wells maintains that the story has the appearance of a legend, a view which, if true, would support the antiquity of the practice. A. C. Gobineau, *Histoire des Perses* (Paris, 1869) 2:195, sees in the story a Persian custom intended to make those one wished to preserve from harm pass between two parts of a sacrificial animal and the more valuable the victim the greater the efficacy of the charm. Whatever the Persian use might have been, there is little doubt that the custom had very early origins.

[41] Actually the statement in Eur. *Helen* 1235 is σπονδὰς τάμωμεν καὶ διαλλάχθητί μοι, describing a reconciliation or a state of change from enmity to peace and friendship; see D. Fehling, *Glotta* 58 (1980) 11.

[42] For the antiquity of this practice see Gen. 9 ff. where God ordered Abraham to get a three-year-old heifer, a three-year-old goat, a three-year-old ram, a turtledove, and a young pigeon and to cut them in half in testimony to their covenant. On the surface at least, the covenant seems to be a mere promise by God and no exchange. In truth, this promise is nothing but part of the original agreement made by God and Abraham which Abraham accepted voluntarily. The practice of cutting up animals in confirmation of a promise or agreement continued uninterruptedly into the Hellenistic times. Livy 40.6.1-3 describes it in association with a lustration by the Macedonian army of Philip V. The fore part of a dog was cut off and placed on the right side of the road, and the hind part, with the entrails, placed on the left. Between these two parts of the victim marched the troops. At the head of the column were the arms and standards of all the preceding kings of Macedonia, then followed Philip accompanied by his children, and then the royal cohorts and the bodyguards and the rest of the rank and file. The practice demonstrates the persistence of many ancient customs and constitutes a lesson for those who accept so easily the theory of discontinuity of cultures, including the Mycenaean and Homeric cultures.

THE LINGUISTIC EVIDENCE 65

Conversely, the absence of *temnein* from this standard phrase would indicate a subcategory of oaths or agreements which, because of their informal, secondary character, or brief duration did not require solemnization by the formalism of sacrifice and the allied ritual of *spondai*. Similarly, the reference to *synthesiai* and *horkia* in *Il.* 2.339 should not be taken to mean the absence of sacrificial ritual and the taking of oaths, for obviously the occasion was much too important not to have been formalized by the established ritualistic ceremonies. But Nestor did not have to elaborate on acts which had so recently been performed and which everybody knew well. His intention was solely to remind the Achaeans of their common agreement and the oaths and sacrifices that accompanied it. The force of Nestor's remarks was to reaffirm the alliance of the Greeks and its initial objective by pointing out that if the Achaeans went home they would be stigmatized as oath-breakers in their own eyes as well as in the eyes of the gods whom they had undoubtedly invoked as witnesses at the time of the ceremonies. Nestor appeared indignant at the apparent irresponsibility of his fellow Achaeans and their failure to pursue what they had set out to do, namely, to live up to the obligations stemming from their oaths. Although they all seemed to have been autonomous rulers, Nestor did not think that they had the right of secession from a freely formed alliance before they had done their utmost to achieve its end.

Hence, the word *horkia* iimplies that a relationship exists between two or more autonomous parties and that any subordination or obligation involved in that relationship has been established by means of *horkia*. In short, the standard case of *horkia* implies an element of reciprocity and mutuality of obligations, the extent of which is defined by the relationship which the *horkia* creates or alters. Such a relationship is usually of two types. The first and the more common involves what is hoped by the parties to be a permanent modification of their existing status, extending beyond the immediate transaction in which they are involved. The second type of relationship occurs in situations where *horkia* does not bring about permanent changes in the relationship of the parties or the assumptions of obligations beyond the completion of the immediate objective. In a way, *horkia* was frequently preceded by the contracting of friendship which set the stage and the psychological climate that would enable the participants to enter into their oaths and stipulations in a positive mood. The religious ritual of the *horkia* ceremony prepared the contracting parties to enter into the type of binding political relationship which imposed reciprocal obligations and duties upon the parties. For lesser promises or for pronouncements between unequals in the hierarchical scale of social and political relationships, particularly when the socially inferior party wishes to establish his credibility, only an oath was required, while for agreements between friends an oath was not needed. Formality proved unnecessary in the case of Penelope and the beggar Odysseus. Likewise, no oath was required between

66 THE LINGUISTIC EVIDENCE

Achilles and Patroclus. The binding force of the promise between Achilles and Patroclus seemed to flow from the pre-existing relationship which made formalism or a simple oath gratuitous.

It is notable that the term *horkia* and its singular form *horkion* survived throughout history and were used repeatedly by Herodotus and Thucydides, though sparingly by the latter and in a different context. Responding to Croesus's proposal for an alliance, the Spartans swore to be his friends and allies, ἐποιήσαντο ὅρκια ξεινίης πέρι καὶ συμμαχίης, (Hdt. 1.69.3; Bengston, No. 113). Prior to this alliance, Croesus had made an alliance with the Egyptian king Amasis and the Babylonian Nebuchadnezzar (Labynetus), παρακαλέσας τοὺς Αἰγυπτίους κατὰ τὸ ὅρκιον, Hdt. 1.74.2. In 585 B.C., a total eclipse occurred during the war between Lydians and Persians, and in the religious climate of that day the phenomenon was interpreted as an omen in consequence of which the two antagonists became reconciled through the services of the Cilician Syennesis and the Babylonian king Nebuchadnezzar. These two advised the contesting parties to come to terms (ὅρκιον οἱ σπεύσαντες γενέσθαι, Hdt. I.74.4; Bengston, No. 107). This settlement was sealed by a marriage alliance. Herodotus also adds the fascinating information that while these oriental nations made treaties in a manner similar to the Greeks (ὅρκια δ᾽ ποιέεται ταῦτα τὰ ἔθνεα τὰ πέρ τε καὶ ἕλληνες, Hdt. 1.74.6), they cut the skin of their arms and licked each other's blood.

In another instance, Herodotus tells us that of all the Ionians, only the Milesians were not attacked by Cyrus, because of their formal treaty with him (πρὸς μούνους τούτους ὅρκιον Κῦρος ἐποιήσατο, Hdt. 1.141.4; Bengston, No. 115), a fact which he repeats a little later in his narrative: Μιλήσιοι ... αὐτῷ Κύρῳ ὅρκιον ποιησάμενοι (Hdt. 1.143.1, 169.2). Because of the Persian threat to the Asian Minor Greeks, the Phocaeans decided to leave their city and go West. Although they made an agreement (ὤμοσαν) to that effect among themselves and took an oath, half of them soon experienced a change of heart and broke their oaths (ψευδόρκιοι) while those who adhered to their oaths (ὅρκιον) sailed off (Hdt. 1.165.3).

When Cambyses succeeded his father Cyrus to the throne of Persia, he embarked on a war of conquest by which he added Egypt to his kingdom. He also contemplated the taking of the territory of Carthage, and to this effect asked the Phoenicians to provide assistance with their navy. The Phoenicians refused, alleging that they had been bound to the Carthaginians by great oaths (ὁρκίοισι γὰρ μεγάλοισι ἐνδεδέσθαι, Hdt. 3.19.2). Among Cambyses' enemies were certain important Babylonian priests who organized a plot against him. They invited other enemies of Cambyses, such as Prexaspes, to participate, after they made Prexaspes swear that he would never reveal their treacherous plans (πίστιν τε λαβόντες καὶ ὁρκίοισι, Hdt. 3.74.2).

THE LINGUISTIC EVIDENCE 67

Following the failure of the Persian attempt to occupy Greece, the Greeks assumed the offensive against Persia. The islanders were soon liberated from the Persian yoke and, wishing to secure their newly found liberty, they asked the Athenians to accept them in their alliance. Among these islanders Herodotus prominently mentions the Samians, Chians, and Lesbians, all of whom promptly bound themselves to the alliance: αὐτίκα γὰρ οἱ Σάμιοι πίστιν τε καὶ ὅρκια ἐποιεῦντο συμμαχίης πέρι πρὸς τοὺς ἕλληνας, 9.92; οὕτω δὴ Σαμίους τε καὶ Χίους καὶ Λεσβίους καὶ τοὺς ἄλλους νησιώτας, ... ἐς τὸ συμμαχικον ἐποιήσαντο, πίστιν τε καταλαβόντες καὶ ὁρκίοισι ἐμμενέειν τε καὶ μὴ ἀποστήσεσθαι, 9.106.4; καὶ τούτους [Σαμίους] καταλαβόντες ὁρκίοισι, 9.106.4. When Solon was commissioned to reform the Athenian constitution, Herodotus says that he bound the Athenians with solemn oaths (ὁρκίοισι μεγάλοις) to abide by the laws he framed for at least ten years (Hdt. 1.29.2; How and Wells *ad loc.*; Plut. *Solon* 25).

In four remarkable instances, however, Herodotus employed the Homeric formula to indicate the making of agreements. Speaking of those Greeks who banded together to withstand the Persian onslaught, Herodotus adverts to their historic agreement, using the statement ἐπὶ τούτοισι οἱ ἕλληνες ἔταμον ὅρκιον...· τὸ δ᾽ ὅρκιον ὧδε εἶχε (Hdt. 7.132.2; Bengtson, No. 130). In still another case he refers to the agreement between Amasis and the Barcaeans made in the following, rather interesting fashion: both parties stood on a hidden trench and swore to the agreement (τάμνοντες ὅρκια, Hdt. 4.201.2). The agreement (ὅρκιον) was to remain valid for as long as the trench endured. Shortly after the agreement was consummated (μετὰ δ᾽ τὸ ὅρκιον), the Persians destroyed the trench in order to claim that the agreement had expired. Similarly, Herodotus informs us that in Plataea the Tegeans and Athenians claimed the right wing of the battle, the left having been awarded to the Spartans. Both attempted to support their pretensions by reciting stories of great deeds performed by their ancestors or by themselves. The Tegeans adduced the story of the single combat between Hyllus, the son of Heracles, and king Echemerus, the son of Phegeus's son Eeropus. Herodotus describes this legendary agreement with the ἔταμον ὅρκιον (9.26.4). In the last case, Herodotus explains the making of agreements by the Scythians. The Scythians, he says, make agreements with other people in the following way. First, they draw blood from the parties to the agreement (τῶν τὸ ὅρκιον ταμνομένων), by piercing the body with an awl or a knife. Then they pour the blood, mixing it with wine, into a great bowl, into which they dip a scimitar, arrows, an axe, and a javelin. When this has been done the makers of the agreement (αὐτοί τε οἱ τὸ ὅρκιον ποιεύμενοι), along with their most important retainers, drink of the blood, uttering solemn imprecations (Hdt. 4.70).

68   THE LINGUISTIC EVIDENCE

From Herodotus's references to *horkion* and *horkia* certain conclusions can be drawn. First, Herodotus uses *horkion* and *horkia* interchangeably and without differentiation. Since there is no other word in the passages given above that would refer to the agreement apart from the oaths, we have to conclude that *horkion* and *horkia* stand for the oaths and the stipulations contained in the agreement. Secondly, the Homeric formula *horkia temnein* is still in use in the fifth century B.C., although it is often replaced by what seems to be more contemporaneous jargon such as ὅρκιον ποιήσασθαι (Hdt. 3.74.2). The use of the Homeric formula *horkia temnein* in the fifth century B.C. thus demonstrates the endurance of traditions in the ancient world, particularly those traditions associated with religious practices. The cutting of the skin and the licking of the blood by the parties of the non-Greek agreements must also have their origins in very ancient practices. The licking of each other's blood implied the establishment of brotherhood by the lickers, while among the less civilized people who followed this practice it took the place of oral or written stipulation contained in the treaties we have already examined. Thirdly, *horkion* and *horkia* denoted the contraction of an agreement by autonomous parties and the change of condition in the relationship of these parties either from a neutral state to a state of friendship (Hdt. 1.69.3; 1.143.1; 1.169.2; 3.74.2; 9.106.4) or from a state of enmity to that of friendship (Hdt. 1.74.4-6). Thus the conditions produced by the agreements in Herodotus are similar to those described by the agreements in Homer. Only on one occasion (Hdt. 1.169.3) were the contracting parties on friendly terms before the compact. Lastly, Herodotus uses the formula ὀρκίοισι μεγάλοισι (3.19.2; 1.29.2) to emphasize the solemnity of an occasion. This formula is reminiscent of the Homeric formula μέγας or δεινὸς ὅρκος, and there cannot be much doubt that the Herodotean phrase draws its origins from archaic Greek usages. In sum, the Herodotean *horkion* and *horkia* denote compacts solemnized by oaths. Although no sacrifice is mentioned in the formalization of these compacts, there should be no doubt that the ceremony of treaty-making included a sacrifice, as the custom of animal sacrifice on important private or public business continued among the Greeks into the classical times and beyond.

The references of Thucydides to *horkia* and *horkion* are few, but they are important in that they indicate the evolution of these terms by the end of the fifth century. Thus in three out of the six times that Thucydides uses the words, he employs them as a modifier (ὀρκίους θεοὺς; Thuc. 1.71.5; 1.78.5; 2.71.4). In 6.72.6 *horkion* is tantamount to *horkos*, while in 6.19.1 it is both the oath and the formalized agreement. The same is true of 6.52.1 which alludes to a formal treaty (see also Gomme, Andrewes, Dover *ad loc.*) Thucydides' meager use of *horkion* and *horkia* leads to the inevitable conclusion that the Homeric usage of *horkia* as a formalized agreement by the second half of the fifth century B.C. was rapidly replaced by other

THE LINGUISTIC EVIDENCE 69

contemporaneous terms, since Thucydides mentions a great number of agreements in his text but under different rubrics.

If thus far the focus of *horkia* has been on the establishment of conditions of reciprocity among two or more parties or the reestablishment of old relationships, other expressions in Homer associated with *horkia* implied the breach or dissolution of relationships. This breach of relationships established through *horkia* was indicated by the use of such words as *pateein* (*Il.* 4.157, 266) *sygcheein* (*Il.* 4.269), *dêlêsasthai* (*Il.* 4.67, 72), and *pêmainein* (*Il.* 3.157, 299). All of these terms suggest injury, cancellation, or other harm to the *horkia*, that is, to the agreement and the oaths taken in conjunction with the agreement.[43] Zeus (*Il.* 4.72) ordered Athena to go among the Trojans and bring about the violation of their earlier agreement with the Greeks (*horkia dêlêsasthai*). Athena accomplished this end by persuading Pandarus to shoot an arrow against Menelaus. The arrow found its target, and Menelaus was lightly wounded, whereupon Agamemnon protested that the Trojans *patêsan* their *horkia*. To rupture, i.e., *patein,* the *horkia* was tantamount to violating the oaths and reciprocally sanctified agreements which had bound them to abstain from activities of war.[44] Appropriately, Hector began his address to the Achaeans about a new combat between himself and one of the Achaeans by explaining that the earlier treaty and the peace settlement that ought to have followed did not materialize because Zeus wished otherwise.[45] No mention was made about violation. Nonetheless, a vague sense of guilt seems to have weighed upon the Trojans. In consequence, Hector proposed a new single combat on the grounds that, whatever had gone astray in the earlier arrangement (of Book 3), the Achaeans were not to blame. The deep dislike of the Trojans for Paris (*Il.* 3.453-54) had, no doubt, increased after Paris's duel with Menelaus, and there were clearly those among them who felt that their own side was accountable for violating the arrangements. Antenor was obviously one of them, and, since he felt that the Trojans had betrayed their oaths and agreements, he proposed that they ought to fulfill their obligations by carrying out the terms of the

---

[43] Plat. *Leg.* 4.753 D; Bikerman, *Archive d'histoire* 5 (1950) 165.

[44] Interestingly, there is a similar expression in modern Greek, πατῶ τὸν ὅρκο μου, denoting the violation of an oath by the speaker. For the nuances in the meaning of the terms denoting disrespect for oaths see Eust. *ad loc.*, cited in the text.

[45] The argument of Cohen, RIDA 27 (1980) 60, that *horkia patein* or *dêlêdasthai* is not tantamount to *epiorkia* remains doubtful. It is true that the Trojans had not sworn falsely and were not eager to see Paris escape from his encounter with Menelaus (*Il.* 3.453-54), but they were as confused as the Greeks by the mysterious disappearance of Paris. Nor could Homer describe it as *epiorkia* for ostensibly the escape was strictly owing to the divine intervention, and if the gods approved of it how could anybody speak against the divine? Paris, on the other hand, was glad to escape from the duel and was not much concerned with the moral or legal implications of his escape.

70   THE LINGUISTIC EVIDENCE

treaty, thereby putting an end to the fighting. The Trojans had violated the
agreement and broken the truce, and could not continue fighting, pretending
that nothing had happened, when their oaths obliged them to establish peace
by returning Helen and her property. It was within this context that Hector's
initiative for a new duel was taken, with the intention that the duel would
serve as an antidote that might banish the guilty feeling of the Trojans and
restore their dignity. Although the new single combat between Aias and
Hector diverted attention from the duel of Menelaus and Paris, it was not
designed to have the finality of that earlier duel. Even the use of similar
terms in the description of this second duel stopped short of ascribing finality
to it. When Trojans and Achaeans swore to *philotêta*, following the end of
the Paris-Menelaus combat, everybody understood this *philotêta* as designed
to establish permanent peace along with the withdrawal of the invaders. On
the other hand, the friendly separation of the two sides subsequent to the
indecisive outcome of the Aias-Hector encounter was only for the day, owing
to the oncoming darkness.[46] Measures were taken to make sure that both
sides agreed to the termination of the combat. The usual aristocratic
compliments were exchanged, and a mutual agreement vouchsafed cessation
from strife for the day, since there would be time to continue the fight in the
future.[47] Appropriately enough, the friendly outcome of the duel prepared the
atmosphere for the truce necessary for the burial of the dead. Idaeus, the
Trojan herald who came to the Achaean camp in pursuit of this mission,
revealed on his own initiative the prevailing Trojan sentiment about Paris
and hinted at the Trojans' inability to coerce Paris to return Helen. The
seemingly undiplomatic statement from a career diplomat distinguished for
wisdom (*pepnymenôi*) was designed to be a conciliatory gesture whose
purpose was to expunge from the Trojans generally any guilt for Paris's
conduct. The important thing here is that the agreement for the truce was
designated by the word *horkia* unaccompanied by *temnein* but with a reference
to Zeus (*Il.* 7.411). Although the agreement entailed certain stipulations such
as the right to strip the other's armor and the return of the corpse for burial,
no *horkia* were cut—that is to say, the text does not mention the cutting of
horkia, as was customary with other agreements. This is due to the unofficial
and secondary importance of the duel, which required a simple gentlemen's
agreement without *horkia* of any kind, rather than to its being perceived as
merely the continuation of the unfinished single combat between Menelaus

---

[46] Whether this single combat was meant to be a substitute for the duel between Menelaus
and Alexander is doubtful. At any rate, there is no mention of the solemnization that would
indicate such a thing. Nor was Hector bent on finishing what was left unfinished by Paris.
The epic presents this duel as a simple agonistic combat providing some sort of relief to the
epic plot.

[47] *Il.* 7.302.

THE LINGUISTIC EVIDENCE 71

and Alexander. Hector's promise, backed by the invocation of Zeus as witness, was tantamount to *horkos* and was hence expected to suffice, especially as nothing was really at stake. Later, when Hector was about to fight Achilles, he was to ask for an agreement which he sought to seal by *horkia* because he rightly suspected that Achilles, in a state of extreme agitation, would not respect the aristocratic tradition dictating the return of the corpse for burial. In fact, driven by a gust of passion, Achilles did not wish to hear Hector's "gibberish" regarding oaths of any kind.

Horkia occurs in another passage in the *Iliad*, in a problematic context which raises serious questions concerning its translation. In *Il.* 19.55 ff., Agamemnon, conceding his folly in the affair of Briseis, was grateful that Achilles had decided to resume fighting against the Trojans, thereby putting an end to their dispute. On his part, Agamemnon, wanting to display his repentance, announced that he was eager to compensate Achilles with gifts described earlier in the Embassy (Book 9). Achilles' response shows indifference to offers of gifts and compensation since his sole desire was to do battle with the Trojans immediately (*Il.* 19.146-53). On the advice of Odysseus, however, Achilles curbed his martial spirit and his rage until a formal ceremony solemnized the new era of good feelings. Odysseus suggested that the gifts destined for Achilles be displayed before the assembly and that Agamemnon swear an oath that he had never even touched Briseis. Eager to take such an oath, Agamemnon urged the Achaeans to remain where they stood until the gifts were brought from his hut and the *horkia* were cut (*Il.* 19.190-91). Subsequently, a ceremony similar to that described in *Il.* 3.271 ff. was carried out, in the course of which Agamemnon took an oath as promised.[48] The mention of *horkia* is unique in that it is juxtaposed to *horkos* in the Homeric epics. This uniqueness becomes more intriguing since Odysseus had merely asked for an *horkos* and Agamemnon responded with the wish to cut *pista horkia*.

Leumann interprets this passage as involving an oath and nothing more.[49] It seems more plausible that, as other scholars also believe, Agamemnon topped Odysseus's suggestion with one of his own, recommending the solemnization of the oaths, as was done on more official occasions during which not only important agreements were made but where also the formality and ritual of the ceremonies symbolized mutuality of the obligations established.[50] Thus Agamemnon used the occasion to convert his reconciliation to Achilles from a merely personal affair to a Pan-Achaean

---

[48] *Il.* 19.187, 190-91; 250-69. Here a boar is slain whose meat is not consumed by the Achaeans but is thrown into the ocean.

[49] Leumann, *Hom. Wörter*, nn. 2 and 85.

[50] Arend, *Die Typische Szenen*, 122-23; Herzel, *Der Eid*, 38; 194.

72 THE LINGUISTIC EVIDENCE

event that signified the end of the deleterious division in the Greek army and the beginning of a new era. Agamemnon correctly perceived the importance of the change in his relationship with Achilles to mean a sharp turn in the politico-military situation affecting all the Greeks. For this reason he wanted to celebrate it officially with all the Achaeans participating as witnesses. A mere oath, as Odysseus had suggested, would have deprived the occasion of its dramatic character, of the pomp and ceremony to which the Greeks were prone. Like the sacrificial ceremony in Book 4 which signified the end of the conflict with the Trojans, this celebration, reestablishing concord between the two leaders and incidentally among all the Achaeans, signaled their final victory over the Trojans. Not only had Achilles by his secession (a secession which was itself justified because Agamemnon had violated the fundamental aristocratic principles on which the original *synthesia* and *horkia* had been based) broken his alliance with Agamemnon but he had ipso facto deprived the Achaeans of their best hope for victory. With this reconciliation with Agamemnon the equilibrium was restored, and a speedier end to the war was almost certain.

Lastly, there are passages in Homer where an agreement is intimated but no *horkos* or *horkia* are involved. In the affair between Priam and Othryoneus, for example (*Il.* 13.363 ff.)—though their earlier relations are somewhat obscure—both parties seem to have been dealing from an independent position. Nevertheless, upon hearing of the war Othryoneus came to Priam and volunteered to help fight against the Achaeans, if Priam would give him Cassandra's hand. Priam responded affirmatively with a nod of his head. No oath or sacrifice took place by way of formalizing this private compact. Doubtless a change took place in the relationship of the two parties and obligations were undertaken as part of the arrangement.[51] The same formula used by Homer to signify the acceptance of a contract between Priam and Orthryoneus was used in another passage where another type of agreement is clearly involved. In both cases the absence of *horkia* was not owing to the disparate status of the contractants, since they were independent of each other and free from bonds of friendship such as those binding Achilles to Patroclus. After a crisis Agamemnon approached the Cretan Idomeneus to ask him to remain faithful to his earlier pledges. Idomeneus reassured Agamemnon of his intention to carry out the pledges he had originally given prior to the Achaean departure for Troy (*Il.* 4.257). Undoubtedly, these

---

[51] Apparently, Othryoneus was a guest within the wall of Troy, according to Leaf *ad loc.*, who considers *kythêrothen endon eonta* as a more natural locution since it is followed by *en megaroisin*. The location of Kabesos is problematic. As for Homer's description of Cassandra as *eidos aristên*, a compliment paid to Laodice in *Il.* 3.124; 6.252. The critics seem to have been puzzled over this supposed inconsistency, some actually taking *eidos* here to mean *tên eidesin,* knowledge of prophecy, which, as the scholion on *Il.* 24.699 remarks, the Homeric Cassandra did not possess.

THE LINGUISTIC EVIDENCE

pledges had tied both parties to reciprocal obligation which did not exist earlier. But no *horkia* was used because the personal agreement between Agamemnon and Idomeneus might or might not have been solemnized by sacrifice. Obviously, Idomeneus accepted Agamemnon's invitation to participate in the Trojan campaign without serious objections.

2. Horkos

Like *horkia*, *horkos* was employed in the Homeric world on a variety of occasions.[52] However, if—as was argued above—*horkia* implied oaths, sacrificial victims, various objects involved in the oath-taking ceremonies, and agreements concluded by two or more parties, what is then the meaning of *horkos* and for what purposes was it used by the Achaeans? The best way, perhaps, to answer the question is to make use of some of the examples contained in Homer.

When Achilles became angry at Agamemnon over Briseis, he took an oath in the presence of all the Greeks that he would not fight again (*Il.* 1.123, 239, *megas horkos*). Achilles had correctly foreseen that without his aid the Achaeans would face an impossible task in fighting the Trojans. Indeed, things turned out as he had predicted. Agamemnon, feeling remorse for the clearly unjust act which he committed in a moment of rashness, and plagued by the burden of public responsibility for the unprecedented losses of the Achaeans, began to search for avenues of reconciliation with Achilles. He consequently sent goodwill envoys with apologies and presents along with promises of rich recompense, and was ready to swear an oath (*megan horkon omoumai*) that he had not touched Briseis (*Il.* 9.132, 274). The effort at reconciliation failed. However, following the death of Patroclus the object of Achilles' anger changed, and he became willing to make his peace with the rest of the Achaeans. Odysseus suggested that in order to clear up the misunderstanding completely and to dispel all doubts, Agamemnon should take the proffered oath (*Il.* 19.175).

Meanwhile, stationed in front of the Achaean camp, the Trojans did not remain entirely complacent. They knew that Achilles would be coming in all his strength again. Hector himself was in a quandary. One of the alternatives he mulled over involved going to the Achaean camp to inform them of the Trojan readiness to return Helen and her possessions with half of the city's treasures as recompense. The proposal, however, had to be approved by the council of Trojan elders (by a *gerousion horkon*, *Il.* 22.119). In the end, Hector rejected this approach and decided to brave Achilles in battle. Yet even

---

[52] Cohen, RIDA 27, 53-59. References to *horkos* are as follows: *Il.* 1.239; 2.377, 755; 9.132, 274; 14.280; 15.38; 19.113, 175, 108, 129; 20.313, 23.42, 441; *Od.* 2.378; 4.253, 746; 5.178, 186; 10.299, 348, 346, 381; 12.304, 298; 14.151, 171; 15.436, 438; 18.55, 58; 19.369; 20.229.

74   THE LINGUISTIC EVIDENCE

the death of Hector did not appease Achilles' desire for revenge. He therefore took an oath not to wash himself from the stains of battle until he had given proper burial to his friend Patroclus. A proper burial entailed, among other things, the celebration of funeral games. During the chariot race, Menelaus charged Antilochus with tripping him, and vowed not to permit him to win the prize before taking an oath (*horkon oise aethion, Il.* 23.44) that he was guilty of no misconduct.

These examples demonstrate the frequency and variety of oath-taking, explained in turn by the strongly personal character of the Homeric relationships and the usually oral nature of personal agreements. A man could make a promise to himself and then, in a subsequent and more public act, take an oath that he would fulfill his promise. The same thing could happen when a man promised something to an absent friend or one deceased. One also took an oath to fulfill a promise to someone present or assumed to be present, though not necessarily present in a physical sense.

In connection with the personal feud between Agamemnon and Achilles, the oath taken by Achilles severed the relationship established earlier by the treaty mentioned by Nestor (*Il.* 2.339-41). The reciprocal obligations which bound the two parties were broken, and the oath served to confirm the rupture. No sanctified animals were needed to solemnize the event because the determination was chiefly one-sided. Thus, Agamemnon had to swear the oath about the chastity of Briseis as he was the only one who could attest to such a fact. Similarly, the only party other than Menelaus who could swear that the game rules were violated was Antilochus, the violator himself. No agreement or formalization of an agreement was involved here, but only the demand for a simple confession on the part of the violator that he had indeed broken the rules.

As we have seen, oaths were taken where no reciprocally binding pacts were involved but instead in personal cases where one person promised something to another or requested something from another without the elaborate ritual of sacrifices and the killing of sacrificial animals appropriate to more intricate and formal relations. *Horkos* could be demanded of a person by a social and political equal or by someone of socially superior rank. Sometimes the socially inferior person was also bound to the superior by special relationships. Thus Telemachus made the old servant swear to him not to divulge to Penelope his impending trip to Sparta (*Od.* 2.377-378). Similarly, Odysseus demanded from his men an oath that they would not touch Helios's cattle (*Od.* 12.304). But in his palace Odysseus, posing as a beggar, asked the suitors to take an oath that they would not harm him by some foul play. Not only was any formalization of this agreement out of the question, involving no real *quid pro quo* between the apparent beggar and the suitors, but also the granting of the favor specified by the oath was

THE LINGUISTIC EVIDENCE 75

something that only the suitors could bestow. Odysseus as beggar could do nothing to compel the suitors to act otherwise.[53]

In the Homeric world it was customary when making a promise to call upon some higher power to assure that the promises would be carried out. The oath presumably set its seal upon the transaction and made it binding. Violation of the oath would bring down upon the transgressor the divine wrath. Frequently, the Homeric gods themselves became involved in business in which they felt oath-taking by them was necessary. The divinities invoked by the gods in these circumstances were not necessarily higher than themselves, but were nonetheless effective witnesses because, under the jurisdictional allotment in the ancient pantheon, the invoked gods presided over the area of oaths. Thus Hera, in her agreement with Hephaestus, called upon the Titans to witness her oaths (*Il.* 14.279). In another case she swore by Heaven and Earth and the Styx, an oath considered the most dreadful for all gods (*Il.* 15.37).[54] Even the supreme god Zeus took oaths, but in so doing he invoked no other divinities as witnesses or avengers, even though the oath was described as mighty (*karteron*; *Il.* 19.108, 113, 127). The absence of other divinities pointed, no doubt, to the superiority of Zeus and accentuated his omnipotence. For Zeus to have invoked others would have been to ascribe to himself a subordinate status, or at least to circumscribe his authority. Consequently, in making a promise, Zeus neither swore by himself, nor called upon others as witnesses.

Here we may recall that in the Old Testament, when God made a promise to Abraham, He swore in His own name because there was no higher force He could call as witness. The validity of the promise was thus doubly attested, in the first place by the solemn promise itself, and then by the oath which God Himself added to the promise to make it still more secure. Both

---

[53] Greeks universally believed that perjury was a moral infraction drawing the most terrible punishment upon the perpetrator; so, they occasionally sought to avoid the appearance of perjury by cleverly framing their oaths so as to leave loopholes. Autolychus, Odysseus's maternal grandfather, was notorious in his times for his ability to "steal oaths," *Od.* 19.395. This was a form of dodging that many Greeks sometimes commended (Hdt. 4.201; Thuc. 3.34.3). Odysseus himself, copying a leaf from his grandfather's book, practiced trickery in the *Iliad* (10.382) where, without any definite promise, he encouraged Dolon to hope for mercy and then let him be killed by Diomedes. But such practices were not usually deemed commendable. Sophistry might have temporarily fascinated some Greeks, but it failed to captivate the Greek imagination permanently. Odysseus's role in Sophocles' *Philoctetes* was not presented as flattering to its performer while Thucydides' poignant comment on the behavior of the Athenians at the truce of Pylos was hardly approving, 4.23. See also Boisacq, *Dictionnaire Etymologique de la langue Grecque4* (Heidelberg, 1960), s.v. *horkos*; J. L. Myres, *The Political Ideas of the Greeks* (New York, 1927) 209. *Horkos* was made into an anthropomorphic or demonic being, and as such it appeared as a god of the underworld with the function of receiving the perjurer into the infernal regions of Hades and punishing him; Hesiod, *Theog.* 783-806.

[54] *Od.* 5.184-85; Hes. *Theog.* 793-806; *Il.* 3.19.260; Rhode, *Psyche* 41.

promise and oath alike were immutable and inviolable, thus guaranteeing the covenant and making it absolute (Heb. 6.13 ff.; Gen. 22.16-17). The nature of the Yahweh-Abraham agreement was bilateral, both parties having undertaken rights and obligations, Yahweh to protect Israel as his people and Israel to worship and obey Yahweh. Both parties joined in the agreement of their own free will, although the initiative and resolution derived from one of the two parties, in this case Yahweh. The agreement between Yahweh and Abraham follows the general format of treaties concluded between tribes, societies, or persons in the ancient times, except that in this case one of the parties is God.

In sum, *horkos* was used to strengthen personal agreements or promises. The two parties involved in the transaction might be equal in status, with the first party pledging something to the second without reciprocal oaths or obligations. The oath implied the improvement of relations between the two parties or the maintenance of the status quo. Failure to abide by one's oath inevitably led to the failure of the anticipated betterment in the mutual relationship or a definite change for the worse. Furthermore, when the oath was taken in the presence of witnesses, a future violator would be branded a perjurer with the firm belief by everyone that divine punishment would be imminent. In some compacts (Telemachus-servant) the oath was imposed upon the inferior party to safeguard compliance with the superior's wishes. Elsewhere, the parties affected by the oath might be autonomous (Agamemnon-Achilles, Achaeans-Trojan Council of Elders), but again the obligation of the oath bound one of the parties only inasmuch as it was that party that could have presumably been implicated in the commitment of an injustice. In other cases (Yahweh-Abraham) the superior party volunteered to take an oath in confirmation of a transaction initiated by him. Even though this last instance involved a *quid pro quo* relationship, the superior party could do harm to the second party by the violation of the newly established terms of the agreement without risking harm to himself. Needless to say, when the superior party was God, it was inconceivable that He would actually wish to violate His agreement. By the same token, God could not be coerced by the inferior party to do something contrary to His will. Since the Homeric oaths dealt primarily with personal matters where only one of the parties had to take an oath, it follows that formalization and ritual ceremonies, beyond the oath taken, would be unnecessary. Thus *horkos* differed from *horkia* in that it could imply a variety of relationships in which promises were made and oaths were involved. *Horkia*, on the other hand, could denote pledges accompanied by oaths, pledges accompanied by sacrifice in confirmation of the pledges, the sacred items employed in confirmation of the newly established relationship, and, by extension, the agreement consecrated by the ceremonial procedure.

THE LINGUISTIC EVIDENCE

3. *Omnymi*

In the final part of this chapter we shall consider the verb *omnymi-omnyein* which was principally employed in connection with the noun *horkos* as *temnein* was frequently used with *horkia*. Whereas the term *temnein* juxtaposed to *horkia* denoted an action at the end of the pronounced formula, *omnymi* involved chiefly the oral pronouncement of the prayer, except where accompanied by some form of the verb *spendein*. More specifically, the verb *omnymi* implied an act of sealing a promise to someone by referring to a god or gods, or to an object that was considered sacred because it was a symbol of some authority whose own origins were divine. Thus Achilles took an oath in the name of the scepter he was holding at the time he spoke. This scepter had been passed on to him in the assembly by a herald as a sign of the "possession of the House," meaning Achilles' right to speak.[55] In the same way, after Hector had received the scepter and swearing in its name, he uttered his oath to Dolon (*Il.* 10.328). However, Sleep asked Hera to swear to him in the name of the waters of the Styx, an oath which was considered the greatest of oaths (*Il.* 14.271). Likewise, Menelaus asked Antilochus to swear while laying his hand on his horses that he had not intentionally hindered Menelaus's chariot (*Il.* 23.585). On another occasion Hera took an oath to Zeus in the name of their bridal bed which, as a token of conjugal fidelity, was considered a very private and sacred object not to be taken lightly.[56]

In addition to swearing upon objects invested with an aura of sanctity because of their particular use in human affairs, people swore upon the gods whose invocation was understood even when the gods themselves were not explicitly mentioned. In this sense Agamemnon assured the other Greeks that he would not swear falsely in the name of the gods (*Il.* 19.188, οὐδ' ἐπιορκήσω πρὸς δαίμονος) and that whoever took the name of the gods falsely committed a sin (*Il.* 19.265, *alilêtai*).

In several cases the verb *epomnyein* was used by Homer in place of *omnyein* even though foreswearing is intended by the oath giver. Homer employed *epomnyein* simply because the oath turned out to be idle, owing not to the responsibility of the oath-giver but to circumstances beyond his control. The promissory character of the oath was then derived from the intention of the oath-taking party to commit himself to what he would and would not do if the other party fulfilled his part of the bargain. It did not

---

[55] *Il.* 10.321; Leaf *ad loc.*

[56] *Il.* 15.40. Modern Greeks still swear by their bridal chamber as an indication of the seriousness of their oath. Several prayers of the wedding ceremony of the Orthodox Church refer to the sacredness of the bridal bed. These practices demonstrate again the tenacity and longevity of ancient customs which have lasted until the arrival of modernity, which now threatens to swallow up, as Cronus swallowed his children, most of the age-old customs, including those which pose no threat to progress and the evolution of civilization.

78   THE LINGUISTIC EVIDENCE

mean that what the first party promised to do would inevitably happen. A promissory oath committed someone to an act, but this commitment might itself be contingent upon an anticipated outcome, as Hector's oath depended on Dolon's completing the undertaken mission. Hector could not have suspected the twist of fate destined for Dolon. At the end, Hector's promise not to allow anybody else to ride the horses reserved for Dolon proved futile because of Dolon's capture and subsequent death, something that neither Hector nor Dolon could have foreseen (*Il.* 10.330-32). By the same reasoning, the spiriting away of Paris by Aphrodite in Book 3 of the *Iliad* could not be interpreted as a breach of the Trojan oaths, as neither Greek or Trojan was responsible for the act and neither could have predicted it. Naturally, the Greeks, who suspected that Paris had escaped to avoid his ultimate fate, viewed the escape as a breach of the oaths. They were inclined to this view not only because it was legally valid but also because it provided a good piece of propaganda with which the Greek leaders could convince their troops that, since the Trojans had apparently violated their pledges, justice lay on their side. However, despite this war of words the truce between the two armies continued until the sly and unprovoked attack of Pandarus on Menelaus provided the technical grounds for the truce violation. Before this happened the Trojans could and did claim that they had not sworn falsely and that they had done no violence to the relationship sanctified by oath.

In another sense the verb *omnymi* signified the forming of an agreement by two parties who were independent of one another. The nature of the agreement was personal and its validity was limited to certain activity or activities. The activity might be either long-lasting or circumscribed in time. Calchas, for example, agreed to prophesy about the cause of the plague on the condition that Achilles would protect him from Agamemnon's wrath whenever this wrath might be manifested. Achilles consented, but his promise of protection was not meant to extend to acts other than Calchas's prediction about Chryseis. If in the future Calchas antagonized Agamemnon unjustifiably, he could not have expected Achilles' protection in such matters. On the other hand, Achilles' promise of restricted protection was to cover Calchas for the duration of the war. What made this open-ended promise reasonable was the fact that the third person involved, Agamemnon, was liable to hold a grudge for as long as he lived. In other cases, the act prescribed in an oath was supposed to be performed within a limited span of time, and by the nature of the promise it had to be accomplished relatively quickly. Although no time-limit is normally mentioned in connection with the oath, the promise may be meant to be fulfilled shortly. Dolon was to depart immediately after Hector's oath-taking. Dolon's mission was to be of limited duration, and the fulfillment of Hector's promise was understood to follow on the heels of Dolon's completion of that mission. The same is true of Agamemnon's promise to Achilles, which was to be consummated upon

THE LINGUISTIC EVIDENCE   79

acceptance of reconciliation by the latter (*Il.* 9.132); it is also true of Hera's promise to Sleep (*Il.* 14.271), and Zeus's oath to Hera (*Il.* 19.108, 113).

As has already been observed, an act of swearing could be undertaken by a superior in authority (Zeus-Hera, Agamemnon-Achilles, Hector-Dolon, Calypso-Odysseus, etc.) or a superior in status or class (Achilles-Patroclus, Odysseus-Eumaeus). An oath could also be given by someone inferior in authority and status (Eurycleia-Telemachus, Eurylochus-Odysseus) if the demanding party happened to be the superior in class, status, or authority. In either case, the common denominator was the favor asked. If the favor was asked by the superior party, then the party that initiated the demand had to assure the bestower of the favor by an oath. This type of transaction generally presupposed the existence of some kind of neutral or friendly relationship between the two parties, with the implicit promise of improvement in the existing relations because of the supposed gratitude of the grantee toward the grantor. In some instances, however, the pre-existing state of the relation was marked by suspicion on the part of one party. The suspicion would be dissipated after the taking of the oath demanded by the suspecting party (*Il.* 19.108; *Od.* 10.343). At any rate, there was no slavish subordination of one of the parties, for the demand of an oath to be taken by the inferior in class or authority is predicated by the asker himself on the assumption that the inferior party enjoys some degree of autonomy. In most instances the parties involved were free agents or at least enjoyed some degree of freedom to act. Eurylochus and his comrades, though formally subjects of Odysseus, could and finally did act independently of the wishes and commands of their lord. Even Eurycleia, the maid of Odysseus, could be influenced to divulge the secret departure of Telemachus because of her loyalty to Penelope. It was therefore necessary for Telemachus to coax her into an oath not to disclose his secret mission. At other times, the oath might be volunteered by someone on behalf of an absent friend so that the oath-giver could enhance his persuasiveness. Thus Odysseus volunteered to take an oath in order to convince Eumaeus of the veracity of his information, although Eumaeus, skeptical of such news, chose to forego the offer.

The Homeric epics point to the existence of different oath formulas, depending upon the gravity of the circumstances. The formula "to swear a mighty oath" should not be dismissed as a stereotyped expression of little consequence. It must have carried great weight for the parties that resorted to it, because it invoked dreadful powers and by consequence dreadful punishment in case of a breach. Such parties exercised the right to ensure themselves against future infractions by asking for greater guarantees, as Sleep did from Hera when he asked her to swear the oath he wanted (*Il.* 14.278, *hôs ekeleuen*). While the verb *omnymi* almost always appeared with the singular form *horkos*, the plural form of the noun could also be used, if only rarely. In Homer it appeared once to signify the agreement between

80 THE LINGUISTIC EVIDENCE

Athena and Hera (νῶϊ πολέας ὠμόσσαμεν ὅρκους, *Il.* 20.313). This use of the plural form, according to Leaf, purportedly alluded to the "many different objects" by which the swearing party took the oath to make it the most solemn sort.[57]

Before the conclusion of this chapter, some additional details associated with *omnymi* and the taking of oaths are in order. The oath-taking parties were usually two, but each party could represent either a single individual or a collective entity. Thus in *Od.* 12.298, 304 the two parties are Odysseus and his men. Similarly, in *Od.* 15.438 the oath-taking parties are the maid and the Phoenician sailors, while in *Od.* 18.55, 59 the parties were Odysseus and the suitors. In the above instances the collective party took an oath collectively and not individually since the verb is in the plural but the noun is in the singular (πάντες ὁμόσσατε καρτερὸν ὅρκον, *Od.* 12.298; ὅμοσάν τε τελεύτησάν τε ὅρκον, *Od.* 15.438).

From the language of Homer it becomes obvious that the people conceived some of the *horkoi* as simple and others as more serious. The difference lay either in the seriousness of the situation represented by the oath or in the mood of the swearer. "Mood" here means the incredulity of the party receiving the oath.[58] It appears that despite the strong implications of oath-taking and the deep reverence for oaths in the ancient world, the widespread practice of oath-taking must have led at times to a dangerous familiarity with them which lessened their awesome character. The net result was that some people used oaths rather lightly. This is explained by the repeated emphasis on dreadful or solemn oaths or by the additional explanation by some oath-givers that they would not have used such dreadful oaths were they not swearing to the truth or that they would not foreswear in the name of gods. The insistence of the oath-giver that he would not use the name of the gods in vain suggests that some individuals did indeed do so.[59]

Finally, while the solemnization and formalization of oaths were denoted by the combination *horkia temnein* or *horkia pista temnein*, the use of *horkos* and *omnymi* did not as a rule point to further action on the part of the swearer except where the verb *omnyein* was accompanied by the verb *apospendein*. In that case the term *apospendein* pointed to further action, namely, to the pouring of libations in sealing oaths just concluded (*Od.* 14.331; 19.288).

---

[57] *Il.* 2.755, 15.36; Leaf ad *Il.* 20.313.

[58] *Il.* 9.132, 274; 15.40; 19.113, 108; *Od.* 4.253; 5.178; 10.299; 12.298; 18.55; 20.229.

[59] *Il.* 19.264-65.

C. CONCLUSION

The practice of promise-giving among the Greeks was an institution that went back to the very dawn of Greek history and which followed certain universally accepted formats. Formal or informal oaths sworn in the act of promise-giving by the Greeks were taken very seriously. With few exceptions, themselves readily accounted for, the practice of swearing was viewed very seriously by the Greeks and not as a mere game or an object of philosophic speculation.[60] Promise-giving was elevated into a serious duty associated not only with the speech ritual but other rituals as well, such as religious rituals and the ritual of personal honor. One's reputation and stature in society were measured by the fulfillment of one's promises. Therefore a gentleman's word was his honor. In this sense promise-giving was an integral part of the culture of that society which viewed it most seriously and considered the violation of given promises as infractions capable of leading to disastrous consequences. Significantly, the ritual and formulas associated with oaths seem to have had very ancient roots that antedated the composition of the Homeric epics. These ancient rituals and formulas had also been closely associated with the religious beliefs and practices of the people of the Near East. It is hoped that the knowledge of the history and importance of oath-giving will make understanding the discussion in the chapter that follows somewhat easier.

---

[60] See, for instance, M. Midgley, *Heart and Mind* (New York, 1981), esp. 133-50.

CHAPTER THREE

THE STRUCTURE OF THE HOMERIC AGREEMENTS

Although Homer makes no pretense of describing legal texts in his works, there is no doubt that the agreements contained in the epics are quasi-legal transactions establishing what amount to legally binding bilateral or multilateral rights- and duties-relationships among the covenanters, relationships that are either explicitly or implicitly stated. The present chapter analyzes the Homeric agreements in order to clarify their structure and the formulaic expressions contained in them. To begin this analysis we shall consider the parallels that exist between the Homeric agreements and the treaties of the Near East, especially those of the Hittites.

One of the very earliest of the Near Eastern treaties that we have today is the one preserved on the Vulture Stele of Eannatum of Lagash.[1] From this ancient Mesopotamian treaty as well as others—especially those of the Hittites—that have been uncovered by the archeological spade, we can infer to the existence in the Near East of a long legal tradition of a much more highly sophisticated form than that of the Homeric agreements. Because of their more developed form, as well as the geographic proximity of the Hittite state to the Greek world and the probable contacts of the Hittites with the Mycenaean civilization, the Hittite treaties will constitute the principal reference point of this and subsequent chapters.[2] Fifteen treaties in all have been preserved (nine in Akkadian, six in Hittite), most of which were concluded by the Hittite kings from Suppiluliumas to Tuthaliyas IV with their vassals in Asia Minor and Syria.[3] In addition, other treaties are found in the archives of Ras-Shamra (Ugarit). Also, information is provided by the

---

[1] F. Thureau-Dangin, *Die sumerischen und akkadischen Königs Inschriften* (Leipzig, 1907); Korosec, *Heth. Staats.*, 23, 34, believes it is possible that the Hittites borrowed the format of their treaties from Mesopotamia. See also Landsberger on the treaty of Eannatum of Lagash with the people of Umma ca. 3110 B.C., in B. Meissner, *Babylonien und Assyrien* (Heidelberg, 1920) 1:24.

[2] They have been published by Weidner, *Polit. Dok.*; see also J. Friedrich, *Die Staatsverträge des Hatti-Reichen in hethitischen Sprache* (Leipzig, 1926-30), as part of the *Mitteilungen der Vorderasiatisch-Agyptischen Gesellschaft*, vols. 31 and 34:1.

[3] Whether indeed there is a direct or indirect connection between the Homeric world and the Near East remains a tricky question. This study assumes an association between the two. As others have been struck by the fact that the developed form of the Hittite treaties and the details of their content have parallels in the Old Testament, so we find similarities in wording and spirit between the Homeric and Near Eastern accords. On the question of potential relationships see A. E. Cowley, *The Hittites*, "The Schweich Lectures," (London, 1920) passim; A. F. Puukko, *Die Altesyrischen und hettitischen Gesetze und das alte Testament*, "Studia orientalia," 1 (Helsinki, 1925) passim; A. Jespin, *Untersuchungen zum Bundesbuch* (BWANT, F.3, H.5, Stuttgart, 1927); M. Noth, *The Old Testament World* (Philadelphia, 1966) passim; A. Götze, *Kleinasien* (Munich, 1957) passim.

THE STRUCTURE OF THE HOMERIC AGREEMENTS 83

Old Testament about treaties elsewhere in the Near East, as well as by the Sfire treaty and the Esarhaddon treaties, all of which show similarities with the Hittite treaties.

A quick review of these treaties shows that most of them have a five-part structure, whose elements are: (1) The Preamble, (2) The Recounting of Antecedent History, (3) Stipulations, (4) Invocations of the Gods as Witnesses, (5) Curses and Blessings.[4] With some variations, this structure can also be discerned in many of the Homeric agreements, and so the present chapter is arranged accordingly. However, as we examine these parallels we should constantly keep in mind that in the Homeric epics the various agreements are not separately created documents that the poet incorporated into his narrative, but rather themes to be distilled by us from the poems, themes which are usually not couched in anything like the highly stylized language of the Near East treaties.

A. THE PREAMBLE

As a rule, the preambles of the Hittite treaties contain the name and title of the ruler issuing the document, followed by the names and titles of his father and more distant predecessors, the last of whom bears the sobriquet "hero." Thus the standard formula of the Hittite treaties reads as follows: "Thus speaks *A*, the Great King, the king of the land of Hatti, the son of *B*, the Great King, the hero." Also, after the mention of the "king of the land of Hatti" it is not unusual to find the insertion: "the favorite of the god."[5]

In contrast, the Homeric preambles are much more simple and direct, serving the purpose of introducing the speaker or the party proposing the treaty. There are two obvious reasons for the absence of a long and formal titulary. The first has to do with the poetic nature of the surrounding context. As a poet, Homer would not have tried to reproduce the documents of the Mycenaean era, even if such documents existed. Instead, he elaborated on the narrative technique of his essentially oral art as it had been developed by his predecessors; in other words, the object of his concern was story, not history, though the kernel of his story might have been history. Indeed, even historians in much later times did not feel compelled to reproduce documentary texts verbatim in order to support their work, preferring to describe the essential part of the document in their own language and manner (Thuc. 5.18.19). The second reason that there are no long titularies in the

---

[4] For variations from this scheme see A. Götze and J. B. Pritchard (eds.), ANET (Princeton, 1955) passim; Korosec, *Heth. Staats.* 12-14; K. Baltzer, *The Covenant Formulary* 9-38; Hillers, *Covenant* 72-79; Hillers, *Treaty-Curses and the Old Testament Prophets* (Rome, 1964) 1-4; G. E. Mendelhall, *Law and Covenant in Israel and the Ancient Near East* (Pittsburgh, Biblical Colloquium, 1955) 26-46.

[5] Korosec, *Heth. Staats.* 12.

Homeric agreements is that Homer tends to provide titles ad hoc and in piecemeal fashion; that is, parts of the titulary of the kings mentioned in the epic are given whenever he had occasion to refer to them. Intentionally or otherwise (but why otherwise?), Homer has achieved variety and poetic grace by not arraying the full titulary whenever a king or god was first mentioned, but rather parceling it out gradually and according to the demands of the context. In fact, most of the titles with which Homer introduced or reintroduced his characters can be divided into two major categories: (1) the general, and (2) the personal. To the general category belong those titles or epithets which as a rule are employed for more than one hero or king. For example, *dios* is not only used for Agamemnon (*Il.* 4.223; 7.313) but also for Diomedes (*Il.* 5.844, 837, 846), Odysseus (*Il.* 5.669), Hector (*Il.* 5.601; 7.1, 42), Areteon (*Il.* 6.31), and Alexander (*Il.* 7.354). The title *diogenês* Homer applies to Odysseus (*Il.* 2.173; 4.258), Achilles (*Il.* 1.7), and Aias (*Il.* 4.489; 7.234). The adjective *daiphron* is applied among others to Pandarus (*Il.* 4.93) and Tydeus (*Il.* 4.370). *Antitheos* is used for Teuthras (*Il.* 5.705), Sarpedon (*Il.* 5.629, 663), and Mygdon (*Il.* 3.186). *Diotrephês* is applied to Menelaus (*Il.* 7.107) and Priam (*Il.* 5.463). *Diiphilos* is used for Achilles (*Il.* 1.74) and Apollo (*Il.* 86), while *poimên laôn* describes Agamemnon (*Il.* 2.243; 4.413), Aeneas (*Il.* 5.513), and Glaucus (*Il.* 6.214), and *phaidimos* is used for Aias (*Il.* 5.617), Hector (*Il.* 6.472), and others.

On the other hand, the personal titles are distinctive of single individuals, be they heroes, kings, or gods. Thus the title *eury kreiôn* is characteristic of Agamemnon in *Il.* 1.355, 441; 3.178-79, 269, and many other places. The same seems to hold true for *Anax andrôn*.[6] The term appears several times in the *Iliad* and *Odyssey,* mostly in connection with Agamemnon. The phrase is used either in a descriptive sense or as a form of address. No other Achaean king in Troy is described or addressed with this title. This

---

[6] The title is of the type of what is called a noun-epithet formula. For the origin of titles like *anax* and *koiranos* see Ehrenberg, *The Greek State* (Oxford, 1960) 11; L. Palmer, *Mycenaeans and Minoans,* 130; Mylonas, *Mycenae and the Mycenaean Age,* 159; 208; B. Hemberg, Ἄναξ, Ἄνασσα und Ἄνακτες als Götternamen unter besonderer Berucksichtigung der attischen Kultur (Uppsala, 1955) passim; G. Pugliese-Caratelli, *La Parola del Passato* 14 (1959) 401-31; Chadwick, *The Decipherment of Linear B,* 112; Finley, *The World of Odysseus,* 83; G. S. Kirk, *The Songs of Homer* (Cambridge, 1962) 70-81; D. L. Page, *History and the Homeric Iliad* (Berkeley—Los Angeles, 1959) 150-60, 188, especially his discussion of epithets. See also H. R. Simpson and J. G. Lazenby, *The Catalogue of the Ships in Homer's Iliad* (Oxford, 1970) 157-58, 164. Also the following modern critical treatments are relevant to the Homeric catalogue of ships: B. Niese, *Der homerische Schiffscatalog als historische Quelle* (Kiel, 1893); T. W. Allen, *The Homeric Catalogue of Ships* (Oxford, 1921); B. Burr, Νεῶν Κατάλογος, 1944); G. Jackmann, *Der homerische Schiffscatalog und die Ilias* (Cologne, 1958); R. G. Buck, *A History of Boeotia* (Edmonton, 1979); G. S. Kirk, *The Iliad* 1985) 168-239; J. T. Hooker, *Minos* 20-22 (1987) 257-67; *Il* .1.7; 172; 442; 506; 2.402; 434; 9.96, 163; 10.103, 110; *Od.* 8.77; 11.379; 24.121.

THE STRUCTURE OF THE HOMERIC AGREEMENTS 85

exclusivity in the description and the form of address supports the hypothesis that *anax andrôn* was part of the formal titulary belonging to Agamemnon, the leader of the Achaeans. The other instances in which this form is employed are *Il.* 11.701; 15.532; 23.288. All three instances refer to heroes of the pre-Trojan war period or non-participants (Augeas, Euphetes, Eumelos). On the Trojan side, Anchises (a non-participant), and Aeneas are mentioned as *anax andrôn* (*Il.* 5.268; 311). It is possible that Anchises carried that formal title, which was inherited by his son Aeneas. Only in the case of Idomeneus and Orsilochus (the latter the grandfather of the Homeric hero of the same name), is a somewhat similar form used (for Idomeneus, see *Il.* 13.452 πολέσσ' ἄνδρεσσιν ἄνακτα [sic, LCL]; and for Orsilochus, see *Il.* 5.546 πολέσσ' ἄνδρεσσιν ἄνακτα). In both cases the form is used in a descriptive sense. In *Od,* 19.181 Idomeneus refers to himself simply as *Idomenêa anakta.* The consistency of the address form for Agamemnon leaves little doubt that we are dealing here with a title, something equivalent to the titles of the Near Eastern potentates.

Among Agamemnon's other characteristic epithets are *kydistos* (*Il.* 1.279; 2.434) and *scyptouchos* (*Il.* 1.279), while Agamemnon's brother Menelaus was known as *areiphilos* (*Il.* 4.13) or *areios* (*Il.* 4.205). Aias is characterized as *herkos* or *herkos Achaiôn* (*Il.* 3.229; 6.5; 7.211), while Hector carries the distinctive epithet *korythaiolos* (*Il.* 7.233). The list of the Homeric heroes and their titles, general and personal, runs on and on, but the above sample illustrates Homer's use of titles for the leaders of the Achaeans.

Of equal interest is his use of titles for the gods, in the sense that the practice of ascribing such titles to them is an extrapolation of the aforementioned custom of ascribing titles to humans. As the supreme god of Olympus, Zeus was often addressed with the title of *anax* (*Il.* 1.502; 3.351), "Father" (*Il.* 1.503; 3.365; 5.757), or "Father of men and gods" (*Il.* 5.426). He was also described as "Cloud-gatherer" (*Il.* 1.511, 517; 5.872, 888), "Bolt-sender" (*Il.* 1.609; 7.443), and so on. His daughter Athena is called Pallas (*Il.* 1.400; 4.541; 5.1, 61), *glaucopis* (*Il.* 206; 2.166, 172), Tritogeneia (*Il.* 4.515), and Alalcomenea (*Il.* 4.8; 5.908). This latter title may be derived from a place name in Boeotia or it may simply mean "guardian" or "defender." In either case the tradition of toponymics or other titles ascribed to gods or goddesses in the ancient Greek world has been carried into the Christian era, and is particularly characteristic of the Mother of Christ.

Poseidon was frequently mentioned with the title "Earth-shaker" (*enosichthôn* or *enosigaios, Il.* 7.445, 455), while Apollo was called Phoebus (*Il.* 1.43, 72), "Far-shooting" (*hekêbolos,* 1.438), "Silver-bow" (*Il.* 1.37, 450), and "Far-working" (*hekaergos, Il.* 1.479). The god of war was Chalceos (*Il.* 5.859), "Man-destroyer," "Murderer," and "Destroyer of Walls" (*Il.* 5.455, 519). Finally, Hera, the wife of Zeus, was described by a variety of epithets such as *presba thea* (*Il.* 5.721), Argive (*Il.* 5.908), and *boôpis potnia* (*Il.* 1.551, 568).

The profusion of epithets used in the Homeric world supports the hypothesis that similar epithets were used on more formal occasions such as the making of treaties by the kings of that time. That is, the extensive use of titles by the Near Eastern and the Homeric cultures makes it rather improbable that no such titles were employed by the Mycenaeans. Whether the Mycenaean courts had the stiffness and rigidity of the oriental chancelleries, however, is not clear. Extrapolating from what we know of the Homeric world, it would seem there was a much greater proximity between ruler and ruled, made possible by the relatively smaller size of the Mycenaean district-states, in contrast to the larger scale of the Near Eastern kingdoms, whose rulers were remote, aloof, and almost other-worldly as far as their subjects were concerned. It is true that the Mycenaean kings, like their Near Eastern counterparts, frequently claimed divine or heroic antecedents. It may also be true that many of the titles of the Homeric kings and the mythical traditions described in the Homeric texts were designed to strengthen these stories of divine antecedents. However, the Mycenaean courts could not have possessed the same degree of aloofness as those of the Near Eastern world.[7] It could not have been simply a historical accident that led to the democratization of life in the Greek world while the East adhered to despotism. The lack of formalism, so dominant in the Eastern world, must have been one of the reasons for the final break-down of the Mycenaean and Dark Age kingdoms and the subsequent emergence of the Greek city-state. Be that as it may, a pale reflection of the oriental treaty titulary seems discernible in the Homeric agreements. For example, in Idomeneus's promise (agreement No. 4), he is introduced as *Cretôn agos*, while in Hera's oath (No. 10) she is called the "lady" or "queenly Hera." In addition, Hera addressed Sleep as the "Brother of Death" or the "Lord King of all the gods and men" (*Il.* 14.233).

That the Homeric epithets served the double purpose of providing a mnemonic device and satisfying the requirements of the meter has already been noted by classicists, and is a fact that needs no further elaboration here. But it could also be possible that epithets reflect a tradition concerning titles whose origins could be traced back to Mycenaean times. The existence of titles in the world of Linear B has not been seriously disputed. What has

---

[7] The possession of the scepter manifests a special category of rulers, such as Agamemnon (*Il.* 1.279), Odysseus (*Il.* 5.9), and others. Not all the Achaean leaders possessed a scepter but only those who as *archoi boulephoroi* took part in the council. They came to the council holding the scepter. Achilles took an oath in the name of the symbol, something that has been interpreted as showing him an independent ruler, despite or perhaps because of the fact that he represented his father. The interpretation is not beyond question.

THE STRUCTURE OF THE HOMERIC AGREEMENTS 87

frequently been a topic of controversy is the interrelationship of titles to functions. Naturally, without a precise knowledge of such an interrelationship, the position of title-bearers in the Linear B society and its administrative apparatus cannot be established. Nevertheless, considerable agreement exists among scholars about the connection between title and function in a few of the cases. For example, it is agreed that the title *wa na ka* was always applied to the king, who stood at the head of the state and who had duties in the secular and cultic sphere. This is illuminating because in Homer both Agamemnon and Priam, who each bore the title of *anax*, had combined in their persons cultic and secular authority. Both stood at the head of the state, Priam as the head of Troy and Agamemnon as the head of all the Greeks in Troy, and both presided over state and cultic business. It is therefore possible that the Homeric address-form employed for the other Argive kings may also reflect something of their true titulary. If so, then the address-forms would not only serve as mnemonic device or fulfill the requirements of the meter; they would also reflect the usage of titles whose roots will have to be traced in the Mycenaean times. In addition to this admittedly slight evidence, common sense dictates that in a stratified society like the Mycenaean, forms of address would not have been unusual. If the above line of argument is correct or at least plausible, it follows that the Homeric epics are the depositories of more historical kernels than we are often disposed to admit.

B. THE RECOUNTING OF ANTECEDENT HISTORY

As noted above, the Near Eastern treaties, especially those of the Hittites, include a historical review of the previous relationships between the Hittite ruler and the other party to the covenant.[8] This review is more than a mere year-by-year recitation of events, since it is arranged according to the sequence of the ancestors of the parties to the treaty. The list may go back as far as the fifth generation, though the references are not always by name.[9] As several scholars have pointed out, the summary of pre-treaty history is a form of historiography whose purpose goes beyond the neutral one of merely enumerating generations in that it led up to a brief but pointed description of the key events prefatory to the treaty. Thus the emphasis of the antecedent history presented in the lord and vassal treaties is weighted on the side of the lord, and the relationships are evaluated positively or negatively.[10]

Although the nature of Homeric poetry precludes the formal recording of agreements in the typical manner form of the oriental chancelleries, the epics

---

[8] Weidner, *Polit. Dok.*, 9 ff.; Korosec, *Heth. Staats.*, 13.

[9] Weidner, *Polit. Dok.*, 35 ff.; Friedrich, *Staatsverträge*, 1:4 ff.

[10] Friedrich, *Staatsverträge*, 2:50 ff.; A. Malamat, *Vetus Testamentum* 5 (1955) 1 ff.

88 THE STRUCTURE OF THE HOMERIC AGREEMENTS

contain declamations of an agreement's historical antecedents—or purported historical antecedents—that are analogous to those of the Near Eastern treaties. Idomeneus's promise (No. 4), for example, was nothing more than a somewhat oblique historical reference to a previous agreement between Agamemnon and Idomeneus. The reference to earlier relations between two parties is somewhat more clearly depicted in Hera's oath (No. 10), in which she unabashedly alluded to a dialogue between herself and Sleep: "If ever you listened to my words, hear me now." The request of Hera was accompanied by the memory of a debt of gratitude owed to Sleep for former benefactions. Unfortunately, Sleep's benefactions would have ended up with his own destruction were it not for the intervention of Night (*Il.* 14.255 ff.).

References to the history of earlier relations of the heroes is very frequent in Homer. When Patroclus was killed, Achilles lost not only a friend but also the armor he had loaned his friend. Unable to go to war without it, Achilles asked his mother Thetis to get him new armor, whereupon she went straight to the most sophisticated armorer of the time. Hephaestus was delighted to see her, since her request afforded him the opportunity to repay Thetis for her previous benefaction, which he proceeded to describe with feeling (*Il.* 18.394 ff.). A similar capsule history of antecedent relations is given by Homer in the story of Achilles to Thetis about the latter's aid to Zeus in a faraway time (*Il.* 396-406).

The death of Patroclus had several concomitant effects, one of which was the reconciliation of Agamemnon and Achilles. In his attempt to explain away his foolish behavior regarding Briseis, Agamemnon attributed his action to Ate, the dreadful goddess. Not entirely satisfied with his own explanation, he then proceeded to recite Ate's biography: how she had overpowered even Hera, was banned from visiting Olympus, and was whirled among men (*Il.* 19.126-31). In still another episode, Apollo, in the guise of Lycaon, son of Priam, suggested to Aeneas that he fight against Achilles. Partially annoyed by the suggestion, Aeneas nonetheless decided to follow Lycaon's advice, but only after explaining to Lycaon how he had earlier fought against Achilles on Mount Ida, where the latter had gone to seize cattle, and how Achilles had laid waste the towns of Lyrnessus and Pedasus. At that time, Aeneas explains, he had saved himself thanks to the swiftness of his feet (*Il.* 20.83 ff.). Since Achilles was renowned for the swiftness of his own feet, we are invited to imagine how much faster Aeneas must have run to escape his doom. Eventually, when Achilles and Aeneas faced each other for the second time, Achilles reminded the latter of their previous encounter and expressed his wonder at Aeneas's decision to meet him on the battlefront again. Achilles then assured Aeneas that there would be no escape for him this time.

We have another example in Nestor's speech (agreement No. 2). When Hector proposed a duel between himself and one of the Achaeans, Nestor

THE STRUCTURE OF THE HOMERIC AGREEMENTS   89

grasped the opportunity to narrate still another purported achievement of his youth. In an attempt to arouse the martial spirit of his fellow warriors, he described his duel against Ereuthalion the Arcadian (*Il.* 7.123 ff.). Phoenix did likewise on another occasion (*Il.* 9.434-605). Angry with Agamemnon for having slighted his personal honor earlier, Achilles had stubbornly refused to entertain any ideas about reconciliation, contemptuously rejecting Agamemnon's profuse offers of apologies coupled with marvelous gifts. In the face of this stubbornness, Phoenix sought to soothe Achilles by resorting to the use of historical examples. He reminded Achilles that such conduct could only lead to catastrophic results, and used the example of Meleager to illustrate his argument. Admittedly, historical accounts cited within this episode as well as within the earlier one of Nestor, are not at all obvious analogues to the historical declamations that are the second element of Hittite and other Near Eastern treaties. However, both of these stories as well as the others mentioned above point to an established practice in Homeric society of underscoring an idea or a decision by recounting the history of prior events, as well as a fondness for dramatizing or otherwise expatiating on one's arguments by the use of pertinent historical antecedents. Such anecdotes were important mnemonic devices in an age when literacy was limited, and helped to set the appropriate stage in the audience's mind for the event that was supposed to follow. They further served as educational devices for instructing people to capitalize from the experiences of past events. The custom of recounting antecedent history obviously was not limited to public occurrences such as the making of agreements; it was also followed in the course of arranging personal commitments and relationships, as the Homeric experiences exemplify. The materials which Homer found and worked into shape seems to incorporate this technique, but it would have been fascinating to have been able to compare them with a few interstate treaties of Mycenaean provenance. Would they have contained the history of the contractants' previous relationships with each other? We can, of course, only speculate on this matter as of now, but considering the Near Eastern evidence we do possess and the aforementioned Homeric examples, the odds are in favor of their having had historical declamation as one of their components.

C. STIPULATIONS

The third, stipulative part of the Hittite treaties comprised two sections which were the most developed. The first described the future relationship of the partners to the treaty and was intimately connected with the antecedent history which had given the facts that constituted the basis for the treaty relationship. Furthermore, this first section sketched the purpose of the stipulations that followed. The second section contained the specific stipulations of the treaty normally cast in the form of conditional statements

90   THE STRUCTURE OF THE HOMERIC AGREEMENTS

of the form: "If the following takes place, you shall comport yourself as follows." The condition could be expressed in either the first, second or the third person. The syntax of the stipulations is invariably the standard if-then format of an apodosis following a protasis. Further examples of this format, some in the subjunctive mood and others in the optative, are common in the treaties of the Near East including of course the Hittite treaties which along with the epics are the principal reference of the present chapter. In the treaty between Suppiluliumas and Mattiwaza it is stated:

> If the city belonging to Biyaššili sent a secret embassy to Mattiwaza and Mattiwaza discovered it, he ought to place the envoys of the embassy under arrest and to deliver them to Biyaššili, his brother. Similarly, Mattiwaza ought not to send to the city of Biyaššili an embassy for the purpose of harming him.[11] If Biyaššili summoned Mattiwaza to Carchemish for talks, Biyaššili ought not to address him in vituperative and offensive language.

In still another treaty between Suppiluliumas and Tette, king of Nuhašši, we read:

> If I, the king of Hatti, tarried in the land of Harri (Armenia), or Misri (Egypt), or Kara-D[uni]yas (Babylonia), or Astata (southwest of the Euphrates, south of Carchemish), or in any other land bordering his which is either hostile or friendly to me, he [Tette] should in turn march against the land of Muski[si] (south of Aleppo) or Halpa (Aleppo), or Kinza (Kades) which are enemies of the Hittites.[12]

Another form often employed in the Near Eastern area was the apodeictic, particularly in dealing with the sacral realm of Man's relation with the divine, or the moral sphere. The apodeictic may be in the precative or imperative mood, but in either case runs as follows: "Whosoever strikes his mother or father shall be put to death."

Significantly, we find the same thing when we look to the Old Testament. Once again, the format of the covenant between Yahweh and Israel is conditional. Here, however, we face the additional question of dating the redacted material, since the covenant is purportedly very old but its date of redaction is not. Thus there is some distance between the Hittite treaties recorded in their original form in the fourteenth century B.C. and the Israelite covenant, which must have been written down at least three centuries later. According to the Israelite tradition most of the legal ordinances observed in Israel were laid down by the divine will of Yahweh, and had been revealed by Him in the last generation before the tribes came out of the desert to settle in Palestine. The laws of the Old Testament are therefore given a context in the

---

[11] Weidner, *Polit. Dok.*, 25.

[12] Weidner, *Polit. Dok.*, 27; 61.

history of that early period. The theory that God gave the whole law at one moment in Israelite history may be implausible because of its lack of logical or historical consistency or for other reasons, but this is not our concern at this point. Regardless of the exact date of the redaction and any inconsistencies in form and content, it is generally recognized that whoever put it together was working with older materials.[13] By now it is an open secret among biblical historians that the Israelites gave literary expression to their spiritual traditions only gradually. This could only mean that the oldest written compilations of laws are separated from the real origins of the law by a considerable period, during which the law had been developed and handed down orally. Work carried out in other branches of Old Testament literature, in particular epic narratives, is also suggestive in this regard. As the proponents of *Gattungs-* or *Formgeschichte* have shown,[14] the most appropriate method of research into the pre-literary origins of the material embedded in written works is the study of their formal characteristics as related to the circumstances in which they were produced. The method relies on the observation that within the individual literary form, the ideas are always connected with certain fixed expressions. This characteristic is not imposed arbitrarily on the material by the literary redactors of a later period. The connection between form and content goes back behind the written records to the period of popular oral composition and tradition. The distinctive formal characteristic of this tradition is that it is invariably introduced by an objective conditional clause beginning with "If." Throughout, all those concerned in these conditional cases are spoken of in the third person. The syntax of the laws, like that of the treaty stipulations, invariably follows the order of the protasis and apodosis of a conditional sentence.

It should be kept in mind that the range of cases covered by the casuistic law corresponds most nearly to the character of ordinary Israelite secular jurisdiction. The provisions of the casuistic law fit without exception into the field of the ordinary secular jurisdiction. They make no reference whatsoever to priests, only coming in contact with the sacral sphere where they legislate for procedures that had to be carried out before God (Exod. 21.6, 22.7). It is equally important to remember that the Israelites were formulating these laws while in the process of settling down in their new land, which makes it likely that the principal features of these laws had

---

[13] J. Morgenstern, HUCA 5 (1928) 1-5; Morgenstern, HUCA 7 (1930) 19-25; Morgenstern, HUCA 8-9 (1932) 1-23; R. H. Pfeiffer, *Harvard Theol. Review* 24 (1931) 29 ff.

[14] J. Morgenstern, HUCA 5 (1928) 1-5; Morgenstern, HUCA 7 (1930) 19-25; Morgenstern, HUCA 8-9 (1932) 1-23; R. H. Pfeiffer, *Harvard Theol. Review* 24 (1931) 29 ff.

92 THE STRUCTURE OF THE HOMERIC AGREEMENTS

already been adopted by the Israelites before they were in Palestine. Therefore they must have already been of much earlier provenance. Regardless of their actual date, these laws are historically significant largely because of their universality in the Near East, in that there are numerous similarities between what transpired in this part of the Near East and the Homeric developments in Greece and Ionia. The chances then are that the covenants in the Homeric material follow a similar format with that of other parts of the Near East, irrespective of the exact date of the redaction of that material. As in the Israelite case, the form and content of the Homeric material go back to a period of popular oral composition. Also—again, as in the Israelite case—the casuistic format corresponds to a secular jurisdiction of the law at a time when, in the absence of any priestly authority to impose sanctions on the international scene, the only final arbiters remained the gods. It is impossible to be sure whether the conditional form of the Homeric epics is an adaptation of the forms prevalent in the Near East or (as seems more likely) of forms prevalent in a pre-Mycenaean world that had ideas and institutions similar to those of the Near East. What is certain, however, is that Homeric agreements are often cast in the conditional format, and that the same is true of many of the archaic Greek inscriptions dealing with treaties or laws.

When Hector proposed the duel between Alexander and Menelaus, he set as a condition that the victor would take Helen and her property and would return home,

> ὁππότερος δέ κε νικήσῃ κρείσσων τε γένηται,
> κτήμαθ' ἑλὼν ἐὺ πάντα γυναῖκά τε οἴκαδ' ἀγέσθω·
> *Il.* 3.92-93

The subjunctive is here expressive of the speaker's purpose, serving as a hortatory with the quasi-imperative meaning of allowing the winner of the contest to take the human prize and her property. The protasis of the sentence is in the subjunctive while the main part of the apodosis is in the imperative. In a subsequent duel agreement Hector proposed the stripping of the vanquished but the return of his body for the proper burial.

> εἰ δέ κ' ἐγὼ τὸν ἕλω, δώῃ δέ μοι εὖχος Ἀπόλλων,
> τεύχεα σύλησας οἴσω προτὶ Ἴλιον ἱρήν,
> καὶ κρεμόω προτὶ νηὸν Ἀπόλλωνος ἑκάτοιο,
> τὸν δὲ νέκυν ἐπὶ νῆας ἐϋσσέλμους ἀποδώσω,
> ὄφρα ἑ ταρχύσωσι κάρη κομόωντες Ἀχαιοί,
> *Il.* 7.81-85

The protasis in the subjunctive is again expressive of the speaker's purpose, with the principal clause referring to a future action. Likewise, the proposed agreement by Agamemnon, by which he would accede to relinquish his prize, is put in a similar format.

THE STRUCTURE OF THE HOMERIC AGREEMENTS 93

ἀλλ' εἰ μὲν δώσουσι γέρας μεγάθυμοι Ἀχαιοί,
ἄρσαντες κατὰ θυμόν, ὅπως ἀντάξιον ἔσται·
εἰ δέ κε μὴ δώωσιν, ἐγὼ δέ κεν αὐτὸς ἕλωμαι
ἢ τεὸν ἢ Αἴαντος ἰὼν γέρας, ἢ Ὀδυσῆος
ἄξω ἑλών· ὁ δέ κεν κεχολώσεται, ὅν κεν ἵκωμαι.
Il. 1.135-39

The statement expresses simple will or determination. The subjunctive stands to the future indicative nearly as in careful English "will" stands to "shall." The apodosis is left unexpressed. It is only in the case of the second of the two alternatives ("If they do not give me...") that any consequences are stated. As Eustathius remarked the schema is elliptical because of the absence of a complementary verb like *ephesyhazô* or *paunomai*.[15] Achilles, presumably speaking for the other Greeks as well as for himself, promises triple and quadruple recompense to Agamemnon when Troy is finally captured (a foregone conclusion for the Greeks), explaining that Agamemnon had always received a greater share of the looting in virtue of his position, irrespective of his efforts.[16] Also, in Hector's proposal (No. 14) he introduced his proposed agreement to Achilles in a conditional form, where the *ou* in association with the subjunctive takes an emphatic meaning so distinct in Homer.

οὐ γὰρ ἐγώ σ' ἔκπαγλον ἀεικιῶ, αἴ κεν ἐμοὶ Ζεὺς
δώῃ καμμονίην, σὴν δ' ψυχὴν ἀφέλωμαι·
ἀλλ' ἐπεὶ ἄρ κέ σε συλήσω κλυτὰ τεύχε', Ἀχιλλεῦ,
νεκρὸν Ἀχαιοῖσιν δώσω πάλιν· ὥς δ' σὺ ῥέζειν.
Il. 22.256-59

A conditional is also present in Odysseus's refusal to believe Calypso's intentions to let him go. The condition is set in the optative with the infinitive in the apodosis.

εἰ μή μοι τλαίης γε, θεά, μέγαν ὅρκον ὀμόσσαι
μή τί μοι αὐτῷ πῆμα κακὸν βουλευσέμεν ἄλλο.
Od. 5.178-79

---

[15] Eust. *ad loc.* considers this scheme elliptical, for the syntax is not, according to him, complete. It should have been completed by the addition of an expression such as *ephêsyhazô* or *pauomai,* here merely understood. See for similar cases, Arist. *Plut,* 468-7; Menander frg. 779 in *Relinquiae,* vol. 2, ed. A. Koerte (Leipzig, 1959); Plato (Comicus) frg. 24 in *Comicorum Atticorum Fragmenta* ed. T. Kock (Leipzig, 1880-88).

[16] Agamemnon demanded a worthy present to replace Chryseis. His emphasis on the worthiness of the substitution is deliberate, according to Eustathius, so that he will have the chance of rejecting it if he does not consider it his due. Similarly, in Book 3 of the *Iliad* he demands from the Trojans adequate compensation along with the return of Helen, thereby leaving the door open for the continuation of the war if the compensation offered is not deemed sufficient (Eust. *ad loc.*).

94 THE STRUCTURE OF THE HOMERIC AGREEMENTS

Again, in an almost identical construction, Odysseus refused to satisfy Circe's sexual desire unless the latter complied with his condition:

οὐδ' ἄν ἐγώ γ' ἐθέλοιμι τεῆς ἐπιβήμεναι εὐνῆς
εἰ μή μοι τλαίης γε, θεά, μέγαν ὅρκον ὀμόσσαι
μή τί μοι αὐτῷ πῆμα κακὸν βουλευσέμεν ἄλλο.
Od. 10.342-44

The statement expresses concession, i.e., willingness that something take place along with a deprecation.

The limited evidence derived from Homer demonstrates the similarity of the stipulatory form of Homeric agreements and Near East treaty-making. The interesting feature in Homer is that despite the preponderance of the parity treaties, a similar casuistic style is nonetheless very much in evidence. Even in suzerainty agreements which, owing to their strictly personal and friendly character, cannot be considered vassal treaties in the Hittite sense, a conditional element is present. For instance, the friendly agreement between Achilles and Patroclus (No. 11) contains a conditional clause expressive of supposition and wish, whose purpose is to underscore the heroic point of honor which was not abstract but required its realization in the form of ransom or other material recompense:

ἐκ νηῶν ἐλάσας ἰέναι πάλιν· εἰ δέ κεν αὖ τοι
δώῃ κῦδος ἀρέσθαι ἐρίγδουπος πόσις Ἥρης,
μὴ σύ γ' ἄνευθεν ἐμεῖο λιλαίεσθαι πολεμίζειν
Τρωσὶ φιλοπτολέμοισιν· ἀτιμότερον δέ με θήσεις·
Il. 16.87-90

Consequently, Patroclus was commissioned to save the Achaean ships but not to push the Trojans back to their city.

If a few of the above-mentioned agreements do not follow the same casuistic style in their stipulatory section, this is due to the fact that Homer's references to them are indirect and incomplete. Thus the marriage treaty between Priam and Othryoneus (No. 9) most probably conformed to the casuistic format in its complete form. The same is true of the Homeric reference to the marriage alliance between the houses of Menelaus and Achilles (No. 16). Only in Odysseus's covenant (No. 22) is it doubtful that the conditional syntax is used since this pact is not the result of bargaining between two parties but an imposition from above. If anything, the apodeictic form is more suitable in the case of No. 22, because the divine compromise implied a threat against the party that dared disobey god's will: "Whosoever disobeys our will ... will be punished."[17]

---

[17] *Od.* 24.544.

THE STRUCTURE OF THE HOMERIC AGREEMENTS   95

That the use of the conditional in the Homeric agreements antedates Homer and that its origins hark back to the misty times of the Mycenaean era is supported by other evidence in the Greek world. Commenting on the inscription which contains the archaizing law code of Gortyn, Willetts observed that many people, including the Achaeans, had contributed to the complex Gortynian tradition over the years before the area came under the mastery of Dorian immigrants.[18] Willetts also cites Plato in support of his view that Gortyn was founded by Achaeans from the Peloponnese.[19] Homer's reference to the walled city of Gortyn in his catalogue of ships may hark back to the times when Gortyn and central Crete were dominated by the Achaeans.[20] To this period can also be reasonably attributed the Achaean pedigrees, cults, cult names, and cult modifications that feature in later Gortynian tradition. The name of Gortyn itself is found in Arcadia and may have been brought to Crete by Achaean settlers.[21]

The regulations contained in the code are formulated as conditional sentences in the third person, with the protasis consisting of the assumed facts and the apodosis containing the legal consequences or provisions. When the optative is used, it is sometimes a mere variant of the subjunctive in like or identical circumstances, but at other times has a functional difference from the subjunctive, expressing a more remote contingency. The subjunctive appears more often than the optative, in the ratio of about five to three, with the optative serving to indicate the occasions in which the contingency is more remotely anticipated.[22] The apodosis is expressed either in the infinitive, the imperative mood, or the future tense, with the infinitive being more frequently employed to express a general recommendation, the

---

[18] R. F. Willetts, *Cretan Cults and Festivals* (London, 1962) 162-68.

[19] Plat. *Leg.* 708 A; see also Paus. 3.2.6; Willetts, *Cretan Cults,* 154, n. 51; C. D. Buck, *Greek Dialects.* (Chicago, 1928) 7-8.

[20] *Il.* 2.646; Eust. *ad loc.* For the chronology of the catalogue see also A. Giovannini, *Etude historique* 45-50 and passim.

[21] Willetts, *The Law of Gortyn* (New York, 1967) passim. Several other scholars share with Willetts the view about the antiquity of this and similar laws: C. M. Bowra, *The Meaning of a Heroic Age* (Newcastle, 1957) 6-7; Sterling Dow, "The Greeks in the Bronze Age," *XIIe Congress Internationale des sciences historique*" (Stockholm, 1960) passim. Talking about the organization of the Mycenaean states, Dow claims that the people appear to have developed an elaborate framework of systems, features of which were specialization under central control, and *writing* used to communicate and preserve orders and records; p. 24. Bowra also admits that the Mycenaean civilization was in fact closer to that of the Hittites than to any we have in Homer, who reflects a simpler and less ambitious order of things, *The Meaning of a Heroic Age* 6-7; see also M. I. Finley, *Historia* 6 (1957) 135. For Gortyn and Amyclaros see Willetts, *Law of Gortyn,* col. III, 7-9; I.C. 4.172.

[22] Willetts, *Law of Gortyn,* 53.

imperative (in the third person) for specific cases and the future when payment is involved.[23]

The dating of the inscription has posed problems. Willetts and Buck are inclined to believe that it was written in the middle of the fifth century B.C. But the date of its engraving and the date of its composition, along with the origins for its stipulations, may be widely different.[24] The later date of the inscription does not necessarily preclude an early origin of the ideas it expresses. Just as the Homeric epics were transmitted by a process of oral tradition before being committed to writing, so legal codifications seem to have had a pre-history that long antedates the use of public records on stone. Thus Greek city-states in their highest cultural achievements still retained many of the usages peculiar to their early tribal character. Pointing to the antiquity and reverence for Law in Crete, Plato remarked that the Cretans called Zeus their law-giver and that Minos, like his brother Rhadamanthys, had been ostensibly inspired by Zeus.[25] No one would have dared to change this customary law had there been a strong prevailing belief that its provenance was divine. In this belief the Cretans and the other Greeks were not much different from the Near Eastern peoples who held a similar conception of the law.[26] It is unfortunate that the legislation of the early law-givers such as Zaleucus of Locris and Charondas have not survived. Had it survived not only would our knowledge of the early Greek history have been much richer but it also would have enlightened us about the format of the ancient Greek law which, most probably, was cast in the casuistic form similar to that of Crete.

The archaic and archaizing inscription from Dreros (650-600 B.C.), which contains what is perhaps the earliest surviving Greek law on stone from the period of the Greek polis, presents regulations cast in the conditional form with the protasis in the aorist subjunctive and the apodosis in the infinitive, ἐπεί κα κοσμήσει, ... μή κόσμειν, or else the protasis in the optative with

---

[23] Willetts, *Law of Gortyn*, 53. The directives of the code are as a rule expressed in the form of a conditional sentence in the third person with the protasis consisting of the assured facts and the apodosis expressing the legal provisions, the assured facts, according to Willetts. Among the limited number of variant type of clauses one should include those introduced by ἒ, though αἰ is not identical with ἐ, for ἐ κα or ἐ δ' κα introduces an indefinite contingency while at the same time suggesting that a definite occurrence is necessary to make the meaning specific. It is the subjunctive mood which supplies the indefiniteness. While the ἒ introduces the contingency, the κα implies the definite occurrence; see Willetts, p. 67.

[24] CAH, 3.3.238; J. W. Headlam, JHS 13 (1982) 48-69; E. Kirsten, *Das Dorische Kreta* (Würzburg, 1942) 1:53.

[25] Plat. *Leg.* 624 B.

[26] R. J. Bonner and G. Smith, *The Administration of Justice from Homer to Aristotle* (Chicago, 1930) 1:67-75.

the apodosis again in the infinitive, αἱ δ' κοσμήσιε, ... διπλεῖ κάϝτὸν ... ἄκρηστον ἦμεν.[27]

Other evidence is provided by the stele with the law of Chios, c. 575 B.C. Although the stele is very difficult to interpret because of its extremely fragmentary nature, its regulations unquestionably entailed a conditional format. The presence of ἤμ ... δεκασ[θῆ] ... with the apodosis in the imperative ἀποδότω clearly shows that this form follows the archaic pattern.[28] The second part of the inscription (Back C) is equally interesting because it follows the apodeictic style employed by later decrees.[29] The use of this format in the early Greek treaties of the Hellenic cities is not surprising. In the much-debated treaty of the Delphian Amphictyony (c. 700 B.C.) partially rendered in archaizing Dorian by Aischines, the conditional predominates in the cursing section of the treaty where Apollo, Artemis, Leto, and Athena Pronoia are invoked as guardians of the treaty.[30] The protasis of the cursing is in the optative, while the apodosis is in the imperative.

Lastly, in the early Elean documents the use of the optative in the conditional clause is much more frequent than elsewhere in Greece, where the subjunctive predominates. Thus in the treaty between Elis and the Arcadian town of Heraea, both the protasis and the apodosis are in the optative, though no remote contingency is anticipated as in the Law of Gortyn, where once again the optative is used, αἰ δέ τι δέοι· αἴτε ϝέπος αἴτε ϝάργον· συνέαν κ' ἀλάλοις· αἰ δὲ μὰ συνέαν· τάλαντόν κ' ἀργύρω· ἀποτίνοιαν. The same is true of a recently found Spartan treaty in which the conditional construction dominates the stipulatory segment of the text. In this inscription the identity of the Exardeeis, who were Sparta's junior partners, is of little relevance here. The date of the inscription is more significant: according to epigraphists it ranges from somewhere in the latter part of the first half to the end of the fifth century. The later date is even of greater importance for the present study, since the survivability of the conditional form strengthens the hypothesis to be discussed below concerning the likelihood of very early Greek treaty-making having an influence upon the later ages, extending well into classical times. It is not surprising that this

---

[27] M/L No. 2; Willetts, *Aristocratic Society in Ancient Crete* (London, 1955) 106; Buck, *Gr. Dial.*, 116; P. Demargne and H. van Effenterre, BCH 61 (1937) 327-41; Demargne and van Effenterre, BCH 62 (1938) 194-95; Ehrenberg, CQ 37 (1943) 14-18.

[28] M/L No. 8; L. H. Jeffery, BSA 51 (1937) 157-67; J. A. O. Larsen, CP 44 (1949) 170-72; H. T. Wade-Gery, *Essays in Greek History* (Oxford, 1958) 198; J. H. Oliver, AJPh 80 (1959) 296-301.

[29] M/L No. 14.

[30] Bengtson, No. 104; G. Busolt and H. Swoboda, *Griechische Staatskunde* (Munich, 1926) 2:1292-94; Larsen, CP 39 (1944) 146-47; F. R. Wüst, *Historia* 3 (1954-55) 140-42; G. Daux, BCH 81 (1957) 95 n. 4; Ehrenberg, *The Greek State*, 254.

format would be predominant among the Spartans who, among the Dorians, were the most conservative people.[31]

D. THE INVOCATION OF GODS AS WITNESSES

It was an ancient tradition when a treaty was concluded to call upon witnesses, whose function was not only to certify that the treaty was made but also, by their own authority and power, to ensure that it was kept. In the international treaties of antiquity this service was performed by gods as well as human beings.[32] To this purpose the Ancient Near Eastern treaties include a detailed list of gods, which as a rule comprised most of the principal gods of both parties. In addition, personified physical objects considered divine were frequently included in the list, namely, mountains, rivers, springs, the ocean, heaven and earth, winds, clouds, and so on.[33] This long and august list of witnesses and potential avengers was necessary for practical reasons. Then even more than now, no collective power existed to enforce the agreements between sovereign political units. No matter how obviously dominant one side was over the other, the stronger party had no guarantee that the other signatory would not seek an opportunity to disregard the stipulations of the treaty. Thus, a king who could not afford to adequately garrison a newly conquered area might hope that the vassal people would not rise in rebellion as soon as he turned his back, or that a recently conquered subject king would not conspire with another ruler against his new overlord. Similarly, he might hope that someone else who ruled as his junior (or even equal) partner would support him with troops when the day of the battle came; but if he were disappointed in such hopes, he had no remedy at law, but only force. Consequently, in their desire to establish some sense of responsibility and good faith among their states, leaders had recourse to the invocation of gods and oaths.

---

[31] F. Gschnitzer, *Ein neuer Spartanischer Staatsvertrag und die Verfassung des Peloponnesischen Bundes*, in *Beiträge zur klassischen Philologie* (Meisenheim am Glan, 1978) 93:2. Gschnitzer dates the inscription ca. 460-50 B.C., while others prefer a date closer to the end of the century. For the Elean inscription see M/L No. 17.

[32] Weidner, *Polit. Dok.*, 29, 49, 69; Korosec, *Heth. Staats.*, 94 ff. It is to be assumed that in the concluding paragraph of the treaty between Mursilis II and Rimi-sarma the highest dignitaries and officials of the Hatti empire were in attendance at the official signing of the treaty. Among them the high priest, the chancellor of the palace and the high scribe (again assuming that the latter was in charge of the composition of the treaty) are mentioned. This points to a complex chancellery staffed by well-educated officials; Weidner, *Polit. Dok.*, 89. It is possible that something analogous prevailed in the Mycenaean chancelleries and that a similar procedure was followed during the making of agreements.

[33] Weidner, *Polit. Dok.*, 51.

In addition to its obvious promise-making function of stabilizing expectations, the oath had another, subsidiary role in law proper, that of establishing sanctions by means of the conditional self-cursing that made the speech act in question an oath. This role was exercised when the community lacked any other techniques for discovering the truth or for enforcing the right. We can see then, that the ancient use of oaths made much sense, for they filled important gaps in the law. As in modern times, in antiquity the value of agreement or consensus had a strong moral dimension. The main difference is that in modern thought (with its heavy contractarian emphasis), social rules and legal norms are thought to flow from explicit agreements that constitute the major premise of a practical syllogism, whereas in antiquity social and legal rules depended not only on explicit acts of promising made between contracting parties but also (and more fundamentally) on religion and morality, which dictated for everyone an implicit obligation to abide by the explicit promises one made. In this respect the likeness in treaty-making between the Near East and the Greek world is very striking. In both worlds the oath, with its conditional self-cursing, was in the beginning of the history of law most closely connected with religion, and appeal to the gods to punish the oath-breaker is the basic legal form which made the promise binding.

It was particularly in the realm of international relations that treaties upheld by oath were presumed to be valid as binding forms, for it was exactly in this area of human relations that adequate legal procedures (i.e., non-military, secular sanctions for pledges) were most difficult to impose.[34] The self-cursing part of the oath is perhaps the most essential component of the treaty, and as a result the treaty stands wholly within the realms of both secular and sacred law since, though secular in origin, the most significant sanctions mentioned are religious. It goes without saying that in the cases of suzerainty treaties the stronger party would proceed against the weaker with military force if it could afford to do so. However, this contingency does not reduce the sacral character of the treaty because the aggressive party as the agent of the "divine will" presumed the right to attack the violator in order to bring down upon him the divine punishment he deserved, thereby restoring the disturbed equilibrium. In the parity treaties, where supposedly the disparity of forces was not so pronounced as to enable the offended party to easily assume the role of the instrument of the divine will, punishment would be left to the discretion of the gods. Such was clearly the case between Achaeans and Trojans when Alexander ostensibly violated his pledge to fight until death. The Achaeans had temporarily no other recourse but to appeal to

---

[34] Mendelhall, *Law and Covenant*, 43; Hillers, *Covenant*, 27. L. M. Wéry, RIDA 14 (1967) 201 about oath-taking. See also Tenekides, *Droit international*, 52.

100 THE STRUCTURE OF THE HOMERIC AGREEMENTS

the gods and to derive confidence from the belief that justice was on their side. Needless to point out, many among the Trojans considered Alexander's sudden departure from the duel an omen foreboding evil for their future (*Il.* 7.351-53, 390).[35]

In an age of profound religiosity, within which the Ancient Near East operated without question and from which the more enlightened Greeks of the Homeric times were by no means free, fear of the gods was enough to motivate a party to keep its oaths. It is not in the least surprising, therefore, that the Achaeans in the *Iliad* attributed the plague to the wrath of Apollo, ostensibly aroused by Agamemnon's mistreatment of his priest.[36] A similar plague, which had struck the land of the Hittites and for twenty years had been claiming its victims, was attributed by King Mursilis and his people to the anger of the gods. Mursilis inquired as to the cause of the divine displeasure, only to discover that a treaty with Egypt, sworn before the storm-god, had been broken in the days of Mursilis's father. Clearly, the gods were regarded as the guarantors of treaties, punishing transgressors sooner or later. This belief in the inevitable expression of divine vexation was voiced in the familiar Near Eastern dictum that the sons paid for their fathers' sins. Thus the invocation of the gods is a common feature of Homeric accords, when agreements in the Homeric times are capped by sacrifices which share common traits, even though some of the times several gods are called upon as witnesses while at other times only one or two are invoked. Thus in *Il.* 3.104, 276, 298, Zeus, along with the other gods, including the *pantepoptês* Helios, the rivers, the Earth and the gods of the netherlands (who were believed to punish sinners after death) were invited as witnesses, whereas in *Il.* 7.76 Hector invoked only Zeus.[37] Elsewhere Zeus and Hera are the only

---

[35] Line 353 has been athetized by Aristarchus; see Kirk, *The Iliad,* 2 *ad loc.* Unfortunately, Kirk's second volume appeared too late to be used in the present study. According to legend, reliance on pledges and oaths seems to have been wide-spread among the early Romans as well. In Book 12 of the *Aeneid,* for instance, we read of Aeneas's suggestion about a treaty with Latinus on a basis of equality. Whereupon, Latinus, looking toward the sky and extending his right arm to heaven said: "By these same I swear, O Aeneas, by Earth, Sea, Sky, and the twin brood of Latona and Janus the double-facing, and the might of nether gods and Pluto's grim shrine..."197-205; Macrobius, *Saturnalia,* 3.9; Phillipson, *International Law and Custom,* 1:394-95.

[36] *Il.* 1.7 ff.; Korosec, *Heth. Staats.,* 98; B. Campbell, *History of Pol. Thought* (1986) 7:265-67.

[37] In the treaty between Hannibal and Philip V of Macedon, 215 B.C., the oath was taken in the name of Zeus, Hera, Apollo and the Carthaginian gods Hercules, Iolaus, Ares, Triton, Poseidon, the Sun, the Moon, the Earth, the rivers, harbors, waters, and all the gods who ruled Carthage or Macedon or the rest of Greece; Polyb. 7.9. It is not surprising then that in Book 18 of the *Iliad* (483-608) Hephaestus depicted on the Shield of Achilles, inter alia, the Earth, the Sky, and the Ocean, all of them important and sacred constitutive elements of the ancient oath-taking and treaty-making. The reference to Heaven and Earth in affirmation of oaths was obviously in use in the Early Christian times, since the author of the epistle of James urged his readers not to swear in their names; James, 5.12.

THE STRUCTURE OF THE HOMERIC AGREEMENTS 101

witnesses mentioned by name, although the other gods are collectively subsumed in the witness list.

In general, Homer makes no apparent distinction between Trojan and Greek gods, leaving it to be understood that both sides worshiped the same divinities. Nonetheless, in *Il.* 22.245-55 he employs the locution *theous epidômetha*, which indirectly points to the existence of some difference between the Greek and Trojan gods, since the expression is to be read as "Let us call on one another's gods." The use of the verb *epidosthai* in this passage was typical of Near Eastern practices and is of considerable significance as a formulary nexus between the Near Eastern customs and Homeric procedures.[38] Likewise, in *Il.* 3.276, 320, Agamemnon and Priam use the formula *Zeu pater, Idêthen medeôn*, by which they invoke Zeus of Ida, the local mountain of Troy, to be the witness of their accord along with the local rivers and other divinities. Even the gods themselves were not above calling upon their colleagues in support of promises and agreements. Thus Sleep, his resistance melted by the vision of female charms so aptly described by the wily wife of Zeus, refused to succumb entirely to Hera's cajolery until he received an oath from her in the name of the dreadful Styx. Impatient to achieve her objective, Hera volunteered to add all the other gods along with the waters of the Styx.

The invocation of Zeus, Hera, Sun, the Erinyes, the Ocean, etc., in the Homeric accords is of considerable interest because, as we shall see, it points to the genuineness of the Homeric oaths of early provenance that were employed on occasions of oath-taking. This practice strengthens the hypothesis regarding the putative format of Mycenaean treaties, their nonsurvival notwithstanding, because several of the deities invoked in the Homeric agreements have been shown by some scholars to have existed in Mycenaean times.[39] Additional information regarding divinities worshipped by the Mycenaeans is provided by the tablets in Linear B found in Cnossus. These tablets were inscribed at the time when the capital of Minos was under the control of mainlanders, and they allegedly refer to Mycenaean religious practices and provide us with a list of the gods who were recipients of offerings.[40] The Olympians included are Zeus, Hera, Poseidon, Hermes, and Artemis.[41] Furthermore, among the divinities worshipped in the Mycenaean period seems to have been the sun-god Helios, frequently referred to as Hyperion. His representations are found on rings from Cnossus.[42] As time

---

[38] No doubt, Priam invoked the Trojan gods when he performed the animal sacrifice, though Homer as the first syncretist in the Greek world refused to differentiate between the two sets of gods.

[39] Chadwick, *The Mycenaean World* 86; Palmer, *Myc. and Minoans,* 132-33.

[40] Mylonas, *Mycenae,* 158.

[41] Chadwick, *The Mycenaean World,* 86, 95.

[42] T. B. L. Webster, *From Mycenae to Homer* (New York, 1964) 41.

102 THE STRUCTURE OF THE HOMERIC AGREEMENTS

passed, apparently the name Helios as a god faded to be replaced by and eventually to be identified with Apollo, most probably originally an oriental god, but one who won his place among the Olympian gods. Apollo's oriental origins seem to be alluded to by Homer, who has him siding with the Trojans, whereas other and older gods of the Mycenaean firmament, such as Hera and Poseidon, fought on the Greek side. Apollo's later addition to the Greek pantheon is further attested by Homer (*Il.* 21.440), who represents him as a younger and less experienced god than Poseidon. The citing of Helios and not Apollo in the Homeric oath formula probably had its roots in the early Mycenaean times. As is often the case, Homer simply quotes traditional poetic forms. The Ocean also seems to have been another early Mycenaean divinity, although whether it was an Indo-European or indigenous deity is not clear; at any rate, it was worshiped before Poseidon became gradually associated with the waters (*Il.* 14.200; 21.195; *Theog.* 133; 137).

Likewise, the Erinyes seem to be of Mycenaean provenance, with a history of dreaded consistency throughout the ages which is deplored by Aeschylus (*Eum.* 68-73). Their special task was to punish persons guilty of the homicide of a kinsman, perjury, unfilial conduct, and inhospitality. They were originally believed to act immediately, causing the offender's death. That belief explains their part in the ordeal by oath, which was said to have been instituted by Rhadamanthys, the legendary lawgiver of Minoan Crete (Plat. *Leg.* 948). The accused uttered a conditional curse on himself, praying that, if guilty, he might perish together with his clan. In Homer they share with Persephone the duty of punishing the souls of perjurers and are definitely Mycenaean or even pre-Mycenaean divinities (*Il.* 9.454-57).[43]

Lastly, the question of *Ge, Ga*. One of the definite names in the Mycenaean tablets is Demeter, appearing in its earlier form as "Damater." Since Demeter is unquestionably the earth-goddess, and since *mater* or *mêter* is the Greek word for mother, *Da* must mean "earth." Although we simply cannot be certain, it is most probable that the form *Da* had changed to *Ga* or *Ge* by the Homeric times though the *Da* or *De* remained in the name of the goddess.[44] In the Mycenaean times Demeter and her daughter Persephone, often referred to as Potnias, were worshipped as Earth divinities, as the

---

[43] A. S. Diamond, *Primitive Law* (London, 1935) 52; G. Thompson, *Studies in Ancient Greek Society, The Prehistoric Aegean* (New York, 1965) 341-42; Bekker, ad *Il.* 9.454; M. C. Astour, *Hellenosemetica* (Leiden, 1967) 96 ff.

[44] Chadwick, *The Mycenaean World,* 93. For the importance of Earth in oaths in ancient times see also Albrecht Dieterich, *Mutter Erde* (Leipzig-Berlin, 1925) 36-58; J. v. Andreev, *Klio* 70 (1988) 20. The interpretations of scholars differ regarding *DA*. O. Kern, RE 4,2 (1901) 2713-64; B.C. Dietrich, *The Origins of Greek Religion,* (Berline, 1974); Albrecht Dieterich *MHtter Erde* (Liepzig, 1905); L. R. Palmer, *Mycenaean and Minoaus* (London 1961), and Palmer, *The Interpretation of Greek Texts* (Oxford, 1963), L. W. Taylour, *The Mycenaean* (London, 1964).

THE STRUCTURE OF THE HOMERIC AGREEMENTS   103

presence of figurines and pictures of all kinds throughout the Bronze Age abundantly attests. Their pre-Hellenic cult continued into the classical times and dominated religious practices all over the Aegean world. The Homeric epics themselves also attest to her antiquity. In the course of enumerating the many love affairs of Zeus (*Il.* 14.317 ff.), Homer mentions a few of the women Zeus had slept with and the offspring of these unions. Chronologically, the fruits of Zeus's liaisons are a younger generation, while his partners in love are from the older generation. It is then reasonable to accept Zeus and his love partners as personified pre-Homeric divinities. Demeter is demonstrably one of Zeus's partners (*Il.* 14.326), and this Homeric reference to Demeter's antiquity buttresses the archaeologically-based view that Demeter was one of the very early Mycenaean or pre-Mycenaean divinities worshiped in Greece.

A noteworthy feature of the account concerning the worship of Mother Earth is the abiding influence, from the earliest generation to the latest, of Gaia, who was not a supreme ruler herself but universally acknowledged as the power behind the Olympian throne. She gave Cronus the iron sickle and was responsible for his rise to kingship. By her counsel and action Zeus was saved and shown how to usurp the throne. By her counsel he ruled, and by it he was saved from being overthrown himself. These things are described as fated, but Gaia has both foreknowledge of what is to be and power to make herself the instrument of fate. All this narrative reflects a genuine religious phenomenon. Throughout the religious changes which took place in Greece, culminating in the lively anthropomorphism of that Olympian religion inherited by the classical Greeks from Homer, the awe inspired by the Earth-Mother never ceased, even though she was recognized to be, as indeed she was, a far older power in the land than the Olympians. Gaia and Apollo as well as other divinities, along with the mythology accompanying them, probably came to the inhabitants of Greece from the lands of the Near East.[45] Hera herself, who for the later Greeks was the legitimate consort of Zeus and the patron and guardian of marriage and fecundity, must have originally been a local form of the Earth Mother, although by the time of Homer her Chthonian associations had sunk into the background.[46]

In sum, the Homeric picture of a pantheon of active and ever-watchful deities suggests that although a king might break his sworn oath when the occasion offered, the religious climate was such that any subsequent disaster would be regarded as fulfilling the curse of the broken oath, worked out on him and his people by the vexed divinities. After the unexpected outcome of the Alexander-Menelaus combat, Agamemnon assured the Achaeans that the

---

[45] C. Picard, *Les religions prehellènique* (Paris, 1948) 225; 231.
[46] CAH3 22.900.

104 THE STRUCTURE OF THE HOMERIC AGREEMENTS

oaths to the gods and the sacrifice of the animals were not by any means made in vain, notwithstanding the apparent escape of Alexander. Even if it appeared for a while that the gods had failed to carry out the oath's curse, when the appropriate time came the culprits would pay the punishment due them, as would their wives and children.

The evidence thus far shows similarities between the Ancient Near East treaty-making and the Mycenaean or Homeric world. Whether these similarities are due to synchronic practices independently developed or are the result of infiltration from one culture to another is difficult to ascertain, although some of the religious similarities are probably not coincidental. There seems to be a common thread running backward in time to the Sumerian culture, many of whose features survived despite the diversity of languages and peoples and the passage of centuries. Throughout the changes that the Near East sustained during its long and turbulent history, certain features of the treaty-making process remained constant, whether in written or oral form. These persistent features included giving one's word, making a pledge, and taking an oath in the name of the gods. Indeed, the very naming of a treaty implied an obligation assumed under oath.

E. CURSES AND BLESSINGS

The Hittite treaties usually concluded with a statement about the consequences of compliance or non-compliance. They invoked the gods, who were not considered passive onlookers of the transaction but participants and the final arbiters. These gods were expected to pursue violators relentlessly and to reward those who kept their oaths. This final component of curses and blessings is significant from a legal point of view, serving as it does to place the treaty squarely within the realm of sacred law (since the most effective sanctions of the covenant were the religious ones). It goes without saying that if the treaty were breached the stronger party would proceed against the weaker. However, this harsh matter-of-fact reality does not negate the sacral character of the treaty inasmuch as the punishment frequently inflicted upon the vanquished was likely to be interpreted as the visitation of divine justice upon the transgressor. There is no mention of this in the treaty itself, but the idea was universal albeit usually implicit.[47] Among the Israelites, with their religious interpretation of history, the covenant stands wholly within the sacred law; even when the other party is not God, a treaty's sacredness and therefore its validity depends upon God's approval.

Because the curse was thought to be the most effective inducement to obedience, it frequently appeared before the blessings and in greater detail.[48]

---

[47] G. R. Driver and J. C. Miles, *The Babylonian Laws* (Oxford, 1952) 1:11.

[48] Weidner, *Polit. Dok.*, 29, 33, 35.

THE STRUCTURE OF THE HOMERIC AGREEMENTS 105

When the Trojans and Achaeans agreed upon a duel between Alexander and Menelaus, they solemnized the agreement by a sacrifice in the course of which any future violators of the agreement were cursed. These curses included the symbolic pouring out on the ground of the brains of the violators and their children, exactly as the wine of the libation ritual had been poured out during the covenant meal. For the wives a fate more dishonorable to both themselves and their husbands was reserved: concubinage (*Il.* 3.296 ff.). Even when the punishment was not immediately forthcoming, the Greeks believed that divine retribution would eventually be visited upon the transgressors, their wives and children (*Il.* 4.161-62; 3.299-300)—a belief which, as we saw above, was also held by the Near Eastern peoples. It is not surprising that the *Iliad* itself begins with such a retribution, one eventually responsible for the great quarrel between the two Achaean leaders. Without the tormenting suspicion that the plague among the Greeks might have been inflicted for some infringement of a vow or a failure to fulfill a promise to one of the gods, the quarrel would not have ensued (*Il.* 1.43.ff.). Finally, when the two protagonists were reconciled, the occasion was solemnized by the sacrifice of a boar. In the process of sacrificing, Agamemnon swore that he had not touched Briseis, invoking in confirmation of his honesty Zeus, the Earth, the Sun and the Erinyes, who punish false swearers. He then wished upon himself all the evils attendant upon false swearing. Whereas curses were a matter of the future, to become operative only if and when a breach took place, blessings were in the here and now and continued forever or at least as long as the agreement was respected. Promised blessings included the protection of the gods, prosperity of the land, eternal reign, abundant harvest, joy of heart, and fruitfulness of sperm. In specific instances, success in one's purpose or action was wished. Thus Chryses blessed the Greeks by wishing them success in the taking of Troy and safe return to their homes.[49]

As a rule, the curses expressed in the Homeric epics are brief. This is significant as the practice of cursing in the Near East, judging from the treaties of Esarhaddon, seems to have undergone a steady enlargement. Early Near Eastern treaties contained a brief and general statement dealing with curses. In the first millennium B.C., however, the formulaic development of cursing apparently became much more elaborate, with the result that there were long segments in the treaties of that time devoted to curses. In this

---

[49] *Il.* 1.19. In fact, Chryses' wishes ran contrary to the interest of his compatriots. He therefore either wanted to flatter the Greeks or, if he were sincere in his wishes, to hold the Trojans responsible for the war. He might have believed that if Alexander had not kidnapped Helen, the Greeks might not have made war against Troy, and that they would not have captured his daughter. Consequently, he wished for the Greeks that they capture Troy and that they return to their home safely (Eust. ad *Il.* 1.7).

106 THE STRUCTURE OF THE HOMERIC AGREEMENTS

respect, Homer is *not* typical of the Near Eastern trends of his day, probably
either because the poetic conventions of his day did not accommodate
elaborate enumerations of this type of material, or because they simply did
not fit well into his own poetic scheme, or else because Homer represents an
older format of treaties.[50] In a few Homeric treaties curses and blessings are
not even alluded to, although it is almost certain that they were originally
constitutive parts of such agreements. When Nestor chided the Greeks for
their desire to return home with their objective unaccomplished, he warned
them that such a wish stood in violation of their agreements, *synthesiai te
kai horkia*. Clearly, the reference to *synthesiai* and *horkia* entailed ritualistic
sacrifices accompanied by curses and blessings. It would be very unusual if
the formalization of the agreement by the participants in the Trojan War did
not follow the archaic formula which, as a general rule, included blessings
and curses. This was too much of an official occasion not to have included a
sacrifice accompanied by curses. It would be very unusual if the agreement
referred to here were not formalized by sacrifice, accompanied by formulaic
curses, especially if the Aulis agreement is alluded to here (*Il.* 2.303-332).
Likewise, the presence of *spondai t' akrêtoi* in Book 2 of the *Iliad* connoted
the use of sacrifice and curses or blessings in connection with the libations
(339-41). That curses and blessings are not expressly mentioned at this point
is owing primarily to the fact that the passage in question is merely an
allusion to a past event, whose details did not need to be repeated here.

On the other hand, in Book 3.390 ff. of the *Iliad*, where sacrifice and
spondai akrêtoi also take place after the slaughter of the sacrificial animals,
Agamemnon expressed the wish that the brains of any violators would flow
on the earth like the *spondai* of wine. In the agreement proposed by Hector to
Achilles, curses and blessings might have been included had Achilles
concurred with the proposals. But since Achilles rejected any notion that
would have bound him to the established practices, Hector's proposal failed
to materialize (*Il.* 22.254 ff.).

Unfortunately, curses associated with Homeric agreements are very few
and scattered. This is largely due to the absence in the entire agreement of
that formalism so typical in the Near Eastern treaties. Furthermore, some of
the Homeric agreements are between men and gods or between gods. In both
cases, curses would usually be inappropriate, although they are not entirely
absent.[51] Lastly, among those agreements is a type of personal arrangement
for which some formalism is evidenced in the post-Homeric sources: the
marriage alliance. It is unfortunate that only a few rapid references are made
by Homer to marriage agreements. Yet somewhere along the way from the

---

[50] D. J. Wiseman, *Iraq* 20 (1958) 60 ff.
[51] *Il.* 14.267-74; *Od.* 5.177-86.

engagement to the nuptial ceremonies, the formalization of the happy event must have entailed some sort of treaty-like rituals, within which curses or blessings would have had a natural role.

The presence in Homer of *any* formulaic curses and blessings is particularly striking (though welcomed) when we consider that the Homeric world was one of international aristocratism, in which a gentleman's word was tantamount to an oath.[52] Such an ethos is in strong contrast to the practice of swearing oaths and incanting curses, but the contrast seems less paradoxical when we also consider that curses and blessings were an established practice with origins firmly rooted in the history of the Near East. Although not needed among true "gentlemen," this practice nonetheless was available as a back-up strategy on those occasions where gentlemanliness could not be assumed. Thus oaths and blessings in the Menelaus accord can be explained not only by the solemnity of the occasion but also by the unreliability of Alexander given his past history. Elsewhere, however, their absence can be explained by the more informal character of these compacts, by the aristocratic ethos of the covenanters, and more so by the nature of the *epos* itself, which is not interested in the full details of agreements as is the case with the legal or the historical documents.

F. CONCLUSION

Our analysis of the general format of the Homeric agreements shows that there were striking similarities between their format and that of the Near Eastern treaties. The similarities are most evident in the titulary, the recounting of antecedent history which preceded the exchange of pledges, in the stipulatory part of the agreements, where the conditional form predominates, and in the accompanying acts of blessing and cursing. Even gods abided by these conventions when, as witnesses of the oaths taken by the contractants, they committed themselves to play an active role in guaranteeing compliance with the agreements by meting out the appropriate punishments or blessings.

In this chapter we have considered the most important common features of ancient treaties and agreements. Even so, the list of similiarities is not exhausted by these features. There are still other interesting and by no means unimportant common features, some of which will be discussed in the next chapter.

---

[52] The modern Greek expression "A man's word is his contract," probably goes back in history to a time when written contracts were rare and difficult to arrange. A similar locution is to be found in the historical section of the Mattiwaza-Suppiluliumas treaty, translated by Weidner as "Das Wort daß meinem munde ausgeht, wird nicht rückgängig" (*Polit. Dok.*, 43).

CHAPTER FOUR

OTHER FEATURES OF HOMERIC AGREEMENTS

In the last chapter we considered five specific components of formal treaties, which are found most clearly in Near Eastern treaties but are also echoed in the Homeric agreements. The present chapter considers some other practices which, though not themselves constituent parts of the formal structure of treaty agreements, are interesting because they again show parallels between the promise-making practices of the Near East and those represented in the Homeric epics. The practices we shall discuss are (1) maledictions that, like the curses at the end of formal treaties, ensure the fidelity of the promise-makers, (2) rituals which underscore the solemnity of the agreements, and (3) suzerainty agreements between lords and vassals, which, though not treaties per se, are what might be called treaty-analogues.

In each of these three areas, the task of collecting examples for discussion is somewhat problematic because of the general difficulty of determining what constitutes a significant parallel between the Near Eastern treaties and the Homeric agreements. Here as elsewhere in this study, the only viable strategy seems to be that of letting the texts speak for themselves and using common sense to determine their significance. Our efforts will be doubly fruitful if, as indeed seems to be the case, the examples presented in this chapter turn out not only to be significant but also to show the same sort of Oriental-Homeric parallelism that was discerned in previous chapters. We can then conjecture—as always, doing so tentatively but not groundlessly—that of the two alternative explanations, viz., the influence hypothesis and the separate development hypothesis, the former is much more plausible. That is (to speak in general terms), when there are only a few parallels between social practices of one culture and those of another, then in the absence of any further information there is a high likelihood that the respective practices of those cultures developed separately and that the parallelisms were coincidental. But as the number of parallelisms increases, the likelihood of coincidence decreases, so that at a certain point it becomes more likely that some sort of causal connection exists between the two cultures. Of course (still speaking generally) the causal link need not be direct: some third factor, perhaps common geographical conditions or perhaps a third culture, might be a common cause for both cultures having developed as they did, just as similarities between two children may be explained not by their influences on each other but by their common parents and shared living conditions. Furthermore, regardless of whether a causal line found between two cultures is direct or indirect, further investigation would be required to establish its direction. In the case under discussion in the present study, the causal line

A. OTHER MALEDICTIONS

could hardly have been moving from Homer backwards in time to the Ancient Near East, but of course many imponderables remain even if one chooses in favor of an influence theory over against a parallel development theory.

A. OTHER MALEDICTIONS

In general, ancient curses carry as their sanctions evils and calamities that sometimes really happened. However fantastic or bordering on the ridiculous these curses may seem to us today, they were meant to be taken seriously in their time, as indeed they must have been, considering their universality. None of the following curses or curse-like maledictions appears to be a simple copy from one culture to the other, but the absence of perfect similarity does not preclude the possibility of direct influence from the Near East on the Homeric world or indirect influence in the sense of dependence on common sources. On the one hand, the influence, direct or indirect, may be explained by the sojourn of the so-called Achaeans (whoever they actually were) in the area of Asia Minor before their final settlement on the mainland of Greece—provided of course, that this theory of migration is correct. On the other hand, long before the Achaeans arrived in Greece there were people living in the Near East and on the Greek peninsula, whose cultural influence upon the Achaeans must have been considerable, particularly in the areas of religious ideas and practices. The example of the Hittites, whose religious ideas were strongly shaped by the Hurrian culture, constitutes a good analogue. Later, in Hellenistic times, the Greeks absorbed much more in the area of religion from the Eastern cultures than they were able to give. It seems that Near Eastern religious ideas were extremely influential for the common man and it would have been a miracle if the average Mycenaean were not affected by them. Such practices include magical formulas and ceremonial curses employed on a variety of maledictory occasions, only one of which was the treaty curses. Such cursing seems to have been prominent early in the history of the Ancient Near East in connection with interstate treaties, and became still more prominent in the first millennium B.C. Though cursing is not so pronounced in Homer where there are no formal treaties as such, it does nonetheless exist throughout the Homeric literature, particularly in certain segments whose maledictory purpose is definitely clear. This tradition of maledictions will continue into the post-Homeric period.

Cursing in Homer takes several forms, which can be categorized in several ways. One way, already discussed, is to distinguish between formal and informal curses, which corresponds more or less closely with the distinction between treaty-curses (as reviewed in the last chapter) and other forms of malediction. But within each of these categories we can further distinguish according to the kind of evil that is projected as the curse's sanction. In

110 OTHER FEATURES OF HOMERIC AGREEMENTS

Homer, the most prominent of these latter categories are the prospects of (1) having one's city turned into a dwelling place for animals, (2) being devoured by animals, (3) the ravishing of wives and enslavement of one's children, (4) weapons being destroyed, (5) warriors becoming women, (6) refusal of burial, and (7) devastating floods. As we shall see, Homer reserves some of his choicest language for these curses.

1. The destruction and transformation of cities

References in connection with verbs like *ekperthô-perthô* or *haliskomai* convey the image of a city's destruction and its transformation into a grazing place for animals (*Il.* 4.291; 19.296, and elsewhere).[1] In *Il.* 16.706-708, Apollo throws Patroclus back from the walls of Troy three times. When Patroclus attacked the walls yet a fourth time, Apollo addressed him with the serious warning that Troy was not fated to be laid waste (*polin perthai*) by Patroclus's spear, nor even by Achilles, even though he was a far better warrior than Patroclus.

2. Ravenous wild animals

Several treaty-curses state that ravenous wild animals will be brought upon a land as punishment. Thus we find in SF I A 30-32: "May the gods send every sort of devourer against Arpad and against its people,"[2] and in the *Iliad* (15.630-36) Hector is described as falling upon the Greeks as a hungry lion falls upon kine grazing in the bottom land of a great marsh (ὡς τε λέων ὀλοόφρων ἐπελθών). The Homeric literature is peppered with other such similes as well.[3] We may, for example, recall Odysseus's admonition to the Greeks to persevere in fighting, reminding them of the portent of Aulis where the Greeks sacrificed to the Olympians prior to their departure for

---

[1] Such expressions bear close similarity to Near Eastern treaty-curses. In Sf I A 32-33 the following curse is pronounced: "And may Arpad become a mound to [house the desert animal and the] gazelle and the fox and the hare and the wild-cat and the owl ... and the magpie"; A. Dupont-Sommer, *Les inscriptions araméennes de Sfire*, Steles I and II (Paris, 1958) 47-48. This curse is without parallel in the Near Eastern treaties, but has definite parallels in other texts. In Esarhaddon's letter to the god Ashur there occurs the following description of a ruined city: "Foxes and hyenas made their home there"; R. Borger, AFO Beiheft 9 (1956) 107. A similar curse made by Marduk is to be found in the annals of the same king; see D. Hillers, *Treaty-Curses and the Old Testament Prophets* (Rome, 1964) 44. Compare also the Hittite malediction on a conquered city which states that the city is to be perpetually desolate and that the bulls of the weather god will graze it for ever, J. Friedrich, *Aus dem hethitischen Schrifttum. Vol. 2: Religiöse Texte* ; AO 25, 2 (Leipzig, 1925) 22-23; 11.18-31. For biblical parallels see F. C. Fensham, ZAW 75 (1963) 166-68; Hillers, *Treaty Curses*, 53-54.

[2] Fitzmyer, JAOS 81 (1961)181, 185.

[3] *Il.* 16.485-90, 751-52.

OTHER FEATURES OF HOMERIC AGREEMENTS   111

Troy. A serpent had appeared during the sacrifice, blood-red on its back, terrible in its appearance. He glided from beneath the altar and darted to the plane tree under which the sacrifice was held. On the topmost bough of the tree was a sparrow's nest containing eight younglings. The serpent devoured them all as they twittered piteously, and then caught the desperate mother who fluttered around them. He devoured her and then disappeared. As the Achaeans stood and marvelled at the event, Calchas interpreted the devouring of the younglings and of their mother to mean that the Achaeans would destroy Troy in the tenth year of their campaign.[4]

3. The ravishing of wives

In the treaty-curses that Agamemnon uttered at the conclusion of the duel agreement between Menelaus and Paris, he wished upon the oath-breakers that their wives be made concubines to others (*Il.* 3.100-301). Likewise, in the generally formular language of *Il.* 236-39 the violators of oaths are cursed to die and be exposed to devouring vultures, while their wives and children are taken captives. Meleager's wife reminds him of the fate of captive cities: the men are slain, while the children and women are led away as captives of strangers. It was needless to repeat that the wives became concubines of their captors (*Il.* 9.590-94). This degradation of the defeated was openly urged upon the Greeks by Nestor, who sought to dissuade the Achaeans from thoughts of return to their homeland before they had lain with the wives of the Trojans in requital for their campaign and for the groanings of Helen (*Il.* 2.354-56).[5]

4. The destruction of weapons

This curse is an *hapax legomenon* in Homer and appears in the prayer of Hecuba to Athena, the purported guardian of Troy. Hecuba asked Athena to break the spear of Diomedes and grant that he fall headlong before the Scaean gates, ἄξον δὴ ἔγχος Διομήδεος; *Il.* 6.305-10. Although unusual in the

---

[4] *Il.* 2.308-329. For examples in the Bible, cf. Lev. 26.22: "Then I will send among you wild animals, which will make you bereft of children, and destroy your cattle, and make you few in number and your ways desolate." Also Deut. 32.24; Isa. 14.29, where the enemy is like a snake; Isa. 5.29-30 (the enemy as a lion).

[5] For a parallel see the curse in Wiseman, *The Vassal Treaties,* p. 62 11.428-29: "[May Venus, the brightest of the stars,] make your spouse lie [in the lap of your enemy before your eyes]"; also Jer. 8.10 offers another parallel: "Therefore, I will give their wives to others." The imprecatory lead tablets (*tabellae defixionum*) buried in the ground by Athenian citizens in the fourth century B.C. called upon various demons and evil spirits to destroy a neighbor's crops and render his flocks sterile, and his wife as well. See Finley, *Use and Abuse of History* 2nd ed. (New York, 1987) 179.

112 OTHER FEATURES OF HOMERIC AGREEMENTS

Homeric corpus, this type of curse appears frequently in the Near Eastern cursing repertory as well as in the Bible.[6]

5. Warriors becoming women

A related curse seems to be the loss of men's courage or virility and their transformation into cowards. Thersites criticizes the Achaeans for losing their courage and bowing cowardly to the arbitrariness of their leaders: "Fools! Shameful creatures! You women of Achaea, men no more" (*Il.* 2.235). Hector reminds the fleeing Diomedes that the Achaeans will scorn him although they earlier honored him, since now he proved no better than a woman, a cowardly puppet (*Il.* 8.163-64). Although neither Thersites nor Hector expresses an imprecation here, the derogatory criticism of this statement seems to reflect a common stock formula similar to the curse formulae found in the Near Eastern treaties, especially in the expression "You women of Achaea, men no more." The same seems to be true of No.4, the precatory request of Hecuba.[7]

6. Refusal of burial

One of the more frequent type of curse to be found in Homer is that which proscribed an essential religious rite, the proper burial of the dead, a threat that was looked upon as an extremely serious form of punishment. Thus Agamemnon threatened his troops not only with death but also with exposure of their corpses to the dogs and birds, if they were ever caught eschewing the battle near the curved ships (*Il.* 2.391-93). In the duel agreement between Hector and Aias one of the stipulations was the return of the vanquished's body for proper burial (*Il.* 7.67 ff.). Athena comforted the worried Hera by assuring her that many Trojans would glut the dogs and birds with their fat and flesh when they died near the Achaean ships (*Il.* 8.379-80). Likewise, Poseidon suggested to Idomeneus that no Achaean who shrank from the fighting should return to his home, but instead he should be the sport of dogs (*Il.* 13.232-34). On the other hand, Hector threatened Aias that he would fill with his flesh and fat the dogs and birds of the Trojans when he fell by the ships of the Achaeans (*Il.* 13.831-32). When Zeus's beloved son Sarpedon fell in battle, Zeus ordered Apollo to get Sarpedon's corpse, bathe it in the river, anoint it with ambrosia, clothe it with immortal garments, and give it to speedy conveyers who would transport it to Lycia. There

---

[6] Thus in Sf I A 38-39 we read: "Just as this bow and these arrows are broken, so may Anahita and Hadad break [the bow of Mati'el] and the bow of his nobles." For biblical parallels; see Fitzmyer, JAOS 81 (1981) 200; Hillers, *Treaty-Curses*, 60.

[7] Curses in the Ashurnirari treaty express the same idea as in Hillers, *Treaty-Curses*, 66; Ishtar is portrayed as having the power to change the men into women as in the Old Babylonian prayer; R. Borger, AFO Beiheft 9, 99. For examples in the Old Testament see Nahum 3.13; Jer. 50.37.

OTHER FEATURES OF HOMERIC AGREEMENTS   113

Sarpedon's brothers and folk would give it the proper burial, building for it a grove and mound, for such was due to the dead.[8] Priam sought to persuade Hector to get behind the walls of Troy whence he should defend the city, reminding him that otherwise the city might fall and Priam himself might be killed and left to rot, while hungry dogs lapped up his blood and devoured his flesh. When Priam's solicitations fell on deaf ears, Hecuba pleaded with Hector using arguments similar to those of Priam (*Il.* 22.66-76, 89). Finally, when the two major antagonists, Achilles and Hector, met in their last encounter, Hector asked Achilles for a pledge to respect his body and give it up for burial, promising to do the same if he were the victor. But Achilles was in no mood to listen to a request that asked respect for moral principles. Blind with anger over Hector's killing of Patroclus, he threatened Hector with the ultimate indignity: exposure of his body to be eaten by dogs and birds (*Il.* 22.335-36). Here again we are reminded of the language of the Near Eastern curse formulae.[9]

7. Devastating flood

Rising and seething around Achilles, the angry water of Scamander beat down on Achilles' shield and overwhelmed him. Unable to maintain his stance, Achilles laid hold of a full-grown elm. But the tree came out by the roots, carrying with it the whole river bank as it crashed into the middle of the river and damming it from side to side, clogging the stream with a tangle of branches. Achilles struggled out of the current, and in his terror made a dash for the bank, where he hoped his speed would save him. But the great god Scamander, who was bent upon saving the Trojans from destruction, was not yet finished with Achilles. He rose and menaced him with a black wall of water. "The son of Peleus fled, gaining a spear-throw's start by swooping away with the speed of the black eagle, that great hunter who is both the

---

[8] *Il.* 16.675: τὸ γὰρ γέρας ἐστὶ θανόντων. For keeping dogs away from a corpse by night see 2 Sam. 21.10; *Il.* 23.185-86; C. H. Gordon, *Homer and the Bible*, 91.

[9] The same principle about the burial of the dead prevailed in the Near East. A curse which occurs three times in Esarhaddon's treaty states that the oath-breaker will not receive proper burial but will be eaten by animals; McCarthy, *Treaty and Covenant*, 202; Hillers, *Treaty-Curses*, 68: "May Palil feed your flesh to the eagle and jackal"; Wiseman, *The Vassal Treaties*, 62.11.426-27: "May dogs and swine eat your flesh"; Wiseman, *The Vassal Treaties*, 64.1.451. A *kudurru* contains the curse, "May the [violator's] corpse drop and have no one to bury it"; L. W. King, *Babylonian Boundary Stones and Memorial Tablets in the British Museum* (London, 1912) 127, vv. 54-55; McCarthy, *Treaty and Covenants*, 203; Hillers, *Treaty-Curses* 68. Like Agamemnon and Achilles, Esarhaddon tells of carrying out the threat of leaving the enemy bodies exposed: "I will let the vultures eat the corpses of their warriors"; Hillers, *Treaty-Curses*, 68. This curse is extremely common in the Old Testament. It occurs in typical form in Deut. 28.26: "And may your corpse be food for all the birds of the heavens and for the beasts of the earth." Similar curses occur in Jer. 34.20: "And their corpses shall be food for the birds of the heavens and for the beasts of the earth." The curse is stereotypical; see 1 Kings 14.11; 21.24; 2 Kings 9.10, 36-37; 1 Sam. 17.43-46.

114 OTHER FEATURES OF HOMERIC AGREEMENTS

strongest and fastest thing on wings.... Achilles was a great runner, but the gods are greater than men, and time and again he was caught up by the van of the flood, like a gardener who is irrigating his plot by making a channel in among the plants for the fresh water from a spring.... Sometimes the swift and excellent Achilles tried to make a stand and to find out whether every god was chasing him. But whenever he stopped, a mighty billow from the heaven-fed river came crashing down on his shoulders. Exasperated, he struggled to his feet. But the water still raced madly by, gripping him round the knees and sweeping the loose earth from under him. The son of Peleus groaned aloud and looking up into the broad sky he cried [to Zeus]."[10]

Before the destructive might of Scamander could be checked by the intervention of the gods, the river-god doubled his fury and, summoning the assistance of other rivers, attempted to overwhelm Achilles. "Simois," Scamander says, "let us unite to overpower this man, who will soon be sacking Priam's royal city, with not a Trojan to put up a fight. Come quickly to my help. Fill your channels with water from the springs, replenish all your mountain streams, raise a great surge and send it down, seething with logs and boulders, so that we may stop this savage who is carrying all before him."[11] At the end, the attempt of Scamander to drown Achilles failed because Hera induced Hephaestus to employ his fire (a force deemed superior to flood) in order to stop Scamander. Thus, even though there are no formulaic curses related to fire in Homer, this precative passage as well as analogous execratory formulae in the Near Eastern documents (see n. 12, below) seem to point to the existence of formulaic curses dealing with consumption by fire, very early in the history of the entire Near East. Hera's vow not to avert from the Trojans their day of evil, not even when all Troy should be burned by the consuming fire of the sons of the Achaeans, strongly suggests such a curse (*Il.* 21.372-73).

---

[10] *Homer: The Iliad,* trans. E. V. Rieu (Baltimore, 1961) 386-87.

[11] Also cf. Rieu's *Homer*, 388. It should be pointed out that the flood metaphors do not abound in Homer: the phenomenon could not have been very frequent in Greece because of the peculiarity of its terrain. Torrential rains could easily cause even small rivers to overflow for a short while, but since fields could flood, the Greeks generally built on elevated places or places least affected by such torrential outbursts. Flood metaphors would have occurred more naturally to residents of Mesopotamia, where destructive inundations were a more common experience than in Greece or even Syria-Palestine. A curse having to do with a flood is to be found in two places in the Esarhaddon treaty: "May an erratic flood come up from the earth and devastate you"; Wiseman, *The Vassal Treaties*, 66, ll. 488-89, and "[May the god submerge] your land"; Wiseman, *The Vassal Treaties*, 62, l. 442. In Esarhaddon's annals, Enlil curses Babylon with a terrible curse and a flood destroys the city; Borger, AFO Beiheft 9, p. 13. In Isa. 8.7 there occurs a similar idea where the waters of the Euphrates river (a metaphor for the king of Assyria) would rise over its channels and overflow all its banks, and would sweep over Judah, flooding as it goes. See Jer. 47.2, which also foretells a flood-scene where the waters will grow into an overwhelming stream and will overflow the land.

OTHER FEATURES OF HOMERIC AGREEMENTS 115

There are indeed similar parallels to fire in the Near East and the Greek world. An Aramaic document from the eighth century B.C. may constitute the bridge between Mesopotamia and the Greek world. It concerns an oath formula in an international treaty where we read that the violators should be consumed by fire like the wax figures burned for symbolic purposes. We find something similar in the seventh century B.C. treaty of the Assyrian king Esarhaddon with his vassals.[12] Analogous to the above practice is the oath of the Cyrenaeans in the foundation inscription (which may reflect a seventh century original, at least in its oath section), according to which the colonists formed wax statues and burned them, praying in the meantime that those who failed to honor the oaths taken would become melted down like the statues.[13]

Summary

The foregoing examples indicate that as a linguistic performance and literary genre, the "curse" was very common in the Ancient Near East and that it could not be rigidly fenced off from the rest of the literature. Instead, the authors of lists of curses, epic compositions, hymns, annals, magical texts, and so on, all drew from the same existing stock of traditional maledictions. Homer, in turn, employed traditional material in composing threats of doom. Secondly, the Greek maledictory material resembles, at many points, curses from the Mesopotamian treaties. As noted above, although exact parallels are often missing, the possibilities of direct or indirect influence and dependence on common sources cannot be disregarded. After all, we possess only a relatively small body of the pre-Homeric literature. Moreover, we would expect the indigenous pre-Mycenaean residents of Greece to have played a role as intermediaries in the flow of such ideas, but our knowledge of their language and literature is practically nil. But, even if we must assume some closer relation between Mycenaean and Homeric literature on the one hand and the Near Eastern texts on the other, we cannot say, on the basis of evidence presented thus far, whether in using these maledictions, people like Homer were conscious of their source or not, considering its remote antiquity. The parallels between the Near Eastern curses and the Homeric ones may reflect a linguistic fact, for instance, that throughout their early history the Greeks shared with the East common stock phrases which a poet might have readily put into his heroes' mouths.

---

[12] Sfire Inscription I A ANET 660; Fitzmyer, CBQ 20 (1967) 14; 16 ff. (I 35 42) ll. 608-10; D. J. Wiseman, *Iraq* 20 (1958) 75 ff.; McCarthy, *Treaty and Covenant*, 76 ff.; 204; W. Burkert, *Die orientalizierende Epoche*, 68: Fitzmyer, JAOS 81 (1961) 181 ff.

[13] SEG 9 (1944) No.3; M/L, No. 5, 11.44: κηρίνος πλάσσαντες κολοσὸς κατέκαιον. A. R. Nock, *Arch. für Religionswischenschaft* 24 (1926) 172 ff.; S. Dusanic, *Chiron* 8 (1978) 55-76; A. J. Graham, *Colony and Mother City* (New York, 1971) 225 ff.

116　　OTHER FEATURES OF HOMERIC AGREEMENTS

That the association of curses with the signing of treaties or the making of internal laws continued in the post-Homeric period admits of little doubt. Thus the early treaty of the amphictyonies cited in Aischines refers to curses pronounced against the future violators.[14] The same is repeated in Aisch. *Against Ctes.* 3.110, where sterility of land and women, as well as birth monstrosities and other forms of misfortunes are wished upon the violators.[15] Finally, in the Law of Gortyn, exactly as in treaties, one can find curses against the potential violators, although by then it was easier for the community to inflict its own punishment upon the culprits through legitimately constituted authority.[16]

B. RITUAL

The list of similarities between Greek and Near Eastern treaties is not limited to the genre of curses. The ceremonial rituals associated with promise-making and oath-taking also present interesting parallels. For instance, Hittite treaties usually contained no reference to sacrificial animals and gave little hint of curses dramatized in connection with sacrifices. This is not to say that such rites were not practiced by the Hittites, because they were. In contrast to the Hittites, Semites regarded the ritual as more important than the word. According to D. J. McCarthy, among the West Semites it is impossible to separate the oaths and the killing of an animal. While the type of animal sacrificed and the method of killing it could vary (Israelites, according to McCarthy, generally used goats or calves or heifers, whereas Aramaeans and Assyrians used sheep), the meaning remained the same.[17] In either case, care was taken that the rite be performed correctly, for correct performance established the efficacy and the validity of the bond between parties.[18] The same care was exercised in the Homeric era. The sacrifice of the two lambs was made by Agamemnon himself, standing in front of both armies and having Odysseus at his side. Representing the Trojan side was Priam, flanked by Antenor. The choice of the *aides-de-camp* may be indicative of some of the forces at play on both sides. Odysseus was the

---

[14] Aisch. *Peri Parapr.* 2.115.

[15] Sterility of women, animals, land, etc. is a frequent curse in the Ancient Near Eastern treaties, as we have seen. Its presence in Aischines buttresses the argument about the stereotype form of the ancient curses and their early origins. See also the treaty between Rome and Carthage, which Polybius places (probably correctly) in 508-507 B.C. For similar curses, cf. Bengtson, No. 121.

[16] Willetts, *The Law of Gortyn,* 40.

[17] McCarthy, *Treaty and Covenant,* 53-54. In the Mari documents an official is represented as having sacrificed an ass or an ass's foal; Munn-Rankin, *Iraq* 18 (1956) 85; ARMT, 2:37.13.

[18] McCarthy, *Treaty and Covenant,* 55.

OTHER FEATURES OF HOMERIC AGREEMENTS 117

diplomat par excellence (*Il.* 3.310 ff.), while Antenor was the chief of the Trojans most inclined to negotiate (*Il.* 3.205-224; 7.345-64). The passage portrays the procedure of sacrifice with considerable precision. Agamemnon begins by cutting the hair from the victim's head, and the heralds distribute it among the chiefs. Thus the ritual associates the participants directly with the sacrifice.[19] Then through a second oath accompanied by libations (*Il.* 3.259-96), each binds himself individually, his own life and the lives of his family and of his people in general.[20] A special knife called *machaira* (*Il.* 3.271-72; Leaf *ad loc.*), not to be confused with the sword, was further used for the sacrifice of the victims. In the instances where the sacrificial animal was not accursed, the flesh of the animal was consumed. The ritual usually entailed the washing of the hands prior to the beginning of the sacrifice with the throwing of barley grains into the fire or on the victims' head (*Il.* 11.1.449; *Od.* 3.430-63; Arist. *Peace* 948 ff.). Only then was the throat of the victim cut, the animal flayed, and the thighs severed and covered with a double layer of fat on which raw flesh was laid to be burned along with the thighs. When all of this was done libations were poured. The remaining meat was then cut up, spitted, roasted, and eaten, and the participants once again poured forth drops of wine in the form of libations.

It was believed essential for the validity of a treaty that the right kind of animal should be sacrificed. This combination of animal and treaty is shown by a letter of king Ibal-El in which he reported that a puppy and a goat had been brought for the sacrificial ceremony.[21] In the Homeric instances, the sacrifice of lambs and the choice of their color seem to be related to this idea of choosing a victim to fit the occasion (*Il.* 3.103). In the course of the ritualistic sacrifice, the animal was cut up or dismembered, and the making of treaty was metonymized as "cutting a covenant," or "to cut a covenant." It was commonly accepted that one was dealing here with a sign or symbol of what would happen to any covenanter who dared to be faithless to the

---

[19] The hair in ancient times was regarded as the special seat of life. Scholars conjecture that this idea was connected with the fact that hair continues to grow, and so to manifest life, even in mature age, and this conjecture is supported by the fact that among many people nails are the object of similar superstitious regard. The practice of cutting off hair, as symbolic of a serious or sacred act, was fairly widespread. Related to the idea of the hair as the special seat of life seems to have been the notion of the hair as a source of strength; W. R. Smith, *The Religion of the Semites* (New York, 1957) 324; Judges 16.16-19.

[20] P. Mazon, ed., *Homère* (Paris, 1961) 8. Regarding the question of libation, Wéry admits that the text is not precise as to the author(s) of the libation, yet it is evident to her that only the four chiefs who are standing in front of the troops perform it, RIDA 14 (1967) 203. In Exod. 19.7-9, when Moses reported to the people the words of Yahweh, they answered with one voice: "All the words which Yahweh has spoken we will do."

[21] ARMT, 2:37.9-12.

118 OTHER FEATURES OF HOMERIC AGREEMENTS

agreement. In such rituals there is, in other words, a conditional "acting out" of immanence.[22]

It should be mentioned at this point that among modern scholars there is another view which takes exception to the theory proposed here.[23] In that view, the ritual of sacrifice is considered as an association of life between the parties symbolized by the animal blood and strengthened by the mystic force contained in the shedding of blood. This claim has been supported by E. Bickerman, who adduces three points in favor of his argument and in opposition to the theory presented in this study. First of all, the ordinary description of "cutting a covenant" makes no express identification of the contracting parties and the victim. Secondly, a number of Hittite rites have the contracting parties passing between severed members of the victim exactly as in Gen. 15.9-10 and Jer. 34.18-19, but these rites do not imply identification with the victim or threat of any kind.[24] Thirdly, the blood is a divine element, released when the victim was slain and giving, by a mystic communion, a special force to the contracting parties and their union.

As to the first point, the aforementioned identification with the victim must be made expressly and while the victim is still alive. In the passage just cited from Jeremiah, victim and covenant-breaker were identified after the event. Yet, while this does not prove that the identification was made during the rite itself, neither does it preclude it.[25] The careful separation made by many between taking an oath which is part of covenant-making and the "cutting of a covenant" (since one does not swear a covenant) apparently suggests to many scholars an original distinction between covenant by oath and covenant by rite.[26] But, we must ask, what is the situation in Homer? Is such a distinction made?

In the *Iliad* (2.339-44) *synthesiai* and *horkia* are juxtaposed, and this juxtaposition leads us to believe that no distinction is made, since *horkia* are the victims on which the covenanters have sworn their oaths. In the duel arrangement between Alexander and Menelaus it appears at first that the stipulations regarding the duel and the oaths are separate from the arrangements provided for Trojan and Achaeans, inasmuch as the expression "but for the others, let us swear brotherhood and oaths of faith with sacrifice"

---

[22] McCarthy, *Treaty and Covenant,* 55.

[23] E. Bikerman, *Archive d'histoire* (1950-51) 5:133-56, follows the earlier view expressed by W. R. Smith, *Religion,* 481.

[24] Livy 40.6.1-3; Curtius Rufus, 10.9.12.

[25] M. Noth, *Gesammelte Studien* 146; E. Vogt, *Biblica* 36 (1955) 565-66; Hillers, *Covenant,* 30. For the traditional interpretation of imprecations where *karat berit* in Israelite history meant "to cut a treaty," and for its similarity to the Homeric *horkia temnein,* see McCarthy, *Treaty and Covenant,* 56.

[26] D. J. McCarthy, CBQ 27 (1964) 181.

OTHER FEATURES OF HOMERIC AGREEMENTS   119

did not affect the duelists themselves. Beyond this distinction, however, *horkia pista tamômen* entailed simultaneous sacrifice and the taking of oaths, exactly as in *Il.* 2.339-41. The same is true in *Il.* 3.105 where there is no distinction between *horkia temnein* and *horkos*. The conclusion, therefore, is that the distinction made by some biblical scholars between oath-taking and oath-cutting is not applicable to Homer.

The method and the object of a sacrifice in the epics could vary. On the occasion of the single combat between Alexander and Menelaus, Agamemnon commanded that two lambs be brought, a white ram and a black ewe, one for the Sun and the other for the Earth, while a third lamb was to be sacrificed to Zeus. In addition, wine which the heralds mixed in a bowl was used while they also poured water over the covenanters in the sacrifice to effect their purification.[27] The invocation by both sides of the list of gods was a sign that the treaty involved not merely the imposition of the will of the superior but also the acceptance under oath of the will of the inferior.[28] This point effectively answers a crucial question about the nature of the suzerainty treaties, namely, whether these types of treaties can really be called treaties. The frequent mention of the guarantee of succession for the vassals' descendants could not have been a mere privilege bestowed but rather also a right that was implicitly or explicitly demanded.[29] Although the cleansing is not explicitly mentioned at this point, it is understood, since from a later reference one learns that it preceded the sacrifice. It is similarly explained a little later in the epic that Hector refused to offer libations or pray to Zeus before he had washed himself of the blood from the battle (*Il.* 6.266). While similar ritual is performed elsewhere in the *Iliad*, the object used in the sacrifice is a boar (*Il.* 19.252). When the sacrificial animals were considered cursed, as with the boar, they could not be consumed but had to be burned or otherwise disposed of.[30]

C. SUZERAINTY TREATIES

The controversy over the question of mutuality in the obligations of vassal and lord was alluded to in the previous paragraph. It stems from the fact that as a rule it was the lord who administered the oath and the vassal who swore

---

[27] *Il.* 3.270. There is something parallel in the Old Testament, at Exod. 19.11.

[28] McCarthy, *Treaty and Covenant*, 39.

[29] Korosec, *Heth. Staats.*, 90-91.

[30] While lambs, goats, heifers, water, wine, etc. were objects of sacrifice in treaty-making, other objects were used on different occasions. At the funeral of Patroclus, Achilles sacrificed sheep, swine, horses, dogs, and human beings chosen from the Trojan captives. He personally cut the throats of the victims, as Agamemnon did earlier, and poured the honey, oil, and wine that the ritual required, *Il.* 23.165. See also ARMT, 2:39.9-12; Munn-Rankin, *Iraq* 18 (1956) 90.

it. Hence there is a fundamental question as to whether the Hittite suzerainty treaties, and by the same token all such agreements, can properly be called treaties. Because of the overwhelming imbalance in these treaties in favor of the lord, the impression is given that they were nothing more than *diktats*.[31] *Diktat* types of agreements—if indeed such arrangements can even be called agreements—involve the question of consent (or the lack thereof) that determines the nature of the agreement and qualifies it as a treaty or not. This question has been answered affirmatively, though with some qualifications, by V. Korosec, who has argued convincingly that in spite of the imbalance in these treaties, the element of free consent on the part of the vassal may very well be present.[32] The care which the Hittites exercised in underscoring the obligations imposed upon the conquered people suggests that the Hittites did not consider the right of conquest sufficient but wanted the conquered to agree to the obligations proposed or imposed. Moreover, the emphasis on the mutual obligations was not riveted on the present right of conquest but allegedly on past relations, favors, honors, help, and good will, all of which were acts extended to the prospective vassal by the Great King.

Because of these many acts, the vassal was to appear as obligated to the Great King and ungrateful if he did not agree to do what he was supposed to do. Thus this donor-recipient relationship assumed not only ethical but also juristic significance. The common people were also included in these benefactions so that they too would feel flattered by them. The vassal's right to pursue an independent foreign policy was in most cases curtailed, but his right to exercise internal rule over his subjects was not. Consequently, if the vassal did not enjoy full sovereignty, he enjoyed at least partial sovereignty. Furthermore, the harms from which the lord promised to protect the vassal included those that would otherwise be wrought by the lord himself. It is clear from the treaty between Tudhaliyas IV and Ulmi-Teshub that if the lord demanded a city or a place of any kind from the vassal but did not use force to take it, the vassal's granting of the place or city to the lord did not bring the lord under the divine oath and curse. The concession presupposed the element of consent, since if Ulmi-Teshub did not wish to give it up, the king of Hatti, his lord, should not take it by force; if he did, the curses pronounced in the treaty should become operative for the lord.[33] Though the imbalance clearly favored the lord, he, too, nonetheless undertook responsibilities and

---

[31] F. Schachermeyr, *Zur staatlichen Wertung,* in Meissner's *Festschrift,* 39.

[32] Korosec, *Heth. Staats.,* 18.

[33] Korosec, *Heth. Staats.,* 29-32, 36; McCarthy, *Treaty and Covenant,* 184; Jos. 24.1-2, 23-27 contains a reference to the suzerainty treaty between Yahweh and Israel. According to it, the people of Israel must not forsake their treaty because of the gratitude due to their God for His many benefactions to Israel. The terms "lord" and "vassal" have been borrowed from feudal terminology. In essence, the Hittite state was a federated state with the Hittites as the senior partner and the allied kings the junior partners.

OTHER FEATURES OF HOMERIC AGREEMENTS 121

made promises which he was under oath and obligation to fulfill.[34] Furthermore, his very position as sovereign led him to be concerned with the welfare of his subjects and tied him to protect them if for no other reason than his self-interest. This self-motivation does not disprove the existence of mutuality of interest but rather strengthens it.

The archives of Alalakh VII have preserved two documents which relate how Alalakh had imposed a vassal relationship upon the ruler of Aleppo in the eighteenth century. The texts are important because they describe the reciprocal duties of lord and vassal. Abbael is the vassal who delivers Aleppo to Yarimlim, the lord. Abbael pledges to remain faithful, and not "take hold of another king's garment"—a figurative expression for "to recognize no other king as his lord." Conversely, Yarimlim and his descendants are bound to remain loyal to the king of Aleppo.[35]

Parity treaties were and are still made on the basis of mutual self-interest. Besides, the unilateral nature of a suzerainty treaty was not conducive to any degree of stability between lord and vassal. The lord would make such a treaty with the full knowledge that there would be absolutely nothing in the newly contracted relationships for the vassal, and that only fear would induce him to abide by it in view of the absence of any benefits. Therefore, morally as well as legally the relationship provided underpinnings for the vassal, flowing out of the self-interest of the lord. Like the medieval lord, the ancient lord must have had to respect his vassal within the context of the newly founded mutuality, for anything less than that would eventually drive the vassal to rebellion. The lord would also have to render him justice when justice was required and pay heed to some of the vassal's needs. These obligations constrained the arbitrariness of the lord, while they increased the readiness of the vassal to abide by the obligations and to make the best of the circumstances. But beyond this tacit reciprocity, there are treaties in which the obligations of the lord were explicitly spelled out.[36] Lastly, there is no

---

[34] In Gen. 9.8-17 we have a covenant between Noah and God where God is definitely the lord and Noah the vassal; yet in the covenant God binds Himself to certain promises. Likewise, in Gen. 15.7-15 God binds Himself through certain obligations to Abraham and his descendants. Even when there were no explicit obligations undertaken by a worldly lord, so that he swore to nothing, implicit obligations gave a *quid pro quo* character to the lord-vassal treaties. The treaty of Suppululiumas and Mattiwaza of Mitanni, though resembling the lord-vassal type, shows a surprising deference on the part of the king-lord of Hatti toward the lesser prince, McCarthy, *Treaty and Covenant,* 23; McCarthy, CBQ 27:179-80. About the mutual character of the covenant in Jewish history, see R. Bultmann, *Primitive Christianity* (Cleveland, 1966) 34.

[35] CAH3 2.1.32-36; G. Bucellatti, *Cities and Nations of Ancient Syria* (Rome, 1967) 46-47.

[36] Such is the agreement between the Hittite king Tudhaliyas VI and Ulmi-Teshub of Datassa, KBO 4.10. The same is true of the covenant between Yahweh and Israel where clearly Yahweh as lord gives certain pledges to His vassal Israel and binds Himself to keep

122   OTHER FEATURES OF HOMERIC AGREEMENTS

absolute model for lord and vassal treaties. Whereas in most cases only the name of the lord is mentioned in the preamble, in the treaties between Suppiluliumas and Mattiwaza of the Mitanni and between Muwattalis and Sunaššura of Kizzuwadna the names of Mattiwaza and Sunaššura along with that of the Great King are mentioned, a departure from the normal usage of suzerainty treaties. Moreover, the king of Kizzuwadna remains free of tribute, yet the subordinate position of both Mattiwaza and Sunaššura was evident since only they were bound by oaths.[37]

The rather clear distinction between the status of superior and inferior lords present in the Near Eastern treaties is absent in the Homeric epics except in a few unimportant cases. Whereas the Greek kings in the *Iliad* form an alliance with Agamemnon as their supreme commander, the position of the partners betokens a loose confederation based on the principle of independence and choice. The relation of these kings to their chief and to each other is governed by the aristocratic conventions, deviation from which was likely to cause division among the partners. Achilles withdrew from the alliance when he felt that his honor had been insulted, pledging not to return. He boldly told Agamemnon that from the beginning he had not intended to obey him in every respect. The freedom from fear with which Achilles addressed his chief bespeaks of the autonomy of the allied kings. It is very doubtful that a mere vassal would have been at liberty to speak and act in the manner of Achilles without fear of immediate and dire consequences. As it was, Agamemnon had to apologize to Achilles at the end and to promise rich rewards in order to entice Achilles back to the battlefield, only to see his efforts and offer rebuffed. By the set of rules governing the relations of the Achaean leaders, Agamemnon was not allowed to use force as a means of coercion since it was ungentlemanly to coerce another gentleman. By these same rules both commander and commanded had undertaken mutual obligations: the one to treat the other as befitted his station as king, and the other to respect and obey the authority represented by the supreme command. During the quarrel between Agamemnon and Achilles, Nestor reminded both of their assumed obligations. The commander had to be tactful in his dealings with his generals, and if he committed an error he should not feel ashamed to admit it. Achilles, on the other hand, had to show respect for authority and not to argue with and revile his commander. Once the split between the two had been patched up, Achilles resumed respect for the rules of the game by deferring to his chief. Although he was in charge of the particular

---

his promises as long as the people of Israel keep theirs; McCarthy, CBQ 27:180-82, and similarly, in the covenant between Yahweh and Noah, Gen. 9.8-17. See also Gen. 15.7-18, 2 Samuel 7.1-17. Even in Exod. 20 Yahweh's obligations are implicit.

[37] Perhaps agreement No. 1 falls in this category. Certainly the agreement between Agamemnon and the other Greek leaders seems to be of this nature. The violation of a fixed principle on the part of Agamemnon enraged Achilles. Later, Achilles bound himself voluntarily to Priam although he had definitely the upper hand.

arrangements for Patroclus's funeral, he acknowledged Agamemnon's general supremacy (*Il.* 23.49 ff.). After the funeral, Achilles similarly asked Agamemnon to command the troops to leave the funeral pyre and take their supper (*Il.* 23.159). Yet, as if to show that he was not completely subservient to Agamemnon, he made an agreement with Priam about Hector's funeral even though he suspected that Agamemnon would not like it.

Not so different is the picture that emerges from the relationship between Agamemnon and Diomedes, notwithstanding the fact that the latter seemed to rule over an area within the territory—or at least in the proximity—of Agamemnon's kingdom. It would be logical to infer that Diomedes was in a condition of dependence upon the greater king. Yet this inference would not be supported by the relationships of the two in the Trojan campaign (*Il.* 9.32 ff.), since in the slight altercation that occurred between them, Diomedes accused Agamemnon in no uncertain terms of cowardice, and vowed to ignore his recommendation to discontinue the war and return home. He also pledged to disregard the advice of his colleagues if they espoused Agamemnon's suggestion. Similarly, after the fall of Troy, Diomedes demonstrably failed to return with Agamemnon, choosing instead to travel with others (*Od.* 3.167). Despite the possession of the supreme command, Agamemnon had to listen to the opinions of the other leaders before he made his decision. He clearly followed this procedure when he kept silent and allowed the other Achaeans to answer Idaeus's peace proposals, thereby letting Idaeus see for himself their determination to continue fighting. True, he did occasionally disregard the advice of others, much to his own and everyone else's chagrin, as Nestor poignantly reminded him (*Il.* 9.108). He also periodically assumed the right to speak on behalf of the rest without prior consultation with them (*Il.* 9.135-39). But Nestor's criticism of the Achaean kings (*Il.* 2.339-41) for the lukewarmness with which they pursued their objective and Idomeneus's response to Agamemnon's inquiry regarding his intentions about the war definitely point to the loose confederate character of the Achaean alliance (*Il.* 4.266-69). The nature of the confederation and the temperament of the confederate partners were such that Agamemnon felt compelled to reassure himself periodically of the willingness of his allies to adhere to their original purpose.

One of the less important cases in which the lord-vassal relationship emerges in the *Iliad* is that of Achilles and Phoenix. But even here Phoenix seems to be motivated by affection and a sense of duty rather than by a vassal's compulsion or fear. Phoenix had earlier escaped to Peleus, who then set him over the Dolopes and charged him with the education of young

124 OTHER FEATURES OF HOMERIC AGREEMENTS

Achilles.[38] When the latter went to Troy, Phoenix followed him as his vassal and adviser. Following the quarrel between Agamemnon and Achilles, Phoenix interceded on behalf of the Achaeans, pleading with Achilles to accept the reconciliation offer. He explained that if Achilles decided to return home, Phoenix would feel bound to follow him. This feeling was the result of his own free decision rather than of coercion. Although Achilles did not seem to mind whether Phoenix stayed or accompanied him to Phthia, he did not fail to remind him of his proper position when he felt that Phoenix had overstepped his bounds by taking Agamemnon's side (*Il.* 9.612-14).

The condition prevailing in the Trojan camp conveys a similar impression of the political and military relationships there. It is true that the Trojans and their allies were more adept at keeping discipline and avoiding disputes. But whereas their unity illuminates their superior cohesion and the superior tactfulness of their commanders, it does not necessarily address the question of what the dominant type of political arrangement was. Homer refers to them as the Trojans and their allies, and describes Priam as their supreme political authority and Priam's son Hector as the supreme commander whose authority and valor are respected by all. In turn, the allies are equally respected and their contribution to the war effort is greatly appreciated. No doubt several of the Trojan allies rushed to Troy's defense because doing so coincided with their own defense interests. Others, like Othryoneus, came because they had hoped to receive, or already had received, some sort of reward for their assistance (*Il.* 13.363-74). Thus Priam, like Agamemnon, enjoyed a position of preeminence among the Trojan allies, but otherwise they do not seem to be subservient to him. Among the Trojans, as among the Achaeans, voluntarism was the cement that kept the alliance together.

---

[38] The Dolopes are not mentioned in the catalogue of ships or the catalogue of the Myrmidons (*Il.* 2.168-97). Nevertheless, they were a historical people, apparently closely connected with the Thessalians, whom Homer equally ignores. See Hdt. 7. 132; Strabo 9.5.5 (431 C), where in the quotation given (ὅς Δολόπων ἄγαγε θρασὺν ὅμιλον σφενδονᾶσαι), Strabo must have had this passage or something similar in mind. See also Apol. Rhod. 1.68. The story of Phoenix's education of Achilles is inconsistent with the legend of Achilles' education by Cheiron (*Il.* 11.832), and is another indication that the Phoenix incident is of a different origin. It shows the variety of material Homer (or whoever the writer of the *Iliad* was) had at his disposal when he composed the epic; Leaf ad *Il.* 9.484. Other scholars use the Phoenix incident as evidence of the non-unitary theory of the Homeric epics.

PART TWO

SOME COMMON CONTENTS AND OTHER FEATURES SHARED BY NEAR EASTERN AND HOMERIC TREATIES

CHAPTER FIVE

THE PEOPLE

The first part of this book dealt with structural aspects of the Near Eastern treaties and the Homeric agreements. The second part deals with some of their standard contents. In it we shall explore some of the basic stipulations set forth in the Near Eastern treaties and in their Homeric counterparts. We shall also briefly consider a few other "technical" factors or procedural matters associated with ancient treaty-making. Our analysis of the Homeric evidence will not be limited to the twenty or so agreements catalogued at the outset of this study, but will extend to whatever in the epics seems relevant to the cases at hand. Thus the present chapter opens with a discussion of the role played by the populace in the making and fulfillment of the treaties and agreements. Our discussion then turns, still in the same people-oriented vein, to their contents or stipulations concerning the disposition and treatment of fugitives. Both of these topics, as well as others taken up in the ensuing chapters, will be discussed by looking first at the Near Eastern evidence and then that of the Homeric world.

A. THE ROLE OF THE PEOPLE

So much has already been written on the subject of popular participation in Greek political life that any new effort to explore this theme in the Homeric world may seem foolhardy. No new material has appeared, and as things now stand no new material is expected. But historians continue to revisit what sources they do have, looking at the old material pertaining to Greek constitutional history in hopes that it may provide them with insights into the political problems contained in the Homeric literature and vice versa. Fortunately for our purposes, new light has been shed by a recent spate of articles on the role of the people in Homer.[1] Our present analysis proceeds in the light provided by these secondary studies, which, let it be said at the outset, generally agree that there is genuine evidence of pre-Homeric texts relating to contacts between Mycenaeans and Hittites. Thus—to reiterate a

---

[1] The following publications are given here as a sample of recent scholarship. Hans van Wees, CQ 36 (1986) 285-303; Ian Morris, *Class. Antiquity* 5 (1986) 81-138; T. Rihll, LCM 11.6.(1986) 86-91; Fritz Gschnitzer, *Festschrift für Robert Muth, Innsbrucker Beiträge zur Kulturwissenschaft* 22 (1983) 151-163; Gschnitzer, *Festschrift für Leonhard C. Franz, Innsbrucker Beiträge Zur Kulturwissenschaft* 11 (1965) 99-112; Gschnitzer, *Studien zum antiken Epos, Beiträge zur klassischen Philologie* 72 (1976) 1-21; Gschnitzer, "Konig, Rat und Volk bei Homer," *Beiträge zum Griechisch-Unterricht* 3 (1980) 1-35; A.M. Snodgrass, JHS (1974) 114-125; John Halverson, *Hermes* 113 (1985) 129-145; W. Donlan, *Historia* 22 (1973) 145-54.

128   THE PEOPLE

point made in the foregoing chapters—the possibility of the existence of
treaties between the two peoples cannot be dismissed out of hand.[2]

A major problem associated with the analysis of popular involvement and
participation practices is the very term "people."[3] While we can be fairly sure
of what the term does *not* mean in Homer, we are not always sure as to what
it does mean, though it is closely keyed to the idea of participating in the
assembly. In Homer the term does not normally include women, children,
slaves, and aliens, none of whom were members of the assembly. We can
also rest assured that while in the *Iliad* the term refers primarily to those arm-
bearing Achaeans not of aristocratic origin, among the Trojans men past the
age of bearing arms could still be included in the assembly. But even this
difference between Achaeans and Trojans may not be safe since certain
allusions, e.g., to "others" (*alloi*; *Il.* 3.94; 256), might not be limited to
those commoners who fought at Troy but rather have been intended to
include all free Achaeans who had stayed behind in Greece and even their
future generations. In the *Odyssey* the use of the term "others" alludes to the
free male population capable of bearing arms as well as those past that stage,
i.e., the participants in the Ithacan assembly (*Od.* 2.6 ff.). In both the *Iliad*
and *Odyssey*, therefore, the references to the people adumbrate some popular
participation in public affairs. The same is true of the Hittite treaty
documents, where the frequent references to the people are not always
indicative of formal popular input in the making of treaties. Nonetheless, the
references to the people in the Hittite treaties, no matter how insignificant
they might seem to be, are elements that a historian cannot afford to ignore.

The Near Eastern evidence

A few examples from the Near Eastern world should help illuminate this
complex problem. The treaty between Suppiluliumas and Mattiwaza contains
the stipulation that the treaty should be read before the king and the people of
Mitanni.[4] There is no corresponding clause for the Hittite king and his
people, a fact which demonstrates that we are dealing here with a suzerainty
treaty. Since the Hittite king was the party that granted the treaty, he was
understandably expected to respect it, for nowhere in these treaties does the
Hittite king appear to be above the law. Formally then, there was no need for
the treaty to be read before his people. On the other hand, the section which

---

[2] E. Forrer, MDOG 63 (1924) 1-24; Forrer, OLZ (1924) 113-18; J. Friedrich, KF 1.1.
(1927) 87-107; A. Goetze, OLZ 33 (1930) 285-92; F. Sommer, *Die Ahhijava Urkunden*
(Heidelsheim, 1975) passim; F. Schachermeyr, *Hethiter und Achäer* (*Mitteilungen der Altorientalischen Gesellschaft*) 9.1-2,1935; Schachermeyr, *Die ägaische Frühzeit. Vol. 5: Die
Levante im Zeitalter der Wanderunagen* (SB Wien, 1982) chap. 1; Güterbock, AJA 87 (1983)
133-38.

[3] Frequent terms denoting the common people are *demos* and *laos*.

[4] Weidner, *Polit. Dok.*, 6, 11, 19, 21, 23, 29, 33; Korosec, *Heth. Staats.*, 101.

THE PEOPLE   129

describes the historical antecedents refers to a revolt by the people of
Turmitta, Terpuziya, Hanza, and Armatana.[5] Still another clause enjoins the
people of Mitanni not to attempt uprisings against their king Mattiwaza or
his successors or to do harm to each other.[6] The treaty also dictates that
refugees from Hatti shall be apprehended by the people of Mitanni and
returned to Hatti. When, however, in accordance with the treaty, the Hittite
king Mursilis II asked his vassal and brother-in-law Mashuiluwas to come
before him to explain some infraction of the treaty, Mashuiluwas refused to
abide by the order and instead took refuge in the land of Masa. But as
Mursilis approached, Mashuiluwas fled to a different land. Mursilis
consequently asked the man who sheltered Mashuiluwas to seize and deliver
him or face the consequences. When the people of the land heard Mursilis's
threat, they seized Mashuiluwas and delivered him up.

Whether this reference is best understood by equating "people" with the
free adult males of the land or merely the aristocratic leadership is not clear,
though it certainly can be read coherently in the former sense.[7] However, in
another Hittite treaty with Mattiwaza the reference to "people" clearly extends
to the common people, that is, to the free adult males.[8] Outside of Hatti,
whenever a group is represented not by a king but by tribesmen, both the
tribal leaders and their followers are included under the rubric "people." In
other instances, the people clearly stand on a lower level.[9] In the treaty
between Suppiluliumas and Huqqanas, the prince of Hayaša and his people
are one of the signatories to the treaty.[10] Whenever vassals are threatened by
the people, the lord king could include a clause in the treaty either to show
that he would support the vassal king against the people or to win their trust
against the vassal. In either case, the stipulations of the treaties contain no
obligations of the vassal toward the people or limitation of the vassal's
power by the people. Finally, in the treaty between Ashurnirari V and
Mati'ilu of Bit-Agusi there is a definite distinction between the people and its
leaders (the nobility).[11]

---

[5] Weidner, *Polik. Dok.*, 5.

[6] Weidner, *Polit. Dok.*, 27-29.

[7] Friedrich, *Die Staatsverträge*, 1, 95-111. Mushuiluwas was from Mira (Lycia? Cilicia?),
but had been expelled by his relatives and had sought the protection of Suppiluliumas. The
latter provided him shelter and gave him his daughter as wife. He also made an agreement by
which he promised to help reinstate Mushuiluwas to the throne.

[8] Weidner, *Polit. Dok.*, 49, 55, 57.

[9] Korosec, *Heth. Staats.*, 6, 10, 57; Friedrich, *Die Staatsverträge*, 2:153.

[10] Friedrich, *Die Staatsverträge*, 2:153.

[11] McCarthy, *Treaty and Covenant*, 195-96; Weidner, AFO 8 (1934) 16 ff. The situation
among the Israelites is clearer (Exod. 19.7-9). There is no doubt that the term "people"
refers to all the people, not just the leaders.

130 THE PEOPLE

In still another type of treaty, the Hittite king Hattusilis III bound together the children (people) of the city of Ura and those of the city of Ugarit. This document involves the people of Ugarit directly, almost without reference to their king who is, however, mentioned in the preface of the treaty and in whose archives the treaty was found. In another context, the king of the city of Ugarit is not even mentioned, the treaty having been made directly between the king of Carchemish and the "men of the country of Ugarit."[12] Similarly, in the antecedent section of the treaty between Suppiluliumas and Mattiwaza it is explained that the people of Irrite (location unclear) gathered to ask for peace from the Hittite king. The same is true of the people of Harran. In both cases no kings are mentioned.[13] Similarly, the people of Wassuganni, the capital of Mitanni, contracted a treaty in which the king of the city is not included. Since it is difficult to visualize a people or town without a king or leader, we may plausibly infer that the king either had abandoned the people for reasons unknown to us, or was killed in battle, or was carried away captive by the conqueror who then concluded a peace treaty with the people whom he had defeated.[14]

Lastly, a striking example of the importance of the people in the transactions of the Near Eastern monarchs is found in the Old Testament. Either as political propaganda or as serious historical evidence the story, if true, constitutes a fascinating example of the degree to which popular reaction was taken into consideration even by an authoritarian ruler like the king of Assyria. Sennacherib, the Assyrian king, sent his cup-bearer to warn the Judaean king and the people against an alliance with Egypt. The cup-bearer addressed Hezekiah's representatives in the Judaean language, explaining his instructions. When Hezekiah's representatives asked him to speak in Aramaic, not Judaean, so that the people would not understand him, the cup-bearer countered that his master had instructed him to speak to the people as well because they were to suffer the consequences of their king's ill-advised policies (2 Kings 18.26-27). The incident seems to have occurred shortly after the death of Sargon and the accession of Sennacherib to power (ca. 705 B.C.). Taking advantage of the change in the throne of Assyria, many tributaries of Assyria sought to regain their independence. Among them was Hezekiah, who, relying upon the help of Egypt and the support of certain Philistine cities, was ready to throw off the Assyrian yoke. As Sennacherib marched against these insurrectionists, several princes hastened to make submission and pay tribute, but the Philistine cities and Judah

---

[12] Buccellati, *Cities and Nations*, 58.

[13] Weidner, *Polit. Dok.*, 47.

[14] Weidner, *Polit. Dok.*, 47. Even in treaties of parity made by strong kings references to people are not absent, whatever they are worth, Weidner, *Polit. Dok.*, 21, 113; O. Gurney, *The Hittites* (Baltimore, 1966) 115-16.

THE PEOPLE   131

continued to defy Assyria. Sennacherib attacked these Philistine cities and Hezekiah who, at the end, submitted and paid heavy tribute. But fortunately for Hezekiah, Jerusalem escaped capture as some kind of plague struck the Assyrian camp.

The limited evidence cited above shows some consideration of the people by their rulers in the making of ancient treaties, even though the parties to the treaties were for the most part the rulers themselves. Yet a puzzling discrepancy appears, for how could the people be kept out of all deliberations and decisions about their land and their fate when they somehow were deemed important enough in the final document to be held accountable—at least partially—for the faithful application of the treaty? A full explanation is not possible, but it is likely that the people did not always remain apathetic or silent spectators to the political games that affected their own lives. For example, Suppiluliumas complained in the treaty with Mattiwaza that certain non-Hittite peoples had rebelled against the rule of his father.[15] Paradoxically, the people, not the king, were blamed for the revolt. Even if we supposed that the revolt had been spearheaded by a person or persons for private reasons and that it was not spontaneous, the people must have had sufficient cause to rise in rebellion. For some unknown reason the people of Mitanni had attempted to kill Mattiwaza, the Mitanni king's son, who saved himself by escaping to his future patron, the king of the Hittites. However justified the popular insurrection might have been, the settlement between Suppiluliumas and his protégé contained a warning that similar popular actions would not be tolerated in the future, unless Mattiwaza failed to respect his oaths. Barring this eventuality, Mattiwaza would have Suppiluliumas's support in dealing with future popular uprisings. Moreover, the people were to be accountable for the apprehension of fugitives from the Hittite kingdom, particularly since such fugitives were apt to foment trouble among them.[16] The inclusion of the people in the curse section of the treaty reveals that despite the prevalence of the authoritarian systems, the people were considered an important component, if only in a restrictive sense. In other words, they were not bound to contribute positively to the fulfillment of the treaty by complying with certain stipulations such as the apprehension of fugitives but they were expected to help in the treaty application by revolting against treaty violations by their leaders.

Thus it seems clear that the people were conceived as a party to the defense mechanism devised by the ancient world to protect itself against the consequences of infractions of international compacts. Inasmuch as copies of the treaties were deposited for safekeeping in the temples, the priests of the

---

[15] Weidner, *Polit. Dok.*, 5.
[16] Weidner, *Polit. Dok.*, 23.

132   THE PEOPLE

temples could always use treaty violations as a reason for denouncing their
political leadership as impious, in order to fan popular resentment against it.
This type of reaction (resentment, discontent, etc.) could also be triggered by
the denunciation of one of the signatories by the other for supposed or real
grievances. In the Near East where religion was—and still is—the most
pervasive force, people were more concerned with religious issues than with
taxes, provided that the taxes were reasonable. An attempt to interfere with
their religion could spell disaster for the political authority, perhaps even
where the king combined the highest political office with that of archpriest.
Aware of this factor, political leaders carefully cultivated an image of piety
by participating in religious festivals, giving donations to temples,
constructing new temples, or reconstructing old ones. If the leader was
perceived as a god-fearing person, his subjects were more inclined to forgive
him even grave mistakes; otherwise, repudiation of a treaty could easily spark
a catastrophic rebellion against him inasmuch as such repudiation entailed the
violation of oaths by which the people had been declared parties to that
treaty. Pretenders to the throne, disaffected elements, opportunists, and many
others could use—or be used—on the occasion of an imagined breach to
incite the people against their leaders.[17] A signatory to a treaty, particularly a
suzerainty treaty, could ill afford to leave himself open to such a "window of
vulnerability." In addition, it was in the worldly interest of the lord to exploit
all avenues against the intransigent vassal.

The Homeric evidence

The information about the Ancient Near East shows that the people
frequently played a role in the making and execution of treaties, if sometimes
in a negative way. The evidence about the Mycenaeans is almost nil, while
the epics do not explicitly enlighten us about such matters. We are therefore
forced to analyze carefully those passages in the epics which have some
bearing on the position of the people in our effort to distill whatever we can
from them and use whatever bits of evidence we possess from the Mycenaean
world to arrive at the pertinent conclusions.

---

[17] Weidner, *Polit. Dok.,* 45, 47. It may be worthwhile to point out here the observation
that no matter how authoritarian the regimes were in antiquity they could not always
disregard with impunity the feelings of their subjects. Thus we learn that as far back as 2350
B.C. Urukagina, the last of the early Lagash rulers, attempted to build an alliance of temple
and clients (semi-free persons) palace and nobility. The attempt failed, a victim of
prevailing international conditions. Urukagina's effort aimed at redressing the complaints
of the class of commoners. A continuous process of royal, priestly, and noble land
purchases had gradually reduced much of the class of commoners to the status of clients of
the palace, temple, and noble estates, where they subsisted on rations of cereals, oil, fish,
and milk, W. W. Hallo and W. K. Simpson, *The Ancient Near East, A History* (New York,
1971) 49-50; Ignace J. Gelb, JNES 24 (1965) 230-43.

THE PEOPLE 133

The political role of the people in Homer has been variously characterized as "active," "passive," or somewhere in between. The Homeric kings, for instance, were frequently disposed to explain their actions to the people if they stood any chance of mobilizing public opinion behind them. When Chryses came seeking the release of his daughter in exchange for a rich ransom, the Achaean warriors, acting like a tragic chorus, voiced their assent to Chryses' reasonable request, bidding Agamemnon to show reverence to the priest's office (*Il.* 1.21-23). But Agamemnon chose to ignore the public reaction, only to discover soon after that ὀργὴ λαοῦ φωνὴ θεοῦ, to use the modern Greek adage. The plague which subsequently decimated the Greek camp forced Agamemnon to call the people to an assembly in order to find some solution. Calchas, who was asked to pronounce the prophecy, bade the Achaeans return the girl as soon as possible if they wished to see the end of the plague (*Il.* 1.109). No matter how hateful the prophet's injunction might have been, Agamemnon could not ignore it this time (*Il.* 1.117, βούλομ᾽ ἐγὼ λαὸν σόον ἔμεννaι ἤ ἀπολέσθαι), since there was no other way out. Unfortunately, he undermined his wise decision to comply with the prophet's prophecy by a foolish act of pettiness and defiance of all accepted practices. In consequence, Achilles warned him that his course of action enjoyed no popular support.

Agamemnon's decision to replace the loss of Chryses by seizing Achilles' concubine ran contrary to the prevailing custom, provoking an angry response from Achilles as well as from the other Achaeans. This incident provided an opportunity for an otherwise insignificant person to become immortalized by seemingly expressing the *communis opinio* against Agamemnon (*Il.* 2.225 ff.). Although the manner in which Thersites made his criticism might have been crude, the criticism itself seems to have reflected the feelings of many in the crowd. Thersites' aspersions against Agamemnon's selfishness and greediness were capped by an exhortation to the Achaeans not to obey Agamemnon any longer but to return home, thereby abandoning Agamemnon in Asia Minor. The implication is clear: without the people—here defined as all warriors, irrespective of class origins—Agamemnon could not have accomplished his objectives, either the capture of Troy in punishment for Helen's abduction or the satisfaction of looting (*Il.* 2.236 ff.). Thersites' criticism sounded the trumpet of revolution, but it was timely silenced by the quick intervention of Odysseus. Odysseus's rough treatment and ridicule as well as his quick action against Thersites supports the view that the latter had struck a sensitive popular chord. Clearly, the affair suggests that, uninformed though we might be about the role of people in the late Mycenaean or the Dark Ages, we cannot deny the possibility that commoners (warriors of non-aristocratic origins in whatever capacity, be they full-fledged warriors or auxiliaries) made a claim to express their view on issues of general interest. We shall return later to the incident

134 THE PEOPLE

of Thersites. In the meantime, let us investigate some other evidence in the epics that points more clearly to the role of people in the Homeric epics.

In *Il.* 6.193-95 the mythical hero Bellerophon performed the labors demanded of him by the king of Lycia and drew the king's admiration. Thus, the king, instead of killing the hero as he had been advised to do, decided to give him his daughter in marriage along with half of his kingdom. At the same time the Lycian people apportioned a *temenos* (plot of land) from the best portion of the land for the use of Bellerophon. The *temenos* in this case is described as a choice piece of land consisting of a tract of orchard and plough-land. In a second case involving a *temenos* (*Il.* 9.574-80), the Aetolian hero Meleager abstained from the war against the neighbors of the Aetolians, the Curetes, because he had been angered for some reason by his fellow Aetolians. The war, however, was not going well for the Aetolians, and the elders came and pleaded with Meleager to change his mind and help the Aetolians in their hour of distress, promising him a great gift of land, a *temenos* of fifty acres (*gyae*), half of which would consist of vineland and the other of plough-land. Again we have here a promise of the best land available, and again it is the people who dispose of the land, for we are to believe that the elders acted as the spokesmen of the people. In addition, this second case shows that it was not only the king who received a *temenos* from the people in the Homeric epics, but also any other important person who served the people in some prominent capacity. In the third case we shall consider, *Il.* 20.184-85, Achilles meets Aeneas in battle and mocks him, as many Homeric heroes customarily did: "How do you dare meet me on the battlefield?" Achilles asks. "You do so, perhaps, in the hope that you will eventually become king of the Trojans? But such a hope is futile because Priam has many sons (184). Or have perhaps the Trojans promised you a *temenos*, a beautiful tract of orchard and of arable land for you to enjoy if you kill Achilles?" We have an almost identical case here to the first, that of Bellerophon. Here as there, a *temenos* is mentioned apart from the office of the king; here again the Trojan people are the givers (*Trôes tamon*).

In all three instances at least two principles become evident. The first principle is that (1) a *temenos* does not always fall as share to the king alone, as is usually the case, but that it may also be given to other prominent personalities as reward for their extraordinary services to the community. The above instances also show that (2) the owner of the land is not the king but the people and that the people dispose of the *temenos*. Does that mean that the people in the Homeric epics stand legally above the king or that the king owes his office to the people? Does the disposing of the *temenos* by the people mean that the king serves only as the representative of the people and that the people compensate him for his efforts on their behalf? Gschnitzer

THE PEOPLE   135

seems to think so, although others are not willing to go that far.[18] Gschnitzer points to the existence of a Linear B tablet [Er 312] from Pylos (ca. 1200 B.C.) that mentions one *temenos* in relation to the *wanax* and another for the *lawagetas* (army-chief). The *temenos* of the *wanax* is at least three times as large as that of the *lawagetas*, and both *temenê* are considerably larger than those of other functionaries. No mention of the people is made in this tablet but other tablets show that the *damos* (community) had sufficient land at hand which it could bestow (*onata*) upon certain persons.

The Pylos tablets support the existence of a remarkable tradition from the Mycenaean times down to the times of the Homeric compositions, a period of more than half a millennium, if we accept the possibility that the Pylos tablets may mirror a practice of land distribution already in operation before the inscribing of the tablets. Naturally, the question of whether the three Homeric references cited above represent practices from the poet's time or are simply archaisms incorporated into the epic becomes pertinent at this point. In all three cases the reference to events that supposedly happened before the time of the speaker supports, at least on the surface, the view in favor of archaisms. On the other hand, all three passages are considered relatively late in the composition of the *Iliad*. In particular, the episode between Diomedes and Glaucus is considered one of the latest sections of the epic. But the epic does not make any other mention of the origins of *temenos*, and thus it does not provide any alternative to the ostensible archaisms which signify the existence of a different practice at the time of the author(s).[19] Thus from this limited evidence we may conclude that the people played an important role in political affairs long before the composition of the Homeric epics.

The cases just cited are not the only evidence in the epics in support of the viewpoint associated with the people's importance. Turning to the *Odyssey*, we find a fourth case in a late passage (*Od.* 7.146 ff.) that has the same kind of context as the ones in the *Iliad*, in spite of the absence of any mention of a *temenos*. Odysseus had appeared in the palace of the Phaeacian Alcinous seeking help and protection, finding Alcinous surrounded by the prominent Phaeacians (ἡγήτορες ἠδὲ μέδοντες) gathered for dinner. Odysseus threw himself at the queen's feet and begged her and the banqueters for help. He also wished them all happiness and that they hand down to their children the wealth and *geras* that the people (*dêmos*) had granted them. Odysseus meant by *geras* the material compensations they had received from the people in return for their services on the people's behalf in the exercise of their office.

---

[18] *Od.* 7.147-152; Gschnitzer, *Beiträge zum Griechisch-Unterricht*, 3-7; Kirk, *The Iliad*, 2, ad 6.192-95. For some of the complexities see also A. Andrewes, *The Greeks* (New York, 1978) 15-51; Walter Donlan, *The Aristocratic Ideal in Ancient Greece* (Lawrence, Kansas, 1980) xi-34.

[19] Gschnitzer, *Beiträge zum Griechisch-Unterricht,* 5.

136   THE PEOPLE

The *geras* is here an inclusive expression that encompassed special grants
such as the *temenos*. Odysseus thus expressed the wish that all present, the
king and the elders, may be blessed to pass on to their descendants not only
their private property, but also the office and the emoluments derived from
that office. Thus it becomes evident that in the Mycenaean and Dark Age
periods private and public inheritance were linked with family position.[20]
    Still another passage in the *Odyssey* points to the importance of the
people (*Od.* 13.7). Odysseus has just finished the narrative of his adventures;
his listeners remain spellbound. Alcinous then assures Odysseus of a well-
provisioned return to his homeland. Already the Phaeacians have supplied
Odysseus with many gifts, but Alcinous now makes an additional appeal to
the elders that they each give Odysseus a tripod and a cauldron. Then in a
stunning twist he assures them that the people would compensate them for
their expense. Otherwise, it would have been an oppressive burden for them
to have to be so generous without any requital. Obviously, the prominence
that kings and elders enjoyed constrained them occasionally to great
generosity. This was part of the obligation of their office. But since there
was no special fund from which they could be compensated for extraordinary
expenses so incurred, these had to be defrayed by the community in the name
of which the generosity was extended.
    Another passage, this one from the *Iliad*, carries us a bit further. In *Il.*
22.111 ff. we see Hector engaging in a conversation with himself as he faces
Achilles for the last time. Torn by fear for his honor, he asks himself
whether he should use this encounter with Achilles to bring about a final
peace between the combatant camps. He could, so he thinks, meet Achilles
unarmed and promise him the return of Helen with all her possessions.
Indeed, he could do even better. He could promise the Achaeans the delivery
of half of the treasures of the city of Troy and later try to extract from the
Trojans the γερούσιον ὅρκον that they would conceal nothing and that they
would divide everything in half with the Achaeans (*Il.* 22.119).
    Does the reference to the oath imply that the elders of the Trojans ought
to swear the oath in the name of all the Trojans and see to its fulfillment, or
does the passage mean that each Trojan would take the oath? The latter seems
more appropriate here inasmuch as the possessions lie in the hands of each
Trojan, who has also the opportunity either to share them equally with the
Achaeans or to hide them. It is obviously easier so to interpret the passage
rather than believe that the elders would swear the oath. In the former case
γερούσιος ὅρκος is a terminus technicus alluding to the oath that the elders
normally took either when they assumed the position as elders or once every
year. The oath held them to the fulfillment of certain tasks, among them

---

[20] Gschnitzer, *Beiträge zum Griechisch-Unterricht*, 5-6.

THE PEOPLE 137

perhaps the obligation to administer the communal property in a certain manner and not defraud the communal treasury. This oath Hector thought to extract from the Trojans (Τρωσίν). The oath obviously contained features applicable to the circumstance Hector mulled over. The exact features are difficult to know, but such an oath fits well in this passage, especially if we bear in mind that only the formal features of the elders' oath are meant here. If this interpretation is correct, what we have here is an oath which underscored the character of the elders' office as a public function on behalf of the community.[21]

What about the role of the people in connection with the assemblies described by the epics? Did the people exercise any influence in the Homeric assemblies? Usually the announcement of such a meeting was made by the heralds, normally in the morning. Soon afterward the people were depicted as going to the assembly place in droves. As a rule, the leadership of the assembly belonged to the king who was instrumental in calling it. In exceptional circumstances, the assembly could meet without the king (as in Ithaca). In such exceptional cases the summons for the meetings was sent out by some other prominent person. Achilles in Book 2 of the *Iliad* called the assembly and explained the reason for doing so, although Agamemnon was present and was the commander-in-chief. In Book 2 of the *Odyssey* Telemachus summoned the assembly and it was he who explained the reason for it. In other cases, when something extraordinary occurred, the people did not need to wait for a call to the assembly; they themselves rushed to an assembly-meeting. Thus when the Ithacans learned of the suitors' massacre (*Od.* 24.413 ff.), they took or sent the corpses home (420) and then proceeded en mass to the assembly and began deliberations about what had transpired. Of course, assemblies of the latter type are rare in the epics. That they are rare is illustrated by the words of the elderly Aegyptius on the occasion of the assembly called by Telemachus (*Od.* 2.15.ff.) "Listen to what I tell you, Ithacans. Never have we held an assembly (*agorê*) or a meeting (θῶκος, *Od.* 2.25; more about this later) since the day when goodly Odysseus departed with the ships for Troy. Who has called us together now? Who among the old or young has felt the need for a meeting? Has he heard some news of an approaching army? If so, he has to tell us exactly, since he was the first to hear of this event. Or is there some other public matter (δήμιον) on which he wishes to address us?"[22] At this point Telemachus got up to explain that

---

[21] Gschnitzer, *Beiträge zum Griechisch-Unterricht*, 13-14.

[22] The term *dêmios* denotes something of public concern and in this sense the term points to the fact that the last and appropriate subject in political life is not the king himself, but the community, the *dêmos*. The term *phêmis* is what one says, a rumor, an expression, a statement. In this sense the word means also a decision and the place where the decision is made, that is, the assembly. See also Gschnitzer, *Festschrift für R. Muth*, n. 25; Roger A. de

138 THE PEOPLE

private matters had forced him to summon the assembly. He asked of the assembly to advise him how to put an end to the deleterious situation at his home which, if allowed to continue, threatened to exhaust his paternal property. Normally, the assembly occupied itself with public matters, but when a person was in dire straits, he could turn to the assembly with the understanding that the problem was of the type in which the assembly could offer help.

From this discussion it becomes clear that the Homeric assembly does not serve merely as a rubber-stamp machine for royal or council decisions. One turned to the assembly for counsel and help. The topics before the assembly were discussed freely and openly and bitter exchanges were not unusual (*Il.* 9.32 ff.). Assembly proceedings may provide a clue as to the development of the institution of debate in the assembly. First, no one could get up and speak in the assembly unless he asked for and was given the scepter by the herald. The scepter was the symbol of authority for kings, judges, heralds, prophets, and served all those who had been invested with permanent or temporary authority which was often conceived as having a divine origin.[23] What does it then mean that one could speak in the assembly only with the scepter in hand? In a practical way it meant that the leader of the meeting delegated to the herald his authority to grant the right to speak or deny it, and that only one person at a time could enjoy that right. Obviously, this is important for the orderly conduct of any meeting. Also obviously, the king was under an obligation to grant the right of speaking to one who was entitled to that right; those entitled to that right were the king's councilors, as we shall see.

The king also possessed a second scepter, which he could use to exercise his right to speak whenever he felt so inclined. This holding of one scepter by the king and another by the herald indicates that originally the right to speak in the assembly was monopolized by the king and his instrument, the herald, who stood by the king ready to help him with his loud voice.[24] If this view is correct, it follows that the assembly of this early time was a rubber-stamp institution, voicing simply its approval of the king's proposals, not much different from the Roman comitia. When the king wanted to make an exception or wanted to give somebody the right to speak, the herald was allowed to give this person the scepter so that he symbolically occupied the position of the herald. But in the course of time the practice of giving the scepter to others was generalized, with the result that the right to speak devolved upon the elders of the king. They are the ones in the Homeric

---

Laix, *Probouleusis at Athens: A Study of Political Decision-Making* (Berkeley and Los Angeles, 1973) 5-7.

[23] *Il.* 2. 100-109; G. Stegakis, *Historia* 15 (1966) 408-19; P. Karavites, RIDA 34 (1987) 44-45, 68-69; J.A.O. Larsen, CP 44 (1949) 165.

[24] Gschnitzer, *Beiträge Zum Griechisch-Unterricht,* 19.

THE PEOPLE   139

assemblies who speak incessantly, while the rest of the people listen silently, as the famous scene in Book 2 of the *Iliad* shows (2.185 ff.). On this occasion Agamemnon made a trial of the army which resulted in a mad rush to the ships. Under these circumstances, Agamemnon passed on his scepter, i.e. the leadership of the assembly, to Odysseus with the authorization to bring back the Achaeans to the place of assembly. Odysseus accomplished this task by addressing the leaders in friendly words and cautioning them to beware of Agamemnon's wrath. Instead they should wait until they understood what Agamemnon really had in mind (198 ff.). In contrast, Odysseus conducted himself roughly toward the commoners, smiting them with scepter and staff (an act indicative of the multiple uses of these instruments) and saying to them: "Miserable people, remain seated and listen to what others, better than you, have to say. You are weak and unfit for war, counting neither in war nor in the council (*boulê*, not *agorê*)." At the end the Achaeans took their places in the assembly and only Thersites complained and behaved in a disorderly manner (οὐ κατὰ κόσμον), i.e., he not only said ugly things about Agamemnon but he also spoke out of order, without permission. This is the picture presented by the conservative poet, whose views must have found response among his listeners. But the Thersites incident could also represent a timid challenge to the elders by those among the people in Homeric society who resented the elders' monopoly on speaking out. Perhaps some among the common people felt that they had intelligence without adequate rights and hence resented the silence to which they were condemned. Thersites dared (ἀκριτόμυθε, 246) to speak out, even though he did not have that right. Yet even Odysseus had to admit that Thersites did not lack intelligence (λιγύς περ ἐὼν ἀγορητής, 246). His main fault might have been that he was ahead of his time. Be that as it may, the picture we have drawn so far is that of a general assembly of men who, for the most part, listen but do not have the right to speak. But what about the Council of Elders?

Since the Council of Elders has been repeatedly mentioned, it might be useful to note its relation to the assembly.[25] In the classical and Hellenistic times council and assembly worked generally together. The assembly fundamentally decided upon subjects that had been prepared and proposed by the council (*probouleuma*).[26] Something similar frequently happened in

---

[25] Gschintzer, *Festschrift Leonhard C. Franz, Innsbrucker Beiträge*, 99-112 considers the Homeric kings elders. They serve the same role that the Phaeacian kings served in Phaeacia. R. Drews, *Basileus, The Evidence for Kingship in Geometric Greece* (New Haven, 1983) follows a similar argument. See also de Laix, *Probouleusis at Athens*, 5-7.

[26] De Laix, *Probouleusis at Athens*; P. J. Rhodes, *The Athenian Boule* (Oxford, 1972) 52-53; B. Keil, *Griechische Staatsaltertümer*, 2nd ed. (Leipzig, 1923) 346 ff.; Gschnitzer, *Festschrift für R. Muth*, 152; Gschnitzer, *Beiträge zum Griechisch-Unterricht*, 21; Larsen, *CP* 44 (1949) 166; 1 Kings 12 presents a similarity. The people make a request of the king

140   THE PEOPLE

Homer. The kings first called the council together and then called the assembly. In *Il.* 7.327 the Achaean assembly rejected the proposal about compensation from the Trojans for Helen but accepted the truce for the burial of the dead. We hear nothing here about the council, but the council had actually held a meeting the evening before and had agreed with Nestor's proposal that the Achaeans should not fight the next day but rather should (1) pick up the corpses and bury them, and that they should (2) strengthen the defenses of their camp (*Il.* 7.327 ff.). The same night the Trojans held a gathering (*agorê*) in the citadel near Priam's doors. Unfortunately, neither of the two meetings is described in detail. Nonetheless, one is led to believe that the Achaean gathering of the army the day after the council convened was for the purpose of ratifying and implementing the decisions reached the day before.[27] Another example of cooperation between council and assembly in the sense of a *probouleutic* proceeding is in *Od.* 7.189 ff., 226 ff., where the council of the Phaeacians convened as was customary in the evening at the royal palace to decide about Odysseus's return.

Exceptions to the rule are not lacking. The assembly can deliberate and decide on topics not previously discussed by the council. At first glance it seems that a good example is the assembly summoned by Telemachus. Yet the council is not generally by-passed. Looking closer, we see that in such cases when, for whatever reason, the council did not meet before the assembly, the two met together, in a peculiar sort of joint session. When such a meeting occurred the council sat in the middle of the assembly and deliberated, reaching its decision with the more or less passive assistance of the assembly. In effect, the discussion in the assembly was carried on among the elders, and it usually happened that the elders came to a resolution. Only in this manner would the decision of the assembly be valid. The elders sat close together in the assembly on special seats with the king in their midst. Hence they acted somewhat as a presiding committee in the middle of the assembly, although an assembly could also meet without the king. In that case, the leadership was provided by the council itself, with the oldest among them serving as the chairman (*Od.* 2.15 ff.).

However, it must be conceded that the foregoing description of the Homeric "parliamentary procedures" is based on textual references that are neither numerous nor sufficiently clear. All that can be asserted with certainty is that the elders had fixed seats in the assembly place. For example, we are told (*Od.* 8.4 ff.) that there was a permanent gathering place for the Phaeacians near the ships. King Alcinous and his guest Odysseus took their places there so that Alcinous could present the wishes of Odysseus before the assembly. They both sat on "polished stones" while the herald in the city

---

who refused to answer until he consulted the council of elders first. It was unfortunate that Rehoboam chose to disregard their advice.

[27] *Il.* 7.327 ff.; Gschnitzer, *Festschrift für Robert Muth,* 152.

THE PEOPLE 141

called the people to an assembly. Soon the assembly places and seats were filled with those who came, ἔμπληντο ἀγοραί τε καὶ ἕδραι, *Od.* 8.16. Were there stone seats for all the participants? The passage seems to indicate there were, although one gets the impression that to provide everybody with a stone seat for an assembly which did not meet very often might have been a great expense. A clearer picture is supplied by the famous "court trial" scene depicted on Achilles' shield, in which "the people come in droves to the assembly place" (*Il.* 18.497 ff.). Both contestants are present and argue their cases in front of the people, among whom each of the contestants found support. In the course of the trial the heralds held the people back (503), while "the elders sat on polished stones in a sacred circle, holding the scepter of the heralds in their hands." With scepter in hand the elders would occasionally stand up and give judgment, each taking his turn.

In this picture it is clear that the "polished stones" lay in the "middle" of the assembly and that they were occupied only by the elders. It is equally clear that it was only the elders (with the exception of the two contestants) who spoke out or passed judgment. But the final verdict lay with the people, although there is no further elaboration at this point. The important feature in this court scene is the depiction of the assembly, in which the elders are seated in the middle of the people who stood or sat on the ground. But then one may perhaps argue that the picture of an assembly for the purpose of a trial may not be typical of the political assemblies. Even so, the picture of this assembly helps us understand better the earlier assembly meeting (*Od.* 8.4-17), that is, the reference to stone seats on which Alcinous and Odysseus sat, as well as the dual term, ἀγοραί τε καὶ ἕδραι (*Od.* 8.16). Something similar is indicated by the assembly of the Pylians (*Od.* 3.31), although in contrast the designation of another assembly as an *agorê* of the Phaeacians (*Od.* 6.266 ff.) is murky. On the other hand, the reference to the assembly in Ithaca is relevant and clear: Telemachus "sat in his father's seat, and the elders made place for him." Here also the elders have their seats next to one another; they are not scattered throughout the crowd (*Od.* 2.14).

We should now return to a passage cited earlier in a different context (*Od.* 15.465 ff.). In the scene described in this passage, the Great Hall in the royal palace of Syria is empty since the young son of the king was gone, kidnapped by the unfaithful female slave. The king and the elders (that is the meaning of ἀνδρῶν δαιτυμόνων) had gone ἐς θῶκον ... δήμοιό τε φῆμιν, to the council at the people's place of debate. Significantly, in order for them to go to the assembly place, they had to leave the palace where the meetings of the elders normally were held.[28] The *thôkos* in this case can be nothing

---

[28] *Od.* 15.465 ff.; Gschnitzer, *Beiträge zum Griechisch-Unterricht*, 23; in the Epic of Gilgamesh people and elders are summoned at the market place where Gilgamesh spoke to

142   THE PEOPLE

else but the meeting of the elders in the middle of the assembly seated in their designated places, as we have seen from the previous references. The dual term ἀγοραί τε καὶ ἕδραι corresponds here to the abstract words θῶκος ... δήμοιό τε φῆμιν.

It is in the same sense that we should understand the statement of the elderly Aegyptius (Od. 2.26) that since the departure of Odysseus there had been in Ithaca neither ἀγορή nor θῶκος. True, there might be an alternative meaning here, namely, a regular meeting of the elders in the palace, something that had not happened during the absence of Odysseus. Nevertheless, the reference in Od. 15.465-70 makes it clear that not only were the elders seated in the midst of the assembly enjoying special places, but also they formed a quasi-presiding committee of the assembly. The positioning of the council of elders in the middle of the assembly brings to mind similar situations in the constitutions of the classical and Hellenistic times, when the presiding committee of the council presided also over the assembly, as happened for instance in Athens with the fifty prytaneis. The committee of the fifty prytaneis formed a committee within the assembly; they obviously enjoyed a special sitting arrangement; they most probably consulted each other when need arose; and they exercised the chairmanship of the meeting. In special assembly meetings such as that in which ostracism was decided, instead of the prytaneis the whole council of five hundred together with the archons had the leadership of the assembly. That is obviously a remnant from the past. So it seems that originally in Athens and throughout most of Greece the council of elders had the leadership of the assembly meetings along with the king, when kings still existed.[29]

What does all of the above mean for our subject? The evidence shows that council meetings took place in the assembly before the ears and eyes of the common people. How important this is for the future process of democratization of Greek life needs no belaboring. But what about the role of the assembly? What is its role in the decision-making process? Does it have any role? Does it only serve as a forum for the airing of the issues without further legal weight and real power? Does the king decide at the end by

---

them. In this assembly, the elders are the ones who speak out against Gilgamesh's proposed enterprise; N. K. Sandars, ed., The Epic of Gilgamesh (Baltimore, 1972) 73 ff.

[29] Similar cases are found in the Ancient Near East. If the Sumerian myths and epics echo an earlier state of affairs, then the institution of the assembly may be as old or older than kingship itself. In the cosmic state of the myths, the chief god ruled his pantheon at the pleasure of the large assembly of the other gods, including a sort of a senate of the senior gods. The epics also show the city-state with a kind of bicameral legislature. Thus Gilgamesh, opposed by the senate of Uruk, appealed to the assembly of the younger arm-bearing men to secure his people's consent for war; see Sandars, ed., The Epic of Gilgamesh, 70 ff. The incident suggests a similarity with King Rehoboam of Israel (1 Kings 12), and Il. 7.237 ff.; T. Jacobsen, "The Early Political Development in Mesopotamia," ZA NF 18 (1957) 91-140. See also de Laix, Probouleusis at Athens, 7; Mogens H. Hansen, The Athenian Assembly (Oxford, 1987) 16-48.

THE PEOPLE   143

himself or together with the elders? Modern scholars have been cautious regarding the importance and the role of the Homeric assembly as well as the effectiveness of the Council of Elders. In his treatment of the assembly and the Council of Elders, A. Andrewes has characterized them as indefinite institutions. In the *Iliad*, he has asserted, the assembly was a simple convention, and in the *Odyssey* it was marked by inactivity and ineffectiveness.[30] Yet, under normal circumstances, the king felt compelled to communicate his decision to the people once he had consulted his council. If the assembly reacted adversely, he could rethink his former decisions. His only concern was the trust of his followers. Thus Andrewes's effort to minimize the institution of the assembly stops short of dismissing the political importance of the will of the people. V. Ehrenberg, on the other hand, appears more certain. In his view, the Homeric assemblies had no right to initiate legislation or even to discuss it.[31] Their right was limited to an affirmative or negative answer to the question put before them by the sovereign. As he observes, this claim is supported by evidence from the epics. For instance, when Achilles sent Patroclus off to stem the Trojan tidal wave that threatened to overwhelm the Achaeans he urged his Myrmidons not to forget the threats they had formerly hurled at the Trojans, and reminded them how they had upbraided him during his anger and his abstinence from the war. Now they had the chance to show their valor (*Il.* 16.200 ff.). This incident may be cited to demonstrate the ineffectiveness of the popular wishes in view of the leader's obduracy that kept them so long from the fighting. But it may also be interpreted as suggesting just the opposite: despite their criticism of Achilles, the Myrmidons must have understood full well the reason for their leader's conduct. The statement of Thersites in Book 2 and that of the elders in the council in Book 9 of the *Iliad* strengthen the assumption that Achilles' rejection, though strong, was not atypical. More important, at least on the surface, is Achilles' rejection of the reconciliatory proposals without prior consultation with his Myrmidons, since the Myrmidons' criticism of Achilles in Book 16 (200 ff.) suggests that they favored reconciliation. The same disregard of the Myrmidons is repeated when Achilles, raving with anger over Patroclus's death, hurried to participate in the battle. Achilles' attitude tends to corroborate the "negative" side of the people's role in the formulation of important public policy. The poet seems to be pointing to an important lesson here. Achilles' angry reaction to his

---

[30] A. Andrewes, *Greek Society* (London, 1971) 46; H. Jeanmaire, *Couroi et Courètes*, 95, 245, 252, 264.

[31] Ehrenberg, *The Greek State*, 40 ff. For a different view see Finley, *The World of Odysseus*, 74-106. See also J. Aubonnet, *Aristote, Politique* (Paris, 1971) 265-66; Vlahos, *Les Sociétés*, 126; M. P. Nilsson, *Homer and Mycenae* (London, 1933) 17; C. G. Thomas, *Historia* 15 (1966) 387.

144 THE PEOPLE

Myrmidons' advice was a violation of existing social conventions. For disregarding the popular voice he subsequently paid dearly by suffering the loss of Patroclus, just as Agamemnon had already paid by suffering repeated military humiliation and tremendous loss of life.

The secondary literature on the importance in the epics of the assembly as an institution is extensive and sometimes bewildering. In spite of the wide variety of views that have been proposed, the Near Eastern evidence as well as analogies with other times strongly suggests that the voices of the people could not be ignored with impunity. After reviewing this literature one must decide just what it demonstrates. But in doing so one should bear in mind that the king received his *temenos* from the community, and that whenever the elders met at the royal palace they ate and drank, not at the expense of the king but at the expense of the people.[32] Why then all this expense of the king in time and money? Why the frequent meetings of the council? Why the less frequent meetings of the assembly? Why all these deliberations if they were nothing more than constitutional formalities, as some scholars believe, with the king being the only real fountain of decisions? Obviously something is awry in this view, a suspicion that increases the more closely one looks at the historical developments in Greece. The constitutional trends after the epics show that kingship became increasingly weak whereas the council and later the assembly became increasingly strong. Consequently, one cannot fail to notice that assembly and council enjoyed considerable influence in the Homeric times (the Dark Ages and perhaps earlier), while kingship was becoming an endangered institution. The difficulties that Agamemnon faced with his elders and his army point to the weaknesses of the Homeric kingship. Similarly, after the massacre of the suitors Odysseus does not try to rule against the wishes of the people in Ithaca but must come to an understanding with the Ithacans.

How can we then justify the views of those who support the theory of the supremacy of the royal authority? It is true that the assembly in the epic does not appear to be vocal. But the assembly does appreciate a nice argument and does express at the end of a speech its agreement or disagreement, on the basis of which king and council often act. When the elders do not agree among themselves there is no resolution of the problem under consideration, and the assembly dissolves, or even worse, divides itself into two camps, each bent upon following its own course, a situation that may lead to civil strife (*Od.* 24.413-468; 3.137-158). Since at this time no majority principle was applicable, failure to reach a decision probably produced a stalemate and inaction in the assembly. At the end, barring civil war, the impasse must have been resolved through persuasion or through an impressive

---

[32] Gschnitzer, *Beiträge zum Griechisch-Unterricht,* 6-9.

THE PEOPLE 145

demonstration by the dominant majority whereby some compromise was achieved.

In *Il.* 7.400 ff. the Trojan envoy brought peace proposals to the Achaeans. Unfortunately, the details of this episode escape us, but we are apprised that the envoy found the Achaeans in an assembly (*agorê*) near the ships of Agamemnon (382) and imparted his proposals to them. No one at first said anything, but when Diomedes broke the silence by recommending rejection of the proposals, everyone cheered. Agamemnon then turned to the envoy and said: "You hear the answer of the Achaeans, with which I concur." Could he have disagreed? Could he have rejected the decision of the assembly at this point as he had done in the case of Chryses? Busolt says that he could have, if the proposals were in his interest.[33] The decision of the assembly was not binding upon the king. But is this true? In the story which is part of the Trojan cycle, Agamemnon did sacrifice his daughter for the sake of the common interest. What is then the king's interest in the Homeric world? Is it something above himself and his family? But let us assume that the king would not do anything contrary to his interest, whatever that is; that he is the king—as indeed he is—and that in practice no one can force him to do something against his will. However, the question here is whether in making his decisions he depends on the approval of others. Thus one perhaps should ask not whether resolutions of the assembly are effective with the approval of the king, but rather how far the king could decide on his own. One can argue that the epic king can disregard what the council or assembly suggested (as in the case of Chryseis, who was after all Agamemnon's personal property), but there is no example that the king did something to which the council or the assembly had refused agreement.[34] Furthermore, one could argue that the epic associates kingship with the gods, especially Zeus. How does then this notion of divine sovereignty harmonize with the circumvention of the power of the king? The answer is simple: the one does not exclude the other.

Finally, there is no need to belabor the obvious fact that by its nature epic poetry deals primarily with the extraordinary feats of prominent people. It is natural that prominent personalities will figure prominently in the epic, whereas common folk and their actions will generally be ignored. During the Homeric battles the activities of the leading personalities are described in detail, while, on the other hand, the actions of the non-aristocratic warriors are either ignored or passed over very quickly. But this internal requirement of the epic should not lead us to assume that the assemblies were equally unimportant in the Homeric world.

---

[33] G. Busolt, *Griechische Staatskunde* (Munich, 1920) 336 ff.; Larsen, CP 44 (1949) 167.

[34] Gschnitzer, *Beiträge zum Griechisch-Unterricht*, 29.

146   THE PEOPLE

What is surprising in the epic is that Homer did not mention any bureaucratic institutions when he described the meetings of the elders or the assembly. Everything is arranged orally. At first one has the impression that the debates were improvisations of the moment, not planned in accordance with established formalities and procedures. Yet the frequent references to heralds who summoned the assemblies and to other significant details point to the existence of institutional (i.e., not improvised) meetings that follow some sort of agenda.[35] Unfortunately, it is not known whether minutes of the meetings were kept by the scribes or if everything was committed to memory. No evidence exists of written records. Nonetheless, it is very likely that certain texts and documents were written before they were read publicly, since writing must have been known from the time of the Minoan Linear A, long before the transition to the alphabet. We may conjecture that the reference by Nestor to *synthesiae* might denote some written text while the various fixed *horkoi* of the Achaeans and Trojans might have been standard texts. Again, though no tangible evidence can be produced to buttress the assumption that there were written records of the meetings, the assumption is eminently compatible with the Near Eastern treaties we have, especially their long and complicated sections of curses.

For instance, some kind of role played by the common people is suggested by the theodicy implicit in the Near Eastern swearing of the oaths and in the Homeric poems, as well as by the belief in collective punishment as inflicted by the plague of Mursilis's time and the similar plague that befell the Achaeans. Once the opinion prevailed among the people that a group punishment was due to some sort of divine wrath, the leader could not thereafter ignore the feelings of his people. On the contrary: the people expected their leader to move quickly to redress the existing grievance against the culprit so that the offended god would lift his or her wrath. It was no poetic accident that Achilles, complying with the divine advice, summoned the people to an assembly to deliberate about the proper response to the destructive plague. It was fitting that the people be summoned, since it was the popular sentiment that Agamemnon had earlier flouted with his erratic conduct (*Il.* 1.22). Even if Chryseis was his personal property, what happened during the plague affected all directly; consequently, all had a stake in determining what to do about the plague.

---

[35] Telemachus adjured the people in the name of Olympian Zeus and Themis, who summon the people to, and dismiss them from the assembly (*Od.* 2.68-69). The appeal to the two gods connected with the proceedings of the assembly hint at some format. *Il.* 19.40 Erbse *ad loc.* hint at some procedural matter which Achilles, in his haste, failed to follow.

Summary

In conclusion, the evidence from the Ancient Near East shows that the people played a role in the making and execution of treaties, if only in a negative way. In the epics, meetings of the council and the assembly were nothing strange. On some occasion the king and the council held their sessions in the palace. On others, council and assembly met together with the elders seated in a circle in the middle of the meeting. The common people did not speak in these assemblies but they enjoyed the privilege of hearing the pros and cons of the arguments and were thus guided in the formulation of unanimity or some preponderant opinion. In these common meetings the council of the elders served as a quasi-presiding committee and was instrumental in informing the people about the issues at hand, in guiding the proceedings, and in giving its weight and authority to the decisions reached in these meetings. Thus the role of the people in treaty-making must have been of some importance. The conclusion of the treaty between Achaeans and Trojans in Book 3 of the *Iliad* transpired in front of the army. The same happened in Book 7 (400 ff.) where the truce between Achaeans and Trojans was again made in front of the troops. In this case the troops decided to reject the peace proposals suggested by the Trojans and Agamemnon concurred.

Our quick analysis of the history of the Ancient Near East has indicated that the *vox populi* was never completely silenced, even under authoritarian rule. It appears, however, that this popular voice was stronger in the earlier part of the history of the Near East. True, the king and his officials could always be petitioned by an individual either by letter or in person, and as a final resort, a frustrated populace could frequently find a champion to raise the standard of rebellion to redress its grievances. The cultural traditions of the Ancient Near East constantly reminded the king that while the gods had given him unexampled supremacy over the people, he had no moral right to abuse this power. A king's possession of the throne was, supposedly, accomplished through the grace of the gods. But although this privilege implied an obligation on the king's part to deal justly and fairly with the people entrusted to him by the divine, by and large the constitutional organs for collective expression of the popular will have progressively atrophied while, conversely, the power of the king became gradually solidified.

The opposite seems to have occurred among the majority of Greeks. Aberrations notwithstanding, the Greeks strengthened their early organs of constitutional expression, while with the passage of time many Greek cities developed democratic regimes whose embryonic growth, as we have seen, is silhouetted in the misty and semi-legendary times of the Mycenaean era.

148   THE PEOPLE

B. STIPULATIONS CONCERNING THE FATE OF FUGITIVES

Several references to fugitives have already been made in the preceding section. In this section we will investigate the topic in detail, to understand how the early Greeks handled the problem of fugitives and the importance that they along with the Near Easterners placed on it. The many references to fugitives in the Near Eastern treaties, the epics, and several post-epic texts point to two major facts: (1) that the Near Easterners and early Greeks were vitally concerned with the subject, and (2) that they had developed specific means to deal with it. It is not surprising, therefore, that one of the most frequent clauses in the Near Eastern treaties concerned the status of fugitives. The stereotyped fashion of these clauses leads us to believe that they constituted a patent formula inserted almost verbatim into the treaties. True, the formula differs slightly from one type of treaty to another, but the wording as well as the ideas remained essentially the same.

Treaties between equals normally stipulate that fugitives, irrespective of their social status, must be returned to their lords.[36] The treaty between Hattusilis and Ramses contains an interesting addendum to the above stipulation, to the effect that fugitives who were returned to their lords ought not to be punished either by death or by gouging out their eyes, or by cutting off their ears, tongue, or legs. The same protection was extended to their wives and children.[37] In the suzerainty treaties, the fugitive arrangements were different. While fugitives from the lord to the territory of the vassal should be apprehended and returned, fugitives from the vassal to the lord fared much better. They should not be returned to their masters, except where they were clearly involved in rebellion or plotting. No punishment is anywhere cited for those fugitives returned to their lords, but understandably the lord would deal with them according to the customs of the time and his personal whims and interests. The asylum granted to fugitives from the vassals did not apply to all but only to those of higher social status. Since these treaties do not make any distinction between political crimes and felonies, they lead us to the conclusion that no such distinction was intended. In the Pentateuch the concern is apparently confined to felonies, but then the political circumstances of early Israel differ from those of the Hittites.[38]

The Near Eastern evidence

In the treaty between Mursilis II and Tuppi-Tešub of Amurru, a kingdom in Syria, it is explicitly stated that prisoners of Hatti should be seized and returned to the Hittite king, since otherwise the vassal stood in violation of

---

[36] Weidner, *Polit. Dok.,* 121.

[37] Langdon-Gardiner, JEA 6 (1920) 197.

[38] Num. 35.9-13; Deut. 19; Josh. 20.1-7, 9.

THE PEOPLE 149

the treaty.[39] In another treaty between Mursilis II and Targašnalliš of Hapalla, a stipulation enjoins Targašnalliš to seize all fugitives from the Hittite king in his area and return them to Mursilis.[40] This stipulation particularly concerned plotters and insurrectionists fleeing from the king's territory into the vassal's area. They were to be apprehended and returned immediately to the king. The same was true of people who, while marching through the vassal's territory, fell sick and remained behind, as well as those who availed themselves of whatever means to engage in looting at the expense of the vassal's subjects. Seized by either the vassal or his subjects, such persons had to be returned to the king, or to his representative if the latter demanded it. Even when such persons could not be easily located, the vassal must search for them, and upon finding them, deliver them to the king or his representative. Failure to comply made the vassal a violator of his oath. Yet whenever soldiers or other men of distinction from Hapalla (Lu Gis-ku-Gidda) fled to Mursilis, the latter was not bound to return them to Tagaršnalliš, for a clause of the treaty emphatically specifies that it would not be "right" to do so. Obviously, the vassal was placed at a disadvantage here, for what was good for the goose was not deemed equally good for the gander. This clause did not cover the common folk, such as weavers, farmers, masons, tanners, and craftsmen and laborers of all kinds who remained outside the pale of such protection. Exceptions once again were made for those who had fled to the lord's area after having plotted against the person and the family of the vassal or, more generally, against the established authority in their country. In such cases, the lord's obligation to return the culprit flowed instead from that stipulation in the treaty which mandated that the lord and vassal should have the same friends and enemies. In the same treaty Targašnalliš agreed to return to Mursilis the prisoners whom Mursilis and his father before him had captured in Arzawa, evidently prior to the making of this treaty, and whom they had enlisted already as fighters in their army. Such refugees, be they Hittites or of other nationalities, had to be seized and delivered to Mursilis. Failure to do so constituted perjury.[41]

Similar stipulations are included in three other treaties. In one of these Mursilis is again one of the signatories, the other being Manapa-Dattaš, the

---

[39] Friedrich, *Die Staatsverträge*, 1:19. These Amorites were earlier allies of Egypt but, upon the collapse of the Egyptian influence in Syria, they switched their allegiance in order to gain greater independence. See also Weidner, *Polit. Dok.*, 23 and nn. 2, 3, 4, where even a social residence is to be provided to the refugees. The delivery of fugitives by an ally or vassal was a sign of compliance with treaty obligations or submission. The opposite was defiance; see F. Schachermeyr, *Die Levante im Zeitalter der Veränderungen*, 19.

[40] Friedrich, *Die Staatsverträge*, 1:59. Hapalla is presumed to have been somewhere in Lycia or Cilicia.

[41] Friedrich, *Die Staatsverträge*, 1:69. The same holds true in the treaty between Mursilis II and Kapanta-aKal; *Die Staatsverträge*, 1:149.

150   THE PEOPLE

ruler of the land of the river Seha.[42] Again, prisoners from Arzawa who escaped to Manapa-Dattaš's land must be seized and delivered to Mursilis. Manapa-Dattaš is not allowed to let them escape through his land to another area. In the second treaty between Suppiluliumas, the father of Mursilis II, and Huqqanas along with the people of Hayaša, it is enjoined that fugitives from the land of Hatti who had fled to the land of Hayaša are to be returned to the king. Since in this case the parties to the treaty are Suppiluliumas on the one hand and Huqqanas and the people of Hayaša on the other, Huqqanas assumes the additional obligation, in case the people failed to extradite the prisoner(s), to go to them and find out the reason they had failed to comply with the letter of the treaty. Unfortunately, the rest of the inscription is missing and it is not clear what the further role of Huqqanas in relation to the extradition might have been.[43] Finally, in the treaty between Muwatallis, the son of Mursilis II, and Alaksandus of Wilusa, refugees from Alaksandus to Hatti were not to be returned to Alaksandus, for it is not "right" for the Hittite king to return them. Only laborers who had escaped to avoid the performance of their work are to be delivered to Alaksandus.[44] A reverse exchange is not mentioned, but there is little doubt that Alaksandus had assumed the obligation to extradite the Hittite fugitives to the king. Clearly, the discrepancy in the treatment of fugitives enabled the Hittite king to increase his army by the addition to it of refugees from his vassals. It is understandable that as long as the vassal abided by the treaty, he enjoyed the protection of his lord such that his position could not—theoretically at least—be substantially weakened by the flight of fugitives. The opposite, on the other hand, would constitute a definite drain on the army of the king in favor of his vassals, an undesirable situation for the king which could not be allowed to prevail.

The Homeric evidence

The rich stream of human experience which flowed through Homer might have received some of its rivulets from the ancient traditions of the Near East. If true, then these quiet tributaries running underground for millennia in the Near East break into the light of the Homeric epics. Their contributions make the Homeric poetry profoundly moving and revealing; they add to it a

---

[42] This land is allegedly located in the area of Arzawa. E. Forrer places it east of Pisidia and Pamphylia; *Forschungen* (Berlin, 1926) 1:83-85; Forrer, OLZ (1924) 114; Forrer, MDOG (1923) 1-40; F. Bilabel, *Geschichte Vorderasiens und Ägyptens* (Heidelberg, 1927) 265; A. Götze, KIF (Weimar, 1930) 112; Friedrich, *Die Staatsverträge,* 1:124-25.

[43] Götze, KIF (Heidelberg, 1924) 25, places it in the upper Maeander in Phrygia. See also Friedrich, *Die Staatsverträge,* 2:129-31.

[44] The approximate date is 1325-05 B.C.; Götze, *Das Hethiter-Reich in der Alte Orient* (Leipzig, 1928) 27; Friedrich, *Die Staatsverträge,* 2:75-77. Wilusa was supposedly part of the Great Arzawa kingdom.

THE PEOPLE   151

vitality and power which surpass the conventions of Greek life. So, out of
the petty squabble of the Greek chieftains in Troy and their alleged struggle
for the damaged honor of one of their colleagues springs a vastly wider flow
of conventions which may trace its background deep in the history of the
Near Eastern and Aegean practices. Knowledge of these practices could help
explain some of the Homeric customs which might have otherwise appeared
totally novel or insignificant in the life of the epic. These practices may help
explain why Greeks almost always extended their protection to fugitives and
suppliants, irrespective of the causes which had forced them to resort to that
status. Fittingly, the story of Achilles' inseparable companion bears some
similarities to the above stipulations of the Hittite treaties. Patroclus had
also run away from home, coming to Peleus as a fugitive. Patroclus had
committed an involuntary manslaughter against Amphidamas's son
Cleitonymus in a moment of rage over a game of dice. Peleus received the
young fugitive and treated him kindly, making him the companion and squire
of his son Achilles.[45] As in the case of the illustrious Near Eastern warriors,
Peleus sheltered the new arrival in order to add him to his military retainers,
particularly since Patroclus's family stood in no subordinate position to the
family of Peleus.

The same practice apparently illuminates another incident in the *Odyssey*.
In this episode the suitors had plotted to kill Telemachus upon the latter's
return from the Peloponnese, where he had gone to gather information about
his father's whereabouts. Foremost among the plotters was Antinous, the
most aggressive of the suitors. The plot was meanwhile revealed to Penelope
by one of the quasi-double agents in the palace, and Penelope, full of fear and
anger, decided to confront the suitors. She addressed caustic words to
Antinous, scolding him for his conduct and reminding him of the debt his
family owed to the family of Odysseus, since Odysseus had saved Antinous's
father Eupeithes when he had fled as fugitive to Ithaca. Eupeithes was being
pursued because he had joined the notorious Taphian pirates and had harried
the Thesprotians who were friends of the Ithacans. As Eupeithes' enemies
closed in upon him ready to kill him, Odysseus had intervened and saved him
from certain destruction. Yet instead of gratitude Antinous was now repaying
Odysseus's family by plotting against Telemachus.[46] In acting on Eupeithes'
behalf, Odysseus had most probably followed the tradition which assumed
protection for fugitives. As is made abundantly clear from the text, Odysseus

---

[45] Peleus himself had formerly been a fugitive from Salamis to Phthia, where he was
purified by Eurytion, the adopted son of Actor. Actor then gave him his daughter Polymeda
in marriage and one third of his kingdom Apollod. 3.13.1-2; Tzetzes, on *Lycophron*, 175;
Eust. ad *Il.* 2.648.

[46] *Od.* 16.418-33; Eust. *ad loc.*

152 THE PEOPLE

was no vassal but an ally and friend of the Thesprotians, such that he could intervene in Eupeithes' behalf without fear of reprisals from a superior.

Still another story in the *Iliad* (9.434 ff.) provides the reader with the background of Phoenix, son of Amyntor. Phoenix had quarrelled with his father over his father's concubine. Amyntor seems to have showed a preference for this concubine over his wife, who was Phoenix's mother. Consequently, Phoenix's mother contrived to use the young Phoenix to get rid of the concubine and win back her husband. She persuaded Phoenix to make love to the concubine in the hope that her husband would learn of it and reject her. Phoenix, initially reluctant, finally gave in to his mother's solicitations, but when the father heard what happened, he cursed Phoenix, invoking the dreadful Erinyes to punish him with childlessness. Since Phoenix soon found himself unable to beget children, he came to believe that the gods had responded to his father's prayers; full of anger, he thought for a moment of slaying his father, but the gods stayed his anger so that he would not become a parricide. Nonetheless, Phoenix decided to leave his paternal land, and though he was closely watched by relatives, managed to escape them. He wandered over many places until he came to Phthia. There, Peleus welcomed him and treated him as a son, bestowing upon him riches and the territory of the Dolopians, over which he was to rule as a vassal of Peleus.[47] Later on, Peleus entrusted him with the education of his son Achilles, and the older man, unable to beget children, came to love his pupil like a son.[48]

The stories of Patroclus and Phoenix bear some similarities to that of Adrastus, the son of the Phrygian Gorgias, since he too had involuntarily slaughtered someone and was subsequently banished by his father. Without country, family, or home Adrastus fled to Croesus as suppliant, and the latter accepted him as one of his courtiers, making him a squire of his son. Although Croesus welcomed Adrastus gladly because of the existing friendship between the two families, this friendship may not explain Croesus's welcome, since even without it Croesus would probably have welcomed Adrastus, bowing to the age-old practice of accepting prominent persons. He knew that their addition to the household increased the prestige

---

[47] The home of the Dolopes was where the plateau guarding the approach to Malis from the north merges into the mass of Pindos. It was perhaps the most inaccessible and remote spot in the whole Greek peninsula, according to Leaf, yet a necessary outpost for Peleus. War-like hill tribes residing beside the pass must have been a standing menace to the valley of Malis. To command this area and defend it from the raids, Phoenix was sent with a strong force, "many folk." Here we may fancy the young fugitive proving his mettle and his gratitude in defense of his new home at safe distance from his father's anger, *Il.* 9.480-85; Eust. *ad loc.*; Leaf, *Homer and History*, 117-18. The example of Phoenix is probably as close as one can come to the Lord-vassal relationship.

[48] *Il.* 23.83 ff.; cf.9.786-87; Pindar, *Olymp. Ode* 9.69-70; Hesiod quoted by Eust. ad *Il.* 1.337-40; Hesiod, frg. 212 M-W and frg. 84; Hyginus, *Fabula*, 97; Schol. on Apol. Rhodius 4.816; Strabo 9.4.2.

THE PEOPLE 153

and might of the host, exactly as was the case for the Hittite kings. Most kings of antiquity were inclined to welcome men distinguished in war, in council, or by their knowledge in the affairs of other states, especially those with whom they were in contact. Most aristocrats were presumed to be adept in war and in council, and as retainers of their new lord they were frequently expected to return their gratitude by fulfilling whatever tasks their lord requested of them.[49] In this sense the stipulated practices of the Hittite kings were not too far from the traditional practices in Homer and elsewhere in the Near East. The purpose of receiving fugitives could not have been entirely altruistic or a mere compliance with the established tradition, since, as is clear from the Hittite treaties, it represented a custom which originally cleverly blended humanitarianism and self-interest.

Nor was this judicious blending of motives forgotten at a much later time. Unquestionably, it was in this vein that the Persians welcomed the Athenian tyrant Hippias in their court, with a welcome that was motivated not solely by their mere conformity to a long-established tradition but also by their long-established desire to expand their sphere of influence in the Aegean. Exiles like Hippias were useful to them to the extent that they could be manipulated to serve the personal and national interest of the host. Inasmuch as Hippias was overeager to use Persian help to accomplish his return to his homeland, the Persians could bank on him to facilitate their plans in the Aegean. The effect of the activities of Hippias on Athens was visibly disturbing, and since the Athenians could not expect the Persians to deliver Hippias to them without the existence of a legal treaty to that effect, they counseled the Persians not to pay attention to Hippias's importunities. The Persian answer intimated the future plans of the Persians and their danger to Athens, if one is to believe Herodotus's statement (Hdt. 5.96). By campaigning with the Persians against Greece in 490 B.C., Hippias may have been fulfilling his desire for revenge or his ambition to repossess his ancestral city, at the same time that he was wittingly or unwittingly fulfilling an obligation expected of him from his host (Hdt. 5.107).

The Spartan king Demaratus was still another welcomed figure at the Persian court. He was received royally by Darius, who endowed him with certain territories which Demaratus could exploit for his own benefit.[50] Darius thus made Demaratus his retainer and as such Demaratus was to serve

---

[49] Hdt. 1.41-42; How and Wells ad Hdt. 1.34-35. R. Sealey maintains that when a powerful man extended protection to a fugitive both parties benefited. The patron gained a follower who might have various talents and be employed in various ways. Above all the fugitive became totally loyal to his protector, AJAH 8 (1983) 112-13.

[50] Hdt. 5.70; *Hell.* 3.1.6; *Anab.* 2.1.3; 7.8.17. According to Xenophon, Demaratus had received Pergamum and Tenthrania in the Troad, which were later retained by his descendants Proclus and Eurysthenes.

154 THE PEOPLE

his host and lord in the capacity of warrior or counselor, as many other noblemen had done. In fact, it seems that Demaratus was clearly privy to the Persian campaign against Greece and allegedly even played the role of double agent, although Herodotus rightly questions whether he was giving advice to the Persians even while he secretly kept the Spartans abreast of the Persian plans.[51]

The story of the flight of the Greek fugitives to the Persian court is one of many similar stories that cannot be thoroughly reviewed here. Suffice it only to mention the case of Themistocles. Since the hero of Salamis and savior of Greece eventually fell so complete a victim to Greek pettiness and hatred that he was ostracized from his native city, Sparta connected him with the treasonable activities of Pausanias. His political enemies, welcoming these accusations in order to pursue him further, dispatched men to bring him to Athens to stand trial. Forewarned of the Athenians' intentions and aware that return to Athens would spell his doom, Themistocles fled first to the Corcyraeans, who if Thucydides is correct improperly refused him asylum, and then to the opposite coast where he lived among the Molossians.[52] King Admetus refused to extradite him either to the Spartans or to the Athenians, but, granting his wish to go to the Persian court, Admetus provided him with an escort and instructions for the trip by way of Macedonia. Once in Asia Minor, Themistocles dispatched a letter to the Persian king in which he enumerated some of the services he had proffered to Xerxes. Whether or not the arguments were persuasive, Artaxerxes received him in his court, most probably because of the well-established tradition regarding the usefulness of distinguished fugitives. The Persian kings, who had not relinquished their hopes for the conquest of Greece even after Salamis and Plataea, might have expected Themistocles to help them succeed where they had formerly failed (Thuc. 1.132.2). Obviously, the combination of Persian readiness to listen and Themistocles' intelligence convinced the Persian king that such refugees constituted a valuable asset to the Persian diplomacy.

The Homeric and post-Homeric refugee cases do not seem to differ much from those described in the treaties between the Hittite kings and their vassals. Greek fugitives, as well as those whom it would not have been "right" for the Hittite king to return to the fugitives' superiors, apparently served the same purpose. Only the circumstance varied; even though in the Hittite treaties the prominent fugitives increased the number of royal

---

[51] Hdt. 7.239. This story has been justifiably suspected as interpolation by several modern scholars, R. W. Macan, *Herodotus ad loc.,* and How and Wells *ad loc.* Macan considers the story, as here given, a later fabrication; Justin, 2.10, 12-17. It sounds somewhat similar to the story of Themistocles who allegedly chose to kill himself rather than betray his country, despite the alleged ingratitude of his city, whose savior he had been.

[52] Thuc. 1.136; Plut. *Them.* 20.3-4; 24.1.

THE PEOPLE 155

warriors, they were not to be used against the vassals from whose territories they had fled. Furthermore, plotters and rebels against the vassals were to be extradited. In the Homeric stories there are no discernible contractual arrangements between the persons from whom the fugitives fled and those to whom they fled. But the practice did not differ in essentials. The host provided protection for the refugee while the refugee served him as retainer and adviser. The relationship of the country of the refugee to that of his host could be friendly, neutral, or, as in the Persian episode, hostile. In the last situation no treaties could have existed between the two countries regulating their relationship or the status of fugitives. Since the mighty Persian empire was immune from coercion, it could freely exercise the age-old right of protecting refugees with no legal or practical restriction on using them against the country of their origin.

In later Greek history, the right of asylum and the obligation to spare fugitives from extradition because it was not "right" to return them to their pursuers becomes a virtual given for all classes of people. Greek history is full of examples of fugitives who claimed protection long before the right to this claim became a written formula recognized by city-state decrees or treaties. The examples of this principle cited in Greek literature are too numerous to enumerate here.[53] Violations occurred frequently for political or other motives, but these violations, no matter how frequent, did not nullify the principle. While its long history and its parallel presence in both the Near East and Greece do not prove borrowing from one culture to the other, they do not exclude it either, nor do they militate against the possibility of a common source with diverse development and at various times.

Summary

Written evidence of fugitives in the Near East goes back at least as far as the fourteenth century B.C. It is even possible that the contractual agreements about fugitives constituted a modification of pre-existing traditional principles. Be that as it may, the Hittite treaties used a double standard for fugitives from the vassal to the lord and vice versa, ingeniously blending humanitarianism and self-interest. When one comes to the Greek world one has to admit that unfortunately no such hard evidence exists about the Mycenaean era, which was contemporaneous with the Hittite civilization. The Homeric epics were written in a later period, and thus one is faced with a yawning gap of several centuries, unless, as seems possible, the Homeric practices reflected earlier Mycenaean practices. The similarities in the

---

[53] Eur. *Heracles* 1332-37; *Medea* 725-30; *Heraclidae* 61-69, 101-103, 707- 708, 305-31, 362-63; Plat. *Menex.* mentions repeatedly the protection extended to the Heraclidae; Hdt. 1.157-59; Aisch. 3.134; Andoc. *On the Peace* 28; Aesch. *Suppliants* 385-86, 488, 609-10, 613; *Eum.* 232-36 are only a few of the examples.

treatment of fugitives in the Homeric and Near Eastern world are very tempting and certainly point to similarities in the prevailing practices among the Mycenaeans. Unluckily again, the evidence is not adequate to clinch the argument. At any rate, the humanitarian motive is fairly strong in the Homeric instances, though the element of self-interest is not absent either. If the inference about the link between the Mycenaean and Homeric customs is correct, then it cannot be ruled out that provisions for fugitives were present in the political agreements of the Mycenaean world. One thing, at least, is certain: asylum for fugitives is a very old custom which emerged in the ancient Greek and non-Greek aristocratic worlds for the protection primarily of aristocrats, but which in the later Greek world covered all fugitives who were free men.

CHAPTER SIX

WAR CONVENTIONS

The principal function of interstate agreements, in ancient times as now, is that of establishing practices that control aggressive behavior—in short, war conventions. For the most part, treaties blocked war, but sometimes they only regulated its conduct. Hence the first, major section of this chapter is concerned with the way limits were put on the taking and sharing of booty, along with associated practices such as the taking, ransoming, or exchanging of captives. The second section concerns a special aspect of those obligations which a treaty might create upon one party to go to the aid of another in time of war: this is the "surrogate stipulation," whereby the assistance promised in the treaty could be provided by troops led by someone other than the contracting party himself. The final, much briefer section of the chapter concerns the rules under which war was to be initiated, i.e., the conditions for "firing the first shot."

A. THE TAKING AND SHARING OF BOOTY

As is suggested by the fact that looting and booty in their various forms have been mentioned several times throughout the preceding discussion, booty-taking was a widespread practice in the Near Eastern and Homeric worlds, continuing even in modern times. Its function is much more than just an outlet for the warriors' aggressive tendencies. It also has been employed as a punishment of the vanquished, as well as a means of enrichment and reward for the victorious troops.

The Near Eastern evidence

Certain peoples in the Ancient Near East engaged regularly in raiding as means of replenishing their coffers or simply as a form of survival. Thus at the height of the Hittite empire its king Suppiluliumas expected his vassals to provide him with support and protection whenever he went on raids.[1] The distribution of booty in the Ancient Near East conformed to certain established regulations, violation of which could prove disruptive to politico-military balances held together mainly by existing treaties or by commonly understood rules in which booty served a special purpose or, more often, as compensation for privations suffered in battle. In the treaty between the Hittite king Muwatallis and Sunaššura, the king of Kizzuwadna, a stipulation specified the division of booty between them in those cases in which

---

[1] Weidner, *Polit. Dok.*, 71-73.

158 WAR CONVENTIONS

misunderstandings could easily arise. The booty clause clarified that whenever Sunaššura offered his services to Muwatallis in putting down the rebellion of one of Muwatallis's cities, the chattels of the captured city would become legitimate booty of Sunaššura's soldiers, to the exclusion of any other claim.[2] The land, however, would remain the property of the original owner. By the same token, if the Hittite king proffered his services to his vassal against a rebel city of the vassal and the king and his soldiers captured it, they had the right to the movable objects in the captured city, although the king was bound to return the city itself to its former ruler. The same principle applied to larger territories.[3] This practice was more or less universally enforced in the Ancient Near East, its prevalence supported by the similar clause in the later treaty between Rome and Carthage.[4] It explains, partially at least, another stipulation in the Hittite treaties by which the vassals had to give their military services to their lord upon written request by him. The custom of making the request in writing shows that the lord king had no desire to drag his vassals into his internal conflicts unnecessarily, in view of the consequent loss of property to the assisting troops.[5] The vassal, of course, would be equally reluctant, since once additional rules or written stipulations were in place, departures could prove deleterious to freely formed alliances composed of independent partners, who presumably were motivated primarily by a high sense of honor.

Near Eastern booty practices are important here because of their possible affiliation to those of the Homeric world and indirectly to those of the Mycenaean world. For example, when Idrimi, the vassal of Parattarna, the Mitanni king, invaded seven cities on the Cilician coast belonging to the Hittites, the booty he hauled from there was eventually divided between his troops on the one hand, and his lieutenants and himself on the other. Exactly how the division was made and who got what has not been spelled out in detail. What is known is that following the capture of the cities, Idrimi

---

[2] F. Delitzsch, *Assyrisches Handwörterbuch* (Leipzig,1896) 629; H. Ebeling, VAB II, 1464.

[3] Weidner, *Polit. Dok.*, 93; for something similar see *Gen.* 14.10-12. Korosec, *Heth. Staats.*, 74. The practice seems to have been universal in the Ancient Near East and among the colonists of Tyre, the Carthaginians; see the treaty between Carthage and the Etruscans; Bengtson, No. 116. Of the plentiful bibliography on this treaty see especially R. Laqueur, *Hermes* 71 (1936) 467-72, who finds similarities between this treaty and the treaty of the Assyrian king Esarhaddon and his vassal, the king of Tyre, in the year 677. Also Hans Hirschberg, *Studien zur Geschichte Esarhaddons* (Diss. Berlin, 1932) 69 ff.; E. Weidner, *Archiv für Orientforschung* 8 (1932) 29 ff.; San Nicolo, *Archiv. Orientalni* 4 (1932) 325 ff. E. Taübler, *Imperium Romanum,* suggests that the formula of the Carthaginian-Roman treaty cited in Polyb. 3.22.4-13 follows oriental models, and Lauqueur's views seem to support him.

[4] Chroust, *Class. et Med.* 15 (1954) 60-107.

[5] Friedrich, *Die Staatsverträge,* 1:125, 127, 131; 2:63.

WAR CONVENTIONS 159

returned in triumph to Alalakh, his resident city, which he embellished with the spoils of war.[6] In another case, Suttarna, a king in Upper Mesopotamia, having destroyed the palace of the Mitanni king and laid waste the land, seized much movable property and took prisoner many local leaders whom he delivered to the Assyrians and Alshe. This extraordinary generosity and unusual concession to the Assyrians and Alshe were primarily due to motives of realpolitik, for Suttarna aimed at Assyrian and Alshian support against the Hittite king Suppiluliumas, and the Assyrians at least did not disappoint him. Additionally, Suttarna used booty in order to bribe the people of Mitanni and to bring them over to his side.[7] Although these few examples do not provide us with full details about looting practices in the Near East, the main outline seems to foreshadow the Homeric practices.

The Homeric evidence

The main theme of the *Iliad* is the baneful quarrel between the commander-in-chief of the Achaean army and the best of the Achaean leaders over what might be called a human piece of spoil. On the surface, this quarrel was the proximate cause of the larger conflict, although in a deeper sense the main dispute was over a principle, and as is commonly known men do not easily compromise on principles: for better or for worse—often for worse—they divide and fight. Something analogous happened in the Trojan War, whose results could have been even more catastrophic than they were had not reason in the form of some supreme power intervened. The tragic aspect of the quarrel was its futility, for it could have been easily averted had not pettiness, spite, and the human ego given it the turn it took. At the end, the dispute required another tragic event, the death of a noble and well-meaning person, to bring it to its resolution. The whole tragedy could have been avoided had the two protagonists been willing to comply with the existing conventions, the so-called *themistes* of the times which seem to have had their roots deep in history, in the hazy times of the Mycenaean world.[8] These commonly acknowledged Greek conventions were assumed to prevail and to regulate the differences of the allied Achaeans in the pursuit of war, just as they had done earlier in the Greeks' interstate relations. And so we must ask, just what were these conventions, and how did they relate to the capture of enemy cities and enemies?

---

[6] Idrimi, a king in the area of Alalakh, vassal of the king of Mitanni, in the sixteenth century B.C. For the topography of the area see R. Dussaud, *Topographie historique de la Syrie antique et medievale* (Paris, 1927); CAH3 2.2.434.

[7] Weidner, *Polit. Dok.*, 39; 45.

[8] By *themistes* are here meant certain unwritten principles which regulated the conduct of people in their personal and interstate relations, in a way roughly analogous to the Common Law in medieval England (perhaps up to Henry II?).

160 WAR CONVENTIONS

Aristocratic traditions mitigated the general practice of brutality, although it is not clear whether this was always the case when Achaean cities fell into the hands of other Achaean rivals. However, the Achaean practice for non-Achaean cities captured in war was to strip them of their movable property and kill some or all of the men, or take them, along with the women and children, as prisoners. The movable wealth, known as ξυνήϊα, was then concentrated in a central place and immediately portioned out.[9] Instances of Greek cities visited by such a fate are not lacking. Meleager's wife recalled with terror what had happened to people whose city was captured: the men were slain, while their children and wives were led away captives. The emptied city was then put to the torch (*Il.* 9.592 ff.). The same fate was feared for the city of Troy after the death of Hector, particularly because of Achilles' anger over the death of Patroclus (*Il.* 24.732 ff.).

Since armies in the ancient times had no organized supply systems but rather expected to live by pillaging the countryside, any non-Achaean town or village in the territory of Troy during the war was subject to raiding. In addition, kings and their armies hoped to enrich themselves from the loot of war, thus making enemy cities, or even neutral ones, fair game. Friendly territories could not hope to remain entirely exempt from the danger of looting; they must keep the troops friendly by handouts to avoid more serious pilfering.

If slavery is viewed as a fate better than death, then women and children in the Homeric times generally were luckier than men. But in antiquity the treatment of captive women was rarely seen as better than that of men, since victors used the captive women as concubines and housemaids, thus insulting and completely humiliating their male relations. From this standpoint the stigma attached to the raping and enslaving of the women came to be viewed as a fate worse then death. Thus it is no wonder that the scholiast to Homer described the fate of these helpless creatures as worse than that of men.[10] The

---

[9] *Il.* 1.124. For the etymology see H. Frisk, *Griech. Etym. Wörterbuch,* 1:332; and U. Wilamowitz-Möllendorf, *Hesiodos Erga,* 2nd ed. (Berlin, 1926) 120. In Deut. 20.10-18 the attitude of the Israelites regarding capture of cities is described as follows: "When you advance to the attack of any town, first offer it terms of peace. If the town accepts those terms and opens its gates to you, all the people to be found in it should be forced to do labor for you and be subject to you. But if it refuses peace and offers resistance, you must lay siege to it. Your God shall deliver it into your power and you are to put all its males to the sword. But the women, the children, the livestock and all that the town contains, all its spoils, you may take for yourself as booty. This concerns farther away cities. As to nearby cities of the Hittites, Amorites, Canaanites, Perizzites, Hivites, Jebusites, they are to be exterminated so that their people may not teach you all the detestable practices they hold in honor of their gods." Religious considerations made the Israelites harsher towards their neighbors than farther away cities. For differences see also Deut. 2.26-36; 2.30 ff.; Num. 31.1-12; 33.55-56; 1 Sam. 15.9-10.

[10] Bekker ad *Il.* 22.62. The condition of many of these women captives, undesirable and shameful though it might have been, was not as a rule desperate. Many enjoyed a kindly

WAR CONVENTIONS 161

callousness toward them is revealed by the advice of Nestor, who sought to inspire the Achaean troops and banish their thoughts of returning home by urging them to lie with the wives of the Trojans as an act of requital for Helen's groanings.[11] On the other hand, while it was true that men were frequently put to the sword by their captors, especially if, as commoners, they were unlikely to be ransomed, noblemen could be spared. They might better be exchanged for ransom, though even without such an opportunity noblemen had some compunctions about killing other noblemen. Yet in many cases even compunction could not save the noble from their ultimate fate. Achilles, who was reputed to have laid waste many cities, was renowned for the capture of the cities of Lyrnessus and Pedasus, where he put all men to the knife and took the women captive. At Troy, Aeneas escaped death thanks only to the swiftness of his feet. Priam's son, Lycaon, who had already been captured and ransomed once, had the bad luck to fall into Achilles' hands again. Although this time, which was after Patroclus' death, he offered three times the previous ransom payment, Achilles was in no mood to bargain or be lenient. Lycaon consequently clasped Achilles' knees in a suppliant's gesture, hoping that he might escape death. Under different circumstances Achilles might have pitied him, since it was conventional practice to spare suppliants (*Il.* 10.454-55; *Od.* 14.279). Achilles himself admitted that until Patroclus's death he had found it pleasing to spare his captives and incidentally to enrich himself with the hefty ransom their release brought to him. This admission was corroborated by Priam, who complained at one point that Achilles had killed many of his sons while he had taken others as prisoners to sell to faraway islands (*Il.* 22.45). But after the death of Patroclus, Achilles' anger was such that no Trojan could hope to escape alive if he fell into his hands. Lycaon suffered the worst of fates: his body was cast into the river Xanthus by Achilles so that it might be eaten up by the fish and deprived of its proper burial rites (*Il.* 21.120). Similarly, Tros, Alastor's son, having been captured by Achilles, clasped his captor's knees begging for mercy. The effort was futile, since Achilles was not to be assuaged by traditional appeals to convention. As the poet observed, no gentleness or softness was left in Achilles' heart (*Il.* 20.463 ff.).

Achilles was not the only Homeric hero who resorted to such brutal practices. While on a spying mission, Odysseus and Diomedes surprised the Trojan Dolon, who was engaged in counterespionage on behalf of the Trojans. The two extracted from Dolon the disposition and plans of the Trojans by promising to spare his life. Then they killed him. To save

---

treatment as if their captors realized that they were the innocent victims of the war, while others became concubines or maids and soon developed deep feelings of affection for their captors; *Il.* 19.997-98; *Od.* 7.8.

[11] *Il.* 2.353-57; Leaf *ad loc.* for some of the problems connected with the meaning of these verses.

himself, Dolon had tried to clasp the chin of Diomedes in the manner of suppliants, but Diomedes struck before his chin was reached. Thus the Greeks could kill Dolon without guilt-feelings for having transgressed the prevailing moral usages dictating that suppliants be spared. Unfortunately for Dolon, whose presence would have been an impediment to their mission, the modern rule of exchanging spies was not known in Homer's times. Perhaps under different circumstances they might have taken his promise of abundant ransom more seriously (*Il.* 10.378).

There were, however, other cases in antiquity in which, by convention, no quarter was presumed to be given even though ransom or payment might be generously proffered. Such was the case of the suitors. The suitor who had most seriously antagonized Odysseus with his obnoxious and arrogant conduct was Antinous. Because of his arrogance and his sly threat to the life of Odysseus and his son, Antinous was the first to be shot down. Following Antinous's death, Odysseus had the rest of the suitors at his mercy, such that they immediately offered to surrender and reimburse him generously for the damage they had done to Odysseus's property, if only he would be ready to discuss the question. Unfortunately for them, there was no price that could compensate Odysseus for their having wooed his wife while he was still alive. The contemporaneous conventions dictated that they should suffer the ultimate fate at the hands of the insulted husband for the immoral act they had perpetrated. Even Leiodes the soothsayer had to be disposed of, although he became Odysseus's suppliant by clasping his knees, because in his prayers he had asked the gods to grant the wishes of the suitors (*Od.* 22.38, 61-64).

Turning now to the matter of captive women, we see that they served several purposes. They could be used as the maids and concubines of their captors; they could be sold as slaves; or they could, like men, be exchanged for ransom. The effort of Chryses to ransom his daughter, his ill-treatment by Agamemnon, and the latter's refusal to return the girl to her father combined to eventually produce a *cause célèbre* that precipitated the even more celebrated altercation between the two Achaean leaders. The great majority of the Achaeans inclined toward the release of the girl, not only because of her father's profession, but also because of the more than fair offer of ransom proposed by the priest. The troops bade Agamemnon receive the ransom and respect the priest, since Chryses, with the cleverness of his calling, had well orchestrated his plea so as to produce the maximum effect upon the Achaeans. Furthermore, the use of the fillets and the scepter gave the impression that Apollo accompanied him in this mission, and that he was an envoy of Apollo. Chryses hoped that either out of greed or fear of Apollo, Agamemnon would not turn his plea down. But if neither motive appealed to the king and the latter said or did anything offensive, Apollo

WAR CONVENTIONS 163

himself might ultimately be offended and take action against the Greeks, as indeed he did.[12] Eventually, Agamemnon had to return the girl if he did not wish to see his army totally destroyed, or so it was believed. In the process Agamemnon committed the grievous error of replacing Chryses by taking Achilles' concubine, Briseis, who had come into Achilles' possession after the capture of Thebe, Eetion's city. Since Briseis's husband Eetion and all her other relatives had been killed by Achilles, there was no one to ransom her.[13] The spoils from the conquest of Thebe were brought to the Achaean camp, as was demanded by the booty game, whose rules apparently required that the despoilers of cities during joint campaigns act not on their personal accounts in the distributions of spoils but on behalf of all the rest.

Clearly, plunder was considered the common property, and by the tacit rules of the alliance it had to be somehow divided by all, among all, and in the presence of all.[14] Exactly what proportion the common warrior received remains obscure, but the scanty evidence points often to a much smaller compensation in comparison to the leaders. It could be, of course, that our conflicting meager information might reflect only the tendency of the Greek character to grumble and complain, rather than a significant inequality of the distribution of the purloined material. Whatever the case, Book 10 of the *Odyssey* (10.37 ff.) portrayed Odysseus's comrades on the island of Helios as complaining that he carried home from Troy a virtual treasure of spoils, while they carried a few miserable crumbs. Their jealousy at the purportedly uneven distribution of spoils, combined with the suspicion that Aeolus had given Odysseus many additional treasures which the latter planned to keep exclusively for himself, led them to the unfortunate decision to open the skins, with the well-known disastrous effects on the future of their voyage.

Other Homeric instances, however, do not leave the impression of grumbling on the part of Odysseus's comrades, even allowing for the fact that the source of the story is Odysseus himself rather than his attendants. When he sacked the city of Cicones and slew its men, Odysseus took their wives and whatever other possessions he could gather, which he eventually divided among his comrades so as to give each an equal share.[15] He did the

---

[12] *Il.* 1.12-20, 375; Erbse *ad loc.*; Eust. *ad loc.*

[13] Sometimes there was an additional difficulty associated with the ransoming of a wife by the fact that the husband's honor had been violated by the wife's rape. Consequently, she had become an embarrassment to him, and he might not have been too anxious to get her back from her captor. The case of Helen seems rather rare. Homer called Eetion's city "holy" (*hierên, Il.* 1.366) because as a place where people lived and worshipped any city enjoyed a degree of sacredness. Thus the impersonal, the inanimate, the abstract, or the idealized, when it exercised power, as cities did through their institutions, became solemnized and acquired a holy aura. See Leaf, ad *Il.* 1.366; Ameis and Hentze ad *Il.* 1.336.

[14] *Il.* 1.367.

[15] *Od.* 9.39-42. The Cicones were a Thracian people, allies of the Trojans; *Il.* 2.846.

164 WAR CONVENTIONS

same thing after they all left the inhospitable island of the Cyclops. The crews of the twelve ships with him at the time cast lots for the goats seized on the island. It seems that the number of goats presented less of a problem than did the quality, size, and age of the goats themselves. To overcome the inevitable complaints about who would get the better goats, Odysseus and his people resorted to the widely practiced custom of sortition. The single exception was made for Odysseus, who received ten goats (*Od.* 9.160). At first sight, nine goats for the crew of an entire ship and ten for Odysseus alone create the impression of an unfair imbalance. But one should bear in mind that Odysseus's comrades made the distribution, not Odysseus. What might have been the compelling factor that determined the apportionment is not clear. But in view of the fact that Odysseus had several obligations inherent to his position as leader, such as entertaining and sacrificing, ten goats might not have constituted an inordinate portion. At any rate, the distribution must have followed the rules of the day since no complaints were registered at this point. The same procedure seems to have been followed after the miraculous escape of Odysseus and his comrades from the jaws of Polyphemus. The survivors divided fairly the sheep they had taken from Polyphemus, with the single notable exception of the famous ram, which they gave to Odysseus as a gift of honor (*Od.* 9.549-50). Again, in this instance Odysseus emphasized that he did his best so that the division would be fair and no one would be deprived of his due portion. In still another instance in which Odysseus was the leader, he headed a team that raided foreign lands. Accordingly, Odysseus maintained that he chose from the loot what pleased his heart and that he obtained much more by lot. The lot was obviously the fair way of distribution, but Odysseus's also choosing whatever pleased his heart does not fit well with his previously announced concern for fairness. Perhaps this was the custom only among pirates; one cannot be certain. What does seem to be certain is that the king participated in the distribution of the booty and that he received something besides an equal share of the spoils.[16] All participated in the apportionment of what was viewed as common booty, irrespective of their roles in the war.[17] Obviously, the booty was divided in parts equaling the number of participants, and the value of each portion must have been calculated against the value of the cattle.[18] Who exactly did the assessing is not clear, though it is most probable that when the participants' number was small everyone had the

---

[16] *Il.* 9.365-67; *Od.* 9.549-51; 14.232, 331 ff.; Nilsson, *Homer and Myc.*, 236; Werner Nowag, *Raub und Beute in der archaischen Zeit der Griechen* (Frankfurt/Main 1983) 40; A. J. Podlecki, *Phoenix* 15 (1961) 125-33.

[17] A. Debrunner, *Mus. Helv.* 1 (1944) 36.

[18] Nowag, *Raub und Beute*, 42.

WAR CONVENTIONS   165

chance to watch the distribution process. Undoubtedly, even with the best of intentions it would have been impossible to satisfy everybody.[19]

The above analysis shows that the issue of fairness so persistently stressed by Odysseus was one of the most important cultural values of the times. Unfairness, or the appearance of it, could trigger trouble or even spell disaster for a leader, as the suspicions and jealousy of Odysseus's comrades suggested. The issue of fairness became even more clearly pivotal when it concerned an alliance of major dimensions such as the alliance of the Achaeans facing Troy. In that instance, the leader had to take extra pains to convey the impression of fairness; otherwise, he could easily bring upon himself trouble of incalculable dimensions as Agamemnon did over Briseis. This outcome implied unwritten but commonly presumed concepts, disregard of which could promptly disturb the balance of the alliance. The prevailing conventions in connection with booty dictated that the booty remain common property until its distribution took place, generally not much later than the return of the warriors from the campaign in which the booty was taken (*Il.* 1.124). It is not entirely clear whether the division was supervised by the kings only or by the kings and representatives of the troops. The *Iliad* speaks (1.338) of the fairness of the process conducted by the "sons of the Achaeans." It was they who had chosen Chryseis as a prize (γέρας) for Agamemnon. Again, Achilles complained that Agamemnon wished to take away from him the prize whom the "sons of the Achaeans" had given him.[20] The dialogue between the two angry kings further emphasized the fact that the effort of Agamemnon to recoup his loss of Chryseis by a new distribution of spoils or the arbitrary seizure of someone else's prize constituted an unorthodox and unfair practice (*Il.* 1.126). Such prizes were not only given to the commanders who participated actively in battle but also to non-active military leaders in the campaign who served as advisors and who enjoyed the high esteem of their colleagues. In such a case the prize was called πρεσβήϊον.[21]

The use of λαούς in conjunction with the division of spoils implied the participation of the common soldier in the distribution process.[22] Unfortunately, the question of who had the final authority in the assignment

---

[19] Eust. ad *Od.* 9.42.

[20] *Il.* 1.162: Δόσαν δέ μοι υἷες 'Αχαιῶν.

[21] Frisk, *Etym. Wörterbuch*, 2:592 s.v. *presbêion; Il.* 8.289; Nowag, *Raub und Beute*, 37-38.

[22] The use of *laos* (*lawos*) in Homer is interesting especially because of its possible connection with *lêiton* and the Homeric *lêis*; Emile Benveniste, *Le vocabulaire des institutions Indo-Européennes* (Paris, 1969) 1:90, 166-170; Pierre Chartraine, *Dictionaire Etymologique de la langue grecque* (Paris, 1968) 618, s.v. *laos*; Hdt. 7.197; Vlachos, *Sociétés*, 135; G. Kirk, "War and the Warrior in the Homeric Poems," in J. P. Vernant (ed.), *Problèmes de la guerre en Grèce ancienne* (Paris, 1968) 93-117; Nowag, *Raub und Beute*, 77.

166 WAR CONVENTIONS

of prizes to the leaders is complicated by the contradictory statements of Achilles, who in Book 9 (130) of the *Iliad* claimed that he himself chose Briseis as his γέρας ἐξαιρετὸν. To complicate matters further, another version in the *Iliad* Book 9 (328) describes the capture of twelve cities by sea and eleven by land, all of which brought a goodly amount of spoils. Achilles acknowledged that he had brought the loot to Agamemnon who, as Achilles sarcastically observed, had stayed behind in the camp.[23] Agamemnon then apportioned some of the spoils to the chiefs, while he kept the greater part for himself. Achilles' use of δασάσκετο indicates that the apportionment was made by Agamemnon himself, probably by virtue of his position as the commander-in-chief of the Achaean forces. This notion appears to be supported by the threat of Achilles to leave for Phthia and to take with him all the wealth he had accumulated in Troy, except of course the prize that Agamemnon had allowed him at first and then arbitrarily and arrogantly took away from him.[24] The supreme commander's right to perks in the distribution of booty is also implied in Agamemnon's offer to allow Achilles to choose for himself the twenty most beautiful women and much of the gold and bronze upon the fall of Troy (*Il.* 9.135-39). The offer seems to have been spontaneous, made without prior consultation of the Council of Elders or the assembly. It points to the traditional right of the supreme commander to reward individuals for extraordinary contributions, as well as to compensate them for the loss of their prizes (*Il.* 9.135 ff.). Perhaps this privilege had its roots deep in traditions of the Mycenaean times, when the position of the king was much stronger. It is a possibility we cannot entirely exclude.[25] Whatever the right of the supreme commander may have been, his position did not empower him to take back what he had formerly apportioned. If Agamemnon had no right to deprive any of the Achaean leaders of his portion of the loot, the misuse of that action in relation to Achilles was all the more unjust inasmuch as Achilles had gone to Troy to please the Atreids, not because he had any obligations stemming from the oath exacted by Tyndareos (Paus. 3.24.11). Achilles had not obviously been one of Helen's suitors, despite one tradition that portrayed him so. This tradition was rejected by Pausanias on the quite sensible grounds that Achilles was much too young to have participated in the competition for Helen's hand. The *synthesiae* and the *horkia* cited by Nestor to remind the Achaeans of their assumed obligations

---

[23] Bekker ad *Il.* 9.228 ff.

[24] *Il.* 9.367.

[25] F. Gschnitzer, "Politische Leidenschaft im Homerischen Epos," in H. Gorgemanns and E. A. Schmidt (eds.), *Studien zum antiken Epos, Beiträge zur klassischen Philologie*, 72 (Meisenheim, 1976) 1-21; Vlachos, *Sociétés*, 87-128; Nilsson, *Homer and Myc.*, 215-26, 266-72; G. M. Calhoun, "The Homeric Picture," in Stubbings and Wace (eds.), *Companion to Homer*, 434-38.

WAR CONVENTIONS 167

might have applied to Achilles, but not the agreement mentioned by Stesichorus.

The apparent contradictions in the respective roles of Agamemnon and other Achaeans in the division of the spoils may disappear if we assume that certain prizes devolved on the leaders automatically, with the tacit concurrence between the soldiers and the supreme commander, especially where no contradictory claims existed.[26] In other words, the absence of any objections by the supreme commander symbolized his stamp of approval of the transaction. Therefore, Achilles might not have been far wrong when he asserted that Agamemnon had given him what was by tradition his. The distribution connoted at the same time the finality of the transaction. If then by some unfortunate twist of fate one of the leaders—particularly the supreme leader—suffered a loss of his prize, his loss usually drew the sympathy of his colleagues, who sometimes promised to compensate him generously whenever the next distribution materialized. Thus the unexpected twist of Chryseis's return and Agamemnon's deeply felt loss prompted the other Achaean kings to pledge to him a threefold reward upon the capture of Troy. Yet Agamemnon, in a moment of angry outburst and petty spite, unwisely declared that he wanted immediate compensation and singled out the prizes of Odysseus, Aias, and Achilles as potential reward. This foolish threat pinned him in a position from which he could not easily retreat without some loss of prestige. Nevertheless, he probably should have sustained this minor loss of face, opting for the road of compromise and reconciliation, whose escape-hatch could easily have been the pledge given to him of future benefits. This approach would have been the wisest route to follow as it would have preserved the unity so essential to the speedier attainment of the ultimate goal. Unfortunately, Agamemnon chose to indulge his anger and temporarily gratify his pride at the eventual expense of his army's welfare and its much-needed unity. It was an unfortunate choice as well as one apparently contrary to his character, inasmuch as when he was placed in a much more difficult situation earlier, Agamemnon had sacrificed his own daughter for the sake of the common objective.

As soon as Agamemnon implemented his foolish decision to replace Chryseis by Briseis, there surfaced certain complaints associated with the custom of booty and its apportionment. The first of them related to Agamemnon's portion, which had always been greater than that of Achilles and by implication greater than that of the other Achaean kings. This undesirable disproportion occurred despite the fact that Achilles had carried the brunt of fighting. Understandably, Achilles went along with the method of

---

[26] Leaf ad *Il.* 1.118 asserts that the gift of honor was set aside before the division of the spoils.

distribution as long as it conformed to the traditional precepts of fairness requiring that an extra portion be awarded to the supreme commander. But once Agamemnon repaid this honor with ingratitude by his arbitrary violation of the traditional practices, Achilles immediately expressed his resentment for the injustice of the distribution method, assailing the traditional principle that gave the commander the lion's share of the booty. His criticism implied that the commander should not be content with the enjoyment of the traditional privileges but that he should bend over backwards to dispel any appearance of unfairness to all those who had left their families and homes for his sake and the sake of his brother. Otherwise, the Greeks had no personal quarrel with the Trojans, who had never invaded their territories. Consequently, Achilles concluded, Agamemnon's obligation toward the other Achaeans ought to have made him very sensitive to their feelings and keen to their sensitivities.

Besides women like Chryseis and Briseis, whom their respective masters had singled out for their charm and whatever other qualities they possessed (*Il.* 1.118-19), the Achaeans held many other prizes in the form of women or material objects which they highly valued. These possessions were usually carried home to be used in the service and adornment of the palace, as donations to the deities, or as gifts to friends and guests on important occasions or visits. Part of the recompense that Agamemnon promised Achilles as inducement for their reconciliation and as an apology were seven women from Lesbos skilled in handiwork, along with a variety of other valuable prizes (*Il.* 1.120 ff.). Several of these prizes, obtained by the kings through the process of apportionment, were passed on to their immediate lieutenants as reward for their faithful service. Achilles himself had given the girl Iphis, captured in Scyrus, to his beloved confidant Patroclus.[27] In fact, all of the prizes given to the participants of the games in honor of Patroclus came from the collection that Achilles had amassed during the Trojan campaign. Homer enumerated with admiration the prizes and sometimes described their history and origin in order to help his readers appreciate their actual value, which went far beyond the face value of the objects themselves. Several of these prizes had been awarded to Achilles from the common loot, either through sortition or as γέρατα ἐξαιρετά.[28] That the list of prizes was merely suggestive of the plethora of treasures in the possession of Achilles becomes clear from the allusion made in the same passage by

---

[27] *Il.* 9.667; it is presumed to have been a city in Phrygia alluded to in *Il.* 9.329 but not to be confused with the island of Scyrus. Its geographic position remains a matter of conjecture; Leaf *ad loc.*

[28] The first prize of the foot race was a mixing-bowl of silver. This bowl, whose craftsmanship was Sidonian, had been given to Thoas and bequeathed to Thoas's grandson. The latter gave it to Patroclus as ransom for Lycaon, Priam's son, *Il.* 23.741.

WAR CONVENTIONS 169

Antilochus when he protested the sympathy shown to the goodly Eumelus for the unexpected mishap he had suffered during the chariot race. Apprehensive that Achilles might bestow upon the losing Eumelus the prize for which he had competed successfully, Antilochus suggested that Achilles give to Eumelus one of the many prizes he had stored in his ships.

Several of the stored items had been taken in the defeat of an opponent in individual combat. It appeared that in such one-on-one encounters the spoils acquired from the defeated did not go into the common pool for general distribution after the end of the battle but that they remained the property of the victor. In this private expropriation, especially of weapons, the claim belonged to the individual who dealt the final blow to the vanquished. Thus in the death of Patroclus, Hector received the armor, although it was Euphorbus who had critically wounded Patroclus (*Il.* 17.14.ff., 130 ff.). The same is true of other important items belonging to the fallen heroes, such as horses (*Il.* 23.291 ff.). Eumelus received as consolation prize for his participation in the chariot race a corselet that had belonged to Asteoropaeus's armor, which had come into Achilles' possession when he killed Asteoropaeus in battle (*Il.* 23.560).[29] Still another of the prizes from a duel was the armor that had originally belonged Sarpedon, whom Patroclus had killed and whose armor he had stripped. While many of these spoils must have been the cause of special pride to their new owners, several of them served practical purposes as well. They were kept in the huts of the Homeric heroes as weapons to be used if necessary in the war. Thus in Book 13 of the *Iliad* (13.225 ff.), Meriones left the battle to return to Idomeneus's hut for a new spear to replace the one which been broken in the course of the fighting. Idomeneus met him on the way and assured him that he would find as many spears, bossed shields, and breastplates as he wanted (καὶ ἕν καὶ εἴκοσι) stocked near the entrance wall. With equal pride Meriones boasted that his own tent contained quite as many spoils. All of these weapons were trophies of war stripped from the vanquished enemies.[30]

Finally, ransom collected in the exchange of captives remained, understandably, the personal property of the ransomer. The silver mixing-bowl given as the first prize in the foot race was part of the ransom received by Patroclus for the release of Lycaon (*Il.* 21.48 ff.). This bowl of Sidonian craftsmanship was evidently highly valued as an exquisite piece of art. The ransom Priam brought to Achilles for the return of Hector's body fitted the importance of the occasion. It consisted of twelve white mantles, ten talents

---

[29] *Il.* 23.799-883; Eust. ad *Il.* 23.780-800, 826 for the cast of iron.

[30] There seems to have been some confusion in the interpretation of the text at this point. The use of τοι and ἐμοὶ and the answer of Idomeneus (*Il.* 13.268) as well as οὐ σχεδόν ἐστιν ἐλέσθαι seem to leave no doubt that Meriones was on his way to Idomeneus's hut; cf. Leaf ad *Il.* 13.168; 268.

170

of gold, two tripods, four cauldrons, and one valuable cup, which Priam had received as a gift when he went on an embassy to Thrace. Two of these robes and a tunic were used by Achilles to wrap Hector's body. The others he kept, asking Patroclus to forgive him even from Hades for breaking whatever promises he had made to him concerning Hector, particularly since the ransom for Hector's body turned out to be considerable. (This text, *Il.* 24.579, has been rejected by Aristarchus.) The emphasis here as well as in Book 1 on the adequacy of the ransom for Chryseis, and similarly the amount of the recompense to Achilles in Book 9, suggest that refusal to accept a handsome gift in exchange for a legitimate request was considered an excess by the Greeks, a hybris often punished by the gods. Thus Phoenix acknowledged that Agamemnon's gifts to Achilles constituted a more than fair recompense for the wrong Agamemnon had perpetrated against Achilles, and that there was no way for anyone to turn them down.[31] The onus of explanation was thus placed on Achilles should he choose to reject the apologies and many gifts of Agamemnon.

Summary

The discussion has shown that booty played an important role in the Near Eastern and Homeric world. Kings and their allies followed certain commonly delineated conventions, violation of which could give rise to serious misunderstandings: hence they explicitly stated in their treaties some of the rules that ought to guide the distribution of the loot. The Hittite and Homeric distribution practices must provide an inkling to similar practices in the Mycenaean civilization. Whether these were explicitly stated in agreements is difficult to say, but it is also difficult, if not impossible, to doubt that they must have been similar to the Hittite and Homeric practices.

B. THE USE OF SURROGATES

As in modern times, so also in the ancient world not all military treaties were exclusively post-war truces. Many interstate and interindividual agreements were also pre-war compacts, spelling out the obligations of the respective parties to assist one another in future battles. In suzerainty treaties, it was often stipulated that the lord was expected to go to the aid of his vassal in times of danger arising from either insurrection or external invasion, with a reciprocal obligation naturally incumbent upon the vassal. This sort of obligation was not limited to suzerainty treaties, but was also generally found in parity treaties. However, in the latter case there was one slight but for our purposes rather important difference in the formulation of legal principles, a difference reflected in Homeric as well as Near Eastern practices.

---

[31] *Il.* 9.164: δῶρα μέν οὐκέτ' ὀνοστά διδοῖς 'Αχιλῆϊ ἄνακτι·

WAR CONVENTIONS   171

This was the stipulation, to which we now turn, that in parity treaties a partner was not obligated to lead the troops *personally*. If he did not wish to go himself, then he could send his troops under the command of somebody else, who functioned as his surrogate.[32]

The Near Eastern evidence

In the Hittite suzerainty treaties, the vassal did not have the option of sending his troops under a surrogate leader such as his son or a trusted lieutenant, but rather was expected to take the field himself unless compelling reasons excused him. The clause that made it mandatory (though exceptions are to be found even for vassals) for the junior partner to go to the assistance of his senior is extremely important, particularly since the senior partner, always suspicious of his vassal's fealty, sought to bind him by a written promise sealed by oath. Thus in the treaty between Suppiluliumas and Aziru the latter assumed the obligation to go to the aid of the Hittite king when the king was threatened by either invasion or domestic rebellion. As soon as Aziru heard of such a threat, he was expected to hasten to Suppiluliumas's assistance. If he could not personally discharge this obligation, then he was bound to send somebody else in his place: a son, a brother, or one of the princes or high officials. The same of course would be true in the reverse case, except that the obligation of the lord's personal presence was not so compelling as that of the vassal.[33] The same stipulation is contained in the treaty between Mursilis II and Tuppi-Tešub of Amurru. By it the Hittite king even reminded Tuppi-Tešub that when Aziru had become too old and feeble to discharge this task personally, he assigned it to a younger man. Tuppi-Tešub should therefore try to fulfill this duty as faithfully as his predecessor had done, and where it was not possible for him to lead his troops and his chariots against the enemies of Mursilis, then he should place in charge either his son or brother. Failure to do so would be interpreted as violation of the treaty's oaths.[34] The same stipulation is repeated in at least three more treaties. The first of these is a treaty between Muwatallis and Alaksandus of Wilusa, the text of which is much damaged, but thanks to the formulaic statements observed in such treaties the text has been satisfactorily restored.[35] Elsewhere in another treaty it has been agreed that when the king summoned his vassals to appear before him but someone did not wish to go or could not go, he was

---

[32] Weidner, *Polit. Dok.*, 190.

[33] Weidner, *Polit. Dok.*, 73.

[34] Weidner, *Polit. Dok.*, 79; Friedrich, *Die Staatsverträge*, 1:9, 17.

[35] Friedrich, *Die Staatsverträge*, 1:53-55, 133, 2:63-69.

172 WAR CONVENTIONS

to send a representative—preferably a son named by the lord king—who had
no obligation to bring "red purple."[36]

The Homeric evidence

A similar custom seems to have existed in the world described by Homer,
although again the kings of the Homeric epics differed in one very important
respect from those of the Hittite treaties in that they all seem to have stood
in a nearly autonomous relationship to each other. Nevertheless, in those
cases in which the king could not exercise some of his duties or—more
specifically—his military obligations, he would usually delegate this task to
his son or to someone else capable of performing it. This practice of
assigning surrogates in the Homeric world is not one of the stipulations
mentioned in the corpus of Homeric agreements specified at the outset of the
present study, but it was nevertheless a familiar practice in the aristocratic
world portrayed by the epics.

To show that the use of surrogates was indeed common, only a few
examples need be given here. The first is that of Priam. Unable to participate
in the Trojan expedition on account of his advanced age, Priam designated his
eldest son Hector to lead the troops of the Trojans and their allies in defense
of Troy. The arrangement does not seem to have been formalized by a
personal or interstate treaty as no such treaty is mentioned. Yet the mere
presence of the Trojan allies (*epikouroi*) suggests the existence of a treaty or
treaties between them and the Trojans, having a clause which explicitly or
implicitly provided for an arrangement of this type. Here, as the Hittite
treaties anticipated, an impediment prevented King Priam from going to war,
although he remained the reigning ruler and continued to exercise the supreme
political authority in his kingdom. However, the battlefield decisions had
been transferred to Hector who enjoyed the overall military responsibility for
the actual conduct of the war. The Greeks themselves, familiar as they were
with the practice of using surrogate commanders, understood fully the
division of authority among the Trojans. When Nestor addressed the
Achaeans with the advice that they put aside their quarrels in order to proceed
with the business of the expedition, he reminded them that Priam and his
sons would rejoice at the news of the Greek dispute. This reference to Priam
is no mere accident, since Priam was the reigning sovereign in Troy and as
such enjoyed the ultimate power.[37] A similar expression is elsewhere repeated
by Zeus when he spoke to Hera about the Trojans, and by Agamemnon (*Il.*
3.165). In Book 2 of the *Iliad* (2.286 ff.), Iris is sent by the gods to Troy to
deliver a message. Although she found all the Trojans holding an assembly

---

[36] Weidner, *Polit. Dok.*, 95; Delitzsch, *Assyr. Handwörterbuch*, 129; M. Streck, ZA 19
(1905) 225; P. C. A. Jensen, KB 6.1 (1923) 570.

[37] *Il.* 1.225; similarly *Il.* 4.31, 35, 47; 6.447, *et passim.*

WAR CONVENTIONS   173

before Priam's palace gate, she first spoke to Priam. Iris's address first to Priam and only later to Hector is in strict accord with the established protocol by which the envoy had to address himself first to the king. Likewise, in Book 3 of the *Iliad* (3.275-301) Greeks and Trojans promoted an agreement for the purpose of resolving their differences. The oaths which sealed the agreement were to be taken by the supreme authority on each side, despite the fact that the agreement itself was the brain-child of Paris and had been approved by Hector without prior consultation with Priam. The purported unreliability of Priam's sons (a few of them at least), which allegedly led the Greeks to demand the presence of Priam in the oath-taking ceremony, is really only a poetic device for bringing Priam into the agreement. Certainly Hector, who was its carrier and advocate, was a very reliable individual. But the agreement was not restricted to some military phase of the war: it was an all-encompassing arrangement bound to touch both those on the battlefield and those away from it. As such it had to be approved and "signed" by the sovereign in whose name it was conducted. If the transaction concerned a mere military operation, Priam's presence would not have been required.

The above view seems to be further supported by the episode in which Zeus dispatched Iris to the Trojans to offer them military advice. In this instance Iris went directly to Hector, who was the commander in the field (*Il.* 11.200 ff.), not to Priam. In another incident involving an extraordinary battlefield discussion, Achilles reminded Aeneas that even if he, Achilles, was killed in the impending fight between them, Aeneas had no chance of becoming the master of Troy, for Priam was the ruling king, who would naturally bequeath the crown to one of his sons.[38] Needless to say, Aeneas himself fought in Troy in the place of his father Anchises who, if we are to believe the *Aeneid*, was too old and feeble to engage in fighting himself.

In Book 24 of the *Iliad*, Achilles was reminded by Priam of his own father, Peleus, who was as old as Priam and, like him, no longer a fighter (486). Too old to participate in the Trojan expedition personally, Peleus had entrusted the command of the Myrmidons to Achilles, whom he dispatched as a surrogate at about the age of fifteen, after giving him his golden armor, the ashen spear, and the two horses, all of them his own wedding presents. On the other hand, Achilles' mother Thetis, suspicious that the Greeks would request Achilles to join the expedition in the place of his father, had earlier tried to disguise her son as a girl, entrusting him to Lycomedon, king of Scyrus. But Achilles was cleverly ferreted out by Odysseus, a member of the

---

[38] *Il.* 20.182. For the rivalry between the houses of Anchises and Priam see also *Il.* 20.306; 17.461.

174   WAR CONVENTIONS

committee that had visited Scyrus to solicit Achilles' participation in view of his father's inability.[39]

Somewhat different is the case of Nestor, who had lived through two generations of men and despite his advanced age remained a bold fighter. Although he could not have been much younger than Priam and Peleus, Nestor nonetheless went to Troy, where he served primarily as a counselor to Agamemnon, rivaled only by Odysseus in his eloquence and sound judgment. The two always advised the same course for the successful conduct of the war.[40] His old age and feebleness notwithstanding, Nestor entered the war once, only to be extricated from a dangerous predicament by Diomedes (*Il.* 8.80 ff.). Because of his age, Nestor did not take part in the funeral games in honor of Patroclus, as did most of the other leaders, confining himself to advising his son Antilochus, a participant in the games. At the end, Nestor was rewarded with a prize (*keimelion*) as a token of his valuable contribution to the war effort in the capacity of counselor and as a sign of respect for his age (*Il.* 23.626 ff.). Nestor thus constitutes an "intermediate" case, neither entirely sharing the full military duties of a warrior nor totally excluded from the expedition. His son, although at Troy, did not serve as the representative of his father in the way Achilles and Hector did.

Still more variant is the case of Odysseus. His father Laertes was also elderly, probably old enough to be disqualified from participation in the Trojan campaign. Yet he was not so feeble that he could not work around his farm or don his panoply at the return of Odysseus, twenty years later, in order to fight at his son's side. Paradoxically, at the time of the Trojan expedition it was Odysseus, not Laertes (though the latter seems to have been sound in body and mind) who was the reigning king of Ithaca.[41]

Summary

From the evidence adduced so far, we see that Priam, Peleus, and Anchises fit well the pattern outlined by the Hittite treaties. Their cases also point to the existence of similar customs among the Greeks of the Dark Ages and most probably of the Mycenaean times.[42] Nestor's case is slightly different and so

---

[39] *Il.* 9.769 ff., 298; Apollod. 3.13.8; scholion on *Il.* 19.332; Ovid, *Metam.* 13.162 ff.; Hyginus, *Fabula* 96.

[40] *Il.* 2.21; 1.247-52; 4.310; 2.553-55; *Od.* 3.244, 126-29; 7.327.

[41] Hyginus, *Fabula* 95; Servius on Vergil's *Aen.* 2.81; Tzetzes on *Lycophron* 818; Apollod. *Epitome* 3.7.

[42] In parity treaties among the early Greeks (also later) the allies had the obligation to go to the aid of one another. If an ally failed to do so, he stood in violation of his oath and agreements. In the treaty between Elis and Heraea, mutual assistance was stipulated. The party that failed to fulfill this part of the agreement was under obligation to pay a penalty to the Olympian Zeus; Bengtson, No. 110; Buck, *Gr. Dial.* 62. The obligation of kings to go or send surrogates had by now devolved upon the communities and their instruments of governance.

WAR CONVENTIONS   175

is that of Odysseus, but not so different that they constitute counter-evidence to this conclusion.

C. FIRING THE FIRST SHOT

The last war convention that we shall consider in this chapter is a rule which is not always expressly stipulated in treaties and agreements but which seems to have been always present as a tacit expectation of both parties. This is the convention concerning the grounds for starting a war, a rule whose Near Eastern and Homeric versions show the same remarkable similarity that we have found in the other conventions discussed so far.

The Near Eastern evidence

Starting a war without sufficient provocation constituted a serious moral crime and a flagrant violation of the international law of the civilized nations of antiquity. The principle continued to hold true despite its frequent violations. The Hittites seem to have been no exception to the rule. Aware that state leaders frequently sought to circumvent its moral implications by devising arguments to justify their aggression, the Hittites tried to prevent war among their allies by demanding that they either negotiate their grievances or appeal to some authority. More specifically, they demanded that their allies appeal to the authority of the Hittite king, who served as the senior partner in several of these alliances. Naturally, appeal to the Hittite king was virtually tantamount to submission because failure to comply with the negotiatory mechanism recommended by the king would automatically be interpreted as insubordination and violation of the existing treaties.[43] In the case of noncompliance by a party, the king and his allies were bound to take to the field against the recalcitrant party. If that party could defend himself, he could hope to escape punishment; if not, the consequences could be dire, since, as we shall see, the victor presumed the right to do as he wished with the vanquished culprit. Accordingly, in the treaty between Suppiluliumas, on the one hand, and Huqqanas and the people of Hayaša, on the other, Huqqanas is warned that he should not do anything inimical to his senior partner either directly or indirectly (by encouraging others). In either case, the Hittite king would consider it a violation of the agreements between them.[44] In another treaty, Mursilis II warns a junior partner not to provoke war against one of the king's other partners, for Mursilis would consider such an act hostile to

---

[43] Korosec, *Heth. Staats.*, 39, 87; Friedrich, *Die Staatsverträge,* 1:21, where the right of the vassal to file a grievance against some of the stipulations of the treaty suggests the process of arbitration. See also Friedrich, *Die Staatsverträge,* 1:61-63; Friedrich, AO 24, 3, p. 20.

[44] Friedrich, *Die Staatsverträge,* 1:119.

WAR CONVENTIONS

himself personally and would immediately move against the culprit. The opposite also held true. If that particular contractant were attacked by one of the other vassals, Mursilis promised to come to his immediate aid. In either case, the assailant was in the wrong while the assailed was viewed as the victim.[45] Commencing hostilities implied also other unpleasant consequences, for if the initiator of war were defeated, by the rules of war his territory and possessions became fair game for the victor.[46]

The Homeric evidence

Homeric practices seem not to have been too dissimilar in this respect. Menelaus in the duel agreement with Paris accepted the challenge, advising the rest of the Achaeans to go along with Paris's proposal, so as to put an end to the war and the suffering, for which, Menelaus added, Paris was clearly responsible (*Il.* 3.100). The Achaeans as well as the Trojans acceded to the terms of this single combat, and Menelaus prayed to Zeus that the guilty party be punished while the rest should establish friendship and peace and live henceforth in concord (*Il.* 3.314-25, 351-54). The use of πρότερος κακ' ἔοργε by Menelaus leaves no doubt that, in his opinion, Paris was the aggressor.[47] The duel solved nothing in the end, and so hostilities resumed, following Zeus's compliance with Hera's request that the Trojans be made to look as if they were the perjurers.[48] When Pandarus, the son of Lycaon, shot the arrow against Menelaus, the Achaeans forthwith shed any reservation they had about breaking the duel compact since they were convinced that the Trojans were definitely in the wrong. Therefore, Agamemnon now urged the Achaeans to fight the Trojans to the end.

Before Agamemnon swore the oath on behalf of the Achaeans in the duel agreement, he added a requirement about the payment of adequate recompense by the Trojans without which no agreement would have been made (*Il.* 3.286 ff.). Since the Trojans did not offer any objections to this addition, it appears that recompense for wrong-doing was not an unusual expectation in the

---

[45] Friedrich, *Die Staatsverträge,* 1:147.

[46] Weidner, *Polit. Dok.,* 95-97; Korosec, *Heth. Staats.,* 6-7; E. Forrer, KAF, I 2, p. 267, n. 2; Schachermeyr, *Zur Staatsrechtlichen Wertung,* 180-86.

[47] Note the frequent use of *archês-archomai* to denote the aggressor in Homer *Il.* 4.67, 72. It seems that the issue is not as simple as the Greeks believed, viz., that justice was on their side in the matter of the abduction of Helen. The Trojans viewed the issue as part of the East versus West relationship, and from this viewpoint it was the Greeks who had established the inequity by the abduction of Medea; see the use of *arxai* in Hdt. 1.2.1; 4.1. When the king of Colchis sent envoys demanding the return of his daughter and indemnity, the Greeks turned down his request, contending that they had been refused justice earlier for the abduction of Io; Hdt. 1.2. When the Greeks asked for the return of Helen and compensation for the evil act of Paris, the Trojans refused the demand; Hdt. 1.3. The whole issue of abductions had become by now a matter of principle, in which both parties blamed the other for starting the wrong.

[48] *Il.* 4.236: *proteroi...dêlêsanto.*

WAR CONVENTIONS 177

ancient world (Hdt. 1.2, 3). Failure to restore the disturbed equilibrium by returning the victim and making the required recompense for the committed wrong banished all doubts about the guilt of the accused and made him subject to all sorts of punishment in case of his capture or defeat. Because the Trojans failed to respond to the Greek appeals for the return of Helen, the requisite indemnity was paid at the end by the destruction of their city.

Unleashing a war without provocation continued to be a serious offense among the later Greeks who went to extremes to justify such action. When no legitimate excuse existed, the aggressors would concoct one to show that the other side was to blame. This need to explain one's aggression underlines the seriousness with which the Greeks continued to view it, a topic too immense for detailed documentation here. Suffice it at this point to cite the complicated maneuvering preceding the Peloponnesian War, in which neither party wished to be branded the aggressor. Such artifices underscore the seriousness of "firing the first shot." Although the Spartans felt that their Athenian opponents had taxed their patience and forbearance to the limit through their obstinacy and refusal to yield on the points where the Spartans had asked for concessions, even at the end of the war they were not "entirely" convinced that the fault lay with the Athenians, since the latter had seemed ready to submit the differences to arbitration which the Spartans rejected. After the defeat of Athens, the Spartans refused to destroy the city, as some of their allies suggested, no doubt partly because of their initial guilt-feelings. The allies, especially the Corinthians after Epidamnus, had no such scruples about the responsibility of Athens for the coming of the war; therefore they did not share Sparta's reluctance to destroy Athens.

Conclusion

The stipulation in the treaty between Mursilis and Kupanta explained that the Hittite king would go to the defense of an attacked party.[49] The implication here is that over and beyond any question of self-interest the Hittite king would align himself with the victimized. The same moral tendency to defend the victims of aggression surfaces in the *Iliad*, when Achilles admits that he came to Troy not because the Trojans had wronged him but to defend Menelaus, whose honor had been besmirched by the unprovoked action of Paris (*Il.* 1.152-59). Odysseus seems to have felt a similar moral obligation to participate in the Trojan campaign despite his strong personal reservations. Apparently the reasons that moved the other Homeric heroes to go to war did not obtain for Achilles or Odysseus, who were not bound by the suitors' oath. Their motivation to participate derived from a more general sense of moral propriety that gave Homeric society its aristocratic character. In the

---

[49] Friedrich, *Die Staatsverträge,* 1:147.

present context, this sense of propriety took the form of certain moral, generally tacit obligations whose contents were much like the written obligations undertaken in the Hittite and other nations of the Near Eastern world.

CHAPTER SEVEN

CONVENTIONS ASSOCIATED WITH TREATY-MAKING

In addition to those conventions which were part of the "contents" of the Near Eastern treaties and Homeric agreements, there were other practices which regulated the very making or keeping of the promises. These procedural rules were sometimes mentioned in the promise, in which case they can be considered stipulations as well as procedures. However, whether they are thought of as internal or external to the agreement itself, they are interesting in the context of the present study, which is concerned with the resemblances and lines of possible filiation to be found among the social practices of the Near Eastern, Mycenaean, Homeric, and even post-Homeric worlds.

The first convention we shall discuss in this chapter is that of the ceremonial meal, which more than any other single practice reveals the deep affiliative bonds that often existed among ancient peoples. We shall then turn to what might be called the "archival" procedures, whereby the terms of a treaty or agreement were made a matter of collective and public memory. These were the closely related conventions of depositing the treaty documents or their equivalents, and declaiming them in public recitations. Finally, we shall consider the manner by which the duration of agreements was established, discovering here as elsewhere that there are significant parallels between the Near Eastern and Homeric practices.

A. MEALS

Perhaps the most important of the conventions associated with the practices of treaty-making in the Ancient Near East and Greece was the ritual of taking a meal together. The ritual itself had little connection with the contents of the treaty, i.e., the stipulations that were agreed upon and sworn to, but it nonetheless symbolized the new relationship established by the contract and oath. The custom of sealing a union by taking bread together seems to have been fairly widespread, and to have been based on the idea of tribal association and its implications. Since the family group ate together, a common meal with a non-family member implied admission to the family group.

The Near Eastern evidence

Bread-breaking must have been a universal custom in the Ancient Near East, because it has been attested among the Semites as well as the non-Semitic

180 CONVENTIONS ASSOCIATED WITH TREATY MAKING

peoples.[1] That food and drink were part of what was considered a sacramental part of treaty-making is clearly adduced from the treaty of Esarhaddon, wherein the vassal promised not to make a treaty with another ruler by serving food at the table or drinking from a cup.[2] The figurative consummation of the alliance between Yahweh and his people on Mount Sinai was the ceremonial meal in which Moses and the representatives of the people took part. After the terrifying manifestation of Yahweh, the meal symbolized the peace and community established by the covenant between Yahweh and Israel. It signified that the weaker had been taken into community by the stronger; hence it was a reassuring gesture on the part of the superior toward the inferior, not a pledge by the latter (Exod. 24.11). The same practice was followed when Abimelech, the Philistine king, decided to make up with Isaac whom he had once expelled from his kingdom. Soon afterward, convinced that the expulsion of Isaac had been unjust and that God was with Isaac, Abimelech asked Isaac to become a party to a covenant, to which he agreed. Once the agreement had been concluded, the king gave a dinner in Isaac's honor. Oddly, the oaths of this non-aggression pact were taken the morning after the meal (Gen. 26.28-31), something unusual for meals in celebration of treaties since such dinners normally followed the oaths which concluded the treaty and not vice versa.

Similarly, when Laban made a covenant with Jacob (Gen. 31.44 ff.; διαθώμεθα διαθήκην) and as a result set up a cairn as a monument to the agreement (καὶ ἔστω εἰς μαρτύριον ἀνὰ μέσον ἐμοῦ καὶ σοῦ), the two partners sat down on the cairn to a meal which symbolized the settlement of their disputes. Jacob subsequently swore by the kinsman of his father Isaac, offered a sacrifice on the mountain, and then called his friends to a meal. They all ate the food and passed the night on the mountain. By this meal Jacob expressed his gratitude for his acceptance into the family of his in-laws, a fact confirmed by Jacob's own reference to his brothers-in-law as brothers. Neither Jacob nor Laban here acted exclusively on his own behalf; each was the leader of a clan and it is clear that the story depicts the way in which boundary lines between units of this kind came to be established. It appears that the story reflected two traditions, the one of the so-called *mizpah*, the other of *Gilead*.[3] The first tradition takes its name from a word

---

[1] Wiseman, *The Vassal Treaties*, 154; J. Pedersen, *Israel, Its Life and Culture* (Copenhagen, 1926) 1:305-306.

[2] Wiseman, *The Vassal Treaties*, 40.

[3] *Mizpah* means "to look out" or "an outlook point." It is the name of several districts and towns located both East and West of the Jordan river, all presumably situated on elevations, and all probably of ancient sanctity. *Gilead* is a term which probably refers to a memorial cairn or pillar. The sanctity of the meal found expression in the rites which accompanied it. Similar *kudurrus* or boundary stones from Ancient Babylon are engraved with inscriptions that are at once legal and royal and their affinity to treaties is widely

CONVENTIONS ASSOCIATED WITH TREATY MAKING   181

meaning "watch" such that the *mizpah* tradition had become the residence of a spirit, or perhaps the spirit itself, who would watch over the two parties and oversee their bargain even when they could not keep each other under close observation. The name of the other tradition, *Gilead*, refers to a heap of stones (again, probably the home of a spirit) which marked the frontier between the Hebrew and Aramaean people. At any rate, the most significant part of the story for our purposes is that the treaty had been solemnized by a common meal which the families shared and after which Laban took his departure for his own land.

The Homeric evidence

Whatever one thinks of the value that explanations of this sort have when applied to early Greek practices, it seems clear that under primitive conditions every banquet had a sacral significance. Anyone who ate and drank in the company of a group of men was united with them by a sacred bond; as noted above, the admission to a meal was tantamount to admission to mutual peace and protection. That the gods were included in the communion of the banquet is clearly evident in the sacrifice of Eumaeus in the *Odyssey* (14.434-35). Of the seven portions of the animal slaughtered, one was set aside for Hermes and the Nymphs, while the men present received the rest. Thus the common banquet became a communion, uniting the participants in one fellowship in which the gods also took part.[4]

Homer makes several other references to meals, although of course not all of them mark important occasions or treaty-making ceremonies. It is

recognized; F. X. Steinmetzer, *Die babylonischen Kudurru als Urkundenform, Studien zur Geschichte und Kultur des Altertums* (Paderborn, 1922) 96; McCarthy, *Treaty and Covenant*, 109; Hillers, *Treaty Curses*, 15.

[4] Among many peoples a stranger who has been permitted to take part in their meal is thereby received under the protection of the tribe and even becomes a tribal member inasmuch as the meal united with sacred bonds all who partook of it. "Thou has forsaken thy great oath, and table, and the salt," the poet Archilochus wrote reproachfully (Bergk, *Poetae Lyrici Graeci*, frg. 96), while the orator Aischines asked emphatically of his colleagues by whom he thought he had been deceived: "Where is the salt? Where the drink-offering?" (Dem. 19.189). The sanctity of the meal which knit all the partakers together in a sacred community helps us understand the best known and most prominent of all the rites of Greek religion, animal sacrifice. Its meaning and origin have been vigorously discussed by W. R. Smith, who advanced the hypothesis of a totemistic origin; see his *Lectures on the Religion of the Semites* (London, 1927). Nilsson rejects Smith's totemistic interpretation, considering it untenable, at least among the Greeks. He does, however, uphold the sacredness of the meal which he deems sufficient to explain the peculiarities of animal sacrifice. The sacrifice is a meal common to the god and his followers, *Greek Folk Religion* (New York, 1961) 73-74; and *A History of Greek Religion* (Oxford, 1963) 96. Wine was part of the ritual associated with treaty-making, and was consequently mentioned often in connection with treaties and libations. This wine, however, is different from the wine consumed at the ritual meal that followed the conclusion of the treaty. The wine utilized in treaties was not mixed with water (*Il.* 2.341; 4.159). Trojans and Achaeans brought wine which they mixed in one bowl. The obvious significance of such an act is also illustrated in *Aen.* 12.161 ff.

182 CONVENTIONS ASSOCIATED WITH TREATY MAKING

important, however, to review the Homeric material with an eye to the utility of meal-taking and its possible connection to contractual arrangements. Suffice it to say that cases are not always clear-cut, or permitting easy categorizations. However, in spite of their frequent blurrings and overlappings, the descriptions of food and drink in the Homeric epics can be grouped according to distinct uses or functions served by the ceremonial eating and drinking.[5]

The first use of food and drink to be considered is the straightforward one of nourishment. For instance, after the death of Patroclus had achieved what several Achaean embassies to Achilles had failed to achieve, namely the return of Achilles to the battlefield, the question of food arose. In his sudden desire to revenge his friend's death, Achilles prepared to begin hostilities even though his troops would be fighting on empty stomachs (the hour was very early and the soldiers had not yet had their breakfast). The quick-witted Odysseus persuaded Achilles of the inexpediency of his proposal. The battle would be long, Odysseus maintained, and therefore very hard for hungry troops (*Il.* 19.155 ff.). Achilles accepted Odysseus's point and allowed the troops to breakfast before they commenced hostilities. He himself, however, refused to partake of food and drink because his heart remained still heavy over Patroclus's death. Odysseus reminded Achilles that, whatever his own feelings, the rest of the Achaeans could not mourn by denying the belly (*Il.* 19.221). Later on, as will become evident, Achilles himself would urge the mourning Priam to partake of food and drink, explaining that even Niobe, that archetype of the disconsolate mother, ate and drank after she had mourned her children for ten days. So far was this act from interfering with her expression of faithful sorrow that, by the favor of the gods, her grief was immortalized in stone. Priam, therefore, Achilles added, should eat despite his mourning (*Il.* 24.600 ff.; Leaf *ad loc.*; Paus. 5.13.7, 8.8.4).

Meals also served the purpose of hospitality, a pleasure and a duty owed to strangers and travellers at a time when inns and hotels did not exist. Consequently, the offer of food and drink by a host extended beyond the

---

[5] Homer employed very frequently the word *deipnon*, which according to Monro (ad *Il.* 8.53) denotes the midday meal taken before the battle, while by the word *dorpos* Homer means the evening meal. Eustathius seems to support Monro's contention, although in *Od.* 4.574 *deipnon* referred to the evening meal. Both terms include the wine taken at such meals. Several other expressions referring to eating and drinking are *medomai sitou* (*Od.* 24.618-19) or *siton edô* (*Od.* 16.110) and *deipnon hairô* (*Od.* 9.86), all referring to food and drink. *Edôde* (*Od.* 16.293; 19.12) also means food and drink (*esthiein kai pinein*, *Od.* 5.196), and ἐσθίειν βρώμην καὶ πίνειν οἶνον (*Od.* 12.23), while *brotus* refers to food but implies drink as well. Finally, Homer used some periphrastic expressions to refer to food and drink, such as *hoplizomai dorpou* (*Od.* 16.453) and τεύχω δόρπου (τετυκοίμεθα δόρπου, *Od.* 14.408). A beloved expression of Homer is also πόσιος καὶ ἐδητύος ἐξ ἔρον ἕντο (*Il.* 24.628) or δαίνυ δαῖτα, the latter hinting at a form of consultation between king and elders around a common dinner (*Od.* 7.189; 8.42; 13.8, Ameis and Hentze, ad *Il.* 9.10).

CONVENTIONS ASSOCIATED WITH TREATY MAKING

simple human necessity with, what seems to be a mystical or quasi-sacramental element implicit in this conventional obligation. Thus Homer showed how Eumaeus first saved the newly arrived Odysseus from the fierce watchdogs and then invited him into his hut where he offered him food and drink and asked him for news of the outside world (*Od.* 14.45-47). Similarly, before Menelaus sent young Telemachus off, he ordered the maids to prepare a hearty breakfast with the explanation that a good meal was a double boon to man: glory and honor for the host and a comfort for all those who embarked on long journeys (*Od.* 15.75-76). Telemachus himself offered his hospitality to Athena, whom he mistook for a stranger. Bidding her come into his house, he assured her that she would find ample food and drink inside (*Od.* 1.123-24). Homeric etiquette required that no business be transacted and that even the identity of the stranger not be asked before the host had entertained his guest with a dinner. Eumaeus faithfully followed the rule when he entertained Odysseus, as did Nestor when Telemachus visited him in hopes of learning of his father's whereabouts (*Od.* 3.43-46). Alcinous did the same when Odysseus came as a victim of shipwreck to his island (*Od.* 7.166 ff.).[6] This quasi-sacramental quality of the common meal and the bond created thereby were viewed so strongly in the ancient world that failure to honor the established relationship drew opprobrium from gods and men. Thus Homer criticized Heracles, that archetype of heroic strength, for slaying Iphitus, his guest, and thereby flouting all propriety and regard for the wrath of gods and for the table he had set before Iphitus.[7]

Since hospitality was considered a sacred duty owed to visitors, visitors were obliged on their part not to abuse this right. Visitors who, like Odysseus, seemed to overstay their visits were frequently requested to perform various chores.[8] Generally, abusing hospitality in any way came to be viewed as reprehensible. The suitors fell under this category, their ill-conduct aggravated by the additional crimes of courting the wife of a gentleman who was still alive and getting drunk at the expense of their host, thereby abusing and making a sham of the right of hospitality.[9]

---

[6] Guests were expected to identity themselves after the enjoyment of their host's dinner and hospitality. A truthful identification was not always given, as the example of Odysseus illustrates. Odysseus understandably did not wish to divulge his identity and therefore resorted to the invention of a credible story; cf. Standford *ad loc.;* C. O. H. Woodhouse, *The Composition of Homer's Odyssey* (Oxford, 1930) ch. 17.

[7] *Od.* 21.28-29; Eust. ad *Od.* 21.35; τελεία γὰρ ἔκτοτε ἡ ξενία διὰ τὸν κοινὸν ἀγνίτην ἄλα καὶ τὸ ὁμοτράπεζον καὶ ὁμοέστιον καὶ ὁμωρόφιον.

[8] *Od.* 15.309, 16.111, where *maps* in connection with eating and drinking in vain or without purpose was not condoned in Homeric times. In *Od.* 17.17 Odysseus recognized that he could not stay at Eumaeus's place forever and be a burden to him; see also *Od.* 12.27.

[9] *Od.* 1.228, 376-77; 2.55 ff.; 2.139-40. See also *Od.* 16.239; 19.12, where the sanctity of feasting is mentioned.

184 CONVENTIONS ASSOCIATED WITH TREATY MAKING

But food and drink had another still deeper function, namely, that of restoring a lost harmony. Thus the mending of the Achaean schism in Book 2 (421) offered the opportunity for still another meal. Nestor and Odysseus, the two protagonists who had never forgotten the original cause of the Trojan expedition, gleefully saw that cause triumph at the end of the assembly session. The troops had been stayed from returning home, and those who, like Thersites, had sought to whip up a demagogic frenzy against the leader of the army found themselves repressed. This success was celebrated with the offering of a supplicatory and doxological meal, symbolizing the restoration of unity among the Greeks, notwithstanding the withdrawal of Achilles. A similar meal had taken place before the Achaean departure from Aulis to celebrate the end of the long dissatisfaction that culminated with the sacrifice of Agamemnon's daughter.[10] Equally doxological was the feast of the Achaeans immediately after the duel between Aias and Hector. On behalf of all the Greeks, Agamemnon slew an ox which he sacrificed to the gods to express his gratitude for the safe return of Aias to the Achaean camp (*Il.* 7.319 ff.). The doxological nature of the meal bespeaks the mystical element encapsulated in the act of eating and drinking. A similar meal was given upon the return of Diomedes and Odysseus from their spying mission. That the purpose of the meal was ceremonial, probably to give thanks, is indicated by the fact that this was the third meal Odysseus had enjoyed during the course of one night.[11] It manifested the double gratitude of the Greeks: first of all to the gods who had safely returned to them the two colleagues, and secondly to the two comrades who had risked their lives for the common good. Odysseus himself would later offer a doxological meal to the gods to celebrate his miraculous escape from the hands of Polyphemus (*Od.* 9.549-50). Finally, on the occasion of the happy reunion of Laertes and Odysseus, a dinner was organized during which thanks were undoubtedly given to the gods for the safe return of Odysseus and the massacre of the suitors (*Od.* 24.384).

The determination of Achilles to fast until Patroclus had received the funeral he had been promised is indicative of the ceremonial role fasting or eating could play. But Achilles eventually yielded to the protestations of the other Achaean leaders that famishing himself would not necessarily be the best way to honor a pledge to a friend (*Il.* 23.48, στυγερῇ πειθώμεθα δαιτὶ). The clash between Achilles' pledge to celebrate Patroclus's death by a fast and the reaction of the other Greeks to this idea demonstrates that fasting was not a clearly established custom in mourning. On the contrary, the Greeks knew that abstinence from food combined with grief could definitely prove detrimental to one's health and they did their utmost to dissuade

---

[10] *Il.* 2.307-21; Paus. 9.19.7.

[11] *Il.* 9.20, 222; Leaf *ad loc.*

CONVENTIONS ASSOCIATED WITH TREATY MAKING   185

Achilles from his mistaken course (*Il.* 19. 225, γαστέρι δ᾽ οὔ πως ἔστι νέκυν πενθῆσαι ᾽Αχαιούς; cf. Leaf *ad loc.*). If fasting and grieving were not the wisest combination to pursue at any time, they were particularly unwise during war time.

The ritualistic significance of food and drink is further attested to with the practice of capping the funeral ceremonies by a meal. Thus after the burial of Hector's bones, the Trojans went back to Troy where they regathered (they had obviously taken the return road severally) and engaged in a splendid banquet at the palace of Priam. This practice continued down to classical times and took the name περίδειπνα. Indeed, even today in the whole area of the Southeastern Mediterranean no funeral ceremony is considered complete without a ceremonial meal (μακαρία) upon the completion of the burial process. Religious or ritualistic practices are indeed slow to die out despite the various upheavals that mark the march of history and revolutionize life. This is borne out by the discovery by Mylonas that the funeral meals in Greece had their origins in the Mycenaean period, a fact which loudly attests to the persistence of certain customs throughout history.[12] These funeral meals symbolized, then as now, the recognition that life goes on despite the grievous losses that frequently afflict man. Accordingly, Odysseus's advice to Achilles not to famish himself was in turn repeated gently by Achilles to Priam when the latter found himself in Achilles' hut pleading for Hector's body. Forewarned by the gods not to defile Hector's body, Achilles ordered his lieutenants to have Hector's corpse washed, anointed, and wrapped in a tunic. After this was done, Achilles placed the body on a bier on Priam's wagon and then invited Priam to a meal (*Il.* 24.618), with a reference to Niobe, whose twelve children had been slaughtered by Apollo and Artemis because of a childish insult to the latter's mother, Leto. In a way Achilles' dinner invitation to Priam went beyond the Homeric etiquette of hospitality, since it manifested Achilles' acceptance of the reality of Patroclus's death, Priam's acceptance of Hector's death, and the union of Achilles and Priam in a sort of social and political bond. Those who do not eat together remain alien, without fellowship in religion or reciprocal and social duties, while those who share the communion of food cease to be strangers and enemies.[13] It was perhaps fitting that Achilles died shortly afterward, since to have survived and gone on to capture and destroy the city of his table-guest would have been incongruous with the aristocratic ethos. The symbolism implicit in this meal is further attested by the altered outlook that each developed toward the other after the dinner. Priam admired Achilles' divine-like height

---

[12] Mylonas, *Mycenae and the Mycenaean Age,* 106.

[13] Smith, *Religion of the Semites,* 269; *Od.* 7.187; 13.8; *Il.* 4.259, 343; 9.70; and Erbse *ad loc.*

186 CONVENTIONS ASSOCIATED WITH TREATY MAKING

and beauty, while Achilles marvelled at Priam's noble look, his serene face, his lofty speech. Following the dinner, Priam finally entertained the thought of sleep, admitting that he had not slept from the day his son had been killed (*Il.* 24.637 ff.). The sedative effect of food and drink alluded to here by Priam was similarly noticed by Odysseus (*Od.* 7.215-22), who recognized that a good meal acted as a pain-killer, helping him forget what he had suffered throughout his return trip.

Finally, meals in Homer and the Near East signaled a change in the relations of men from a negative to a positive attitude, from the condition of enmity and discord to a state of friendship and concord. The restoration of concord in the Greek camp was celebrated with the offering of sacrifice and a meal. The meal symbolized the peace and harmony that prevailed once more among the Greeks, following the turbulent assembly meeting in which Thersites nearly succeeded in creating a rebellion. The same conciliatory effects of the food and drink occur again and again. Ostensibly, the Achaeans were eventually forced to return Chryseis to her father in order to end the destructive plague. Odysseus, who was chosen to head the embassy to Chryses, prepared a propitiatory sacrifice to Apollo upon his arrival; then Odysseus and his embassy-members sat down to a dinner (*Il.* 1.467). While the sacrifice symbolized the Achaeans' atonement for the insult they had perpetrated upon Apollo's priest, the meal that followed represented the restoration of peace between Apollo's priest and the Achaeans.

This ritualistic significance of meal-taking as the seal of a new set of relationships is probably best exemplified in the encounter between Circe and Odysseus. Since she had failed to convert Odysseus into a pig by means of her potion, as she had done to Odysseus's comrades, Circe became reconciled to Odysseus, gracing this reconciliation with a suggestion of food and drink. Although Circe swore not to harm him, Odysseus would not eat Circe's food when his reconciliation to her was not yet complete, because his comrades were still pigs (*Od.* 10.375). Nor should Circe have asked him to eat and drink at her table as long as she kept Odysseus's comrades in that condition. When, at his request, his comrades were freed, Odysseus sat down to Circe's dinner. A similar scene was repeated between Calypso and Odysseus, following their agreement that Calypso should let Odysseus go. Calypso set the table while she herself ate ambrosia and drank nectar. This dinner, which consummated their agreement, hailed the beginning of reconciliation for both. Certainly the dialogue that followed their dinner reflected the soothing effects it had upon their spirits and upon the restoration of friendly relations between them. Their mutual suspicion and tension had now been dissipated (*Od.* 5.196-97; Eust. ad *Od.* 5.199). Finally, to return to the *Iliad*, after the reconciliation between Agamemnon and Achilles and after Agamemnon's oath that he had not so much as touched Briseis, Odysseus proposed that Agamemnon make amends to Achilles by entertaining him with a

CONVENTIONS ASSOCIATED WITH TREATY MAKING 187

sumptuous feast, "so that Achilles would have nothing lacking of his due" (*Il.* 19.179-80), where ἀρέσκω denotes to make amends or reconcile.

Summary

In concluding this brief analysis of the symbolic significance of food and drink in the life of the ancients, it is worth noting that no mention of banquets appears in formally made treaties, although dinners constituted an indispensable ritual of the concluding ceremonies.[14] The explanation for this omission is obvious. Dinners consummating agreement were part of the celebratory conventions highlighting the newly established legal relationship, but not an integral part of the treaty itself. The role such dinners played could be viewed as greater than the clauses of the treaty itself, in that the meals manifested the fullness of heart, those subtle sentiments expected to follow the contracting or making of a covenant. In some way the food and drink of which the contractants of the agreements partook symbolized the state of mind that superseded the formalities associated with the making of an agreement and which, it was hoped, would serve as the best guarantee of the agreement. From this standpoint, the food and drink at such dinners served to remind the participants that they were expected to perform tasks over and beyond the mere conformity to the letter of the law. It made strangers or even enemies into friends, and dictated that each treat the other in the way he would have wished to have been treated by him. This is the essence of the heroic spirit.

B. DEPOSITION AND RECITATION

Ceremonial means were not the only striking social conventions in the marvelous age of Homeric aristocracy. Equally striking, because animated by the same noble spirit, were the implicit and explicit conventions that, so to speak, "documented" the consummated agreements. These were the practices of depositing and periodically reciting the contents of an important agreement, which we shall discuss in turn.

---

[14] The obligation to entertain the envoys of a newly acquired ally becomes part of the text of the concluded alliances in the fifth and fourth centuries B.C. See for example the treaty between Athens and Segesta, Bengtson, No. 139; SEG 10, 7, 11.14-15. The year of the treaty is most probably 458/7 B.C. It would not be too far-fetched to infer that the Erythrae decree contained a similar stipulation in its missing part, and the same might be true of treaties Nos. 142, 148, b 11.17-21, 169, 207, 208. The evidence thus points to a standing practice in the fifth century with roots very early in the history of Greece and the Near East. Such dinners, following the taking of oaths and the conclusion of treaties, symbolized the beginning of a new era in the relations of the contractants and unquestionably assumed a doxological significance.

188 CONVENTIONS ASSOCIATED WITH TREATY MAKING

Deposition: The Near Eastern evidence

Several Near Eastern treaties contain an explicit clause concerning their depositing and regular recitation. According to the agreement between Suppiluliumas and Mattiwaza, the King of the Mitanni, a copy of the tablet containing their treaty was to be deposited in the temple of the famous Babylonian sun-god Samash, the special protector of the Hittite king and queen, while another copy was to be placed before Tešub, the lord of Kurinnu in Kahat.[15] The contents of the tablet were to be read repeatedly before the king of Mitanni, and no one had the right to tamper with the tablet, hide it in a secret place, break it, or change its contents, under fear of divine punishment.[16] The tablet which contained the treaty between Tudhaliyas IV and Ulmi-Tešub of Datassa had similarly been deposited in Arinna, before the sun-goddess of Arinna. This treaty was shown to Tudhaliyas when he visited Datassa, since Ulmi-Tešub had certain legitimate complaints regarding the excessive tribute imposed upon him by the treaty. Tudhaliyas enjoined that this tablet, made of iron, was not to be taken away from Ulmi-Tešub and his descendants or from the Hittite king's descendants.[17]

The practice of depositing the treaty documents at the temple seems to have served the dual purpose of protection and publication. As guardians of the divine *temenos*, the priests and the gods also served as guardians of the document itself, although, given the accessibility of the temples to all, many inquisitive visitors were probably able to see it and testify to its existence. Thus the physical presence of the tablet at the temple corroborated its existence and its official nature, a purpose which today is served by the publication of official documents in the government gazette, or the newspapers and magazines. Although no mention is made of copies kept in the royal archives, there is little doubt that such a practice was in force. When the tablet containing the treaty between Mursilis II and Mursilis's nephew, Rimi-šar-ma of Halap (Aleppo), was stolen, Rimi-šar-ma asked for a duplicate from Mursilis's son and successor. Muwatallis dispatched a duplicate to him with the addendum that no one was to change the contents of the treaty in the future, denounce it, or break the tablet, under penalty of death. Muwatallis did not explain from what copy the duplicate had been

---

[15] Perhaps a sanctuary, though we cannot be sure; Weidner, *Polit. Dok.*, 28 n. 1.

[16] Weidner, *Polit. Dok.*, 27-29, 49.

[17] McCarthy, *Treaty and Covenant*, 183-84; see also J. Fitzmeyr, SBQ 20 (1959) 444; Fitzmeyer, JAOS 81 (1961) 181-83. In most cases not one but several copies were deposited in various temples belonging to different gods. A copy of the treaty between Suppiluliumas and Mattiwaza was deposited before Samash of Arrina, the protector god of the Harri king and queen. Still another copy was deposited before the god Tešup, the lord of Kirinnu of the city of Kahat, though the significance of this god is unclear. No changes were to be made in the terms of the document, while no removal from the place of its deposition, and no violation to the document were allowed, Weidner, *Polit. Dok.*, 27-29, 49.

CONVENTIONS ASSOCIATED WITH TREATY MAKING 189

produced nor was there any word as to the place from which Rimi-šar-ma's copy had been stolen. One cannot exclude the possibility that the stolen copy was kept at some temple rather than the royal archives where it could be under lock. But no reference was made to any temple nor was it mentioned whether the duplicate was to be deposited at a temple.[18] The injunction that the text of the treaty should be read to the signatory several times a year in order to remind him constantly of his obligations, and that the signatories should teach the treaty to their sons and grandsons, suggests that a copy of the treaty was kept near the palace.[19] After the treaty had been signed by the two parties and before it was deposited in the royal archives or the temples, it would be stamped with the official seal of the signatories, which most probably were the pictures of the signatories' patron gods.[20]

Deposition: The Homeric evidence

The Mycenaean Linear writing points to the maintenance of chancellories by the Mycenaean kings. Whether or not official documents such as treaties were kept there is unclear, since no Mycenaean treaty documents have survived, but such an arrangement was certainly possible. If they were kept there, were copies also deposited at Mycenaean sanctuaries? Again the question cannot be easily answered, since no treaty documents or Mycenaean temples have been unearthed. What is known, however, is that in the post-Homeric era copies of interstate treaties were normally deposited in the archives of temples of the Greek cities, while still other copies were usually set up at such famous pan-Hellenic religious centers as Olympia and Delphi. (Not many examples need be cited here in confirmation of this practice, since the practice itself is well known.) In some cases, because of the worn-out condition of the stelae, no mention of the stipulation regarding the setting up of the inscription at the sanctuary can be traced, but the discovery of the stone itself in places like Olympia and Delphi, often far away from the geographic location of the signatories, leaves little doubt that copies of Greek interstate treaties were customarily deposited there. In the treaty between Elis and Heraea (which some scholars place in the middle of the sixth century) mention is made of fines to be paid to the Olympian Zeus. Inasmuch as the slab itself containing the treaty has been discovered in Olympia, it seems that the Heraeans most probably had their own copy preserved at the temple of their most prominent divinity, a temple which must have served as the repository of public documents. The Eleans kept their copy at the temple of Zeus in Olympia,

---

[18] Weidner, *Polit. Dok.*, 81; KBO 4,4 and 3,15 ff.

[19] Friedrich, *Die Staatsverträge*, 2:77; Wiseman, *The Vassal Treaties*, in *Iraq* 20 (1958) 1 ff.; McCarthy, *Treaty and Covenant*, 200; Korosec, *Heth. Staats.*, 101.

[20] McCarthy, *Treaty and Covenant*, 198-200; Wiseman, *The Vassal Treaties*, 20 (1958) 54, 173.

190 CONVENTIONS ASSOCIATED WITH TREATY MAKING

since, as some scholars believe, at the time of the treaty they had taken over control of Olympia from the Pisatans. But even if Olympia was not under the control of Elis, the presence of the slab underlines the resolve of the two allies to deposit a copy at Olympia.[21] Similarly, the Greek cities of the Anaetoi and Metapioi as well as the cities of Sybaris and the Serdaeans had copies of their treaties (dated between 550-525 B.C.) placed in Olympia where the mutilated texts have been discovered. Unquestionably, copies of these treaties must also have been placed at some temple of the signatory cities.[22]

Significantly, the custom of placing copies of documents at the temples of gods was not limited to treaties. Appropriately, a stone on which the text of the constitution of the Cretan city of Dreros had been inscribed (ca. 650-600 B.C) has been located on the wall of the temple of Apollo Delphinios in Dreros. Though the document does not pertain to the class of documents under discussion, its location confirms the hypothesis that temples served as repositories of important interstate treaties.[23] The same is true, of course, regarding the inscription containing the agreement of the Theraeans about the foundation of a colony on the Libyan coast. The fourth century re-draft of the original agreement (ὅρκιον; IIa 11.23-40) represents a decree of the ecclesia of Thera. This document contains the injunction that an inscribed tablet be placed in the ancestral sanctuary of the Theraeans at Delphi in confirmation of the decree of the assembly.[24]

The progressive democratization of life in the Greek world failed to alter this ancient religious custom. Thus one of the stipulations of the Nicias treaty required the mutual display of the pillars that had been inscribed with the text of the treaty, and which specified their location as well. The Lacedaemonians had to set up the pillar at the temple of Apollo in Amyclae while the Athenians were to place it on the Acropolis at the temple of Athena.[25] The same story is repeated in the treaty of alliance between Athens and Haliaea. The Athenians were obligated to inscribe the text on stone and place it in the city (the Acropolis), while the Halieis were to deposit their

---

[21] W. Dittenberger, and K. Purgold, *Die Inschriften von Olympia*, No. 21. M/L No. 17; Busolt, IG12 (Berlin, 1893) 64, n. 4; 706; L. I. Highby, *The Erythrae Decree. Klio Beiheft* 36 (1936) 63-64; Ehrenberg, JHS 57 (1937) 151; C. Callmer, *Studien zur Geschichte Arkadiens* (Lund, 1943) 80.

[22] Bengtson, Nos. 111,120; F. Kiechle, RhM 103 (1960) 348-50; H. Schaefer, *Staatsform und Politik* (Leipzig, 1932) 80; C. Calderone, *Helikon* 3 (1963) 219-58.

[23] M/L No.2; Willetts, *Arist. Soc. in Anc. Crete,* 106; Buck, *Gr. Dial.* 116; Ehrenberg, CQ 37 (1943) 14-18; Demargne and van Effenterre, BCH 62 (1938) 194-95.

[24] M/L No. 5; SEG 9.3; F. Chamoux, *Cyrene sous la Monarchie des Battiades* (Paris, 1953) 105-11; L. H. Jeffery, *Historia* 10 (1961) 139-46; A. J. Grahamn, *Colony and Mother City,* 27, 40, 224-26; J. H. Oliver, GRBS 7 (1966) 25-29.

[25] Thuc. 5.23.5; 18.10; Gomme, HCT 3, 694.

CONVENTIONS ASSOCIATED WITH TREATY MAKING 191

copy in Apollo's temple.[26] Likewise, in the treaty made by Argos, Athens, Mantineia and Elis in 420 B.C. the same requirement is included. Because of the fragmentary character of the stone this clause is missing, but Thucydides explains that the Athenians had to post the treaty on the Acropolis, the Argives were to post it at the temple of Apollo in the market place, and the Mantineians were to put it in the temple of Zeus and also in their market place. The Eleans were apparently exempted from this requirement because of the common obligation to erect a bronze copy of the treaty in Olympia, the expense of which must have been borne by all.[27]

This practice of entrusting treaties to the temples of the gods went on unabatedly into the Hellenistic times. Thus an inscription from the Troad containing the treaty between king Antiochus III and the city of Lysimacheia enjoins that the text be reproduced in triplicate, of which one copy was to be displayed in Ilium at the sanctuary of Athena, the second in the city of Lysimacheia beside the altar of Zeus, and the third in Samothrace at the sanctuary of the Great Gods.[28] A third century decree bestowing *isopolity* between the Aetolians and the Heracliots orders the cutting of an inscription and its exposition at the temple of Apollo at Delphi. Undoubtedly, copies of this decree must have been set up at the temples of each of the signatories.[29]

Although no information remains from the Mycenaean times on the placing of treaty documents in the temples of gods, the invocation of the gods as witnesses, the curses, blessings and other customs similar to the Near Eastern practices suggest that the practice of temple or palace-temple deposition must have been in existence among the Mycenaeans. Because the practice has been found very early in the history of post-Homeric Greece, and because of the persistent history of religious practices in general, it seems unlikely that placing documents in the temples of the gods was only a post-Mycenaean development. Furthermore, places like Olympia and Delphi evolved as important religious centers because of their significance as cultic centers at least as early as the Mycenaean period.

---

[26] Bengtson, No. 184; IG 13 75; B. Meritt, AJPh 66 (1945) 254; Meritt, AJPh 68 (1947) 313; n. 5; D. M. Lewis, BSA 49 (1954) 23-24; SEG 14.8; D. W. Bradeen and M. F. McGregor, *Studies in the Fifth Century Attic Epigraphy* (Cincinnati, 1973) 123-24.

[27] Bengtson, No. 193; Busolt, IG 32 (1904) 1227-29; Phillipson, *The International Law and Custom* 2:57-59; F. R. Wüst, *Historia* 3 (1954/55) 152-53; Beloch, Griechische Geschichte 12, 347; D. Cohen, *Mnemosyne* (1966) 289-95.

[28] Z. Tashlikioglou and P. Frisch, ZPE 17 (1975) 102-104; OGI 225, 11.24-25,138-39.

[29] L. Robert, BCH 102 (1978) 477-490; J. Bousquet, BCH 83 (1959) 146-92, and BCH 84 (1960) 161-175; IG^9 1; H. Pomtow, *Klio* 18 (1923) 297-98.

192 CONVENTIONS ASSOCIATED WITH TREATY MAKING

Recitation: The Near Eastern evidence

Another similarity between the Ancient Near East and the early Greek world, which complemented the just-discussed habit of entrusting their documents to the temples, was the custom of periodical recitation, whereby the signatories, their successors, and their people would be constantly aware of their contents. Thus the treaty between the Hittite king Muwatallis and Alaksandus of Wilusa (in Asia Minor) stipulated: "...this tablet which I have set [forth] for you Ala-[ksandus] shall be recited to you three times each year and you Alaksandus shall know it."[30] Again, in the treaty between Mattiwaza, the king of the Mitanni, and Suppiluliumas a clause enjoined the frequent recitation of the text before the two kings.[31] In Deut. 31.9 ff., Moses decreed the recitation of the law before the people every seventh year on the occasion of the Feast of the Booths in the year of release. Knowledge of the words of the covenant was an extremely useful imperative, since in an age when literacy was limited, oral recitation before the people served as a constant reminder of their obligations. Similarly, in the treaty between the Assyrian king Esarhaddon and Ramataia, lord of the city of Urakazabanu, the latter was enjoined to teach enthusiastically the contents of the treaty to his sons and grandsons.[32]

Recitation: The Homeric evidence

The custom of treaty recitation is also found in the Homeric epics, although since the Homeric agreements are oral, the mode of recitation was somewhat different. Thus when Hector proposed the duel between Alexander and Menelaus to the Argives, he did so in the full presence of both armies (Il. 3.85-86). Menelaus answered him on behalf of all Achaeans, also in the presence of both armies. As soon as an agreement was reached, Idaeus the herald went to the Scaean Gates where the Trojan elders and Priam were seated to report to them what had transpired (Il. 3.248-249). During the solemnization sacrifice, Agamemnon recited the terms of the treaty again for all to hear (Il. 3.281-91). In Book 7, Hector proposed another duel agreement and again recited publicly the terms of his proposal (Il. 7. 66 ff.). Similarly, when Odysseus was dispatched as Agamemnon's envoy to Achilles to negotiate a reconciliation, he repeated publicly the terms offered by Agamemnon (Il. 9.121, 262). After Idomeneus had killed Othryoneus, he dragged the body toward the Achaean ships, taunting the dead Othryoneus by repeating the terms of the alliance he and Priam had agreed upon. Presumably

---

[30] Friedrich, *Die Staatsverträge*, 2:77.

[31] Weidner, *Polit. Dok.*, 49.

[32] McCarthy, *Treaty and Covenant*, 200.

CONVENTIONS ASSOCIATED WITH TREATY MAKING 193

it was because the contents of this agreement had already been publicly announced that Idomeneus was able to speak as he did. Unless one regards this episode as pure invention, created solely for poetic or dramatic purposes and reflecting nothing at all about the actual social scene (in which case, why stop with this episode?), it must be counted as another bit of evidence in favor of there having been, among the Greeks as well as in the Near East, recitatory practices corresponding to our modern practices of publishing the terms of an important contract or treaty.

The custom of public recitation of treaties is also found in the post-Homeric world. In the absence of any hard evidence of a positive discontinuity between the periods involved, the most coherent explanation is that, like other post-Homeric practices, this one had its antecedents in the Homeric and Mycenaean worlds. Thus the peace treaty between the Lacedaemonians and Athenians contained a clause (Thuc. 5.18.10) that bound both signatories to renew the oaths of the treaty every year (ἀνανεοῦσθαι κατ' ἐνιαυτόν,) a solemnity tantamount to the recitation of the treaty as a reminder of its obligations. The same demand is repeated in Thuc. 5.23.4, where we are told that to renew the oaths, the Athenians had to go to Lacedaemon at the Hyacinthia, while the Spartans had to go to Athens at the Dionysia.[33] In the treaty signed by the Athenians, Argives, Mantineians, and Eleans, the oaths of their alliance had to be repeated every four years. To that purpose, the Athenians had to travel to Elis, Mantineia, and Argos respectively, thirty days before the Olympic games, while the Argives, Eleans, and Mantineians were expected to go to Athens ten days before the Great Panathenaea. Gomme considers this renewal-proviso uncommon, at least in treaties of peace and alliance, although he concedes that the same format was repeated in the treaties between the Athenians and the Halieis and the treaty between Athens and Perdiccas.[34] Interestingly, the constitution of Dreros contains an injunction that the city officials swear an oath every year that they would respect and preserve the constitution. The officials include those elected annually plus two unknown officers (δάμιοι) who were generally identified with financial duties. The annual renewal of oaths must have coincided with the yearly election of officials, who then swore their oath of office to respect the constitution of their city. One can only conjecture whether this ancient Cretan custom is an offshoot of Near Eastern practices, though here again there seems no reason to deny that it may have been.

---

[33] Gomme, HCT ad 5.18.10; Busolt, *Griechische Geschichte*, 2nd ed., 722, n. 2; Hdt. 9.7.11. The custom of oath renewal continued unabatedly in the Hellenistic times. The Achaean League renewed annually the oath of the treaty with Macedon (Livy 32.5.4).

[34] Thuc. 5.18.9; Gomme, HCT *ad loc.;* Bengtson, No. 188; B. D. Meritt, H. T. Wade-Gery, M. F. McGregor, ATL 3 (1950) 346-49; A. Andrews and D. M. Lewis, JHS 77 (1957) 177-88.

194   CONVENTIONS ASSOCIATED WITH TREATY MAKING

Summary

As we have seen, what evidence we have strongly suggests that the Near Eastern peoples and the Greeks shared some practices of recitation and deposition. It further suggests—admittedly, a bit less strongly—that the Greeks' practices were not merely a parallel and coincidental development, but rather had their origin in the practices of the Near East. As we shall see in the next section, the same kind of suggestion is to be found in the evidence we have concerning another treaty-making convention.

C. THE DURATION OF THE AGREEMENT

Another common feature of the Hittite and Homeric covenants is their emphasis on perpetuity. This element of perpetuity is especially significant because along with its social and moral value it had political ramifications that often tended to complicate the relations of the signatories.

The Near Eastern evidence

The permanent character of the political and military alliances of the Near Eastern states is not only the product of contractual stipulations spelling out the duration of the agreement; it is also subtly imbedded in the spirit of the agreement through collateral relationships such as the union through marriage of the houses of the covenanters. Already in the diplomacy of Suppiluliumas, during the heyday of the Hittite empire, marriage alliances by which Suppiluliumas sought to cement mutual relations with adjacent states played a clearly important role. Through such arrangements Suppiluliumas hoped to acquire further support for himself and his successors, while, on the other hand, he promised respect and protection for the succession rights of his co-signatories. In this vein, he arranged for the marriage of his daughter to the fugitive from Arzawa called Mashuiluwas. Suppiluliumas's purpose was to place his new son-in-law on the throne of Mira and Kuwaliya.[35] The elevation of Mashuiluwas's son finally took place in the reign of Mursilis II, who recognized Kupanta-Kal (Mashuiluwas's son by Suppiluliumas's daughter Muwattis) as the presumptive heir to the throne of Mira and Kuwaliya.[36] Suppiluliumas did not hesitate to ally his family through marriage to the semi-barbarous Huqqanas and the people of the land of Hayana.[37] His policy was faithfully adhered to by all of his successors, and thus by the treaty of Ištarmuwas, contracted between Muwatallis and

---

[35] Friedrich, *Die Staatsverträge*, 1:4.
[36] Friedrich, *Die Staatsverträge*, 1:106.
[37] Friedrich, *Die Staatsverträge*, 2:106 ff.

CONVENTIONS ASSOCIATED WITH TREATY MAKING 195

Mašturis, the king of the land of River Seha, Muwatallis gave his sister to be Mašturis's wife.[38] Hattusilis III attempted to bind the Amurru king Bentešina through a double marriage with the result that his son Nerikka-ilis married the daughter of Bentešina, while, on the other hand, Hattusilis gave his daughter to be Bentešina's wife, securing in this fashion the throne of Amurru for his grandson, the hoped-for product of this union.[39] On another occasion Tuthaliyas IV gave his sister to Ištarmuwas of Amurru in marriage, securing at the same time the succession to the throne for the offspring of this marriage.[40] The Hittites were not the only ones to use their daughters and sisters for the purpose of perpetuating relations. The Egyptians did the same by the conclusion of many treaties with the various states in the Near East. The El-Amarna texts are full of references to requests by Near Eastern allies of the Pharaoh for wives from the Pharaoh's household. Finally Ramses II married the daughter of Hattusilis III at the conclusion of the treaty between the two monarchs.[41] Hence we see that the alliances among the courts of Egypt, Babylon, and Mitanni played an important role in the diplomatic game of the second millennium B.C. and constituted the main topic of the diplomatic correspondence of these countries, with the exception of the unabashed begging by Babylonians, Mitannis, Assyrians, and others for Egyptian gold.[42] Babylonian and Mitanni princesses joined the Egyptian harem for diplomatic reasons, with the ulterior purpose of either cementing political relations or channeling some of the purported Egyptian goldstream to their countries.[43]

Still another method whereby leaders in the Near East hoped to bind each other in perpetuity was the practice of making themselves brothers and friends forever. Both concepts brotherhood and marriage, involved social, moral, and legal considerations designed to bind the contracting parties into a permanent political, social, and military relationship. The fact that this permanency may have been contrived, or even elegantly camouflaged by terms that did not reflect the real sentiments and intentions of the parties, does not necessarily negate the scope and intent of the formula and its

---

[38] KUB 23, 1, 2:15 ff.; Götze, *Archiv Orientalni*, 2, 157.

[39] Weidner, BOST, 9.124 ff.

[40] KUB 23, 1. 2:3.

[41] Ed Meyer, GdA, 2:12 484; Korosec, *Heth. Staats.*, 44.

[42] Knudzton, *Die El-Anarna Tafeln*, 71, 73, 137, 145, 153, 179, 189, 229, 241, 245; Meyer, GdA 2:12, 484; Korosec, *Heth. Staats.*, 45; CAH3 2.2.5.

[43] Not all of the princesses could hold the position of queen of Egypt; Meyer, GdA, 2:12 160, 484. In this case the alliance may have had theoretically a lesser chance of perpetuity. The practice of marriage alliances continued among the oriental monarchs, while in most city-states where democratic regimes replaced the aristocratic rule the practice disappeared. Cf. Hdt. 1.74.1-2, where Alyattes and Cyaxares made a treaty and reinforced it with the marriage of Alyattes' daughter to Cyaxares' son.

implications. Alliances were indeed made and unmade then as they are now, but unlike modern statesmen, who generally consider the element of expediency in the making of treaties and who avoid formulas that have a ring of the sacred or give the impression of perpetuity, the people of the Ancient Near East often used traditional expressions charged with moral overtones even though they did not intend to faithfully carry out their spirit. The reason for the use of such formulas is complex. As has already been shown, some of the stipulations were dictated by the superior signatory whose chancellory used and respected formulaic expressions loaded with religious and moral implications. Violations of such treaties conveyed the impression of religious and moral impropriety on the part of the offender. Another factor is the inevitable rigidity produced by pat formulas, for although the chancellories tried their best to adjust the language to the appropriate circumstances, no effort was made to change the spirit of the treaties, particularly in respect to perpetuity. As to the preamble and the oath-taking sections of the document, the scribes who served as the legal staff in its preparation attached to it well-known formulas with the customary implications for the offenders. Although the expression "for ever" was not always present, it was almost always implied by the general spirit of the wording. Beyond that, the nature of leadership in the ancient states conflated aristocratic ideals and the demands of the state as a neutral or superpersonal agency, with the result that leader and state were usually closely identified with each other. Violators of the aristocratic traditions were judged by the ideals of the time even when no written treaties existed between nations. For aristocrats to break with friends or to act contrary to their words and the expectations of their culture was considered offensive.

Thus, whereas the spirit of the age precluded the violation of an alliance and the concomitant abandonment of friends, the letter of the treaty would also forbid such acts, since the perpetuity of the treaty was frequently spelled out in the document or was clearly implied by certain formulas in it. The permanence of the treaties is emphasized by the stipulation for the mutual protection and support of the signatories, and particularly of their successors. Another deals with the depositing of the document. In the treaty between Suppilulimas and the Mitanni king Mattiwaza, the former undertook to protect the great kingdom of Mitanni, giving his daughter in marriage to Tušratta with the stipulation that her son and grandson would inherit the Mitanni throne. Thus the grandson of Tušratta would be the great grandson of Suppilulimas. If for every generation we count thirty years, the treaty implied a duration of over one hundred years, which is to say forever. For although only three or sometimes four generations were enumerated, the

CONVENTIONS ASSOCIATED WITH TREATY MAKING 197

cooperation alluded to was not meant to stop at the end of these generations; such was not the spirit of the treaty.[44]

Similar examples are present in other treaties. Mursilis II asked Kupanta-Kal of Mira to respect and support his son and grandson, the successors to the throne of Hatti. The same obligation was undoubtedly assumed by Mursilis toward Kupanta's sons and grandsons.[45] The same Hittite king promised to support the succession to the throne of Tuppi-Tešub's son, while he demanded the same degree of support from his co-signatory for his own son and grandson, successors to his throne.[46] Alaksandus of Wilusa was bound in his agreement with Muwatallis, the Hittite king, to protect the king of Hatti, his son, his son's son, and so on. The same promise was extended to Alaksandus by the Great King.[47] The promise of mutual respect and protection to the third and fourth generation was equivalent to perpetuity for both contracts. The same promise surfaces in some of the El-Amarna letters which follow up earlier treaties between the Egyptian king and the states of the Near East, obligating both to "eternal friendship."[48] Moreover, the depositing of copies of treaties in the temples of the gods and the injunction that these copies be read again and again before the king, the people, and the successors of the signatories clearly underscore the perpetuity of the documents, particularly since no clause limited the duration of the agreements. In view of the absence of such chronological limits in practically all the Hittite agreements, the conclusion is inexorable: the agreements were made in perpetuity.[49]

The Homeric evidence

The picture silhouetted in the Homeric agreements is similar to that of the Near Eastern treaties, although the interpersonal character of some and the objectives of others differ from the interstate nature of the Hittite compacts. For example, the agreement among Helen's suitors had a limited duration in contrast to the permanent character of the Hittite treaties, simply because the duration was contingent upon Helen's life-span. The same is true of the agreement between Calchas and Agamemnon. Achilles' promise of support and protection was extended only to the lifetime of Achilles in Troy, since Achilles knew that he was going to die in the Trojan campaign. A limitation was also implied in the compact among the Achaean leaders who went to

---

[44] Weidner, *Polit. Dok.*, 19.
[45] Friedrich, *Die Staatsverträge*, 1:121
[46] Friedrich, *Die Staatsverträge*, 1:13.
[47] Friedrich, *Die Staatsverträge*, 2:57-59.
[48] Knudtzon, *Die El-Amarna Tafeln*, 137-38.
[49] Weidner, *Polit. Dok.*, 29, 49; F. Delitzsch, HW, 435; Abr. 2.218; Thompson, *Reports*, 249.

198 CONVENTIONS ASSOCIATED WITH TREATY MAKING

Troy under an offensive alliance, stemming from a defensive pact made earlier for the benefit of Helen and her husband. The object of this defensive covenant was limited in scope to the Trojan campaign, as was the duration of the alliance. Upon the achievement of its goal, the alliance was apparently terminated as each of the Homeric heroes left for home. Likewise, the duel agreement which pitted Hector against Aias constituted a temporary diversionary episode, whose objective was limited along with its duration. The duel itself was not designed to solve any of the major issues that separated the antagonists. Of course the duel could have had drastic results for the Trojans, in that the death of Hector, the most important leader of the Trojan troops, would have profoundly changed the outlook of the war, just as Achilles' withdrawal upset the military balance in favor of the Trojans. Similarly limited in time was the truce for the burial of the dead in Book 7, and so was the agreement between Achilles and Priam for the burial of Hector. To list the several other agreements that were limited in their objective and consequently in their time would be superfluous here, since it is clear from the evidence already cited that personal agreements could be quite divergent in range.[50] A few of these compacts, though limited in their purview, were solemnized by sacrifice and the taking of oaths; others were simply gentlemen's agreements devoid of the formalities of solemnization. In the latter case, the promises of the countries sufficed to seal the agreement.

Some other personal agreements in Homer assumed the character of official interstate treaties, and as such involved not merely formal solemnization but also commitment in perpetuity. Such is the dual agreement proposed by Paris. Upon its acceptance by both parties, it was given the finality of a treaty designed to resolve the hostilities and bring about a permanent peace between the two rivals. No time limit was cited because none was needed, it being understood by all that the friendship specified by the agreement would remain for ever.

Like the Hittite agreements, Homeric pacts were frequently sealed by marriage alliances. Thus the alliance between Othryoneus and Priam was conditional on Priam's willingness to give his daughter to Othryoneus in marriage. This alliance was to last beyond the life-span of the contractors. Even more illustrative is perhaps the case of Agamemnon in Book 9 of the *Iliad*. Repentant for his injustice against Achilles and caught in a dangerous military predicament, Agamemnon proposed reconciliation to Achilles and promised to seal this reconciliation with the hand of one of his daughters. The tenor of the proposal leaves little doubt that the marriage constituted an additional honor offered by the supreme commander to one of his generals.

---

[50] See agreements Nos. 8, 9, 10, 12, 18, which are all limited in scope. The same is true about the agreement between Odysseus on the one hand and Circe and Calypso on the other. Both were solemnized by oaths (sacrifices were not needed) and implied unlimited duration.

CONVENTIONS ASSOCIATED WITH TREATY MAKING

199

The union was intended to bring the two royal houses together in a lasting political and military alliance. The similarity of this offer to the Hittite agreements suggests that similar stipulations were associated with Mycenaean treaties, making it reasonable to assume that marriage alliances were a fairly common practice in the Mycenaean world, and that one of their objectives was to bind the families in lasting peace and friendship. How such alliances among the Mycenaeans might have affected the principle of succession is not known, but again it is not improbable that, like the Hittite kings, the Mycenaeans welcomed the support and protection anticipated from their friends and in-laws.

Several of the treaties from archaic Greece contain a stipulation that points to the everlasting character of such agreements. The treaty between Elis and Heraea found in Olympia was contracted for one hundred years.[51] Here as in the Near East, a temporal span is cited that is, for all practical purposes, an eternity. The number one hundred is equivalent to the three or four generations mentioned in the Hittite agreements. The novel aspect here is the reference to a concrete number of years replacing a number of generations. By the archaic times the hereditary principle of succession had disappeared along with the institution of monarchy, making references to sons and grandsons meaningless. Even so, the evocation of eternity rather than a specific time span was frequent, as is seen in the treaty between the Sybarites and the Serdaeans, whose duration is set to be ἀείδιον.[52]

While there is no doubt about the everlasting character of these two treaties, another alliance dating from about the same time is clearly of limited duration. This treaty was contracted between the Anaetoi and Metapioi, both Greek people.[53] Although its objectives are similar to those of the other two, its duration is set at precisely fifty years. Whether the number fifty is symbolic of an everlasting friendship is very doubtful, though this possibility should not be totally excluded. But the rise of the city-state, where leadership and state interest begin to be differentiated, seems to be responsible for the introduction of greater flexibility in the formulation of treaties. A greater realization of life's fluidity must have impelled the leaders of the Greek city-states to be more circumspect in their use of language. The aristocratic practice of commitment to everlasting friendship is not totally

---

[51] W. Dittenberger and K. Purgold, *Die Inschriften von Olympia* (Berlin, 1826) 21; *Syll.* 13 9; Phillipson, *The International Law and Custom*, 2:54-55; R. Bölte, RE 7 (1912) col. 413; H. Schaefer, *Staatsform* passim; Highby, *The Erythrae Decree* , 63-64; Ehrenberg, JHS 57 (1937) 141; Bengtson, No. 110; M/L No. 18; Buck, *Gr. Dial.*, 62; Jeffery, *The Local Scripts of Anc. Greece* 220, dates it ca. 500 B.C. or later.

[52] Bengtson, No. 120; M/L No. 10.

[53] Bengtson, No. 111; E. Meyer, *Forschungen zur Alte Geschichte* (Halle, 1892) 1:295; Schaefer, *Staatform*, 80; Kiechle, RhM 103(1960) 348.

200   CONVENTIONS ASSOCIATED WITH TREATY MAKING

absent from the archaic treaties, but new trends appear in the formulation of interstate treaties, reflecting the new political configuration of the Greek world. The clash of concepts in this transitional period might have been responsible for some understandable confusion. It definitely accounts for the disappearance of marriage alliances as instruments of state policy in the formulation and duration of interstate treaties in the Greek world, except of course wherever the monarchy or tyranny remained a strong political institution, mostly on the periphery of the Greek world. It re-emerged as an important diplomatic tool with the restoration of royal authority in Hellenistic times.[54]

Summary

Here as in previous chapters we have seen that there was a strong resemblance between certain practices of the Near Eastern world and those of Homeric and archaic Greek times. By extrapolation from the similarities found in the evidence we have from those periods, we are led to the conclusion that these same practices probably obtained in the Mycenaean world. If they did not, then the similarities discussed in the preceding pages would have to be either the result of some large-scale and long-standing event that is utterly unknown, or else utterly coincidental resemblances between randomly occurring events. Compared to the far more plausible conclusion drawn here, neither of the two alternatives is very satisfying, to say the least.

---

[54] In the Near East the royal authority remained supreme. Consequently, the proposal of Xerxes to the victor of Plataea for an alliance through marriage is true to the traditional format of the Near Eastern treaties; Thuc. 1.128-30; Hdt. 5.32; 8.85.3; How and Wells, *ad loc.*

CHAPTER EIGHT

CONCLUSION: CONTINUITY OR DISCONTINUITY?

The common saying that history repeats itself is, with due qualifications, applicable to historical scholarship itself. It often happens that after some aspect of a historical period has been minutely analyzed a scholarly "exhaustion" sets in, whereupon scholars turn their attention to another set of questions or even another period altogether. They feel that enough has been written about a theme, and that until new material is uncovered there is no use discussing the matter further. Of course the sad fact is, new material is not usually uncovered. Students of ancient history are seldom so lucky. Nonetheless, it often happens that after another few years the old material is taken up again anyway and reexamined through the prism of new methodological approaches, typically ones borrowed from other disciplines. Using the new methods a swarm of scholars revisits the previously abandoned question, drawing new insights from the reworked material and illuminating corners of the topic never noticed before. And so the discussion goes through a new cycle which eventually enriches the field of historical scholarship.

Such renewals ought not be surprising, at least not after they have taken place. After all, most historians subscribe to the theory that each new generation has the right to look at history through its own optic glass. The present book is an effort in that direction. It seeks to reopen the question of continuity between cultures, namely the pre-Dark Ages culture of Greece and that of the Dark Ages and after. Many earlier scholars have rejected the notion of continuity between the Mycenaean and post-Mycenaean culture on the grounds that we possess very little information from the Mycenaean culture on which to build a sufficiently strong case for continuity. Supposedly, the Homeric epics mainly reflect the world of the Dark Ages, and whatever morsels of information survived from earlier centuries do not help us unravel the Mycenaean mystery with any degree of certainty. For instance, it has been suggested by Chadwick that the arrival of Dorians constituted a cataclysmic event that shattered the possibility of continuity between the Mycenaean world and the world of the Dark Ages that followed it.[1] This is now the received view, and—to be fair—we must admit that it could also, at some future time, turn out to be the true view, in the sense of providing the most coherent explanation of available evidence. However, notwithstanding its currency and in spite of the apparent facts often cited in its support, such as the virtually simultaneous destruction of numerous major Greek cities or

---

[1] Chadwick, *The Mycenaean World*, passim.

the sudden decimation of the population around the middle of the 12th century, at the present state of historical knowledge this claim does not have the prima facie plausibility that it is often credited with. The conventional chopping up of history into centuries and eras is only a convenient shorthand device for historians and does not mark real points of sudden and total change. Rather, it is doubtful whether complete and total changes ever take place in short historical time spans. Conventional periodizations are convenient tools for historians to tackle historical problems but they should not normally be interpreted to mean sudden changes. On the contrary, changes usually occur incrementally and continually, eventually altering the historical scenario but only becoming visible in retrospect and over a long period of time. Pari passu with such changes, older customs and practices remain embedded in the people's psyche, staying more or less constant even while many other important things change. When, for example, Christianity pushed Greco-Roman and mystery religions off the front stage, many of the religious customs and ideas of the ancient world refused to yield. They simply adjusted to the times and became incorporated into the new religion, often with the blessings of the church leaders, who at the same time thundered against the old religions or ridiculed their ideas.

This essay has been an attempt to challenge the currently received notion of discontinuity and to re-open the question of continuity. The methodology used in these pages has been simple: Near Eastern materials contemporary with the Mycenaean world and the Homeric epics were used to demonstrate the way whereby old problems can be looked at profitably once again. The method itself is not new and, one hopes, not too bold. However, it should be noted that the conclusions which our use of the method has produced *are* rather bold, for they run against the current assumptions of radical discontinuity between the Mycenaean age and the so-called Dark Ages. Thus Finley has argued that Thucydides thought (as did other Greek writers) that there had been a catastrophic collapse of the Mycenaean civilization near the end of the second millennium B.C. and of the "profound discontinuity between Mycenaean civilization and Greek civilization proper."[2] Finley is of course aware of many of the problems connected with the text of Thucydides, particularly those concerning the chronological questions. But there are still other problems, whose cumulative effect is to challenge the credibility of his view. Even if we accept the claim that Thucydides and the other Greek intellectuals subscribed to the notion of a "destruction of the Mycenaean civilization," many potentially unsettling questions remain to be asked. What did this civilization mean to these later Greeks, and how did they interpret its so-called destruction? Did they think it implied that the arrival of the Dorian

---

[2] Finley, *The Use and Abuse of History* (New York, 1987) 19-20. He has made similar claims elsewhere, e.g., *Early Greece*.

CONTINUITY OR DISCONTINUITY? 203

tribes and the changes that took place during the time of their arrival (again supposing that they arrived during a sharply limited time-span, which may very well not have been the case) were so profound as to create a radical discontinuity with the established civilization which the Dorians found? And even if we ascribe directly to the Dorian "invasion" some of the more obvious changes, such as the vulgarization of art, does it follow more generally that the ideas and practices embodying a variety of human experiences were completely abandoned or drastically changed and replaced by new ones? Is it not equally if not more plausible that many of the religious, social, political and other sorts of traditions survived the collapse of the Mycenaean civilization (which might not have been so catastrophic after all), and that having changed somewhat over a period of time these ideas and practices continued to influence life in the post-Mycenaean times? Indeed, it is quite reasonable to argue that unless all or most of the people who lived in the Mycenaean areas occupied by the Dorians were destroyed, the odds are that their customs survived with them. As a matter of fact, we do know that not all of the Mycenaean areas were seized by Dorians. Attica was invaded but not seized, nor was Arcadia. The Dorians did not necessarily constitute the majority of the population wherever they settled. In Laconia they were not in the majority, and we are not sure that they were in the majority in Messenia. The Dorians seemed to have been more concentrated in the Argive and Corinthian plains, but even there we cannot be certain that they constituted most of the population. In the area of Sicyon, we hear of tribal differences down to the times of the Orthagorids. Does that mean that these differences go back in time as far as the Mycenaeans? Also, what of Achaea, Thessaly, and other places in Greece? Were these places overwhelmed by Dorians, and if so did the habits and practices of the residents of all these places change so drastically that they no longer resembled their former ways at all? Such possibilities are unlikely, to say the least.

Furthermore, we have no grounds for supposing that in spite of their differences with the other inhabitants of Mycenae, the Dorians themselves did not also have similar religious, political, and social customs. What evidence we do have suggests just the contrary. As we have seen throughout this book, there were many practices and ideas observable in the Homeric and post-Homeric times that had very early origins, going back at least to Mycenaean times, and these practices and ideas had strong similarities to those of the Near Eastern World.

As classicists have often noted in various contexts, binding the scattered activities and events of the Homeric epics is a continuity, a steady background of social, political, and cultural life. How faithfully this background reflects Mycenaean prototypes is uncertain. However, in view of the international climate characteristic of the time, it is very probable that the Mycenaean civilization borrowed some of its practices from the Near East.

204 CONTINUITY OR DISCONTINUITY?

Some evidence and strong indications to this effect exists, although, unfortunately, no conclusive evidence is available. When we approach the world of Homer, our picture becomes clearer. Similar elements between the Near East and the world of Homer are clearly silhouetted. For instance, the use of the words *tithêmi, syntithêmi, horkos-horkia* and their Near Eastern equivalents are not unusual in the Near East and Homer.[3] The format of the Homeric agreements themselves seems to bear distinct resemblances to that of the Near Eastern treaties, despite the absence of formal treaties in the Homeric texts. As we saw in Part One of this study, common structural features such as forms of address, the recounting of antecedent history, stipulations in the conditional form, invocations of the gods as witnesses, the stock formulas of curses and blessings, fixed rituals, and other features lead us to believe in the existence of practices that were shared by both worlds. The commonality theory is further corroborated by similarities to be found in Part Two, where we considered the content elements and other nonstructural features of Near Eastern and Greek agreements. Among these features were the respective roles of the populace and fugitives, conventions of war governing booty and the use of surrogates as well as the outbreak of hostilities, and conventions governing the making of treaties, such as ceremonial meals and public recitations of the terms of treaties.

In the centuries to come, many of these practices were to continue both in the Near East and the Hellenic and Hellenistic worlds, albeit with modifications wrought by the changing times. The idea of *philotês*, for example, would lose the personal character it had possessed in a world dominated by kings, to be replaced by *philia*, a term that lacked the semasiological variations of *philotês* but carried a strictly political connotation in interstate transactions. Thus it is clear that the broad term *philotês* no longer represented the political climate of the emerging city-state in the Greek world wherein rule was less personal and more collective. Although *philotês* would survive as a political term until classical times, it would eventually be replaced in that context by *philia*, which better suited the new realities of the city states. Something similar happened in the realm of cursings and blessings. While the list of gods and goddesses invoked in corroboration of the Near Eastern treaties became more elaborate, concomitant with the rise of the city-states was the further contraction of the already short list of deities associated with the Homeric agreements. True, the highest divinities and the local patron-gods of the contracting parties continued to be invoked, but the dreadful Styx, rivers, oceans, and many other such powers often fell by the wayside.

---

[3] Barré, *loc. cit.*, 6.

The future held other changes as well. With the emergence of city-state institutions came much greater variety in the typology and the stipulated durations of treaties in the Greek world. However, a fair amount of both sorts of diversity (especially the latter) was already evident in Homer, either explicitly or by ready implication. The same is true of the Archaic Greek treaties. Several of these, like the Near Eastern and Homeric agreements, were made for ever. But whereas the Near East and Homer used implicit methods to denote the length of the agreements they recorded, the Greek cities would explicitly specify the duration of their treaties. And even when agreements were supposedly made for ever, the signatories were careful to state this fact outright. Thus, whereas differences in the evolution of treaty-making are to be expected, they need not necessarily be regarded as at odds with the hypothesis of some remote common origins or even the hypothesis of the one civilization's having influenced the other at some time in the latter's development. It would have been quite natural for the Near Eastern cultures to have left their marks on the Mycenaean and later Greek world, as the evidence suggests was indeed the case. If, generally speaking, earlier cultures are likely to influence the course of later civilizations, then it is reasonable to suppose that the earlier and highly pervasive Near Eastern culture affected the rise of the Greek civilization. Similar parallels abound in the Near East among the Hurrians, Hittites, Mitanni, and other peoples in the area, many of them contemporaries of the Mycenaeans. Greece and the Greeks were not so far removed from these peoples as to have remained immune to their influences. But how these influences were imparted and the degree to which they were effective are questions more difficult to ascertain without a more exact knowledge of the history of the origins of the Indo-European tribes that settled in the Greek mainland after 2,000 B.C., as well as of the customs and ideas they carried with them from their place of origin, the places they stopped on their way to Greece and the customs they might have absorbed at these places, the institutions and practices they found among the earlier inhabitants of Greece, and the number of these practices they absorbed after their intermingling with the local people. That the Indo-Europeans borrowed from the natives is to be expected. But how different—if indeed they were different—the treaty-making practices of these Indo-Europeans were by the time of their arrival in Greece from those of the inhabitants they found there as well as the surrounding world are unanswered, and with our present evidence unanswerable, questions. One thing however is clear. Borrowings by one people from another in the area of the Near East was a common historical development. The focus of the present study has been exactly the investigation of the possibility of such inter-cultural borrowings.

BIBLIOGRAPHY

Adcock, Sir Frank E., and D. M. Mosley. *Diplomacy in Ancient Greece,* in the series *Aspects of Greek and Roman Life* (New York, 1975).

Adcock, Frank E. "The Development of Ancient Greek Diplomacy," AC 17 (1948) 1-12.

—. "Some Aspects of Ancient Greek Diplomacy," PCA 21 (1924) 92-116.

Adkins, A. W. H. "Friendship and Self-sufficiency in Homer and Aristotle," CQ n.s. 13 (1963) 35-45.

Allen, Thomas W. *Homer, The Origins and the Transmission* (Oxford, 1924).

—. *The Homeric Catalogue of Ships* (Oxford, 1921).

Ameis, Carl F., and C. Hentze. *Homers Ilias,* 7th ed., ed. by Paul Cauer (Amsterdam, 1965).

Andreev, Jurij V. "Die Homerische Gesellschaft", *Klio* 70 (1988) 5-88.

Andrewes, Anthony. *Greek Society* (London, 1971).

Arend, W. *Die typischen Szenen bei Homer* (Berlin, 1933).

A. R. M. T. *Archives royales de Mari,* several vols., esp. vol. 4, ed. by G. Dossin, *Correspondence de Samsi-Addu* (Paris, 1954).

Astour, M. C. *Hellenosemitica: An Ethnic and Cultural Study in West Semitic Impact on Mycenaean Greece* (Leiden, 1967).

Aubonnet, Jean. *Aristote, Politique* (Paris, 1960).

Austin, M. M., and P. Vidal-Naquet, *Economic and Social History of Greece* (Berkeley and Los Angeles, 1977).

Aymard, André. "Le partage des profits de la guerre dans les traités d'alliance antique," *Revue Historique* 217 (1957) 233-46.

Baltzer, Klaus. *The Covenant Formulary,* trans. by D. E. Green (Philadelphia, 1971).

Barré, M. L. *The God-list in the Treaty between Hannibal and Philip V of Macedonia. A Study in Light of the Ancient Near Eastern Treaty Tradition* (Baltimore, 1983).

Baunack, J. T. *Die Inschrift von Gortyn* (Leipzig, 1885).

Beaumont, R. L. "The Date of the First Treaty between Rome and Carthage," JRS 29 (1939) 74-86.

Bechtel, F., and H. Collitz. *Sammlung der griechischen Dialektinschriften* (Göttingen, 1884-1915).

Bekker, Immanuel (ed.). *Scholia in Homeri Iliadem* (Berlin, 1825).

Beloch, K. J. *Griechische Geschichte,* 2nd ed. (Berlin, 1912-27).

Benveniste, E. *Le vocabulaire des institutions Indo-europèennes,* vol. 1 (Paris, 1969).

Bender, Franz. *Antikes Völkerrecht* (Bonn, 1901).

Bengtson, H., and H. H. Schmitt. *Staatsverträge des Altertums,* 2 vols. (Munich, 1969-75).

Berne, Eric. *Games People Play* (New York, 1961).

Bernhoft, F. *Die Inschrift von Gortyn* (Stuttgart, 1886).

Bickerman, Elias. "Hannibal's Covenant." AJPh 73 (1952) 1-23.

—. "An Oath of Hannibal," TAPA 75 (1944) 88-99.

Bikerman, Elie. "Remarques sur le droit des gens dans la Grèce classique," RIDA 2 (1950) 99-127.

—. "Couper une alliance," *Archive d' Histoire du droit Oriental* 5 (1950-51) 133-56.

Bilabel, F. *Geschichte Vorderasiens und Ägyptens* (Heidelberg, 1927).

Bonner, R. J., and G. Smith. *The Administration of Justice from Homer to Aristotle* (Chicago, 1930-38).

Bleckmann, F. *Griechische Inschriften zur griechischen Staatskunde* (Bonn, 1913).

Böhl, F. M. Th. "King Hammurabi of Babylon in the Setting of His Time," in *Opera Minora* (Groningen-Djakarta, 1956).

Boisacq, E. *Dictionnaire étymologique de la langue grecque,* 4th ed. (Heidelberg, 1960).

Borger, R. "Die Inschriften Assarhaddons Königs von Assyrien," AFO Beiheft 9 (Osnabrück, 1967).

—. "Zu den Assarhaddon Verträgen aus Nimrud," ZA 54 (1961) 173-96.

Bouzek, J. *The Aegean, Anatolia and Europe: Cultural Interrelations in the Second Millennium B.C.* (Göteborg, Astrom, and Prague, 1985).

Bowra, C. M. *Meaning of a Heroic Age* (Newcastle, 1957).

—. *Homer and His Forerunners* (Edingburgh, 1955).

208 BIBLIOGRAPHY

—. *Heroic Poetry* (London, 1952).
Bradeen, D. W., and M. F. McGregor. *Studies in Fifth Century Attic Epigraphy* (Cincinnati, 1973).
Briant, P. "La Boulé et l'election des ambassadeurs à Athenes au IVe siècle," REA 70 (1968) 7-31.
Bruce, I. A. F. "Athenian Embassies in the Early Fourth Century B.C.," *Historia* 15 (1966) 272-81.
—. "Athenian Politics and the Outbreak of the Corinthian War," *Emerita* 28 (1960) 75-85.
Bucellatti, Giorgio. *Cities and Nations of Ancient Syria, Studi Semitici* (Rome, 1967).
Buchholz, H. G., and J. Wiesner (eds.). *Kriegswesen I-II, Archaeologia Homerica* (Göttingen, 1977-80).
Buck, R. G. *A History of Boeotia* (Edmonton, 1979).
Buck, R. D. *The Greek Dialects* (Chicago, 1955).
—. "The Interstate Use of the Greek Dialects," CP 8 (1913) 133-59.
Buffière, Felix. *Les Mythes d'Homère et la Pensée Grecque*, in the Société d'Edition *Les Belles Lettres* (Paris, 1956).
Burkert Walter. *Greek Religion*, trans. by J. Raffan (Cambridge, MA, 1985).
—. *Die orientalisierende Epoche in der griechischen Religion und Literatur* in the *Sitz. Heid. Ak. Wiss. phil. hist. Kl. Jg.* 1984 (Heidelberg, 1984).
Burr, Bruno. "Νεῶν Κατάλογος," *Klio* Beiheft 39 (Leipzig, 1944).
Busolt, Georg. *Griechische Geschichte*, 2nd ed., 3 vols. (Gotha, 1893-1904).
Calderone, Salvatore. "Sybaris e i Serdaioi," *Helikon* 3 (1963) 219-58.
Calhoun, G. M. "The Homeric Picture," in Stubbings and Wace (eds.), *Companion to Homer* (London, 1962).
Callmer, Christian. *Studien zur Geschichte Arkadiens* (Lund, 1943).
Campbell, Blair. "Constitutionalism, Rights and Religion: The Athenian Example," *History of Political Thought* 7 (1986) 239-273.
Campbell, E. F. *The Chronology of the Amarna Letters* (Baltimore, 1964).
Camps, W. A. *An Introduction to Homer* (Oxford, 1980).
Cauer, Paul. See Ameis and Hentze.
Chadwick, John. *The Mycenaean World* (Cambridge, 1976).
—. *The Decipherment of Linear B*, 2nd ed. (Cambridge, 1970).
Chamoux, François. *Cyrène sous la Monarchie des Battiades* (Paris, 1968).
—. "L'île de Thasos et son histoire," REG 72 (1959) 348-69.
Chantraine, P. *Etymologique de la langue grecque* (Paris, 1953).
Chroust, Anton Hermann. "The International Treaties in Antiquity: The Diplomatic Negotiations between Hannibal and Philip V of Macedonia," *Classica et Mediaevalia* 15 (1954) 60-107.
Cohen, David. "'Horkia' and 'Horkos' in the *Iliad*." RIDA 27 (1980) 49-68.
—. IG I2 86 and Thucydides 5.47," *Mnemosyne* 9 (1956) 289-95.
Contenaeu, G. *La civilization des Hittites et des Jurrites du Mitanni* (Paris, 1948).
Cook, J. M. *The Greeks in Ionia and the East* (London, 1962).
Cowley, A. E. "The Hittites," in *The Schweich Lectures* (London, 1920).
Crossland, R. A., and Ann Birchhall (eds.). *Bronze Age Migrations in the Aegean* (London, 1973).
Dahlheim, Werner. *Struktur und Entwicklung des römischen Völkerrechts im dritten und zweiten Jahrhundert v. Chr.* (Munich, 1968).
Delbrück, H. *Geschichte der Kriegskunst im Rahmen der politischen Geschichte*. Vol. 1 in the series *Das Altertum* (Berlin, 1920), rev. ed. by K. Christ (1964).
Delitzsch, Friedrich. *Assyrisches Handwörterbuch* (Leipzig, 1896).
Demargne, P., and H. van Effentere. "Recherches à Dreros," BCH 61 (1937) 5-32 and 333-48.
—. "A propos du serment des Dreriens," BCH 61 (1937) 327-32.
Desborough, V. R. d'A. *The Greek Dark Ages* (London, 1972).
—. *The Last Mycenaeans and Their Successors* (Oxford, 1964).
Diamond, A. S. *Primitive Law* (London, 1935).
Dickinson, O. T. P. K. "Homer, the Poet of the Dark Age," in *Greece and Rome* 28 (1986).

BIBLIOGRAPHY 209

Dieckhoff, M. "Über Krieg und Frieden im griechisch-römischen Altertum," *Altertum* 12 (1966) 17-28.

Dietrich, Albrecht. *Mutter Erde; Ein Versuch über Volksreligion* (Leipzig, 1925).

Dietrich, B. C. "Some Eastern Traditions in Greek Thought," *Acta Classica* 7 (1964) 11-30.

Dindorf, G. (ed.). *Scholia Graeca in Homeri Iliadem* (Oxford, 1855).

——. *Scholia Graeca in Homeri Odysseam* (Oxford, 1855).

Dirlmeier, Franz. "Homerisches Epos und Orient," RhM 98 (1955) 18-37.

——. *Φίλος und Φιλία im vorhellenischen Griechentum* (Diss. Munich, 1931).

Dittenberger, W. (ed.). *Sylloge Inscriptionum Graecarum*, 3rd ed., 4 vols. (Leipzig, 1915-24).

——. *Orientis Graecis Inscriptiones Selectae*, 2 vols. (Leipzig, 1903-1905).

Dittenberger, W., and K. Purgold. *Die Inschhriften von Olympia* (Berlin, 1986).

Donlan, Walter. *The Aristocratic Ideal in Ancient Greece, Attitudes of Superiority from Homer to the End of the Fifth Century* (Lawrence, KS, 1980).

——. "The Tradition of Anti-Aristocratic Thought in Early Greek Poetry," *Historia* 22 (1973) 145-54.

Dow, Sterling. "The Greeks in the Bronze Age," in *XIIe Congrès Internationale des sciences historiques* (Stockholm, 1960).

Drews, Robert. *The Evidence for Kingship in Geometric Greece* (New Haven, 1983).

Drexler, H. "Justum bellum" RhM 102 (1959) 97-140.

Driver, G. R. *Canaanite Myths and Legends in Old Testament Studies* 3 (Edinburgh, 1967).

Driver, G. R., and J. C. Miles. *The Babylonian Laws*, vol. 1 (Oxford, 1952).

Duchemin, J. "Le Zeus d'Eschyle et ses sources proche-orientales," RHR 197 (1980) 27-44.

Dunbabin, T. J. *The Greeks and Their Eastern Neighbors* (London, 1957).

Dupont-Sommer, André. *Les inscriptions araméennes de Sfire (Stele I et II). Extrait des Memoires presentes par divers savants à l'academie des Inscriptions et Belles Lettres*, vol. 15 (Paris, 1958).

Dusanic, S. "The ὅρκιον τῶν οἰκιστήρων and Fourth-Century Cyrene," *Chiron* 8 (1978) 55-76.

Effentere, van H. *La cité grecque: des origines à la défaite de Marathon* (Paris, 1985).

Ehrenberg, Victor. *The Greek State* (Oxford, 1960).

——. "An Early Source of Polis-Constitution," CQ (1943) 14-18.

——. "When Did the Polis Rise?" JHS 57 (1937) 147-151.

——. *Die Rechtsidee im frühen Griechentum* (Leipzig, 1921).

Engnell, I. *Studies in Divine Kingship in the Ancient Near East* (Uppsala, 1943).

Erbse, Hartmut (ed.). *Scholia Graeca in Homeri Iliadem (scholia vetera)* (Berlin, 1969).

Eustathii Archiepiscopi Thessalonicensis. *Scholia ad Homeri Odysseam* (Berlin, 1825-26).

Fehling, D. "Lehnübersetzungen aus altorientalischen Sprachen im griechischen und lateinischen," *Glotta* 58 (1980) 1-20.

Feldman, A. B. "Homer and Democracy," CJ 47 (1952) 337-43.

——. "The Apotheosis of Thersites," CJ 42 (1947) 219-21.

Fensham, F. C. "Common Trends in Curses of the Near Eastern Treaties and Kudurru Inscriptions Compared with Maledictions in Amos and Isaiah," ZAW 75 (1963) 155-75.

——. "Clauses of Protection in Hittite Treaties and in the Old Testament," VT 13 (1963) 133-43.

——. "Maledictions and Benedictions in Ancient Near Eastern Vassal Treaties and the Old Testament," ZAW 74 (1962) 1-19.

Finley, M. I. *The World of Odysseus*, 2nd ed. (New York, 1978).

——. *Early Greece. The Bronze and Archaic Age* (London, 1970).

——. "Homer and Mycenae: Property and Tenure," *Historia* 6 (1957) 133-59.

Fischer, Weltgeschichte, *Die Altorientalischen Reiche I, vom Palaeolithicum bis zum mitte des 2. Jahrtausends*, ed. by E. Cassin, J. Buttero, and J. Vercoutter (Frankfurt, 1965).

Fitzmyer, Joseph A. *The Aramaic Inscriptions of Sefire*, in the series *Biblica et Orientalia* (Rome, 1967).

——. "The Aramaic Inscriptions of Sefire I and II," JAOS 81 (1961) 178-222.

210 BIBLIOGRAPHY

—. "The Aramaic Suzerainty Treaty from Sefire in the Museum of Beirut," CBQ 20 (1958) 456-81.
Forrer, E. O. "Für die Griechen in den Boghazköi Inschriften," KF 1 (1929) 252 ff.
—. *Forschungen,* vol. 1 (Berlin, 1926).
—. "Vorhomerische Griechen in den Keilschrifttexten von Boghazköi," MDOG 63 (1924) 1-22.
—. "Die Griechen in den Boghazköi Texten," OLZ 27 (1924) 113-18.
Friedrich, Johannes. "Werden in den hethitischen Keilschrifttexten die Griechen erwähnt?" KF 1.1 (1927) 87-107.
—. *Staatverträge des Hatti-Reiches in hethitischer Sprache,* 2 parts (Berlin, 1926-30).
—. "Aus dem hethitischen Schriftum," I, AO 24/3 (Leipzig, 1925).
—. "Aus dem hethitischen Schriftum," II, *Religiöse Texte* AO 25, 2 (Leipzig, 1925).
Foxhall, L., and J. K. Davies (eds.). *The Trojan War: Its Historicity and Context* (Bristol, 1984).
Fraisse, Jean Claude. *Philia. La notion d'amitié dans la philosophie antique* (Paris, 1974).
Frankfort, H. et al. *Before Philosophy* (Baltimore, 1963).
Frisk, H. *Griechisches etymologisches Wörterbuch.* 2 vols. (Heidelberg, 1960).
Garlan, Yvon. *La guerre dans l'antiquité* (Paris, 1972).
—. "Etudes d'histoire militaire et diplomatique," BCH 89 (1965) 332-48.
Garnsey, P. D. A., and C. R. Whittaker (eds.), *Imperialism in the Ancient World* (Cambridge, 1978).
Geddes, A. G. "Who's Who in 'Homeric' Society," CQ 34 (1984) 17-36.
Gelb, Ignau J. "The Ancient Mesopotamian Ration System," JNES 24 (1965) 230-43.
Gelb J., B. Landberger, A. L. Oppenheim, and E. Reiner (eds.). *The Assyrian Dictionary* (Chicago, 1964).
Gernet, Louis. "Droit et prédroit en Grèce ancienne," in *Anthropologie de la Grèce ancienne* (Paris, 1968) 218-23.
—. *Droits et société dans la Grèce ancienne* (Paris, 1964).
Giangrande, Lawrence. "Pseudo-'International' Olympian and Personal Peace in Homeric Epic," CJ 68 (1972-73) 1-10.
Giovannini, Adalberto. *Etude historique sur les origines du catalogue des Vaisseaux* (Bern, 1969).
Gobineau, Arthur C. *Histoire des Perses,* 2 vols. (Paris, 1869).
Goedicke, H., and J. J. M. Roberts (eds.). *Unity and Diversity: Essays in the History, Literature, and Religion of the Ancient Near East* (Baltimore, 1975).
Gordon, Cyrus H. "Homer and the Bible, The Origin and Character of East Mediterranean Literature," HUDA 26 (1955) 43-108.
Gomme, A. W., A., Andrewes, and K. Dover. *A Historical Commentary on Thucydides,* 5 vols. (Oxford, 1945-81).
Götze, A. *Kleinasien. Handbuch der Altertumswissenschaft,* 2nd ed. (Munich, 1957).
—. "Die Annalen des Mursilis," MVAG 38:6 (Leipzig, 1933).
—. "Review of E. Forrer's *Forschungen,*" OLZ 33 (1930) 285-92.
—. "Zur Chronologie der hethiter Könige," KIF (Weimar, 1930) 115-29.
—. "Über die hethitische Königs Familie," *Archiv Orientalni* 2 (1930) 153-63.
—. *Das Hethiter Reich. Seine Stellung zwischen Ost und West* (Leipzig, 1928).
Graham, A. J. *Colony and Mother City* (New York, 1971).
Graetzel, Paul. *De Pactionum inter Graecas Civitates Factarum ad Bellum Pacemque Pertinentium Appelationibus Formulis Ratione* (Ph.D. Dissertation, Halle, 1885).
Grant, J. R. "A Note on the Tone of Greek Diplomacy," CQ 15 (1965) 261-66.
Gresseth, G. K. "The Gilgamesh Epic and Homer," CJ 70 (1975) 1-18.
Gschnitzer, Fritz. "Der Rat in der Volksversammlung. Ein Beitrag des homerischen Epos zur griechischen Verfassungsgeschichte," *Festschrift für Robert Muth* (Innsbruck, 1983).
—. *Griechische Sozialgeschichte* (Wiesbaden, 1981).
—. "König, Rat und Volk bei Homer," in *Beiträge zum Griechisch-Unterricht* 3 (Rheinland-Pfalz, 1980) 1-35.
—. *Ein neuer Spartanischer Staatvertrag* (Meisenheim am Glan, 1978).
—. "Politische Leidenschaft im homerischen Epos," in *Studien zum antiken Epos* (Meisenheim am Glan, 1976) 1-21.

BIBLIOGRAPHY

—. "Βασιλεύς. Ein Terminologischer Beitrag zur Frühgeschichte des Königtums bei den Griechen," in *Festschift für Leonhard C. Franz. Innsbrucker Beiträge zur Kulturwissenschaft*, vol. 11 (Innsbruck, 1965) 99-112.

—. *Abhängige Orte im griechischen Altertum* (Munich, 1958).

Guarducci, M. (ed.). *Inscriptiones Creticae* 4 vols. (Roma, 1935-50).

Gunkel, Hermann. *Kultur der Gegenwart*, Teil I, Abt. 7 (Berlin, 1906).

Gurney, O. R. *Some Aspects of Hittite Religion* (Oxford, 1977).

—. *The Hittites* (Baltimore, 1954).

Güterbock, Hans G. "The Hittites and the Aegean World: Part I. The Ahhiyawa Problem Reconsidered," AJA 87 (1983) 133-38, 141-43.

Haag, Herbert. "Homer und das Alte Testament," *Theologische Quartalschrift* 141 (1961) 1-24.

Hainsworth, J. B. *The Flexibility of the Homeric Formula* (Oxford, 1968).

Hallo, W. W., and W. K. Simpson. *The Ancient Near East, A History* (New York, 1971).

Halverson, John. "Social Order in the Odyssey," *Hermes* 113 (1985) 129-45.

Hammond, N. G. L. *Migrations and Invasion in Greece and Adjacent Areas* (Park Ridge, NJ, 1976).

Hampl, Franz. "Das Problem der Datierung der ersten Verträge zwischen Rom und Karthago," RhM 101 (1958) 58-75.

—. *Die griechischen Staatverträge des 4 Jahrhunderts v. Christi Geb.* (Leipzig, 1938).

Hansen, M. H. *The Athenian Assembly in the Age of Demosthenes* (Oxford, 1987)

Headlam, J. W. "The Procedure of the Gortynian Inscription," JHS 13 (1892-93) 48-69.

Hemberg, B. *Ἄναξ, Ἄνασσα, und Ἄνακτες als Götternamen unter besonderer Berücksichtigung der attischen Kulte* (Uppsala, 1955).

Herman, Gabriel. *Ritualized Friendship and the Greek City* (Cambridge, 1987).

Herter, Christian. "Griechenland und Orient," *Archiv für Soziologie und Ethik* 10 (1967-68) 49-60.

Heubeck, Alfred. "Homer und Mykene," *Gymnasium* 91 (1984) 1-14.

Hillers, Delbert R. *Covenant: The History of a Biblical Idea* (Baltimore, 1969).

—. "A Note on Some Treaty Terminology in the Old Testament," BASOR 176 (1964) 46-47.

—. *Treaty-Curses and the Old Testament Prophets* (Rome, 1964).

Hirzel, R. *Der Eid* (Leipzig, 1902).

—. *Agraphos Nomos (Abh. Sach. Gesel. der Wiss. Phil. Hist. Klasse)* 20 (1900).

Hooker, J. T. "Titles and Functions in the Pylian State," *Minos* 20-22 (1987) 257-67.

—. *Mycenaean Greece* (London and Boston, 1977).

Hopper, R. J. "Interstate Agreements in the Athenian Empire," JHS 63 (1943) 37-51.

How, W. W., and J. Wells. *A Commentary on Herodotus* (Oxford, 1912).

Huxley, L. G. *Achaeans and Hittites* (Oxford, 1960).

Jachmann, G. *Der homerische Schiffskatalog und die Ilias* (Köln, 1958).

Jacobsen, Th. "The Early Political Development in Mesopotamia," ZA 18 (1957) 91-140.

Jacoby, Felix. *Die Fragmente der griechische Historiker* (Leiden, 1923—).

Jeanmaire, Henri. *Couroi et Courètes* (Lille, 1939).

Jeffery, L. H. "The Pact of the First Settlers at Cyrene," *Historia* 10 (1961) 139-47.

Jensen, M. S. *The Homeric Question and the Oral Formulaic Theory* (Copenhagen, 1980).

Jensen, P. C. A. "Assyrisch-Babylonische Mythen und Epen," *Keilinschriftliche Bibliothek* 6 (Berlin, 1900) 1-588.

Jespin, A. *Untersuchungen zum Bundesbuch*, BWANT, F.3 (Stuttgart, 1927).

Jones, Walter J. *The Law and Legal Theories of the Greeks* (Oxford, 1956).

Jirku, A. *Das weltliche Recht im alten Testament* (Gütersloh, 1927).

Kantor, H. J. *The Aegean and the Orient in the Second Millennium B.C.* (Bloomington, 1947).

Keil, Bruno. *Staatsaltertümer* (Leipzig, 1923).

Karavites, Peter. "Diplomatic Envoys in the Homeric World," RIDA 34 (1987) 41-100.

Kempiski, A., and S. Kosak. "Der Ismeriga Vertrag," WO 5 (1970) 191-217.

Kiechle, Franz. "Das Verhältnis von Elis, Triphylien und der Pisatis im Spiegel der Dialektunterschiede," RhM 103 (1960) 336-66.

BIBLIOGRAPHY

King, L. W. *Babylonian Boundary Stones and Memorial Tablets in the British Museum* (London, 1912).

Kirk, G. S. *The Iliad: A Commentary*, vol. 1, Books 1-4 (Cambridge, 1985).

——. *The Nature of Greek Myths* (Baltimore, 1975).

——. "War and Warrior in the Homeric Poems," in J. P. Vernant (ed.), *Problèmes de la guerre en Grèce ancienne* (Paris, 1968).

——. *The Language and Background of Homer* (Cambridge, 1964).

——. *The Songs of Homer* (Cambridge, 1962).

Kirsten, E. *Das dorische Kreta* (Wurzburg, 1942).

Klengel, Horst. *Geschichte Syriens in 2. Jahrtausend vor unsere Zeit*. Teil 1, *Nordsyrien*. Teil 3, *Historische, geographische und allgemeine Darstellung* (Berlin, 1965-70).

Knudtzon, J. A. *Die El-Amarna Tafeln* (Leipzig, 1915).

Kock, Th. (ed.). *Comicorum atticorum Fragmenta* (Leipzig, 1880-88).

Kohler, J., and E. Ziebarth. *Das Staatsrecht von Gortyn* (Göttingen, 1913).

Korosec, Victor. "Völkerrechtliche Beziehungen in der El-Amarana Zeit," RIDA 22 (1975) 47-70.

——. "Quelques remarques juridiques sur deux traités internationales d'Alalah," *Droits de l'antiquité sociologie juridique: Mélange Henri Levy-Bruhl* (Paris, 1959) 171-78.

——. *Hethitische Staatsverträge. Leipzig. Rechtswiss. Studien* 60 (1931).

Laix, de R. A. *Probouleusis at Athens* (Berkeley and Los Angeles, 1973).

Lalonde, Gerard V. *The Publication and Transmission of Greek Diplomatic Documents* (Ph.D. Dissertation, University of Washington, 1971).

Lang, Mabel. *The Palace of Nestor in Messenia* (Princeton, 1966).

Langdon, S., and Alan H. Gardiner. "The Treaty of Alliance between Hattusilis, King of the Hittites, and the Pharaoh Ramses II of Egypt," JEA 6 (1920) 179-205.

Langdon, S. "A Phoenician Treaty of Assarhaddon: Collation of K.3500," RA 26 (1929) 189-94.

Laroche, E. "Suppiluliuma II," RA 47 (1953) 70-78.

Larsen, J. A. O. "The Origin and Significance of the Counting of Votes," CP 44 (1949) 164-81.

——. "Federation for Peace in Ancient Greece," CP 39 (1944) 145-62.

Latacz, Joachim. *Homer: Ein Einführung* (Zürich and Stuttgart, 1985).

——, (ed.). *Homer, Tradition und Neuerung* (Darmstadt, 1979).

Latte, Kurt. *Heiliges Recht* (Tübingen, 1920).

Lawson, John C. *Modern Greek Folklore and Ancient Greek Religion* (Cambridge, 1910).

Leaf, Walter. *The Iliad*, 2nd ed. (Amsterdam, 1960).

——. *Homer and History* (London, 1915).

Leaf, Walter and M. A. Bayfield (eds.). *The Iliad of Homer* (London and New York, 1962).

Lejeune, M. "Le Damos dans la sociéte Mycénienne," REG 78 (1965) 19-30.

Lesky, Allin. "Zum hethitischen und griechischen Mythos," *Eranos* 52 (1954) 8-17.

——. "Hethitische Texte und griechische Mythos," *Anzeiger der österreiche Akademie der Wissenschaften* (1955) 139-59.

Leumann, Mann. *Homerische Wörte*, in the series *Schweizerische Beiträge zur Altertumswissenschaft*, Heft 3 (Basel, 1950).

Lohmann, Dieter. *Die Komposition der Reden in der Ilias* (Berlin, 1979).

Lorimer, H. L. *Homer and the Monuments* (Oxford, 1950).

Luce, J. V. "The Polis in Homer and Hesiod," *The Royal Irish Academy* 78 (1978) 10-15.

Macan, R. W. *Herodotus* (London, 1895-1908).

Malamat, A. "Doctrines of Causality in Hittite and Biblical Historiography," VT 5 (1955) 1-6.

Mallowan, M. E. L. *Nimrud and Its Remains* (London, 1966).

Martin, R. *The Language of Heroes* (Ithaca, NY, 1989).

Martin, Victor. *La vie internationale dans la Grèce de cités, VIe-IVe s. av. J-C* (Genève, 1940).

Mazon, Paul. *Introduction à l'Iliade* (Paris, 1948).

McCarthy, Dennis J. *Treaty and Covenant: A Study in Form in the Ancient Oriental Documents and in the Old Testament* (Rome, 1963).

BIBLIOGRAPHY 213

Meiggs, R., and D. M. Lewis (eds.) *A Selection of Greek Historical Inscriptions* (Oxford, 1969).

Meissner, Bruno. *Festschrift*, vol. 1 (Leipzig, 1929).

—. *Babylonien und Assyrien*, 2 vols. (Heidelberg, 1920-25).

Mendelhall, George. *Law and Covenant in Israel and the Ancient Near East* (Pittsburgh, 1955).

—. "Covenant," in the *Interpreter's Bible Dictionary* (22).

Meyer, Eduard. *Forschungen zur Alten Geschichte*, vol. 1 (Halle, 1892).

Midgley, Mary. *Heart and Mind: The Varieties of Moral Experience* (New York, 1981).

Mondi, R. "Divine Kingship in Early Greece," *Arethusa* 12 (1980) 203-16.

Moran, W. L. "A Note on the Treaty Terminology of the Sefire Stellas," JNES 22 (1963) 173-76.

Moreau, Felix. "Les assemblées politiques d'après l'Iliade et l'Odysseé," REG 6 (1893) 204-50.

Monro, D. B. *Homer, Iliad*, 2 vols. (Oxford, 1893-96).

Morgenstern, Julian. "The Book of the Covenant, Part III," HUCA (1932) 1-150.

—. "The Book of the Covenant, Part II," HUCA 7 (1930) 19-258.

—. "The Book of the Covenant, Part I," HUCA 5 (1928) 1-151.

Morris, Ian. "The Use and Abuse of Homer," *Class. Antiquity* 5 (1986) 81-138.

Mosley, Derek J. "On Greek Enemies Becoming Allies," *Ancient Society* 5 (1974) 43-50.

—. *Envoys and Diplomacy in Ancient Greece, Historia Einzelschriften* 22 (1973).

—. "Crossing Frontiers under Arms," RIDA 20 (1973) 161-69.

—. "Voting Procedure and Election of Athenian Envoys," in *Wiener Studien* N.F. 6 (1972) 140-44.

—. "Diplomacy and Disunion in Ancient Greece," *Phoenix* 25 (1971) 319-30.

—. "Archipresbeutai," *Hermes* 94 (1966) 377-81.

—. "The Size of Embassies in Ancient Greek Diplomacy," TAPA 96 (1965) 255-66.

Muhly, James D. "Hittites and Achaeans: Ahhiyawa *Redomitus*," *Historia* 23 (1974) 129-45.

—. "Homer and Phoenicians: The Relations between Greece and the Near East in the Late Bronze and Early Iron Ages," *Berytus* 19 (1970) 19-64.

Munn-Rankin, J. M. "Diplomacy in Western Asia in the Early Second Millennium B.C.," *Iraq* 18 (1956) 68-110.

Mylonas, George. *Mycenae and the Mycenaean Age* (Princeton, 1966).

—. *Homer and His Critics* (London, 1958).

Neufeld, E. *The Hittite Laws* (London, 1951).

Niese, B. *Der homerische Schiffscatalog* (Ph.D. Dissertation, Kiel, 1893).

Nilsson, Martin P. *History of Greek Religion* (London, 1963).

—. *Greek Folk Religion* (New York, 1961).

—. *Geschichte der griechischen Religion*, 2 vols. (Munich, 1955).

—. *Cults, Myths, Oracles, and Politics in Ancient Greece* (Lund, 1951).

—. *Minoan-Mycenaean Religion and Its Survival in Greek Religion* 2nd ed. (Lund, 1950).

—. *Greek Piety* (Oxford, 1948).

—. *Greek Popular Religion* (New York, 1940).

—. *Homer and Mycenae* (London, 1933).

—. *Mycenaean Origins of Greek Mythology* (London, 1932).

Nock, A. D. "A Curse from Cyrene," *Archiv für Religionswissenschaft* 24 (1926) 172-73.

Noe, M. *Phoinix, Ilias und Homer: Untersuchungen zum neunten Gesang der Ilias* (Leipzig, 1940) esp. pp. 1-124.

Noth, M. *Gesammelte Studien zum Alten Testament* (Munich, 1957).

Nougayrol, Jean. *Le palais royal d'Ugarit IV: Textes Accadiens des archives sud (Archives internationales)* (Paris, 1956).

Nowag, Werner. *Raub und Beute in der archaischen Zeit der Griechen* (Frankfurt/Main, 1983).

Numelin, Ragnar. *The Beginnings of Diplomacy. A Sociological Study of Intertribal and International Relations* (London and Copenhagen, 1950).

214 BIBLIOGRAPHY

Olshausen, Eckart, and Hildegard Biller (eds.). *Antike Diplomatie* in the series *Wege der Forschung* (Darmstadt, 1979).

Oettinger, N. "Die militärischen Eide der Hethiter," STBoT 22 (Wiesbaden, 1976).

Oliver, J. H. "Herodotus 4.153 and SEG IX 3" GRBS 7 (1966) 25-29.

—. "Text of the So-called Constitution of Chios from the First Half of the Sixth Century B.C." AJPh 80 (1959) 296-301.

Otten, Heinrich. "Neue Quellen zum Ausklang des Hethitischen Reiches," MDOG 94 (1963) 1-23.

—. "Ein Brief aus Hathusa an Babu-ahu-iddina," AFO (Graz, 1959-60).

Page, D. L. *History and the Homeric Iliad* (Berkeley and Los Angeles, 1959).

Palmer, L. R. *Mycenaeans and Minoans*, 2nd. ed. (London, 1965).

—. *Achaeans and Indo-Europeans* (Oxford, 1955).

Papachatzis, Nicholas D. *Pausaniou Ellados Periegesis*, 5 vols. (Athens, 1963-69).

Parry, Milman. "Greek Society and South Slavic Heroic Song," TAPA 64 (1933) 179-99.

—. "Studies in the Epic Technique of Oral Verse-Making. II. The Homeric Language as the Language of Oral Poetry," HSCP 43 (1932) 1-50.

—. "Studies in the Epic Technique of Oral Verse-Making. I. Homer and Homeric Style," HSCP 41 (1930) 72-147.

—. "The Homeric Gloss: A Study in Word-Sense," TAPA 59 (1928) 233-47.

Pedersen, J. *Israel, Its Life and Culture* (Copenhagen, 1926).

Persson, A. W. *The Religion of Greece in Prehistoric Times* (Berkeley and Los Angeles, 1942).

—. *Royal Tombs at Dendra Near Midea* (Lund, 1931).

Pfeiffer, R. T. "The Transmission of the Book of the Covenant," HThR 24 (1931) 11-109.

Phillipson, Coleman. *The International Law and Custom of Ancient Greece and Rome*, 2 vols. (London, 1911).

Picard, C. G. *Les religions préhelléniques* (Paris, 1948).

Plescia, John. *The Oath and Perjury in Ancient Greece* (Tallahassee, 1970).

Podlecki, Anthony J. "Guest-gift and Nobodies in Odyssey 9," *Phoenix* 15 (1961) 125-33.

Pomtow, H. "Delphische Neufunde, V: Zusätze und Nachträge," *Klio* 17 (1923) 153-204.

Preiser, Wolfgang. *Macht und Norm in der Völkerrechtsgeschichte* (Baden-Baden, 1978).

Pritchard, James B (ed.). *Ancient Near Eastern Texts Relating to the Old Testament*, 2nd ed. (Princeton, 1955).

Pugliese-Caratelli, G. "Aspetti e problemi della monarchia Micenea," *La Parola del Passato* 14 (1959) 401-31.

Puukko, A. F., *Die altsyrischen und hethitischen Gesetze und das Alte Testament*. Vol. 1 in the series *Studia Orientalia* (Helsinki, 1925).

Rhodes, J. P. *The Athenian Boule* (Oxford, 1972).

Rieu, E. V. trans. *Homer, The Iliad* (Baltimore, 1961).

Rihill, Tracey. "'Kings' and 'Commoners' in Homeric Society," LCM 11 (1986) 86-91.

Robert, Louis "Documents d'Asie Mineure, V-XVII," BCH 102 (1978) 477-90.

Robert, R. *Homère* (Paris, 1950).

Robin, Léon. *La pensée hellénique des origines à Epicure*, 2nd ed. (Paris, 1967).

Rohde, Erwin. *Psyche*, 2 vols., trans. by W. K. C. Guthrie (New York, 1966).

Rose, H. J. *Primitive Culture in Greece* (London, 1925).

Samuel, Alan E. *The Mycenaeans in History* (Englewood, NJ, 1966).

Sandars, N. K. *The Epic of Gilgamesh* (Baltimore, 1965).

San Nicolo, M. "Parerga Babylonica," *Archiv Orientalna* 4.1 (1932) 34-40.

Schachermeyr, Fritz. *Die Levante im Zeitalter der Wanderungen*. Vol. 5 in the series *Die ägaische Frühzeit* (Wien, 1982).

—. *Die ältesten Kulturen Griechenlands* (Stuttgart, 1955).

—. "Hethiter und Achäer," MAOG 9, 1-2 (1935).

—. "Die römisch-punisch Verträge," RhM 79 (1930) 350-62.

—. "Zur staatsrechtlichen Wertung der hethitischen Staatsverträge," in *Bruno Meissners Festschrift*, vol. 2 (Leipzig, 1929) 180-86.

Schaeffer, C. F. A. *Cuneiform Texts of Ras Shamra* (London, 1930).

Schaeffer, F. A. *Mission de Ras Shamra*, vol. 18, *Ugaritica VIII* (Paris, 1978).

Scheil, Viktor. *Memoires. Tome XI Textes Elamites-Anzanites* (Paris, 1911).

BIBLIOGRAPHY 215

Scully, Stephen. "The Polis in Homer: A Definition and Interpretation," *Ramus* 10 (1981) 1-34.

Sealey, Raphael. "How Citizenship and the City Began in Athens," AJAH 8 (1983) 97-129.

Segal, C. P. "The Embassy and the Duals of *Iliad* 9.182-98," GRBS 9 (1968) 101-14.

Seymour, Thomas D. *Life in the Homeric Age* (New York, 1907).

Simpson, Hope R., and J. F. Lazenby. *The Catalogue of the Ships in Homer's Iliad* (Oxford, 1970).

Simpson, Hope R. *Mycenaean Greece* (Park Ridge, NJ, 1981).

Smith, Robertson W. *Religion of the Semites* (New York, 1957).

Snell, Bruno. *Lexikon des Frühgriechischen Epos*, 2 vols. (Göttingen, 1979-82).

Snodgrass, A. M. "An Historical Homeric Society?" JHS 94 (1974) 114-19.

—. *The Dark Age of Greece* (Edinburgh, 1971).

Soltau, Wilhelm. "Die römisch-karthagischen Verträge," *Philologus* 38 (1889) 131-41.

Sommer, Franz. *Die Ahhijawa Urkunden* (Hildesheim, 1932).

Sorgen-Grey, Th. *De vestigiis iuris gentium homerici* (Leipzig, 1871).

Stagakis, George. "Therapontes and Hetairoi in the *Iliad* as Symbols of the Political structure of the Homeric State," *Historia* 15 (1966) 408-19.

Stamm, J. J., and M. E. Andrews. *The Ten Commandments in Recent Research* in *Studies in Biblical Theology*, 2nd series, No. 2 (Naperville, IL, 1967).

Stanford, W. B. *The Odyssey of Homer*, 2 vols. (London, 1958-59).

Starr, Chester G. *The Economic and Social Growth of Early Greece, 800-500 B.C.* (Oxford, 1977).

—. *The Origins of Greek Civilization, 1100-650* (London, 1962).

Steinmetzer, F. X. *Die babylonischen Kuddurru als Urkundenform Studien zur Geschichte und Kultur des Altertums* (Paderborn, 1922).

Steiner, Gerd. "Die Ahhijawa-Frage heute," *Saeculum* 15 (1964) 365-92.

Stella, L. A. "Importanza degli Scavi di Ras Shamra per il problema finicio dei poemi Omerici," *Archaeologia Classica* 4 (1952) 72-76.

Stengel, Paul. *Die Griechischen Kultursaltertümer*, 3rd. ed. (Munich, 1920).

—. *Opferbräuche der Griechen* (Leipzig, 1919).

—. "Zu den griechischen Schuropfer," *Hermes* 49 (1914) 90-101.

Streck, Maximilian. "Bemerkungen zu den 'Annals of the kings of Assyria, I'" ZA 19 (1906) 234-60.

Syriopoulos, C. T. *Eisagogê eis tên archaian Ellênikên istorian. Oi metabatikoi xronoi apo tên Mykenaikên eis tên archaïkên periodon 1200-700 p. x A-B.* (Athens, 1983).

Tasliklioglu, Z., and P. Frisch. "New Inscriptions from the Troad," ZPE 17 (1975) 102-14.

Täubler, Eugen. *Imperium Romanum, Studien zur Entwicklungsgeschichte des römischen Reiches*, vol. 1 (Leipzig, 1913).

Ténékidès, George. *Droit internationale et communautés fédèrales dans la Grèce des cités (Ve-IIIe s. av. J.C.)* (Leiden, 1957).

Thomas, C. G. "The Roots of Homeric Kingship," *Historia* 15 (1966) 387-407.

Thompson, George. *Studies in Ancient Greek Society. The Prehistoric Aegean* (New York, 1965).

Thompson, J. A. *The Ancient Near Eastern Treaties and the Old Testament* (London, 1964).

Thompson, R. C. *Reports of the Astrologers of Nineveh and Babylon* (London, 1900).

Thureau-Dangin, F. *Die sumerischen und akkadischen Königs Inschriften* (Leipzig, 1907), esp. pp. 10-43.

Toynbee, Arnold J. *Hannibal's Legacy*, 2 vols. (Oxford, 1965).

Turney-High, Harry H. *Primitive War* (Columbia, SC, 1949).

Trumbull, Henry Clay. *The Blood Covenant* (New York, 1885).

Trümpy, Hans. *Kriegerische Fachausdrücke im griechischen Epos* (Basel, 1950).

Valk der van, Marchinus (ed.). *Eustathii archiepiscopi Thessalonicensis Commentarii ad Homeri Iliadem Pertinentes*, 4 vols. (Leiden, 1971-87).

van Wees, Hans. "Leader of Men? Military Organization in the *Iliad*," CQ 36 (1986) 285-303.

van Royen, R. A., and B. H. Isaac. *The Arrival of the Greeks* (Amsterdam, 1979).

Ventris, M., and J. Chadwick. *Documents in Mycenaean Greek* (Cambridge, 1956).

BIBLIOGRAPHY

Virolleaud, Ch. "Cinq tablettes accadiennes de Ras-Shamra," RA 38 (1941) 1-25.
Vlachos, George C. *Les sociétés politiques homériques* (Paris, 1974).
Vogt, Ernst. "Vox 'berit' concrete adhibita illustratur," *Biblica* 36 (1955) 565-66.
Vollmer, A. "Die römisch-karthagenischen Verträge," RhM 32 (1877) 614-32.
von Scala, R. *Die Staatsverträge des Altertums* (Leipzig, 1898).
von Schuler, Einar. *Die Kaskäer* (Berlin, 1965).
—. *Staatsverträge und Dokumente hethitische Rechts* in *Hethiter. Historia Sonderheft* (1964).
von Wilamowitz-Möllendorff, Ulrich. *Der Glaube der Hellenen* (Berlin, 1931-32).
Wace, A. J. B., and C. Blegen. "Pottery as Evidence for Trade and Colonization in the Aegean Bronze Age," *Klio* 32 (1939) 131-47.
Wace, A. J. B., and F. H. Stubbings (eds.). *A Companion to Homer* (London, 1962).
Walser, Gerold (ed.). *Neuere Hethiter Forschung, Historia, Einzelschriften,* Heft 7 (1964).
Walther, Fritz. *Die Anfänge der Diplomatie. Die Entwicklung des internationalen Verkehrs bei den Grossmachten des Altertums* (Ph.D. Dissertation, Würzburg, 1956).
Webster, T. B. L. *From Mycenae to Homer* (New York, 1964).
Weidner, Ernst F. "Der Staatsvertrag Assurniraris VI von Assyria mit Mat'ilu von Bit-Agusi," *Archiv für Orientforschung* 8 (1932) 17-26.
—. *Politische Documente aus Kleinasien. Die Staatsverträge in akkadischer Sprache aus dem Archiv von Boghazköi* (Leipzig, 1923).
Wéry, Louise-Marie. "Le fonctionnement de la diplomatie à l'epoque homérique," RIDA 14 (1967) 169-205.
—. *Hesiodos Erga*, 2nd. ed. (Berlin, 1926).
Willcock, M. M. *A Commentary on Homer's Iliad, Books I-IV* (New York, 1970).
—. "Mythological Paradeigma in the *Iliad*," CQ 14 (1964) 141-54.
Willetts, Ronald F. *The Civilization of Ancient Crete* (Berkeley and Los Angeles, 1977).
— (ed.). *The Law of Gortyn* (New York, 1967).
—. *Cretan Cults and Festivals* (London, 1962).
—. *Aristocratic Society in Ancient Crete* (London, 1955).
Wirth, Hermann. *Homer und Babylon, Ein Lösungs. Versuch der homerischen Frage vom orientalischen Standpunkte aus* (Freiburg, 1921).
Wiseman, D. J. "The Vassal Treaties of Esarhaddon," *Iraq* 20 (1958) part I., 1-99.
Woodhouse, W. J. *Composition of Homer's Odyssey* (Oxford, 1930).
Wüst, F. R. "Amphictyonie, Eidgenossenschaft, Symmachie," *Historia* 3 (1954-55) 129-53.

INDEX OF PROPER NAMES AND TITLES

Abbael 121
Abimelech 180
Abraham 8, 75, 76
Achaea, Achaean 5, 17-20, 22-35, 41, 45, 48, 61-62, 65, 69-73, 76, 78, 84-85, 88, 92-95, 99-100, 103, 105, 109, 111-112, 114, 118, 122-124, 128, 133, 136, 139-140, 143, 145-147, 159-163, 165-166, 168, 172, 176, 182, 184-185, 192, 197
Achilles 3, 18-19, 22, 29, 32-36, 42-44, 46, 53-56, 66, 71-74, 76-79, 84, 88-89, 93-94, 106, 110, 113-114, 122-124, 134, 136-137, 141, 143, 146, 151-152, 160-161, 163, 165-170, 173-174, 177, 182, 184-187, 192, 197-198
Acropolis 190-191
Adad-nirari 151
Admetus 154
Adrastus 152
Aegean 103, 151, 153
Aegyptius 137, 142
Aeneas 84-85, 88, 134, 161, 173
Aeneid 173
Aeolus 163
Aetolian(s) 134, 191
Agamemnon 3, 17-22, 24-26, 29, 33, 36, 41, 45, 53, 61-62, 69, 71-74, 76-79, 84-85, 87-89, 92-93, 100-101, 103, 105-106, 111-112, 116-117, 119, 122-124, 133, 137, 139, 144-147, 162-163, 165-168, 170, 172, 174, 176, 184, 186, 192, 197, 198
Aeschylus 102
Ahhiyawa 9, 49
Aias 26-28, 70, 84-85, 93, 112, 167, 184, 198
Aischines 97, 116
Akkadian 82
Alaksandus of Wilusa 150, 171, 192, 197
Alalakh 121, 159
Alalcomenea 85
Alastor 161
Alcinous 55, 135-136, 140, 141, 183
Aleppo 90, 121, 188
Alexander 22, 25-29, 41-42, 45, 54, 57, 71, 84, 92, 99-100, 103-105, 107, 118-119, 192
Alshe 159
Amarna 49-50

Amasis 66-67
Amenophis III 50-51
Amenophis IV 50
Amphictyony 97
Amphidamas 151
Amurru 171, 195
Amyclae 190
Amyntor 152
Anaetoi 190, 199
Anchises 85, 173-174
Antenor 26, 28, 42, 69, 116-117
Antigone 42
Antilochus 74, 77, 169, 174
Antinous 151, 16
Antiochus 191
Aphrodite 25, 78
Apollo 18, 26-27, 32, 84-85, 88, 92, 97, 100, 102-103, 110, 112, 162, 185-186, 190-191
Aramaean, Aramaic 115-116, 130, 181
Arcadia(n) 89, 95, 97, 203
Areteon 84
Argos, Argive(s) 7, 18, 86-87, 191-193, 203
Aristarchus 170
Aristophanes 38
Arinna 188
Armatana 129
Arzawa 149, 150, 194
Armenia 90
Arpad 110
Artaxerxes 154
Artemis 97, 101, 185
Ashurnirari 129
Assyria(n) 49-51, 115-116, 130-131, 159, 192, 195
Astata 90
Asteoropaeus 169
Ate 88
Athena 26, 33, 40, 43-44, 61, 69, 80, 85, 97, 111-112, 183, 190-191
Athens 1, 8, 142, 153-154, 177, 190-191, 193
Athenians 1, 67, 153-154, 177, 190-191, 193
Atreid(s) 25, 166
Attica 203
Augeas 25
Aulis 4, 41, 106, 110, 184
Aziru 171

218 INDEX OF PROPER NAMES AND TITLES

Babylonia(n) 49-51, 66, 90, 188, 195
Barcaean 67
Bede 9
Bellerophon 52, 54, 134
Bente'šina 195
Birds 38
Bit-Agusi 129
Biya'ššili 90
Boar's Tomb 62
Boeotia 85
Bogazköy 49
Briseis 71, 73-74, 88, 105, 163, 165-168, 186
Bronze Age 103
Burnaburias II 50

Calchas 18-19, 63, 78, 111, 133, 197
Calypso 37, 44, 79, 93, 186
Cambyses 66
Canaanite 51
Carchemish 90, 130
Carian 5
Carthage, Carthaginian 64, 66, 158
Cassandra 30-31, 43, 45, 72
Chalcheos 85,
Charondas 96
Chios, Chian 67, 97
Chryses 18, 105, 133, 145, 162-163, 167, 186
Chryseis 78, 145-146, 165, 167-168, 170, 186
Chthonian 103
Cicones 163
Cilicia(n) 66, 158
Circe 18, 37-38, 44, 94, 186
Cleisthenes 22
Cleitonymus 151
Cnossus 101
Corcyraean 154
Corinthian 177, 203
Council of Elders 76, 139, 143, 166
Crete, Cretan i, 6, 72, 95-96, 102, 190, 193
Crito 1
Croesus 66, 152
Cronus 103
Curetes 134
Cyclops 164
Cyprus 49
Cyrene, Cyrenaean 115
Cyrus 66

Danaean 18, 26, 32
Darius 153
Datassa 188

Demaratus 153-154
Dameter, Demeter 102-103
Delos 1
Delphi(an) 97, 189-190
Diomedes 46, 52-55, 84, 111-112, 123, 135, 145, 161-162, 174, 184
Dionysia 193
Dolichium 39
Dolon 29-30, 77-79, 161-162
Dolopes, Dolopesian 123, 152
Dorian 95, 97-98, 201-203
Dreros 96, 190, 193

Eannatum, 82
Earth 23, 31, 36, 75, 85, 100, 102-103, 105, 119
Echemerus 67
Eeropus 67
Eetion 163
Egypt, Egyptian 6, 49-51, 66, 90, 100, 130, 195, 197
El-Amarna 195, 197
Elis, Elean 97, 189-191, 193, 198
Epidamnus 177
Erinyes 101-102, 105, 152
Ereuthalion 89
Esarhaddon 13, 83, 105, 115, 180, 192
Eumaeus 39, 79, 181, 183
Eumelus 169
Eupeithes 151-152
Euphorbus 169
Europe 7
Eustathius 22, 34, 93
Euphetes 85,
Euphrates 90
Euripides 64
Eurylochus 79
Eurycleia 79
Exardeeis 97

Feast of Booths 192

Gaia (Ga, Ge) 102-103
Gilead 180-181
Glaucus 53-55, 84, 135
Gorgias 152
Gortyn, Gortynian 95, 97, 116
Greek x, 1-4, 7-9, 11, 12-14, 17-21, 22-29, 32-33, 35, 38, 41-45, 48, 53-54, 56, 60, 62-63, 65-69, 72-73, 77, 81-82, 85-86, 92-93, 95-97, 99-103, 105-106, 109-111, 115-116, 122, 127, 133, 147-148, 151, 154-156, 159-160, 162-163, 168, 170, 172-174, 177, 181, 184, 186, 189-190, 192-194, 199-202, 204-205
Greece ix, 5-8, 14, 24, 53, 67, 92, 97,

INDEX OF PROPER NAMES AND TITLES

219

103, 109, 115, 128, 142, 144, 153-155, 179, 185, 191, 198, 201, 203, 205
Grave Gamma 6

Hades 170
Haliaea 190
Halieis 190, 193
Halpa 90
Hanza 129
Hapalla 149
Harran 130
Harri 90
Hatti 49, 83, 90, 120, 129, 148, 150, 197
Hattusilis 49, 130, 148, 195
Hayaša 129, 150, 175
Hayana 194
Hebrew(s) 63-64, 181
Hector 22-23, 25-30, 33-35, 38, 41-42, 46, 48, 54, 56, 61-62, 69-71, 73-74, 77-79, 84-85, 88, 92-93, 100, 106, 110, 112-113, 119, 123-124, 136-137, 160, 169-170, 172-174, 184-185, 192, 198
Hecuba 111-113
Helen 7, 21-22, 25-26, 28-29, 41-42, 48, 62, 64, 70, 73, 92, 111, 133, 136, 140, 161, 166, 177, 197-198
Helenus 26
Helios 24, 38, 74, 100-102
Hellenes, Hellenic 1, 97, 103, 189, 204
Hellenistic 109, 139, 191, 200, 204
Helladic 6
Hellespont 27
Hephaestus 30-31, 34, 75, 88, 114
Heracliot(s) 191
Hippias 153
Hera 17-18, 28-34, 42, 44, 75, 77, 79-80, 85-86, 88, 94, 100-103, 112, 114, 172, 176
Heracles 63, 67, 183
Heraea 97, 189, 198
Hermes 36, 101, 181
Herodotean 68
Herodotus 63-64, 66-68, 153-154
Hesiod 37, 55, 57
Hezekiah 130-131
Hittite 6, 9, 11, 13, 49, 51, 57, 82-83, 87, 89-90, 94, 100, 104, 109, 116, 118, 120, 127-131, 148-151, 153-155, 157-159, 170-172, 174-175, 177-178, 188, 192, 194-195, 197-199, 205
Homer 2, 3, 9, 14, 17, 22, 24, 29, 42-43, 46, 48, 53, 55, 59-62, 64, 68-69, 72-73, 77, 79-80, 82-85, 87-89, 93-95, 101-103, 106-107, 109-112, 114-115,

118-119, 124, 127-128, 133, 140, 146, 150, 153, 160, 162, 168, 172, 181, 183, 186, 198, 202, 204-205
Homeric 2-5, 7-18, 31, 42, 45-48, 52, 55-57, 59, 62, 67-68, 71, 73-76, 79, 81-87, 89, 92, 94-96, 100-110 112, 115, 117, 122, 127, 132-135, 137-140, 142-146, 150-151, 154-161, 163, 169-170, 172, 175-178, 181-183, 185, 187, 189, 192-194, 197-198, 200-205; post-Homeric 7-8, 13, 106, 109, 116, 154, 179, 189, 191, 193, 201, 203; pre-Homeric 2, 103, 106, 115, 127
Huqqanas 129, 150, 175, 194
Hurrian 109, 205
Hyacinthia 193
Hyllus 67
Hyperion 101
Hypnos 30

Ibal-El 117
Ida 34, 88, 101
Idaeus 24, 28-29, 42, 45, 123, 192
Idomeneus 25-26, 30, 41, 45, 72-73, 85-86, 88, 112, 123, 169, 193
Idrimi 158
Iliad 2-5, 9, 11, 18, 41, 46, 52-54, 60, 71, 78, 84, 100, 105-106, 110, 119, 122-123, 128, 135-137, 139, 143, 152, 159, 165-166, 172-173, 177, 186, 198
Ilios 27
Ilium 20, 21, 26, 27, 32, 40, 92, 191
Io 7
Ionia 92
Iphis 168
Iphitus 183
Iris 173
Irrite 130
Isaac 180
Išme-Dagan 50
Israel, Israelite 63, 76, 90-92, 104, 116, 180
Ištarmuwas 194-195
Ithaca(n) 40, 54, 61, 128, 137, 142, 151, 174

Jacob 180
Jeremiah 63, 118
Jerusalem 131
Judah 63
Judaea(n) 130

Kabesos 30
Kahat 188
Kkad'šman-Harbe 50
Kades 90

INDEX OF PROPER NAMES AND TITLES

Kara [duni] yas 90
Kinza 90
Kizzuwadna 122, 157
Kupanta-kal 177, 194, 197
Kurigalzu 50
Kurinnu 188
Kuwaliya 194

Laban 180-181
Labynetus (Nebuchadnezzar) 66
Lacedaemon, Lacedaemonian 1, 190-193
Laconia 203
Laertes 174, 184
Lagash 82
Leiodes 162
Lesbos, Lesbians 67, 168
Leto 97, 185
Libya(n) 190
Locris 96
Lycia(n) 112, 134
Lycaon 88, 161, 169, 176
Lycomedon 173
Lydia(n) 66
Lymessus 88, 161
Lysimacheia 191

Macedonia 154
Manapa-Dattas 149-150
Mantineia(n) 191, 193
Mari 50
Masa 129
Mashuiluwas 129, 194
Masturis 195
Mati'ilu 129
Mattiwaza 90, 122, 128-131, 188, 192, 196
Meleager 89, 111, 134, 160
Menelaus 22-28, 36, 43-46, 48, 54-55, 57, 62, 69-70, 74, 77-78, 84-85, 92, 94, 103-105, 107, 111, 118-119, 176-177, 183, 192
Mentor 40
Meriones 169
Mesopotamia(n) 49, 82, 115, 159
Messenia(n) 63, 203
Metapioi 190, 199
Middle Helladic 6
Milesian 66
Minos(an) 96, 101-102, 146
Mira 194, 197
Misri 90
Mitanni 49, 122, 128-131, 158-159, 188, 192, 195-196, 205
Mizpah 180-181
Mosaic Law 37
Moses 180, 192

Mursilis 100, 129, 146, 148-150, 171, 175-177, 188, 197
Muskisi 90
Muwattalis 122, 150, 157-158, 171, 188, 192, 194-195, 197
Muwattis 194
Mycenaea(n) ix, 2-10, 17, 19, 82-83, 86-87, 89, 95, 101-104, 109, 115, 127, 132-133, 135-136, 147, 155-156, 158-159, 166, 170, 174, 179, 185, 189, 191, 193, 199-203, 205; post-Mycenaean 201, 203, 205; pre-Mycenaean 6, 92, 102, 115
Mygdon 84
Myrmidon 143-144, 173

Nebuchadnezzar (Labynetus) 66
Neleus 63
Neoptolemus 35
Nerikka-illis 195
Niobe 182, 185
Nestor 20-22, 41, 46, 65, 74, 88-89, 106, 111, 122-123, 140, 146, 161, 166, 172, 174, 183-184
Nicias 190
Nuhassi 90
Nymphs 181

Ocean 101-102
Odysseus 20-21, 37-40, 43-44, 46, 54-55, 60-61, 65, 71-75, 79-80, 84, 93-94, 110, 116, 133, 135-137, 139-142, 144, 151, 161-165, 167, 173-175, 177, 182-186, 192
Odyssey, 2-4, 9, 11, 14, 40, 43-46, 60-61, 84, 128, 135-137, 151, 163, 181
Old Testament 63, 75, 83, 90-91, 130
Olympus, Olympian 32, 37-38, 43-45, 85, 88, 101-103, 110, 189
Olympic 193
Olympia 63, 189-191, 198
Orsilochus 85
Orthagorid 203
Othryoneus 30-31, 43, 45, 72, 94, 124, 192, 198

Pactolus 5
Palestine 90, 92
Pallas 85
Panathenaea 193
Pandarus 69, 78, 84, 176
Parattarna 158
Paris 22-24, 41-42, 45, 48, 53, 61-62, 69-70, 78, 111, 173, 176-177, 198
Pasithea (Grace) 31, 43
Patroclus 32-34, 43, 56, 65, 72-74, 79,

INDEX OF PROPER NAMES AND TITLES

88, 94, 110, 113, 123, 143-144, 151-152, 160-161, 168-170, 174. 182, 184-185
Pausanias 63, 154, 166
Pedasus 88, 161
Pelasgian 5
Peleus 28, 113-114, 123, 151-152, 173-174
Peloponnese 95, 151, 177
Penelope 60, 65, 74, 79, 151
Pentateuch 148
Perdiccas 193
Persephone 102
Persian 64, 66-67, 153-155
Phaeacian 55, 135-136, 140-141
Pharaoh 49, 195
Phasis 7
Phocaea(n) 66
Phegeus 67
Philistine 130-131, 180
Philoctetes 35
Phoenix 33, 53-55, 89, 123-124, 152, 170
Phoenician 39, 46, 66, 80
Phoebus 85
Phrygian 152
Phthia 124, 152, 166
Pisatan 190
Plataea(n) 67, 154
Plato 12, 56, 64, 95-96
Polyphemus 164, 184
Poseidon 38, 85, 101-102, 112
Potnias 102
Prexaspes 66
Priam 23-24, 26, 29-30, 34-36, 42-45, 62-63, 72, 84, 87-88, 94, 101, 113, 116, 123-124, 134, 140, 161, 169-170, 172-174, 182, 185-186, 192, 198
Pronoia 97
Pylos, Pylosian 135, 141
Pythius 63

Ramataia 97
Ramses 49, 148, 195
Ras-Shamra (Ugarit) 82
Rhadamanthys 96, 102
Rimi-šar-ma 188-189
Roman 64, 202
Roman-comitia 138
Rome 158

Salamis 154
Salmanezer I 51
Samash 188
Samian 67
Samothrace 191

Samši-Adad 50
Sargon 130
Sarpedon 84, 112-113, 169
Scaean (Gate) 26, 111, 192
Scamander 113-114
Scyrus 168, 173-174
Scythia(n) 67
Seha 148, 150, 195
Semite, Semitic 116, 179
Sennacherib 130-131
Serdaea(n) 190, 199
Sfire 13, 83
Sicyon, Sicyonian 22, 203
Sidon, Sidonian 39-40, 169
Simois 114
Sinaih 180
Sleep 17, 31, 44, 77, 79, 86, 88, 101
Socrates 1, 2
Solon 67
Sophocles 35, 42
Sparta(n) 8, 36, 66-67, 74, 97-98, 153-154, 177, 193
Stenyclerus 63
Stesichorus 21, 41, 62, 167
Styx 31, 37, 41, 75, 77, 101, 204
Sumerian 59
Sun 23, 101, 105, 119
Sunaššura 122, 157-158
Suppiluliumas 82, 90, 122, 128-131, 150, 157, 159, 171, 175, 188, 192, 194, 196
Suttarna 159
Sybaris, Sybarite 190, 199
Syennesis 66
Syria 39, 82, 141, 148

Talthybius 28
Taphian 151
Targašnallis 149
Tawagalawas 49
Tegea(n) 67
Telemachus 36, 74, 76, 79, 137, 140-141, 151, 183
Terpuziya 129
Tešub 188, 197
Tette 90
Teuthras 84
Thebe 163
Themistocles 154
Theraea(n) 190
Thersites 112, 133-134, 139, 143, 184, 186
Thessaly 203
Thesprotian 151-152
Thetis 88, 173
Thrace 170
Thucydides 66, 68-69, 154, 191, 202

222 INDEX OF PROPER NAMES AND TITLES

Titan 75
Tritogenia 85
Troad 5, 191
Tros 161
Trojan 8, 17, 21-30, 32-35, 38, 41-42,
    44-45, 48, 53-55, 61-62, 69-73, 76, 78,
    85, 93-94, 99-102, 105-106, 111-112,
    114, 116-118, 123-124, 128, 134, 136-
    137, 140, 143, 145-147, 159, 161, 168,
    172-174, 176-177, 184-185, 192, 197-
    198
Troy 7, 17, 19-21, 24-26, 30, 32-33, 36,
    41-42, 53, 57, 61, 63, 72, 84, 87, 101,
    105, 110-111, 113-114, 123-124, 128,
    136-137, 151, 160-161, 163, 165-167,
    172-174, 177, 185, 197-198
Tudhaliyas 51, 82, 120, 188, 195
Tuppi-Tešub 148, 171, 197
Turmitta 129
Tušratta 196
Tydeus 52, 54, 84
Tyndareos 62, 166

Tyre 7

Ugarit 82, 130
Ulmi-Teshub 120, 188
Ura 130
Urukazabanu 191

Waššuganni 130

Xanthus 18, 33-34, 43, 161
Xerxes 154

Yahweh 76, 90, 180
Yarimlim 121
Yašmah-Adad 50

Zaleucus 96
Zedekiah 63
Zeus 23, 27-31, 33-34, 38, 40-41, 43-45,
    54, 60, 63, 69-71, 75, 77, 79, 85, 88,
    93, 96, 100-101, 103, 105, 112, 114,
    119, 145, 172, 173, 176, 189, 191

INDEX OF TRANSLITERATED TERMS

aethion 74
agorê 137, 139-140, 145
ahuka 50
abûtum 49
ahûtum 49
akritoi 106
alloi 128
aliletae 77
anax 85, 87
anax andrôn
antitheos 84
apomnyon 38
apospendein 80
areiphilos 85
arexein 19
aristê 30
aristos 19
ater 58

boôpis potnia 86
boêtheia 19
boulê, boulae 45, 139

Crêtôn agos 86

daiphrôn 84
damos 135
dêmos 135
dêlêsasthai 69
deinotatos 44
diiphilos 84
diogenês 84
diktat 120
dios 84
diotrephês 84
dôrois 33
dôšo 60

echeuan 26
echei 19
eidêsin 30
eidos 30
eipein 45
eirênê 40, 43
ekeleuen 79
ekperthô 19
endon 30
enosichthôn 85
enosigeos 85
epamynein 41
ephesychazô 93
epidômetha 34, 101
epikertomeôn 36

epikouroi 172
epiorkia 21, 26
epamnyein 77
ergon 45
eros 58
ethêken 40, 61
eury kreiôn 84

geras 135, 136
gerousion 73
glaukopis 85
gyae 134

haliskomai 110
harmoniê, harmonia 34, 46,
hapax 111
hekaergos 84
hekêbolos 85
herkos Achaiôn 85
homoiiou 43
hospitium 49
horkia 24, 26, 29-30, 40-41, 45-46, 48,
   58-73, 76-77, 80, 106, 118-119, 166,
   204
horkion 60, 66, 68
horkos 46, 58-60, 71-80, 204; horkoi 30,
   80, 146
hôs 79
hypestên 21, 26, 45; hypestêsan 21, 26
hypescheto 45-46; hypeschonto 21
hypemeinan 21
heureto 27

Idêthen 101

karteron 75
kateneusa 46; kateneuse 26
keimilion 174
keklyte 45
korythaiolos 85
koton 19
koilêis para nêusi 19
kydistos 85

lawagetas 135
legomenon 111

machaira 117
machêsometha 41
mantikês 30
mater 102
mêdea andrôn 20
mêdeôn 101

INDEX OF TRANSLITERATED TERMS

megas 42, 44, 45, 73; megan 73
mantikês 30
marûtum 49
meter 102
meteipen 45
metopisthen echei koton 19
monomachia 22
mytheomai 45

neikos 43

omnyein 77-80; omosan 38; omosson 19-
  20; omoumai 73
onata 135
ontos 28
oise 74
ophra 62
pantepoptês 100
patein 69; pateein 69; patêsa 69
pauomai 93
pêmainein 69
pepmymenôi 70
phaidimos 84
philia 45, 56, 204
philotês 23, 43, 48-49, 52-58, 71, 204;
  philotês êphemerou 58
perthô 110
pherô 61
pista 24, 29-30, 61, 71, 80, 119
ploutos 40, 43
poimên laôn 84
pelomoio 43
polis, 7, polin 110
polychalchos 29
polychrysos 29
probouleuma 139

probouleutic 140
prophrôn 19

rhêtrê 38-39, 44, 46

scyptouchos 85
spondai 41, 45, 65, 106; spendein 77
sphagê 25
stratôi 19
syncheein 69
synêmosynê 46
synetou 28
synthêkê epi boêtheiai 19
synthesie, synthesa, synthesai 20, 41, 45-
  46, 65, 72, 106, 118, 146, 166
syntithemi 204; syntheo 19-20,

temenos 134, 135, 136, 144, 188
temnein 24, 29, 62-65, 68, 70, 80, 119;
  etamen 40; temnêi 62; tamontes 61;
  tamômen 119
tecmôr
thôkos
themistes 22, 159
theous 100
tithêmi 204
tomia 62-64; tomiôn kaprou 63
troes 134

wa na ka 87
wanax 135

xeniê 53
xenios 54

Zeu pater 101

SUPPLEMENTS TO MNEMOSYNE

EDITED BY A.D. LEEMAN, C.J. RUIJGH AND H.W. PLEKET

4. LEEMAN, A.D. *A Systematical Bibliography of Sallust (1879-1964)*. Revised and augmented edition. 1965. ISBN 90 04 01467 5
5. LENZ, F.W. (ed.). *The Aristeides 'Prolegomena'*. 1959. ISBN 90 04 01468 3
7. McKAY, K.J. *Erysichthon. A Callimachean Comedy*. 1962. ISBN 90 04 01470 5
8. SWEENEY, R.D. *Prolegomena to an Edition of the Scholia to Statius*. 1969. ISBN 90 04 01471 3
10. WITKE, C. *Enarratio Catulliana. Carmina L, XXX, LXV, LXVIII*. 1968. ISBN 90 04 03079 4
11. RUTILIUS LUPUS. *De Figuris Sententiarum et Elocutionis*. Edited with Prolegomena and Commentary by E. Brooks. 1970. ISBN 90 04 01474 8
12. SMYTH, W.R. (ed.). *Thesaurus criticus ad Sexti Propertii textum*. 1970. ISBN 90 04 01475 6
13. LEVIN, D.N. *Apollonius' 'Argonautica' re-examined*. 1. The Neglected First and Second Books. 1971. ISBN 90 04 02575 8
14. REINMUTH, O.W. *The Ephebic Inscriptions of the Fourth Century B.C.* 1971. ISBN 90 04 01476 4
15. YOUNG, D.C. *Pindar Isthmian 7*. Myth and Exempla. 1971. ISBN 90 04 01477 2
16. ROSE, K.F.C. *The Date and Author of the 'Satyricon'*. With an introduction by J.P. Sullivan. 1971. ISBN 90 04 02578 2
17. SEGAL, Ch. *The Theme of the Mutilation of the Corpse in the Iliad*. 1971. ISBN 90 04 02579 0
18. WILLIS, J. *De Martiano Capella emendando*. 1971. ISBN 90 04 02580 4
19. HERINGTON, C.J. (ed.). *The Older Scholia on the Prometheus Bound*. 1972. ISBN 90 04 03455 2
20. THIEL, H. VAN. *Petron. Überlieferung und Rekonstruktion*. 1971. ISBN 90 04 02581 2
21. LOSADA, L.A. *The Fifth Column in the Peloponnesian War*. 1972. ISBN 90 04 03421 8
22. STATIUS. *Thebaidos Liber Decimus*. Edited with a commentary by R.D. Williams. 1972. ISBN 90 04 03456 0
23. BROWN, V. *The Textual Transmission of Caesar's 'Civil War'*. 1972. ISBN 90 04 03457 9
24. LOOMIS, J.W. *Studies in Catullan Verse*. An Analysis of Word Types and Patterns in the Polymetra. 1972. ISBN 90 04 03429 3
25. PAVLOVSKIS, Z. *Man in an Artificial Landscape*. The Marvels of Civilization in Imperial Roman Literature. 1973. ISBN 90 04 03643 1
26. PARRY, A.A. *Blameless Aegisthus*. A study of ἀμύμων and other Homeric epithets. 1973. ISBN 90 04 03736 5
27. GEORGE, E.V. *Aeneid VIII and the Aitia of Callimachus*. 1974. ISBN 90 04 03859 0
28. SCOTT, W.C. *The Oral Nature of the Homeric Simile*. 1974. ISBN 90 04 03789 6
29. BERS, V. *Enallage and Greek Style*. 1974. ISBN 90 04 03786 1
30. GEFFCKEN, K.A. *Comedy in the 'Pro Caelio'*. With an Appendix on the *In Clodium et Curionem*. 1973. ISBN 90 04 03782 9
31. STARR, C.G. *Political Intelligence in Classical Greece*. 1974. ISBN 90 04 03830 2
32. BOEDEKER, D.D. *Aphrodite's Entry into Greek Epic*. 1974. ISBN 90 04 03946 5
33. MATTHEW, V.J. *Panyassis of Halikarnassos. Text and commentary*. 1974. ISBN 90 04 04001 3

34. POE, J.P. *Heroism and Divine Justice in Sophocles' Philoctetes.* 1974.
ISBN 90 04 04165 6
35. EDEN, P.T. *A Commentary on Virgil: Aeneid VIII.* 1975. ISBN 90 04 04225 3
36. SHANNON, R.S. *The arms of Achilles and Homeric Compositional Technique.* 1975.
ISBN 90 04 04249 0
37. SMITH, O.L. *Studies in the Scholia on Aeschylus. 1. The Recensions of Demetrius Triclinius.* 1975. ISBN 90 04 04220 2
38. HIJMANS, B.L. *Inlaboratus et facilis. Aspects of Structure in Some Letters of Seneca.* 1976.
ISBN 90 04 04474 4
39. SCHMELING, G.L. & J.H. STUCKEY. *A Bibliography of Petronius.* 1977.
ISBN 90 04 04753 0
40. WALLACH, B.P. *Lucretius and the Diatribe against the Fear of Death.* De rerum natura III 830-1094. 1976. ISBN 90 04 04564 3
41. ANDERSON, G. *Lucian: Theme and Variation in the Second Sophistic.* 1976.
ISBN 90 04 04735 2
42. CLADER, L.L. *Helen: The Evolution from Divine to Heroic in Greek Epic Tradition.* 1976. ISBN 90 04 04721 2
43. ANDERSON, G. *Studies in Lucian's Comic Fiction.* 1976. ISBN 90 04 04760 3
44. THOMPSON, W.E. *De Hagniae Hereditate. An Athenian Inheritance Case.* 1976.
ISBN 90 04 04757 3
45. McGUSHIN, P. *Sallustius Crispus, 'Bellum Catilinae'. A Commentary.* 1977.
ISBN 90 04 04835 9
46. THORNTON, A. *The Living Universe. Gods and Men in Virgil's Aeneid.* 1976.
ISBN 90 04 04579 1
47. MORGAN, K. *Ovid's Art of Imitation. Propertius in the 'Amores'.* 1977.
ISBN 90 04 04858 8
48. BRENK, F.E. *In Mist apparelled. Religious Themes in Plutarch's 'Moralia' and 'Lives'.* 1977. ISBN 90 04 05241 0
49. HENRY, A.S. *The Prescripts of Athenian Decrees.* 1977. ISBN 90 04 05429 4
50. NORTH, H.F. (ed.). *Interpretations of Plato. A Swarthmore Symposium.* 1977. ISBN 90 04 05262 3
51. SUSSMAN, L.A. *The Elder Seneca.* 1978. ISBN 90 04 05759 5
52. WENDER, D. *The Last Scenes of the Odyssey.* 1978. ISBN 90 04 05710 2
53. NEWMYER, S.T. *The 'Silvae' of Statius.* Structure and theme. 1979.
ISBN 90 04 05849 4
54. BORING, T.A. *Literacy in Ancient Sparta.* 1979. ISBN 90 04 05971 7
55. GRIFFITHS, F.T. *Theocritus at Court.* 1979. ISBN 90 04 05919 9
56. *The Letters of Apollonius of Tyana.* A critical Text with Prolegomena, Translation and Commentary by R.J. PENELLA. 1979. ISBN 90 04 05972 5
57. BOER, W. DEN. *Private Morality in Greece and Rome.* Some Historical Aspects. 1979.
ISBN 90 04 05976 8
58. BRIGGS, W.W. *Narrative and Simile from the 'Georgics' in the 'Aeneid'.* 1980.
ISBN 90 04 06036 7
59. CLAYMAN, D.L. *Callimachus' 'Iambi'.* 1980. ISBN 90 04 06063 4
60. JOHNSTON, P.A. *Vergil's Agricultural Golden Age. A Study of the 'Georgics'.* 1980.
ISBN 90 04 06111 8
61. *Hieronymus' Liber de optimo genere interpretandi (Epistula 57).* Ein Kommentar von G.J.M. BARTELINK. 1980. ISBN 90 04 06085 5
62. MAEHLER, H. *Die Lieder des Bakchylides.* I. Die Siegeslieder. 2 Bde. 1982. 1. Edition des Textes mit Einleitung und Übersetzung. 2. Kommentar.
ISBN 90 04 06409 5
63. HOHENDAHL-ZOETELIEF, I.M. *Manners in the Homeric Epic.* 1980.
ISBN 90 04 06223 8

64. HARVEY, R.A. *A Commentary on Persius*. 1981. ISBN 90 04 06313 7
65. MAXWELL-STUART, P.G. *Studies in Greek Colour Terminology. 1.* γλαυκός. 1981. ISBN 90 04 06406 0
66. MONTI, R.C. *The Dido Episode and the Aeneid*. Roman Social and Political Values in the Epic. 1981. ISBN 90 04 06328 5
67. MAXWELL-STUART, P.G. *Studies in Greek Colour Terminology. 2.* χαροπός. 1981. ISBN 90 04 06407 9
68. ACHARD, G. *Pratique rhétorique et idéologie politique dans les discours 'Optimates' de Cicéron*. 1981. ISBN 90 04 06374 9
69. MANNING, C.E. *On Seneca's 'Ad Marciam'*. 1981. ISBN 90 04 06430 3
70. BERTHIAUME, G. *Les rôles du Mágeiros*. Etude sur la boucherie, la cuisine et le sacrifice dans la Grèce ancienne. 1982. ISBN 90 04 06554 7
71. CAMPBELL, M. *A commentary on Quintus Smyrnaeus Posthomerica XII*. 1981. ISBN 90 04 06502 4
72. CAMPBELL, M. *Echoes and Imitations of Early Epic in Apollonius Rhodius*. 1981. ISBN 90 04 06503 2
73. MOSKALEW, W. *Formular Language and Poetic Design in the Aeneid*. 1982. ISBN 90 04 06580 6
74. RACE, W.H. *The Classical Priamel from Homer to Boethius*. 1982. ISBN 90 04 06515 6
75. MOORHOUSE, A.C. *The Syntax of Sophocles*. 1982. ISBN 90 04 06599 7
76. SARKISSIAN, J. *Catullus. An Interpretation*. 1983. ISBN 90 04 06939 9
77. WITKE, C. *Horace's Roman Odes*. A Critical Examination. 1983. ISBN 90 04 07006 0
78. ORANJE, J. *Euripides' 'Bacchae'*. The Play and its Audience. 1984. ISBN 90 04 07011 7
79. STATIUS. *Thebaidos Libri XII*. Recensuit et cum apparatu critico et exegetico instruxit D.E. Hill. 1983. ISBN 90 04 06917 8
80. KEBRIC, R.B. *The Paintings in the Cnidian Lesche at Delphi and their historical context*. 1983. ISBN 90 04 07020 6
81. DAVID, E. *Aristophanes and Athenian Society of the Early 4th Century B.C.* 1984. ISBN 90 04 07062 1
82. DAM, H.-J. VAN. *P. Papinius Statius, Silvae Book II*. A Commentary. 1984. ISBN 90 04 07110 5
83. MINEUR, W.H. *Callimachus: Hymn to Delos*. Introduction and Commentary. 1984. ISBN 90 04 07230 6
84. OBER, J. *Fortress Attica. Defense of the Athenian Land Frontier, 404-322 B.C.* 1985. ISBN 90 04 07243 8
85. HUBBARD, T.K. *The Pindaric Mind*. A Study of Logical Structure in Early Greek Poetry. 1985. ISBN 90 04 07303 5
86. VERDENIUS, W.J. *A Commentary on Hesiod: Works and Days*, vv. 1-382. 1985. ISBN 90 04 07465 1
87. HARDER, A. *Euripides' 'Kresphonthes' and 'Archelaos'*. Introduction, Text and Commentary. 1985. ISBN 90 04 07511 9
88. WILLIAMS, H.J. *The 'Eclogues' and 'Cynegetica' of Nemesianus*. Edited with an Introduction and Commentary. 1986. ISBN 90 04 07486 4
89. McGING, B.C. *The Foreign Policy of Mithridates VI Eupator, King of Pontus*. 1986. ISBN 90 04 07591 7
90. MINYARD, J.D. *Lucretius and the Late Republic*. An Essay in Roman Intellectual History. 1985. ISBN 90 04 07619 0
91. SIDEBOTHAM, S.E. *Roman Economic Policy in the Erythra Thalassa 30 B.C.-A.D. 217*. 1986. ISBN 90 04 07644 1
92. VOGEL, C.J. DE. *Rethinking Plato and Platonism*. 2nd impr. of the first (1986) ed. 1988. ISBN 90 04 08755 9

93. MILLER, A.M. *From Delos to Delphi*. A Literary Study of the Homeric Hymn to Apollo. 1986. ISBN 90 04 07674 3

94. BOYLE, A.J. *The Chaonian Dove*. Studies in the Eclogues, Georgics, and Aeneid of Virgil. 1986. ISBN 90 04 07672 7

95. KYLE, D.G. *Athletics in Ancient Athens*. 1987. ISBN 90 04 07861 4

96. SUTTON, D.F. *Seneca on the Stage*. 1986. ISBN 90 04 07928 9

97. VERDENIUS, W.J. *Commentaries on Pindar. Vol. I. Olympian Odes 3, 7, 12, 14*. 1987. ISBN 90 04 08126 7

98. PROIETTI, G. *Xenophon's Sparta*. An introduction. 1987. ISBN 90 04 08338 3

99. BREMER, J.M., A.M. VAN ERP TAALMAN KIP & S.R. SLINGS. *Some Recently Found Greek Poems*. Text and Commentary. 1987. ISBN 90 04 08319 7

100. OPHUIJSEN, J.M. VAN. *Hephaestion on Metre*. Translation and Commentary. 1987. ISBN 90 04 08452 5

101. VERDENIUS, W.J. *Commentaries on Pindar. Vol. II*. Olympian Odes 1, 10, 11, Nemean 11, Isthmian 2. 1988. ISBN 90 04 08535 1

102. LUSCHNIG, C.A.E. *Time holds the Mirror. A Study of Knowledge in Euripides' 'Hippolytus'*. 1988. ISBN 90 04 08601 3

103. MARCOVICH, M. *Alcestis Barcinonensis*. Text and Commentary. 1988. ISBN 90 04 08600 5

104. HOLT, F.L. *Alexander the Great and Bactria*. The Formation of a Greek Frontier in Central Asia. Repr. 1989. ISBN 90 04 08612 9

105. BILLERBECK, M. *Senecas Tragödien: sprachliche und stilistische Untersuchungen*. Mit Anhängen zur Sprache des Hercules Oetaeus und der Octavia. 1988. ISBN 90 04 08631 5

106. ARENDS, J.F.M. *Die Einheit der Polis. Eine Studie über Platons Staat*. 1988. ISBN 90 04 08785 0

107. BOTER, G.J. *The Textual Tradition of Plato's Republic*. 1988. ISBN 90 04 08787 7

108. WHEELER, E.L. *Stratagem and the Vocabulary of Military Trickery*. 1988. ISBN 90 04 08831 8

109. BUCKLER, J. *Philip II and the Sacred War*. 1989. ISBN 90 04 09095 9

110. FULLERTON, M.D. *The Archaistic Style in Roman Statuary*. 1990. ISBN 90 04 09146 7

111. ROTHWELL, K.S. *Politics and Persuasion in Aristophanes' 'Ecclesiazusae'*. 1990. ISBN 90 04 09185 8

112. CALDER, W.M. & A. DEMANDT. *Eduard Meyer. Leben und Leistung eines Universalhistorikers*. 1990. ISBN 90 04 09131 9

113. CHAMBERS, M.H. *Georg Busolt. His Career in His Letters*. 1990. ISBN 90 04 09225 0

114. CASWELL, C.P. *A Study of 'Thumos' in Early Greek Epic*. 1990. ISBN 90 04 09260 9

115. EINGARTNER, J. *Isis und ihre Dienerinnen in der Kunst der römischen Kaiserzeit*. 1991. ISBN 90 04 09312 5

116. JONG, I. DE. *Narrative in Drama*. The Art of the Euripidean Messenger-Speech. 1991. ISBN 90 04 09406 7

117. BOYCE, B.T. *The Language of the Freedmen in Petronius'* Cena Trimalchionis. 1991. ISBN 90 04 09431 8

118. RÜTTEN, Th. *Demokrit — lachender Philosoph und sanguinischer Melancholiker*. 1992. ISBN 90 04 09523 3

119. KARAVITES, P. (with the collaboration of Th. Wren). *Promise-Giving and Treaty-Making*. Homer and the Near East. 1992. ISBN 90 04 09567 5

120. SANTORO L'HOIR, F. *The Rhetoric of Gender Terms. 'Man', 'woman' and the portrayal of character in Latin prose*. 1992. ISBN 90 04 09512 8